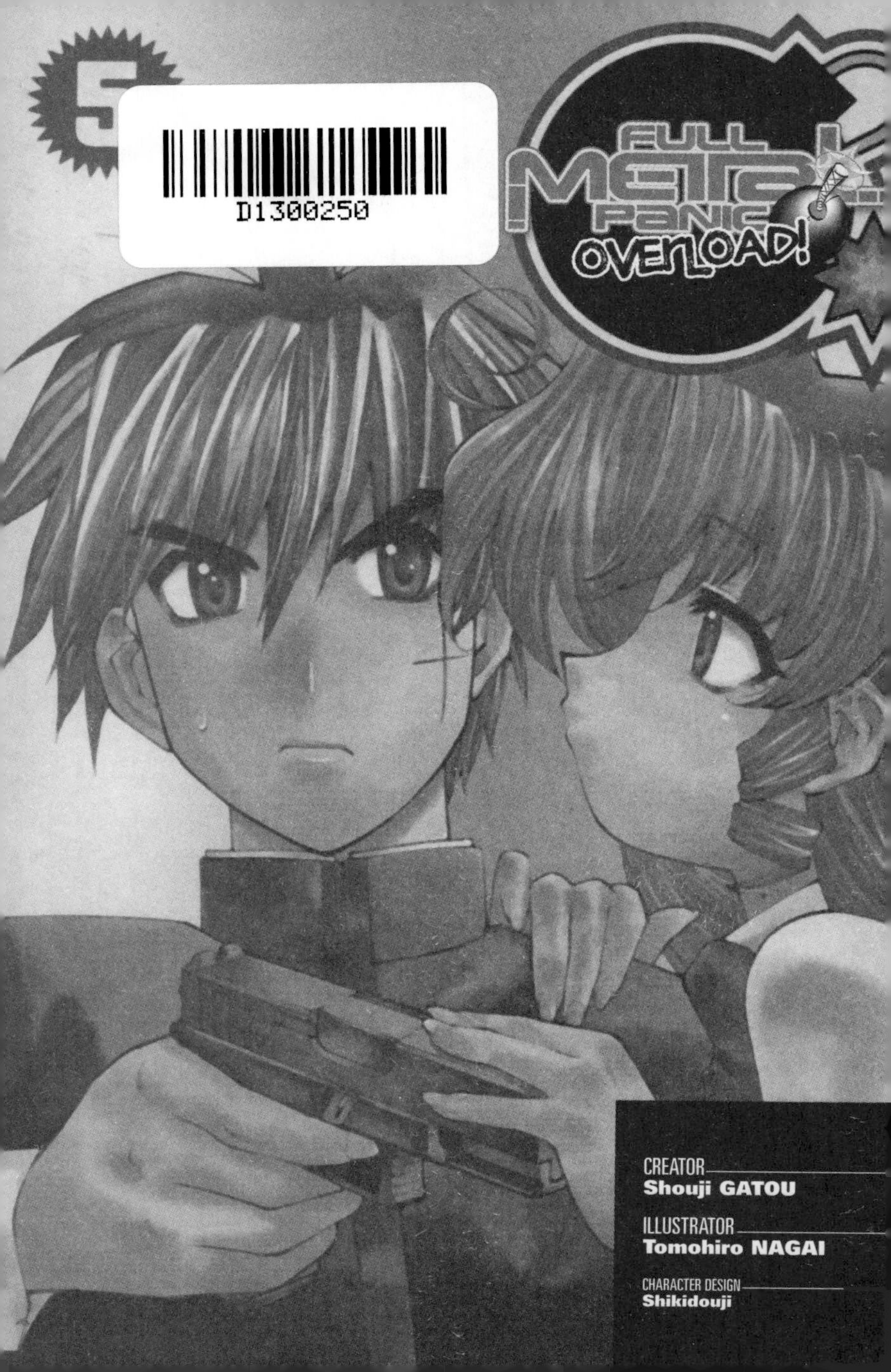
5
FULL METAL PANIC
OVERLOAD!

CREATOR
Shouji GATOU

ILLUSTRATOR
Tomohiro NAGAI

CHARACTER DESIGN
Shikidouji

ONTENTS

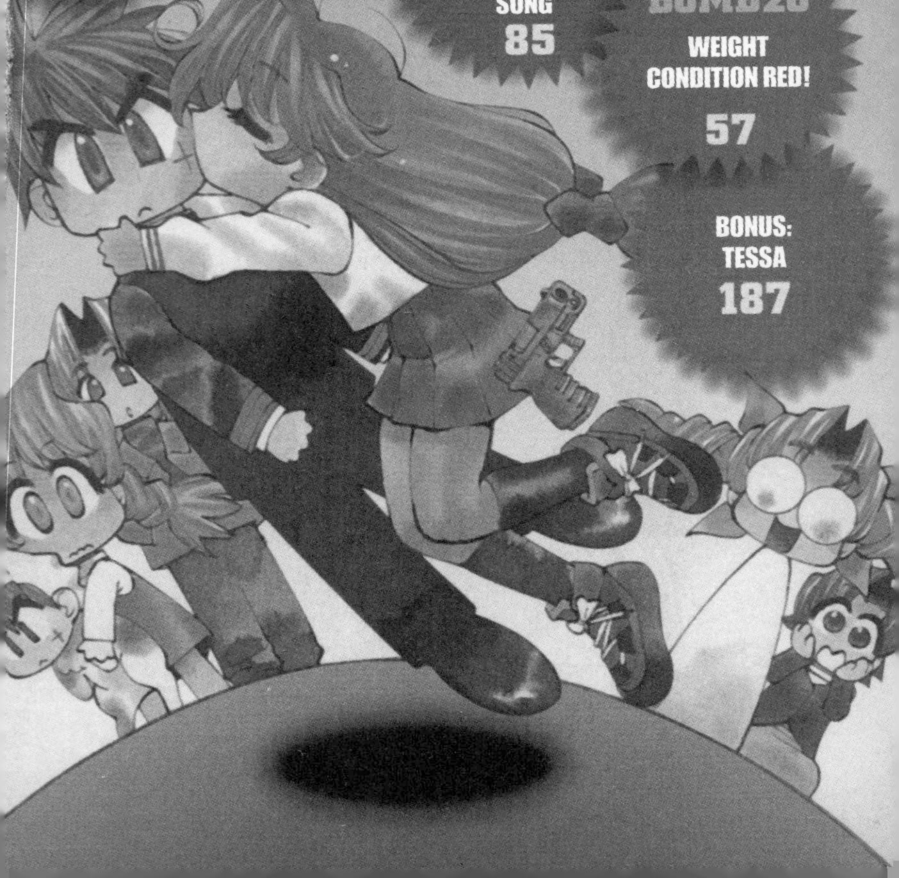

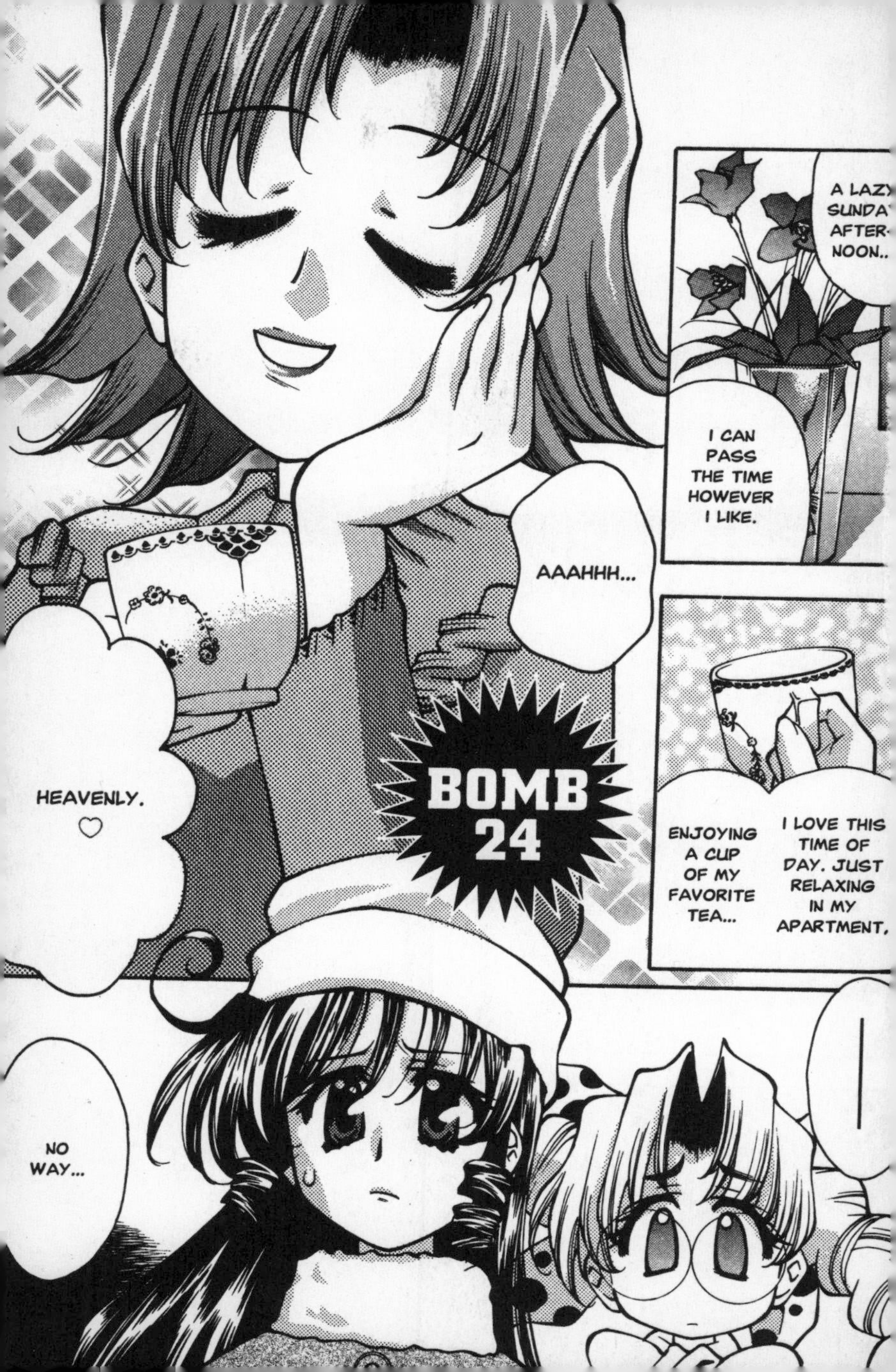
A LAZY SUNDA AFTER- NOON..
I CAN PASS THE TIME HOWEVER I LIKE.
I LOVE THIS TIME OF DAY. JUST RELAXING IN MY APARTMENT,
ENJOYING A CUP OF MY FAVORITE TEA...
AAAHHH...
BOMB 24
HEAVENLY. ♡
NO WAY...

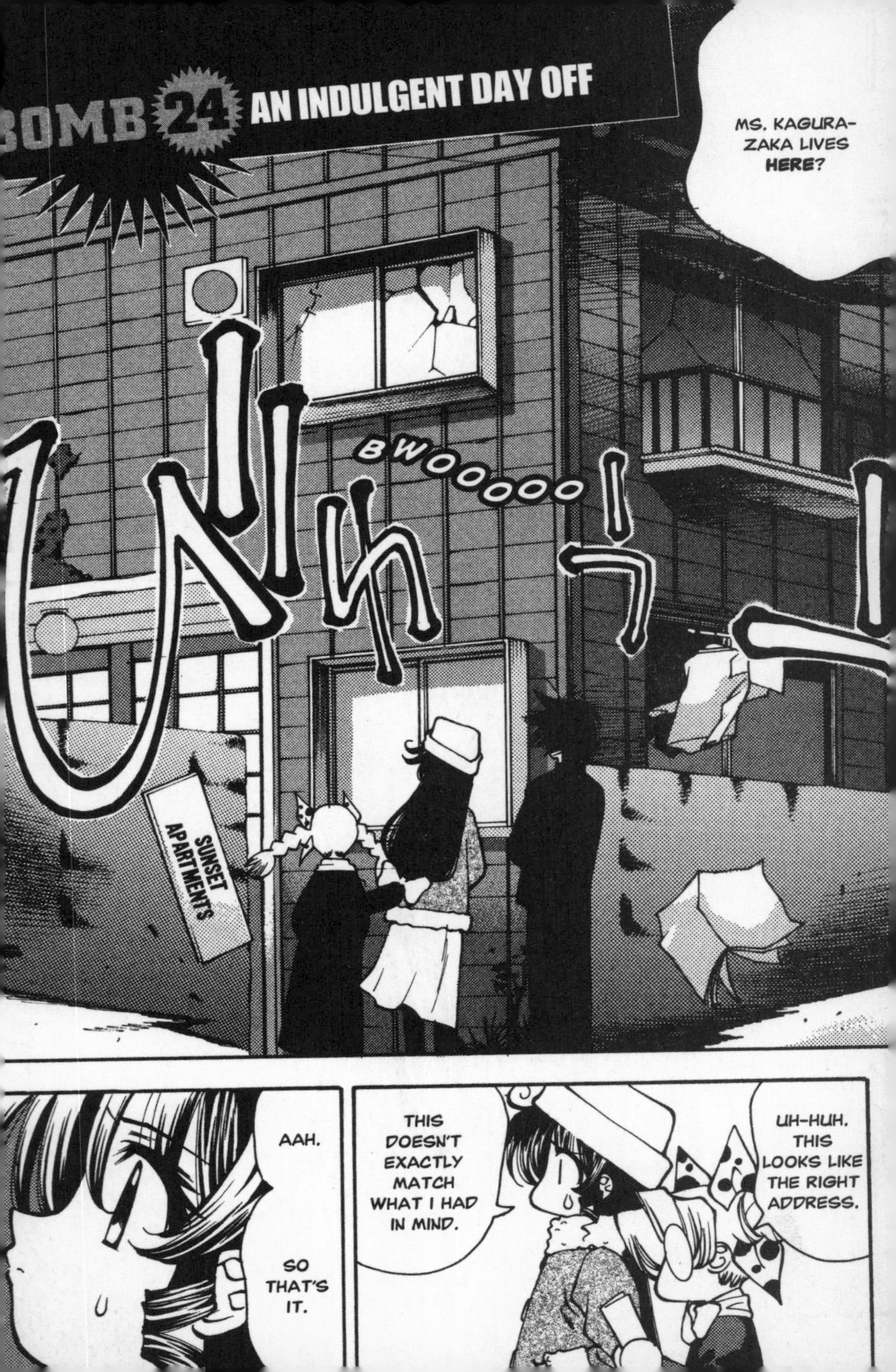
BOMB 24 AN INDULGENT DAY OFF
MS. KAGURA-ZAKA LIVES HERE?
BWOOOOO
SUNSET APARTMENTS
UH-HUH. THIS LOOKS LIKE THE RIGHT ADDRESS.
THIS DOESN'T EXACTLY MATCH WHAT I HAD IN MIND.
AAH.
SO THAT'S IT.

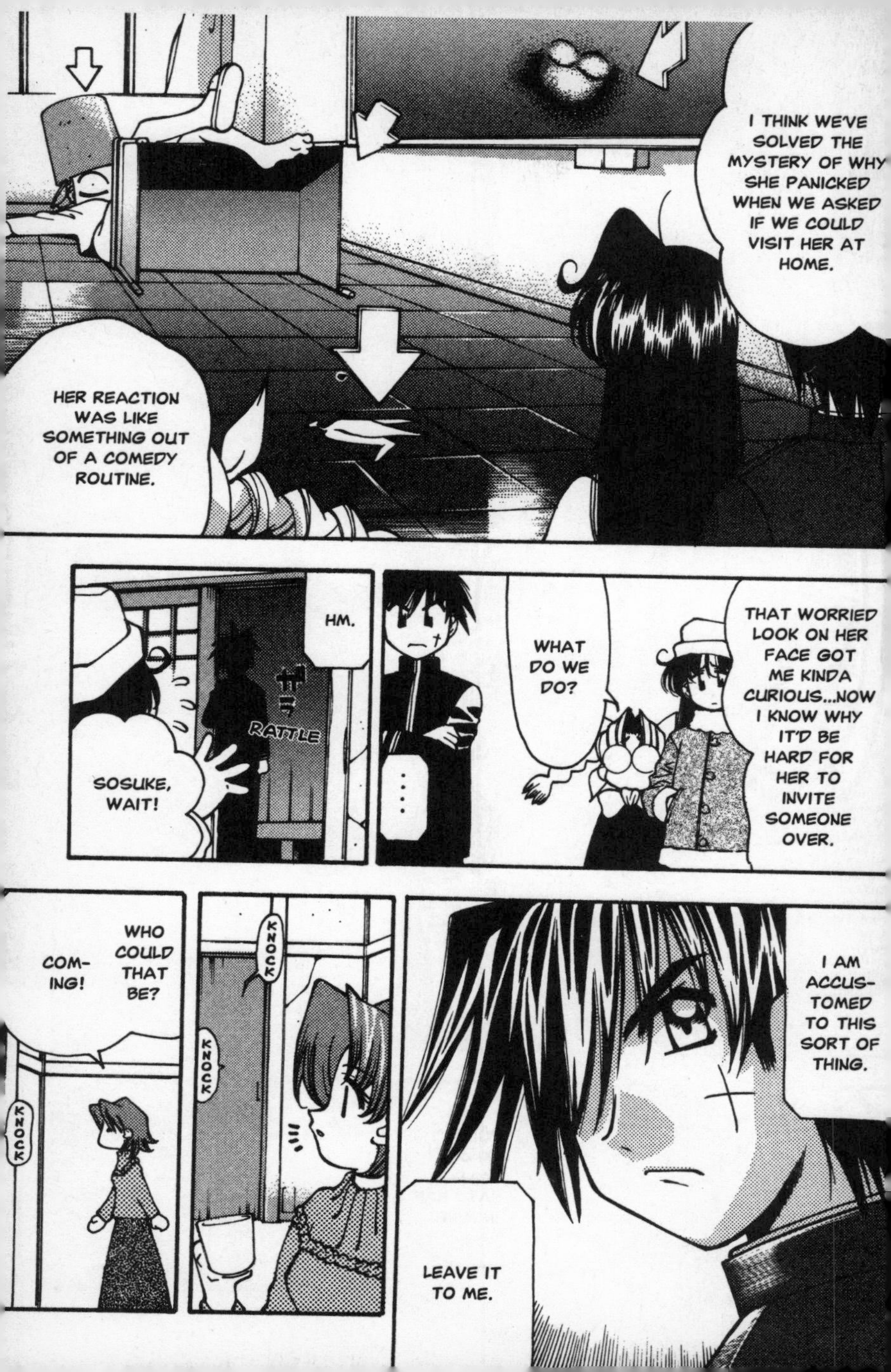
I THINK WE'VE SOLVED THE MYSTERY OF WHY SHE PANICKED WHEN WE ASKED IF WE COULD VISIT HER AT HOME.
HER REACTION WAS LIKE SOMETHING OUT OF A COMEDY ROUTINE.
THAT WORRIED LOOK ON HER FACE GOT ME KINDA CURIOUS...NOW I KNOW WHY IT'D BE HARD FOR HER TO INVITE SOMEONE OVER.
WHAT DO WE DO?
....
HM.
RATTLE
SOSUKE, WAIT!
I AM ACCUS-TOMED TO THIS SORT OF THING.
LEAVE IT TO ME.
KNOCK
KNOCK
WHO COULD THAT BE?
COM-ING!
KNOCK

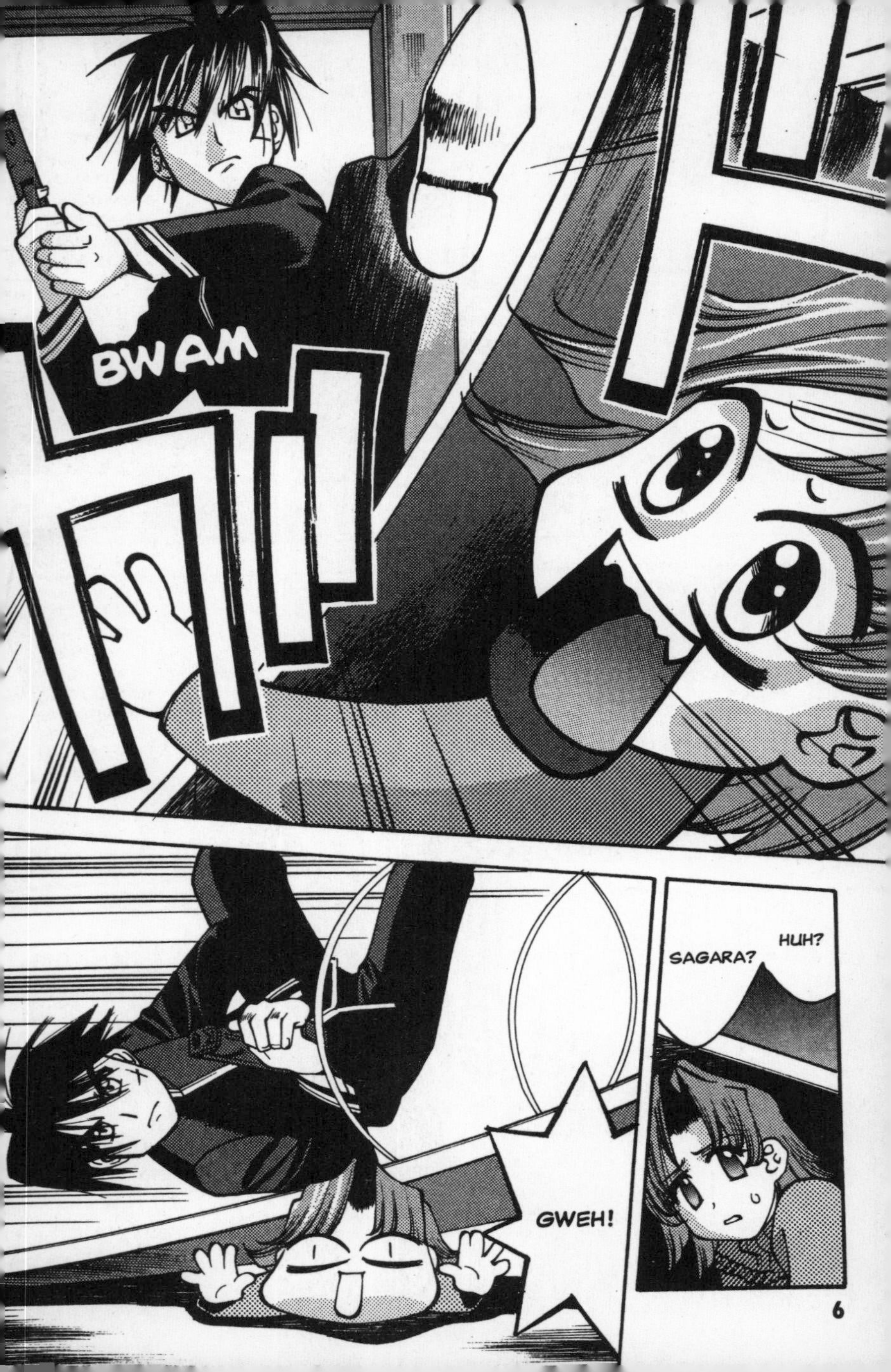
BWAM
HUH?
SAGARA?
GWEH!

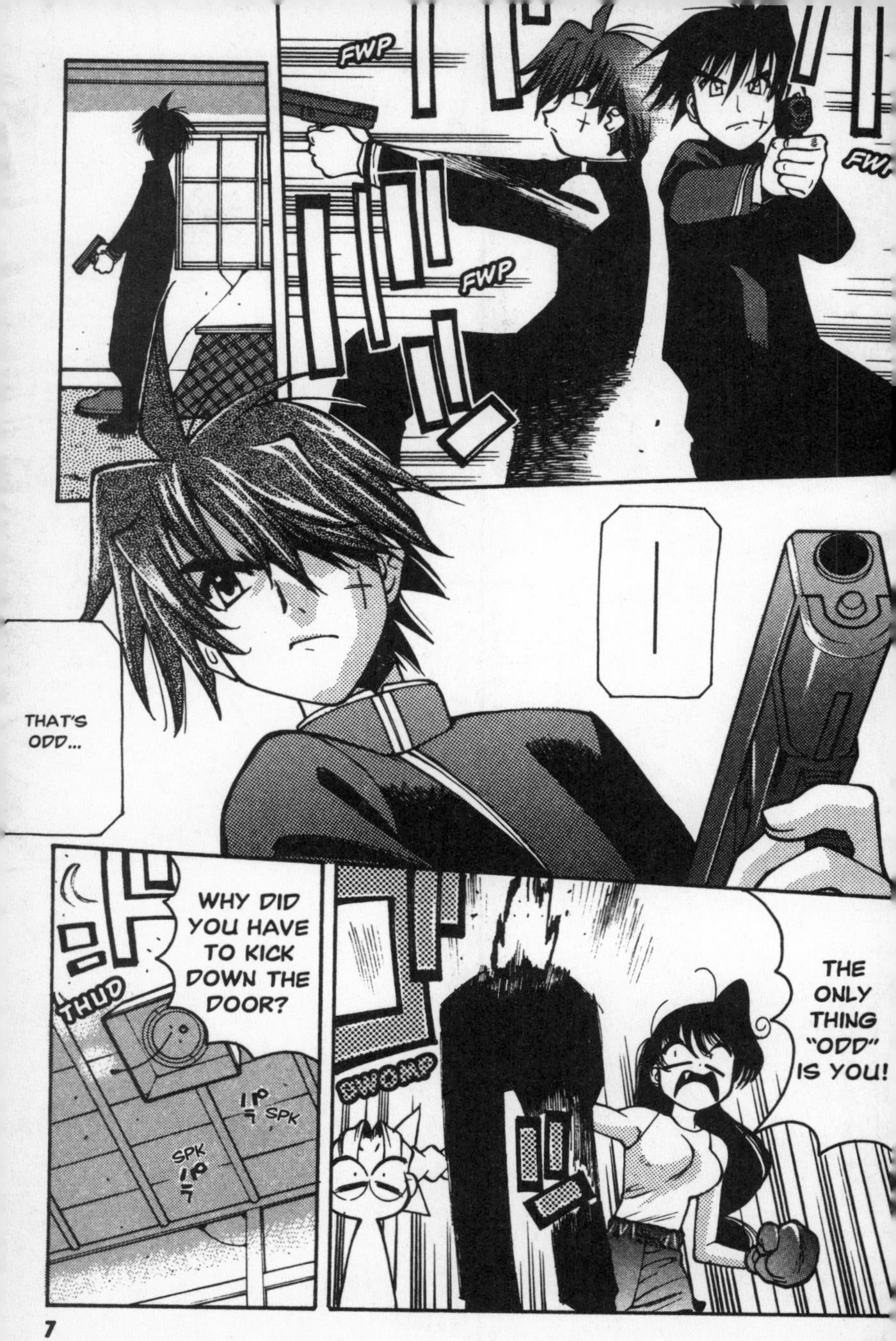
FWP
FWP
FW
FWP
THAT'S ODD...
THE ONLY THING "ODD" IS YOU!
WHY DID YOU HAVE TO KICK DOWN THE DOOR?
THUD
SPK
SPK

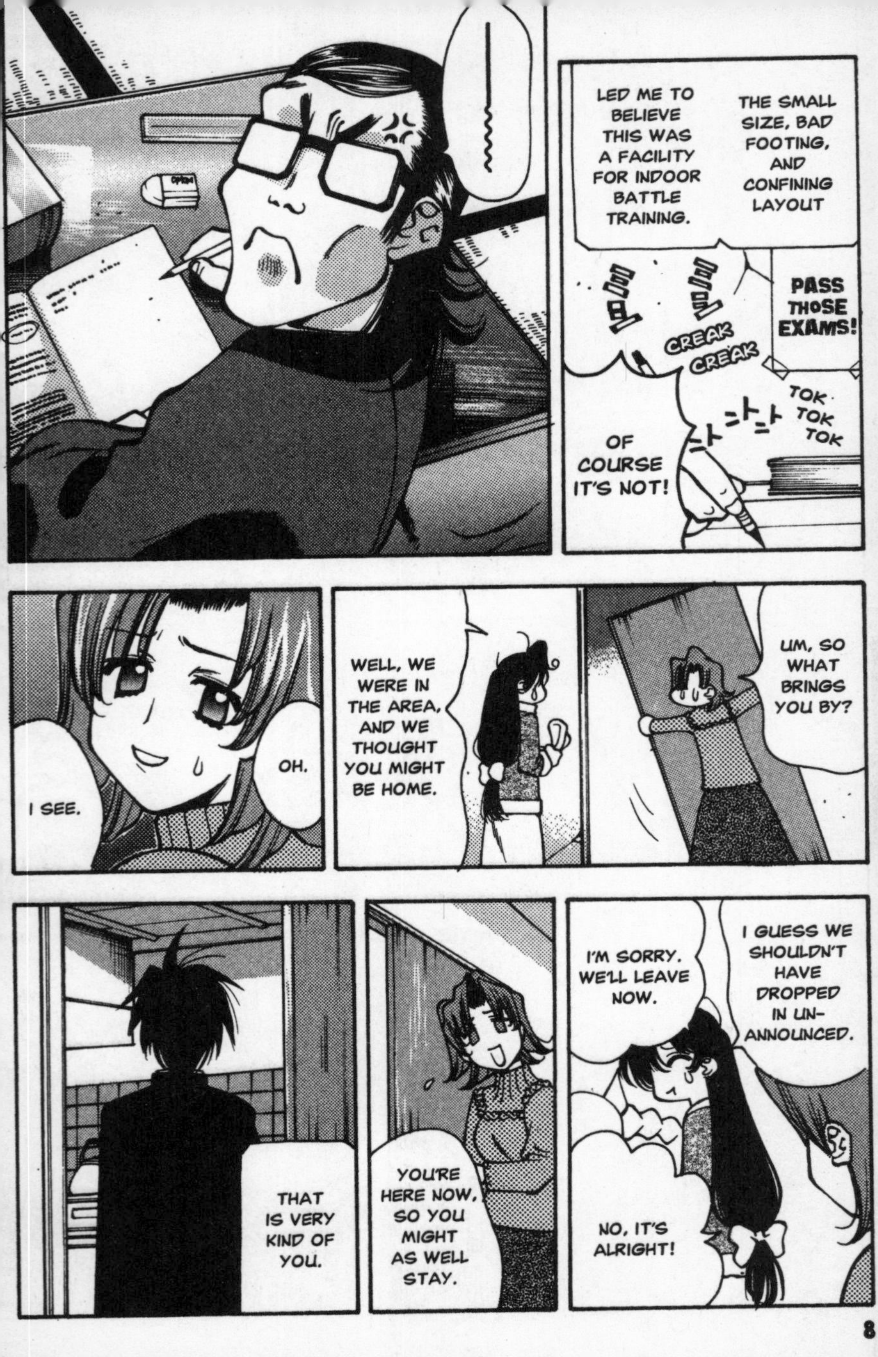
THE SMALL SIZE, BAD FOOTING, AND CONFINING LAYOUT
LED ME TO BELIEVE THIS WAS A FACILITY FOR INDOOR BATTLE TRAINING.
PASS THOSE EXAMS!
CREAK
CREAK
TOK TOK TOK
OF COURSE IT'S NOT!
UM, SO WHAT BRINGS YOU BY?
WELL, WE WERE IN THE AREA, AND WE THOUGHT YOU MIGHT BE HOME.
OH.
I SEE.
I GUESS WE SHOULDN'T HAVE DROPPED IN UN-ANNOUNCED.
I'M SORRY. WE'LL LEAVE NOW.
NO, IT'S ALRIGHT!
YOU'RE HERE NOW, SO YOU MIGHT AS WELL STAY.
THAT IS VERY KIND OF YOU.

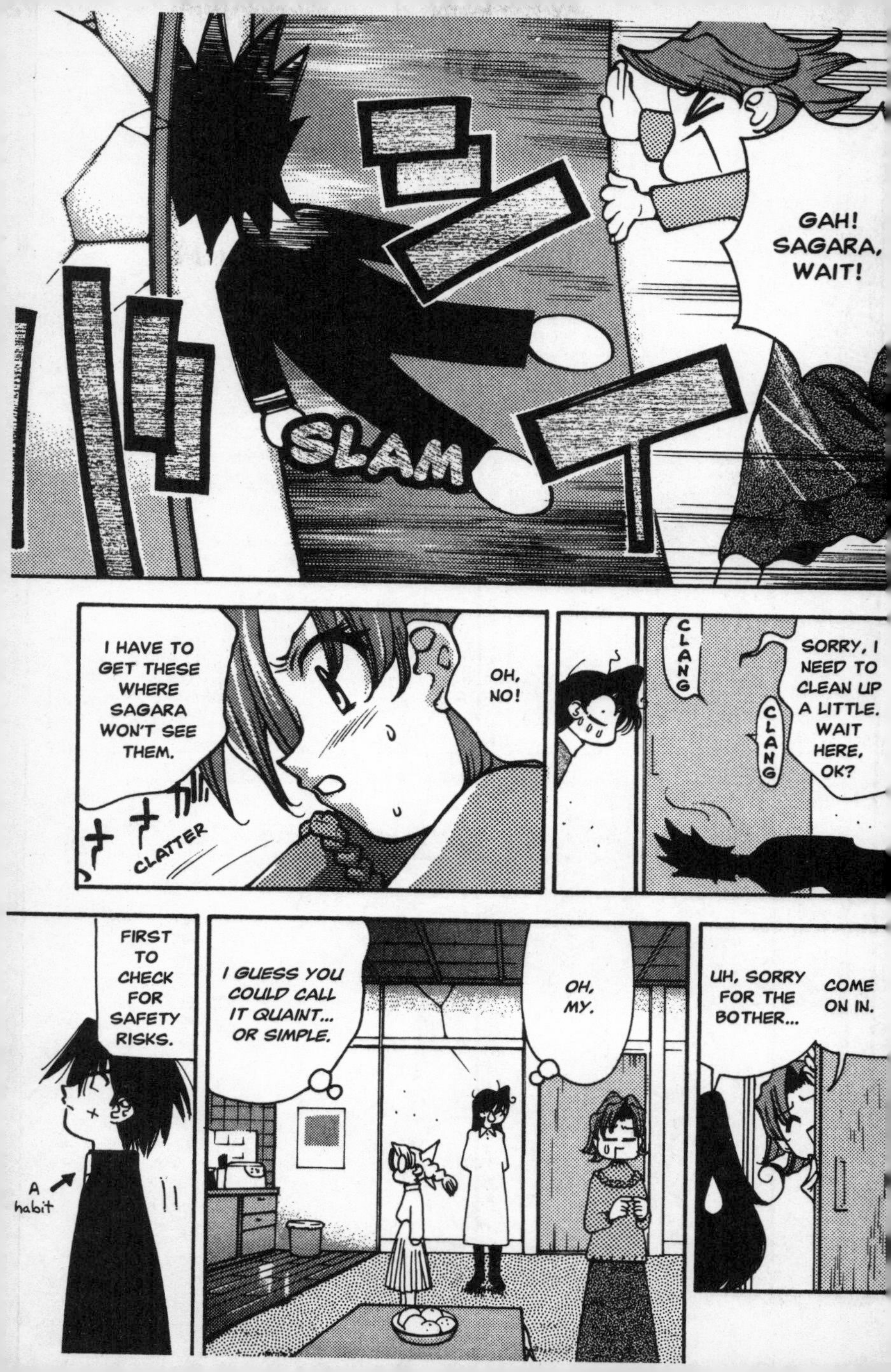
GAH! SAGARA, WAIT!
SLAM
CLANG
SORRY, I NEED TO CLEAN UP A LITTLE. WAIT HERE, OK?
CLANG
OH, NO!
I HAVE TO GET THESE WHERE SAGARA WON'T SEE THEM.
CLATTER
COME ON IN.
UH, SORRY FOR THE BOTHER...
OH, MY.
I GUESS YOU COULD CALL IT QUAINT... OR SIMPLE.
FIRST TO CHECK FOR SAFETY RISKS.
A habit

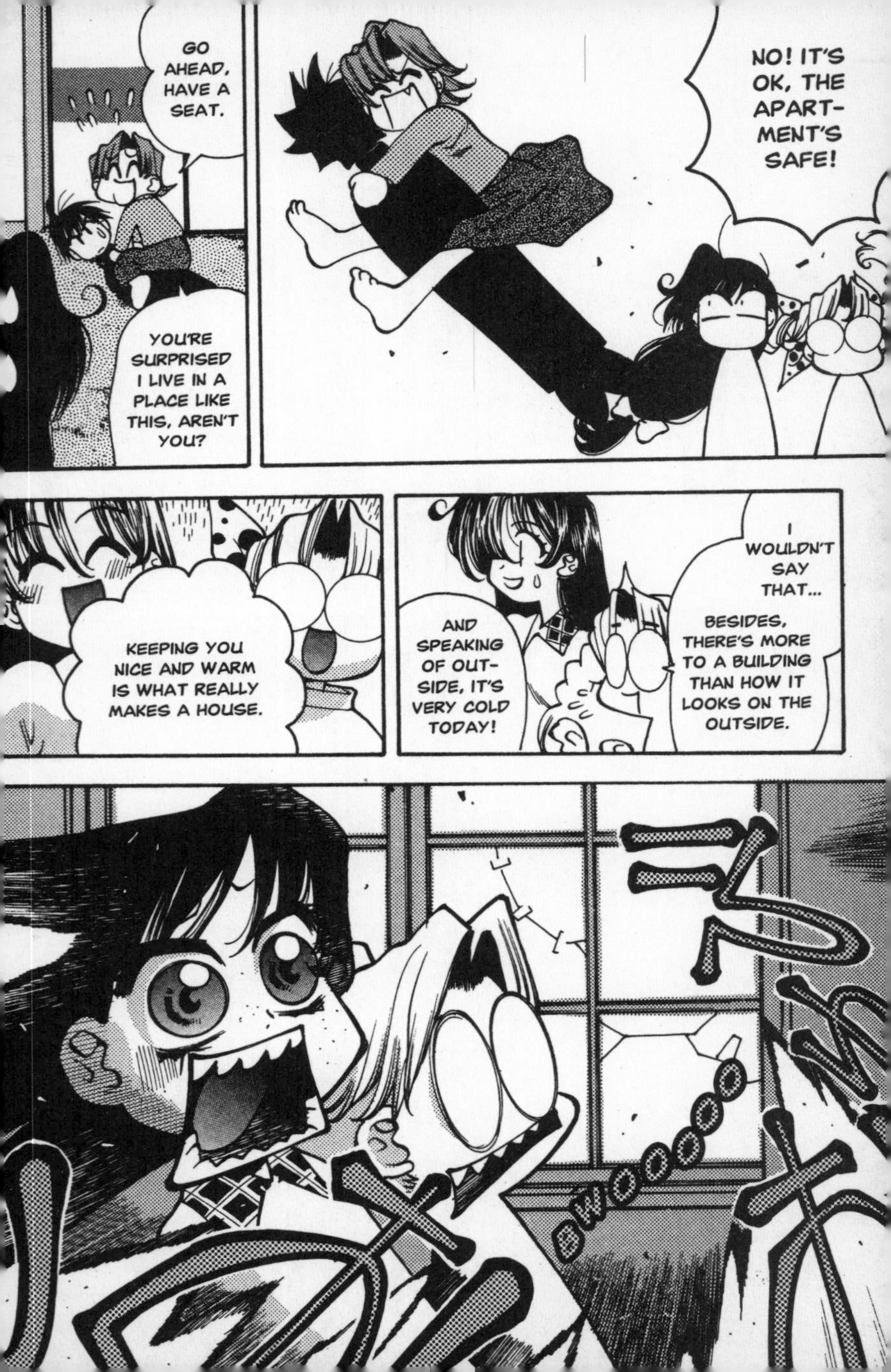
NO! IT'S OK, THE APART-MENT'S SAFE!
GO AHEAD, HAVE A SEAT.
YOU'RE SURPRISED I LIVE IN A PLACE LIKE THIS, AREN'T YOU?
I WOULDN'T SAY THAT...
BESIDES, THERE'S MORE TO A BUILDING THAN HOW IT LOOKS ON THE OUTSIDE.
AND SPEAKING OF OUT-SIDE, IT'S VERY COLD TODAY!
KEEPING YOU NICE AND WARM IS WHAT REALLY MAKES A HOUSE.

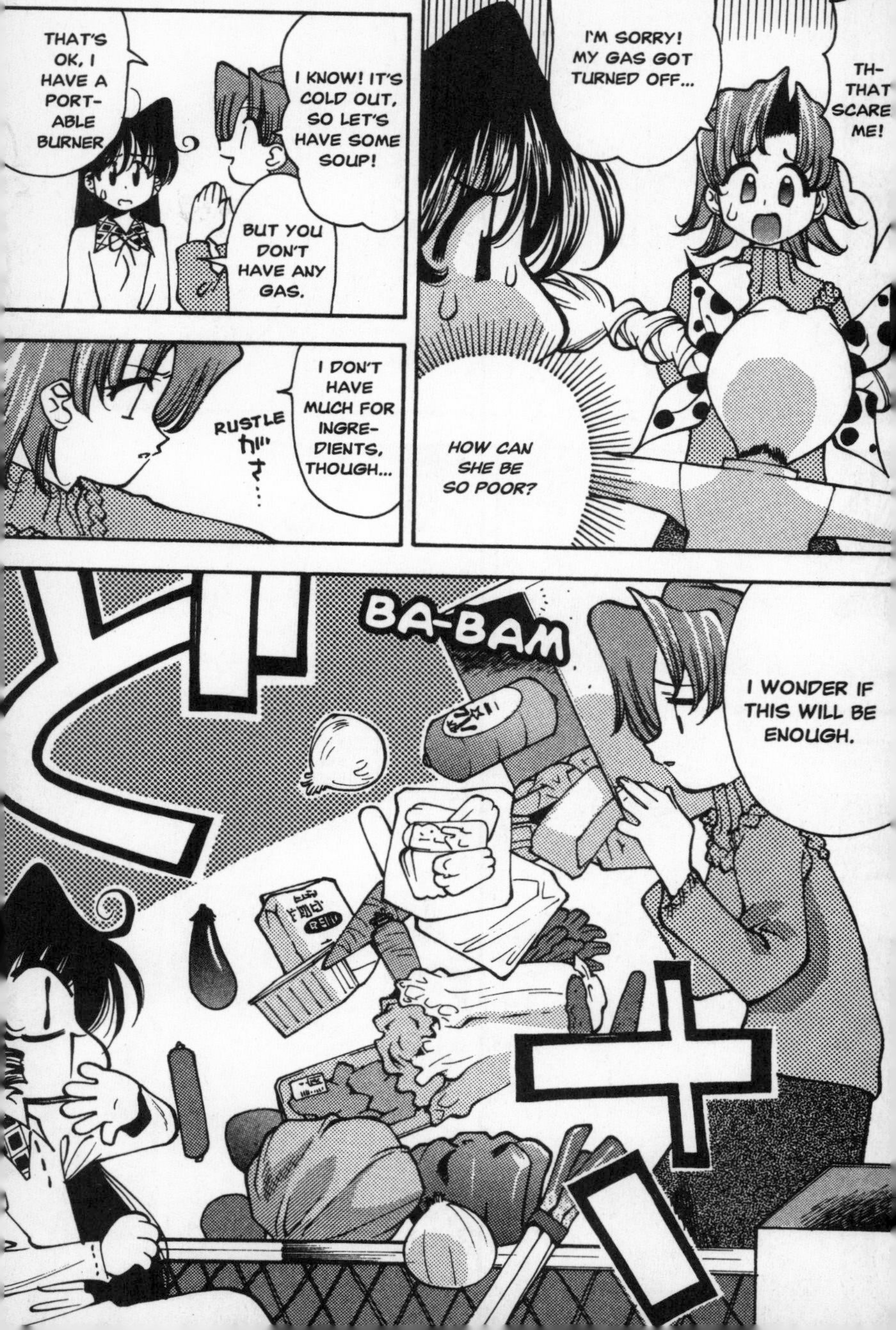

TH- THAT SCARE ME!
I'M SORRY! MY GAS GOT TURNED OFF...
HOW CAN SHE BE SO POOR?
I KNOW! IT'S COLD OUT, SO LET'S HAVE SOME SOUP!
BUT YOU DON'T HAVE ANY GAS.
THAT'S OK, I HAVE A PORT- ABLE BURNER
I DON'T HAVE MUCH FOR INGRE- DIENTS, THOUGH...
RUSTLE
BA-BAM
I WONDER IF THIS WILL BE ENOUGH.

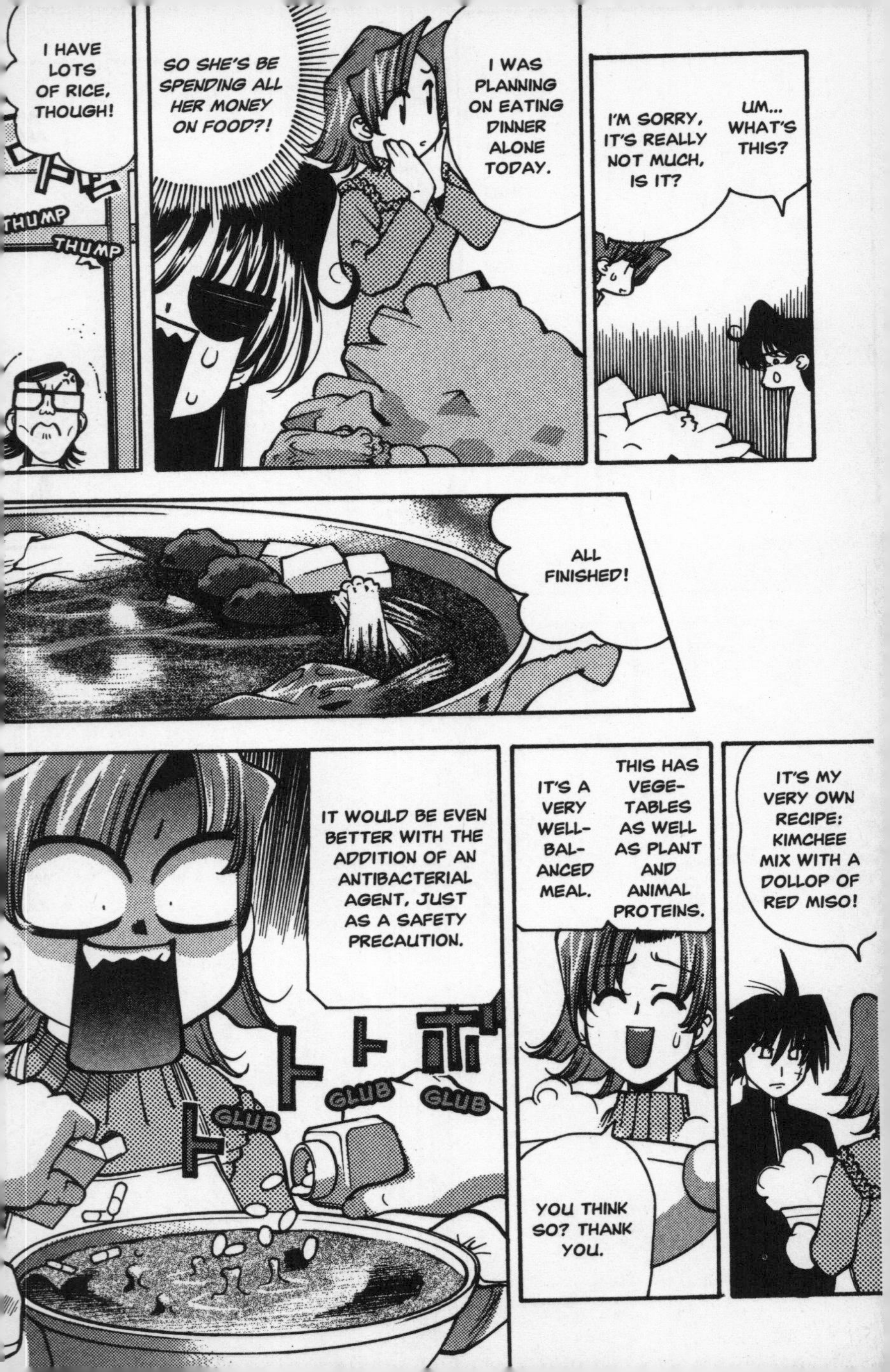
UM... WHAT'S THIS?
I'M SORRY, IT'S REALLY NOT MUCH, IS IT?
I WAS PLANNING ON EATING DINNER ALONE TODAY.
SO SHE'S BE SPENDING ALL HER MONEY ON FOOD?!
I HAVE LOTS OF RICE, THOUGH!
THUMP
THUMP
ALL FINISHED!
IT'S MY VERY OWN RECIPE: KIMCHEE MIX WITH A DOLLOP OF RED MISO!
THIS HAS VEGE-TABLES AS WELL AS PLANT AND ANIMAL PROTEINS.
IT'S A VERY WELL-BAL-ANCED MEAL.
YOU THINK SO? THANK YOU.
IT WOULD BE EVEN BETTER WITH THE ADDITION OF AN ANTIBACTERIAL AGENT, JUST AS A SAFETY PRECAUTION.
GLUB
GLUB
GLUB

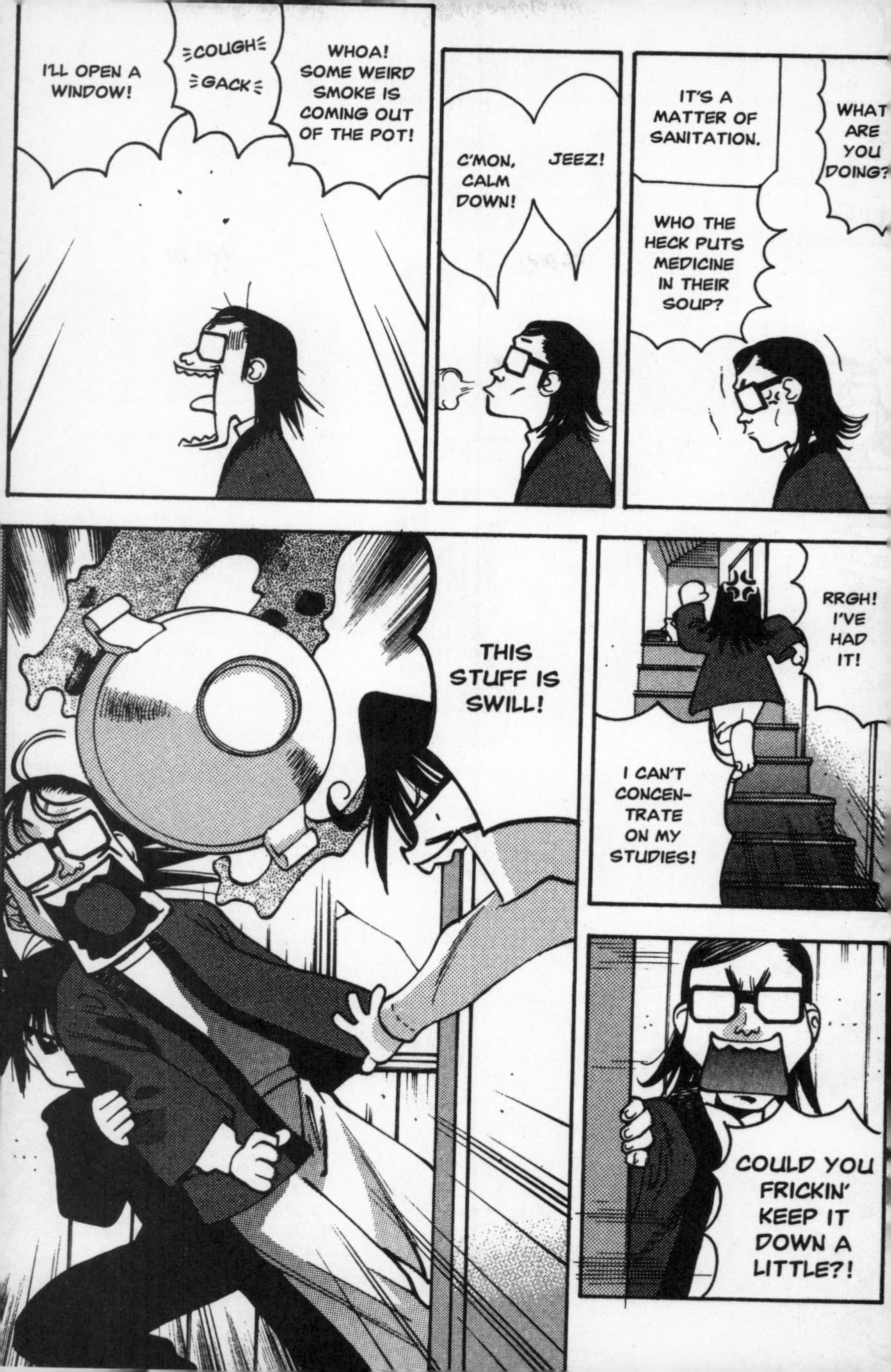
WHAT ARE YOU DOING?
IT'S A MATTER OF SANITATION.
WHO THE HECK PUTS MEDICINE IN THEIR SOUP?
JEEZ!
C'MON, CALM DOWN!
WHOA! SOME WEIRD SMOKE IS COMING OUT OF THE POT!
COUGH
GACK
I'LL OPEN A WINDOW!
RRGH! I'VE HAD IT!
I CAN'T CONCENTRATE ON MY STUDIES!
COULD YOU FRICKIN' KEEP IT DOWN A LITTLE?!
THIS STUFF IS SWILL!

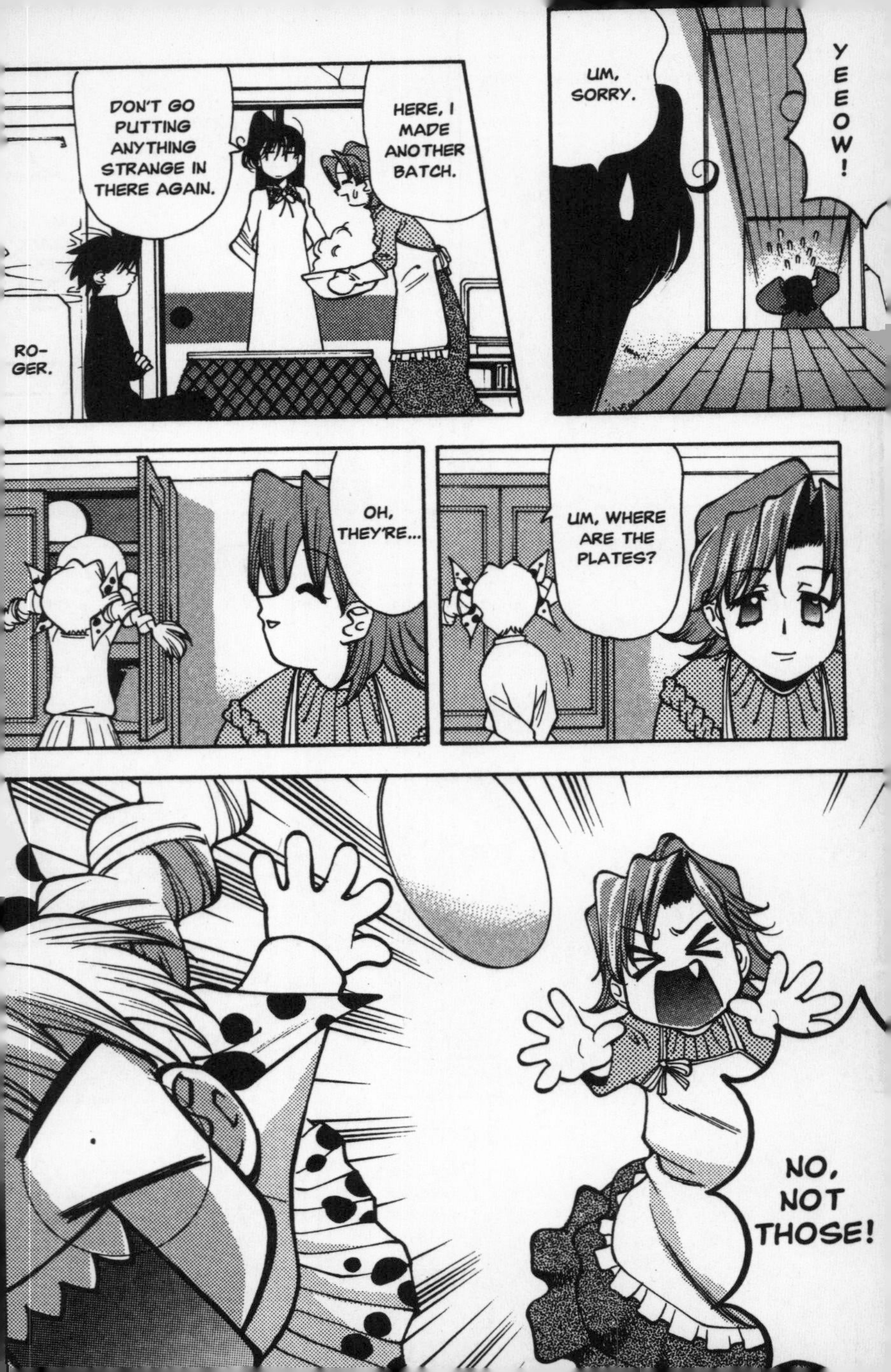
YEEOW!
UM, SORRY.
HERE, I MADE ANOTHER BATCH.
DON'T GO PUTTING ANYTHING STRANGE IN THERE AGAIN.
RO-GER.
UM, WHERE ARE THE PLATES?
OH, THEY'RE...
NO, NOT THOSE!

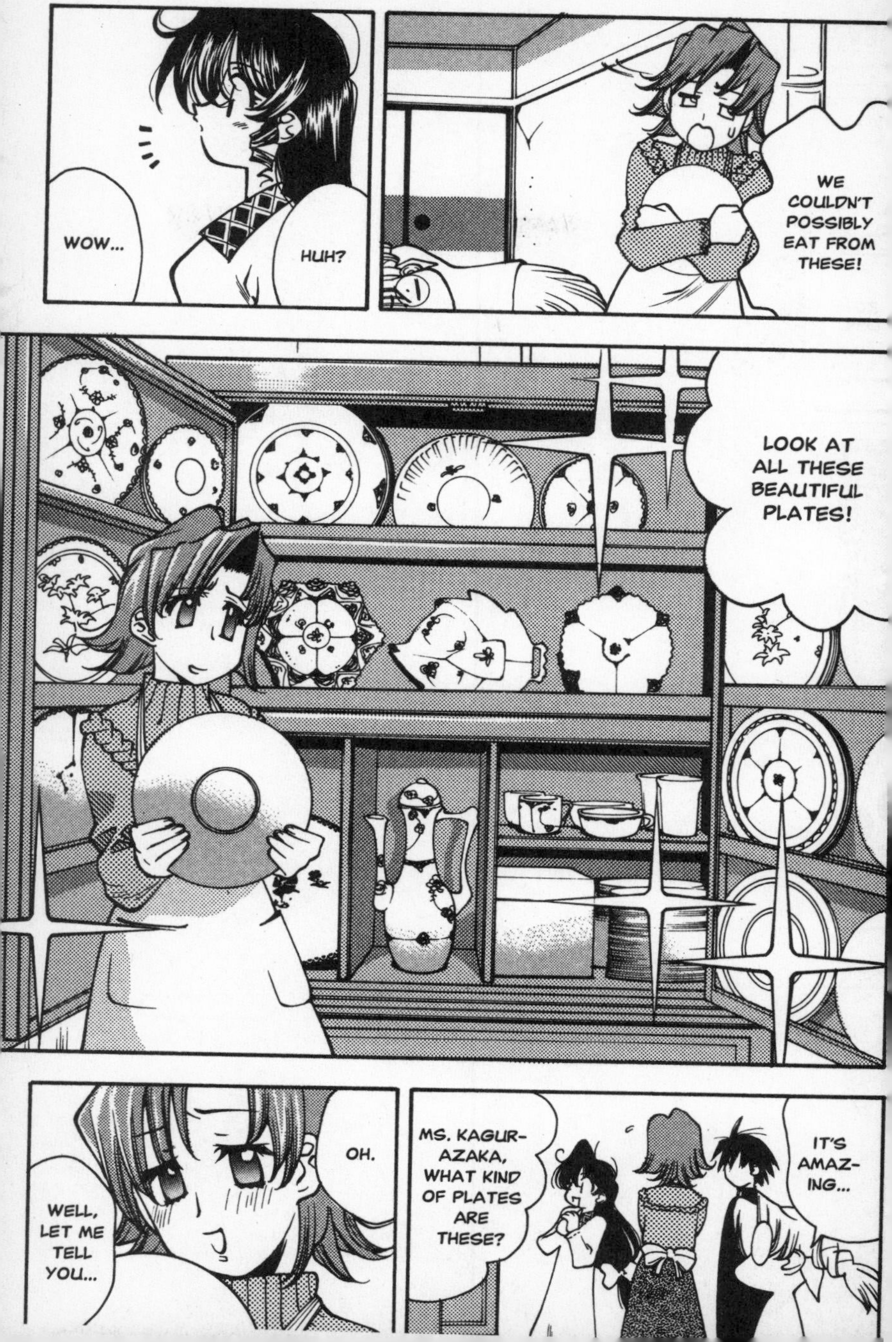
WE COULDN'T POSSIBLY EAT FROM THESE!
HUH?
WOW...
LOOK AT ALL THESE BEAUTIFUL PLATES!
IT'S AMAZ-ING...
MS. KAGUR-AZAKA, WHAT KIND OF PLATES ARE THESE?
OH.
WELL, LET ME TELL YOU...

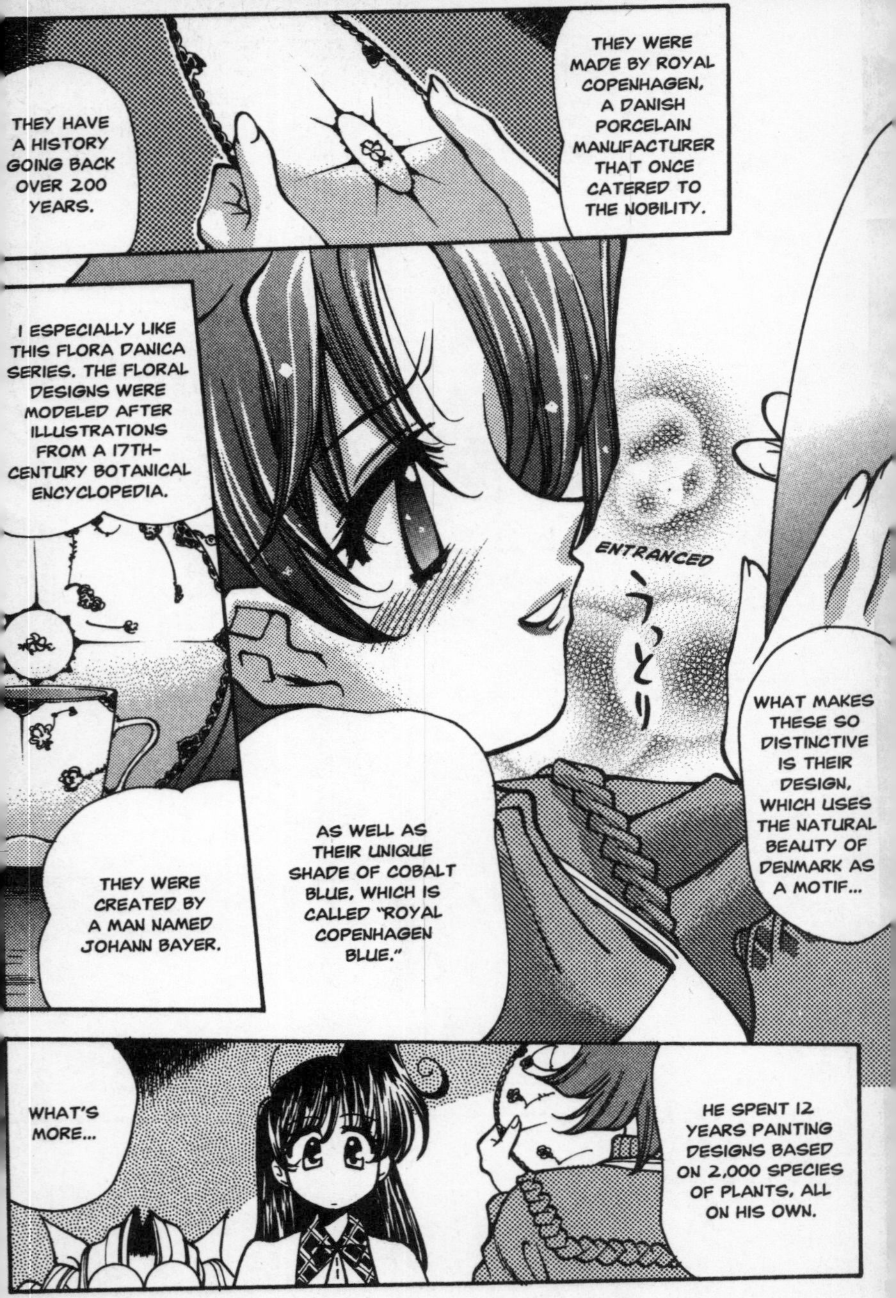
THEY WERE MADE BY ROYAL COPENHAGEN, A DANISH PORCELAIN MANUFACTURER THAT ONCE CATERED TO THE NOBILITY.
THEY HAVE A HISTORY GOING BACK OVER 200 YEARS.
WHAT MAKES THESE SO DISTINCTIVE IS THEIR DESIGN, WHICH USES THE NATURAL BEAUTY OF DENMARK AS A MOTIF...
AS WELL AS THEIR UNIQUE SHADE OF COBALT BLUE, WHICH IS CALLED "ROYAL COPENHAGEN BLUE."
ENTRANCED
うっとり
I ESPECIALLY LIKE THIS FLORA DANICA SERIES. THE FLORAL DESIGNS WERE MODELED AFTER ILLUSTRATIONS FROM A 17TH-CENTURY BOTANICAL ENCYCLOPEDIA.
THEY WERE CREATED BY A MAN NAMED JOHANN BAYER.
WHAT'S MORE...
HE SPENT 12 YEARS PAINTING DESIGNS BASED ON 2,000 SPECIES OF PLANTS, ALL ON HIS OWN.

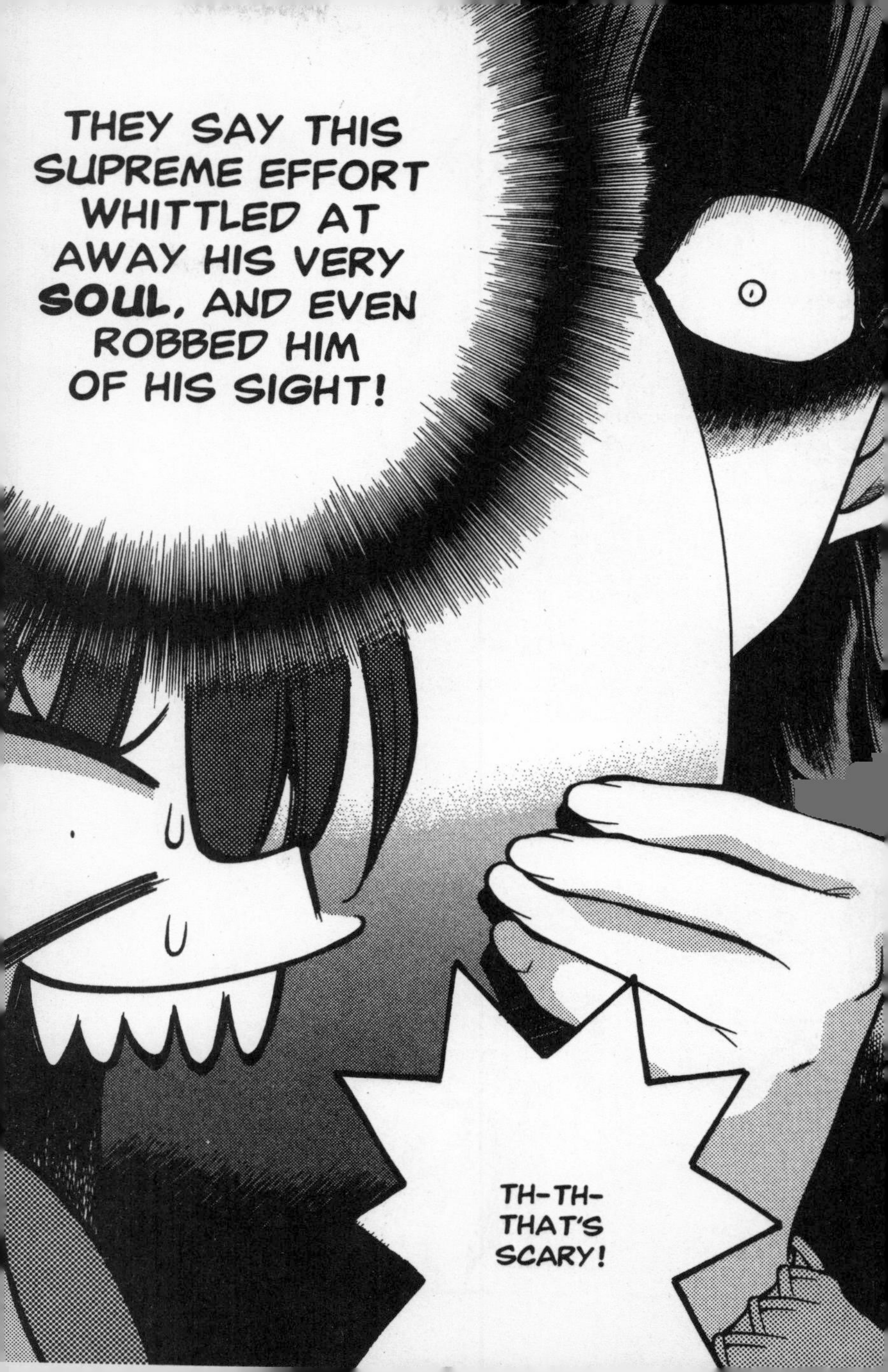
THEY SAY THIS SUPREME EFFORT WHITTLED AT AWAY HIS VERY **SOUL**, AND EVEN ROBBED HIM OF HIS SIGHT!
TH-TH-THAT'S SCARY!

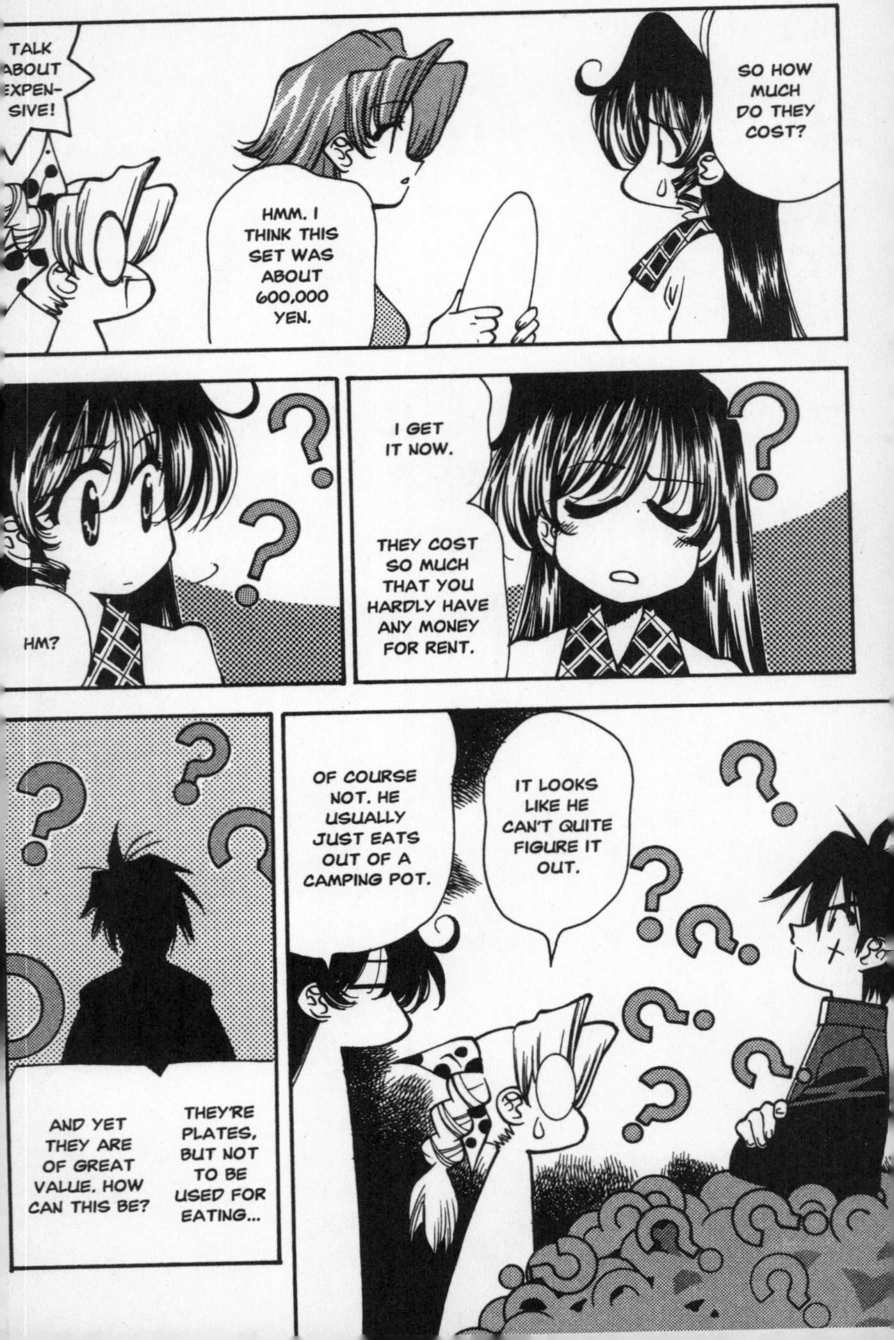
SO HOW MUCH DO THEY COST?
HMM. I THINK THIS SET WAS ABOUT 600,000 YEN.
TALK ABOUT EXPENSIVE!
I GET IT NOW.
THEY COST SO MUCH THAT YOU HARDLY HAVE ANY MONEY FOR RENT.
HM?
IT LOOKS LIKE HE CAN'T QUITE FIGURE IT OUT.
OF COURSE NOT. HE USUALLY JUST EATS OUT OF A CAMPING POT.
THEY'RE PLATES, BUT NOT TO BE USED FOR EATING...
AND YET THEY ARE OF GREAT VALUE. HOW CAN THIS BE?

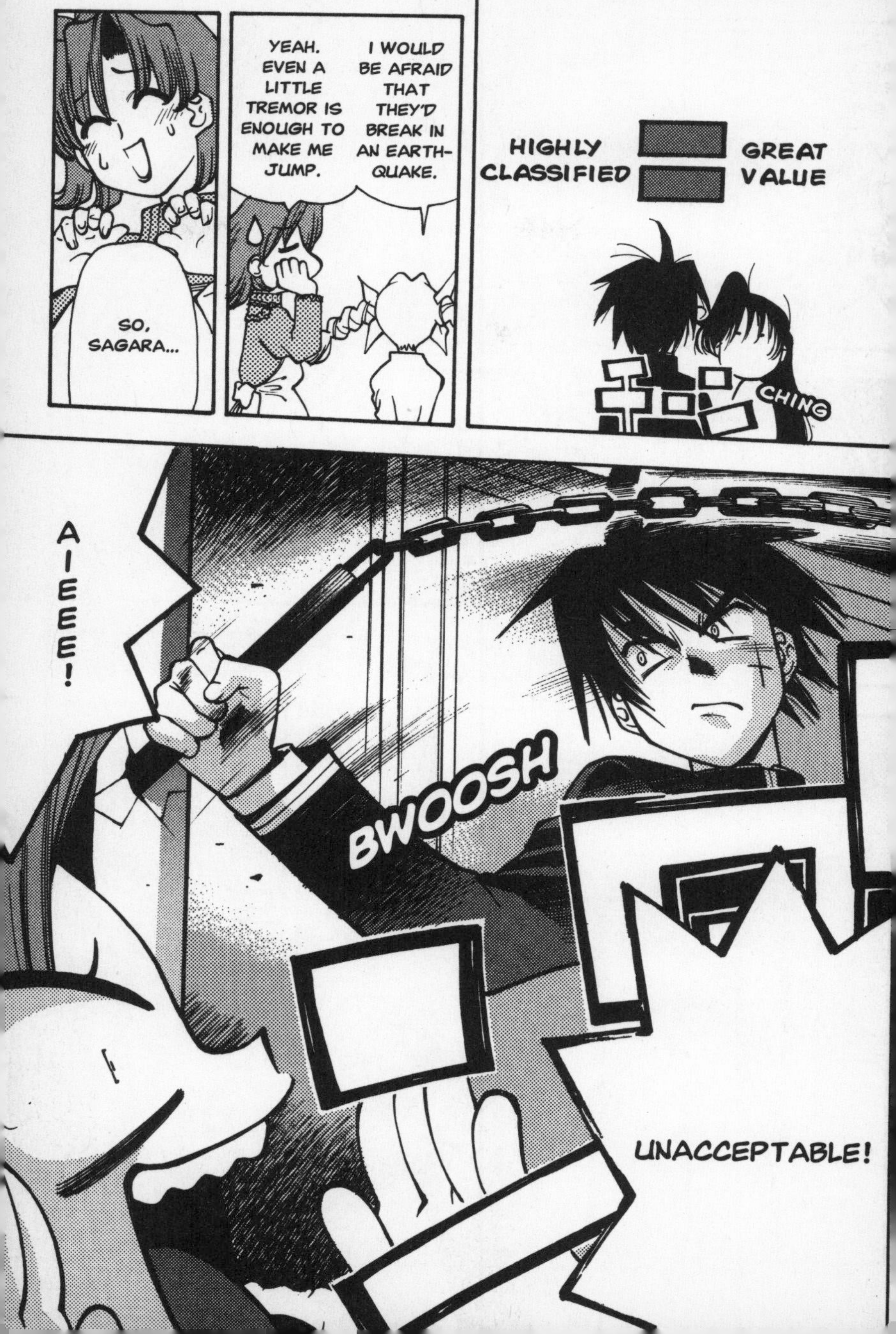
HIGHLY CLASSIFIED
GREAT VALUE
CHING
I WOULD BE AFRAID THAT THEY'D BREAK IN AN EARTH-QUAKE.
YEAH. EVEN A LITTLE TREMOR IS ENOUGH TO MAKE ME JUMP.
SO, SAGARA...
UNACCEPTABLE!
BWOOSH
AIEEE!

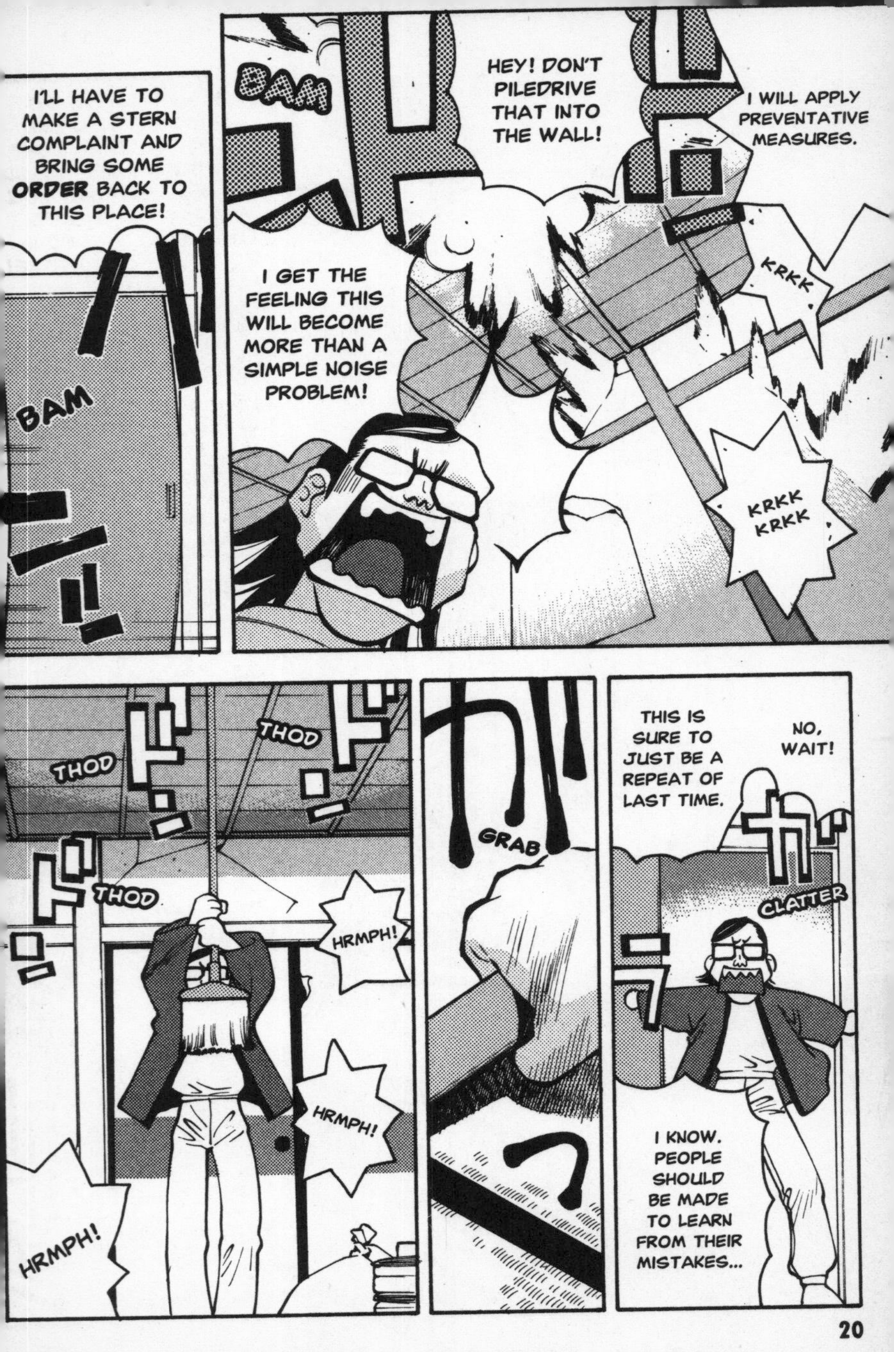
I'LL HAVE TO MAKE A STERN COMPLAINT AND BRING SOME ORDER BACK TO THIS PLACE!
BAM
BAM
HEY! DON'T PILEDRIVE THAT INTO THE WALL!
I WILL APPLY PREVENTATIVE MEASURES.
I GET THE FEELING THIS WILL BECOME MORE THAN A SIMPLE NOISE PROBLEM!
KRKK
KRKK KRKK
THOD
THOD
THOD
HRMPH!
HRMPH!
HRMPH!
GRAB
THIS IS SURE TO JUST BE A REPEAT OF LAST TIME.
NO, WAIT!
CLATTER
I KNOW. PEOPLE SHOULD BE MADE TO LEARN FROM THEIR MISTAKES...

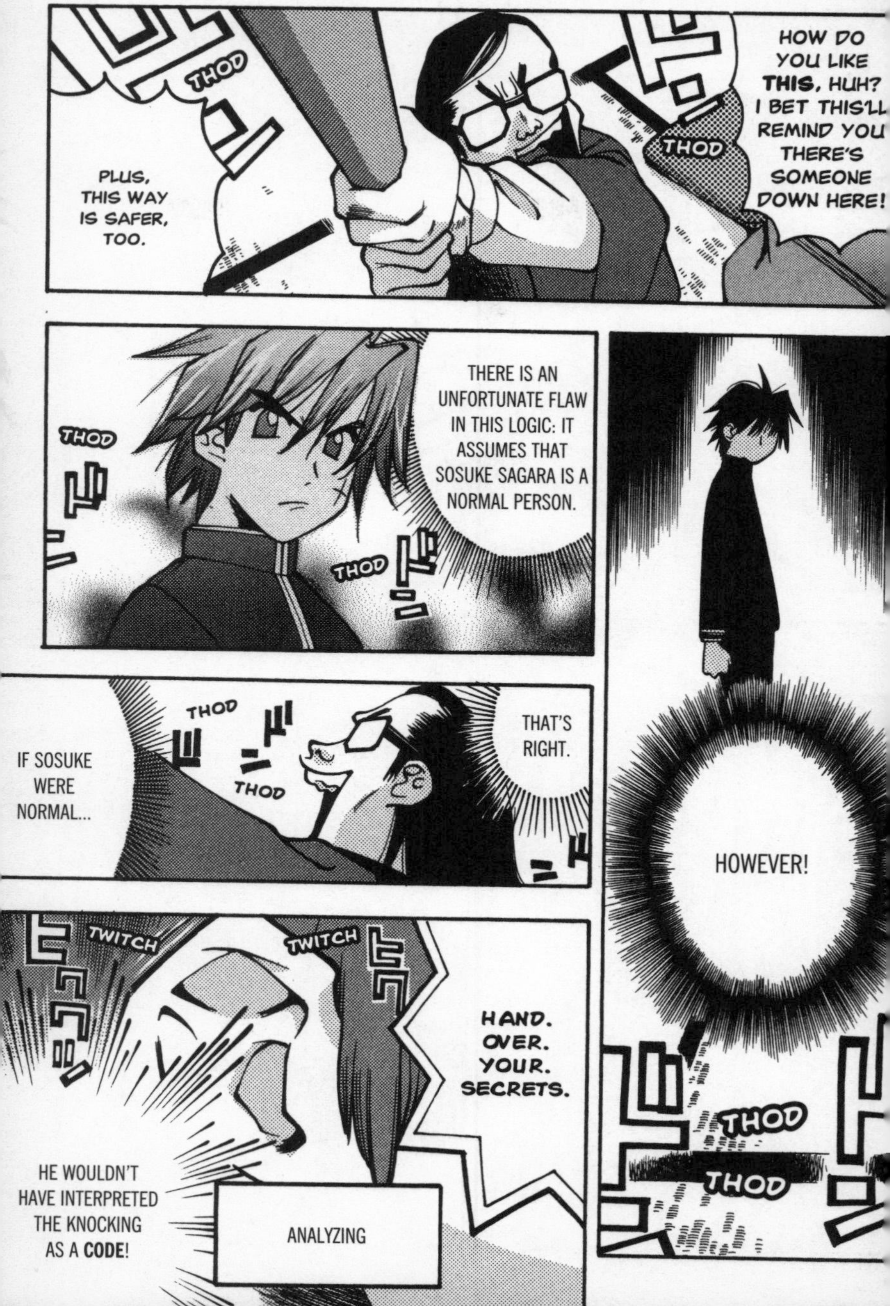
HOW DO YOU LIKE THIS, HUH? I BET THIS'LL REMIND YOU THERE'S SOMEONE DOWN HERE!
THOD
THOD
PLUS, THIS WAY IS SAFER, TOO.
THERE IS AN UNFORTUNATE FLAW IN THIS LOGIC: IT ASSUMES THAT SOSUKE SAGARA IS A NORMAL PERSON.
THOD
THOD
THAT'S RIGHT.
THOD
THOD
IF SOSUKE WERE NORMAL...
TWITCH
TWITCH
HAND. OVER. YOUR. SECRETS.
HE WOULDN'T HAVE INTERPRETED THE KNOCKING AS A CODE!
ANALYZING
HOWEVER!
THOD
THOD

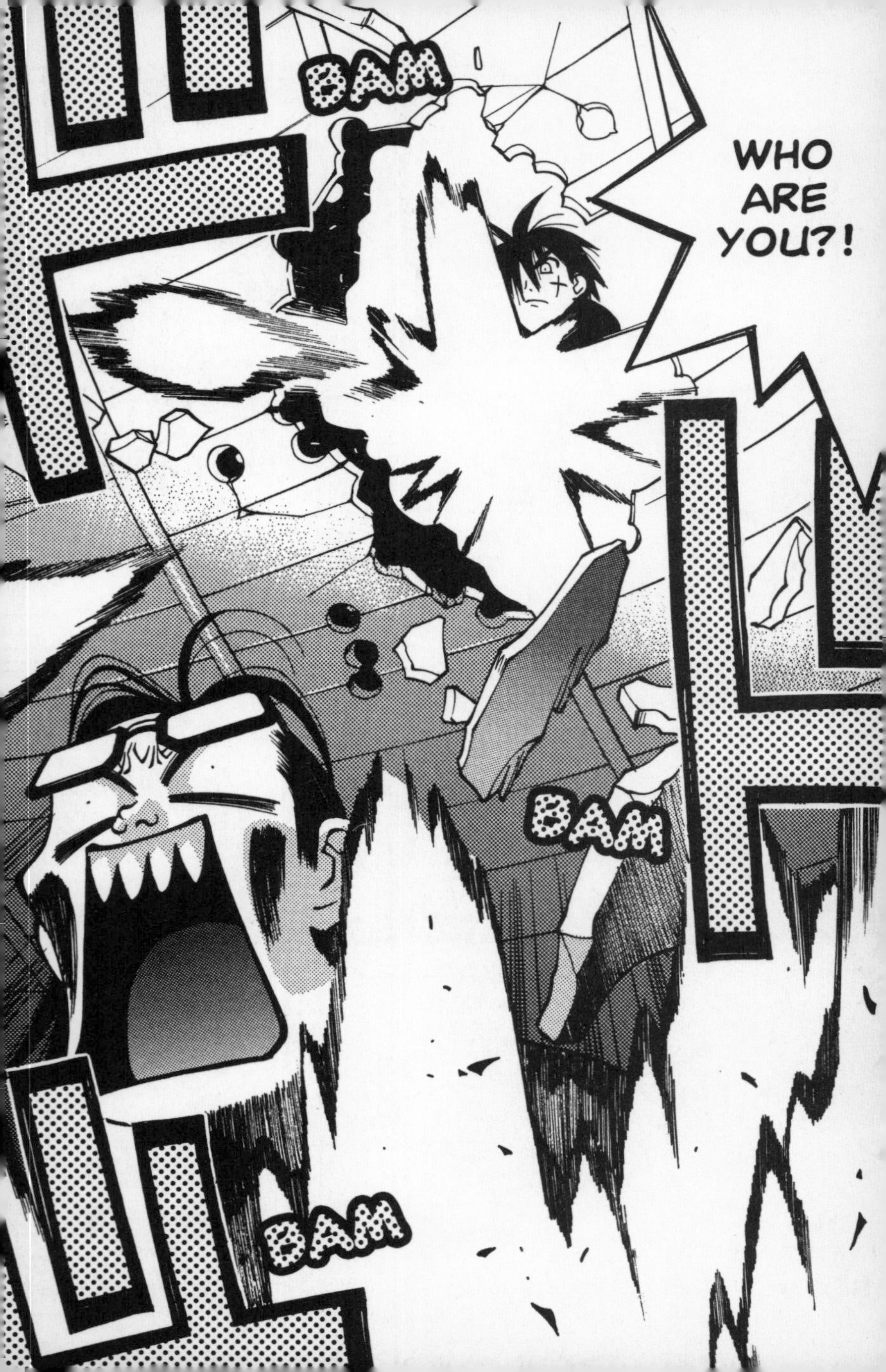
BAM
WHO ARE YOU?!
BAM
BAM

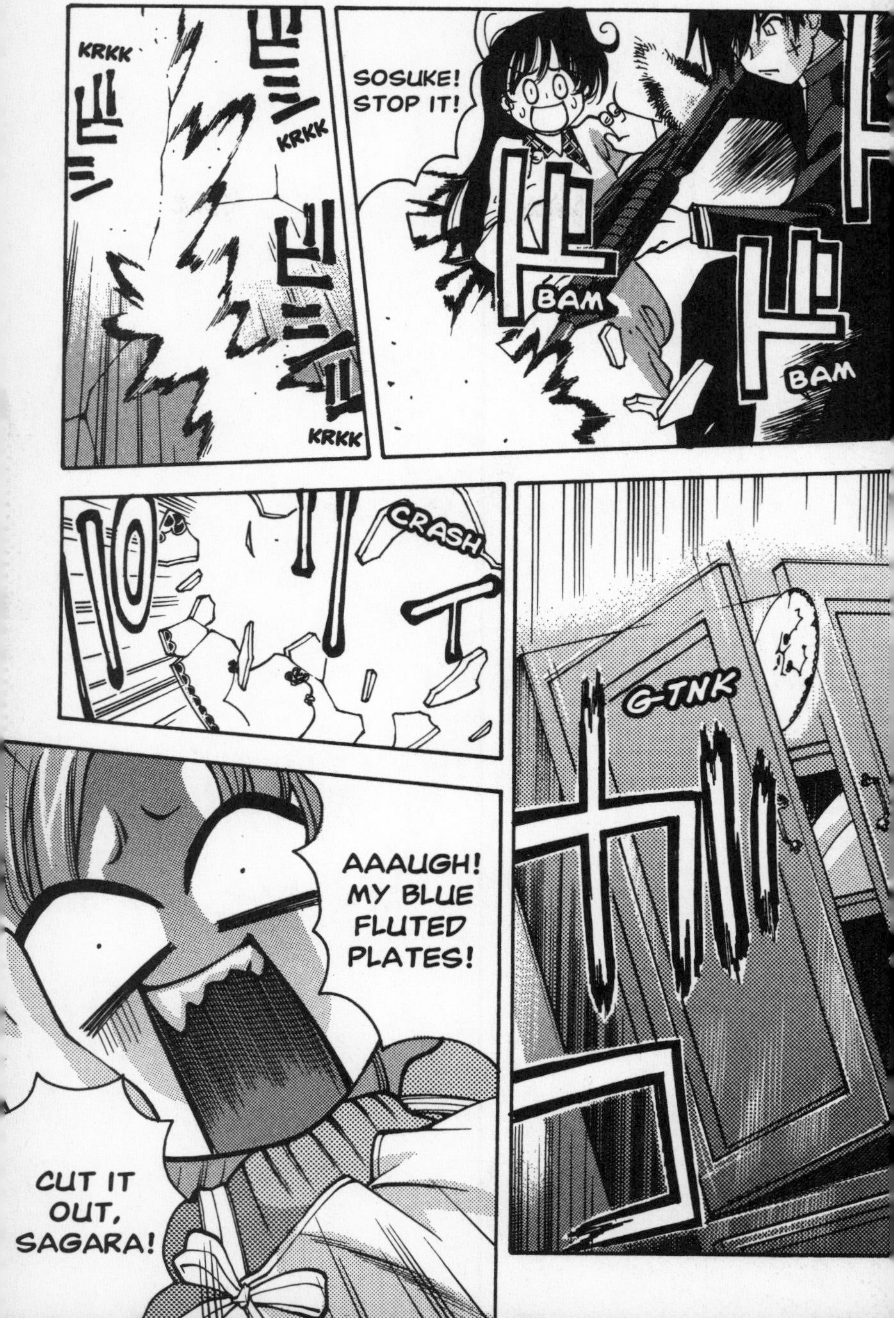
SOSUKE! STOP IT!
BAM
BAM
KRKK
KRKK
KRKK
G-TNK
CRASH
AAAUGH! MY BLUE FLUTED PLATES!
CUT IT OUT, SAGARA!

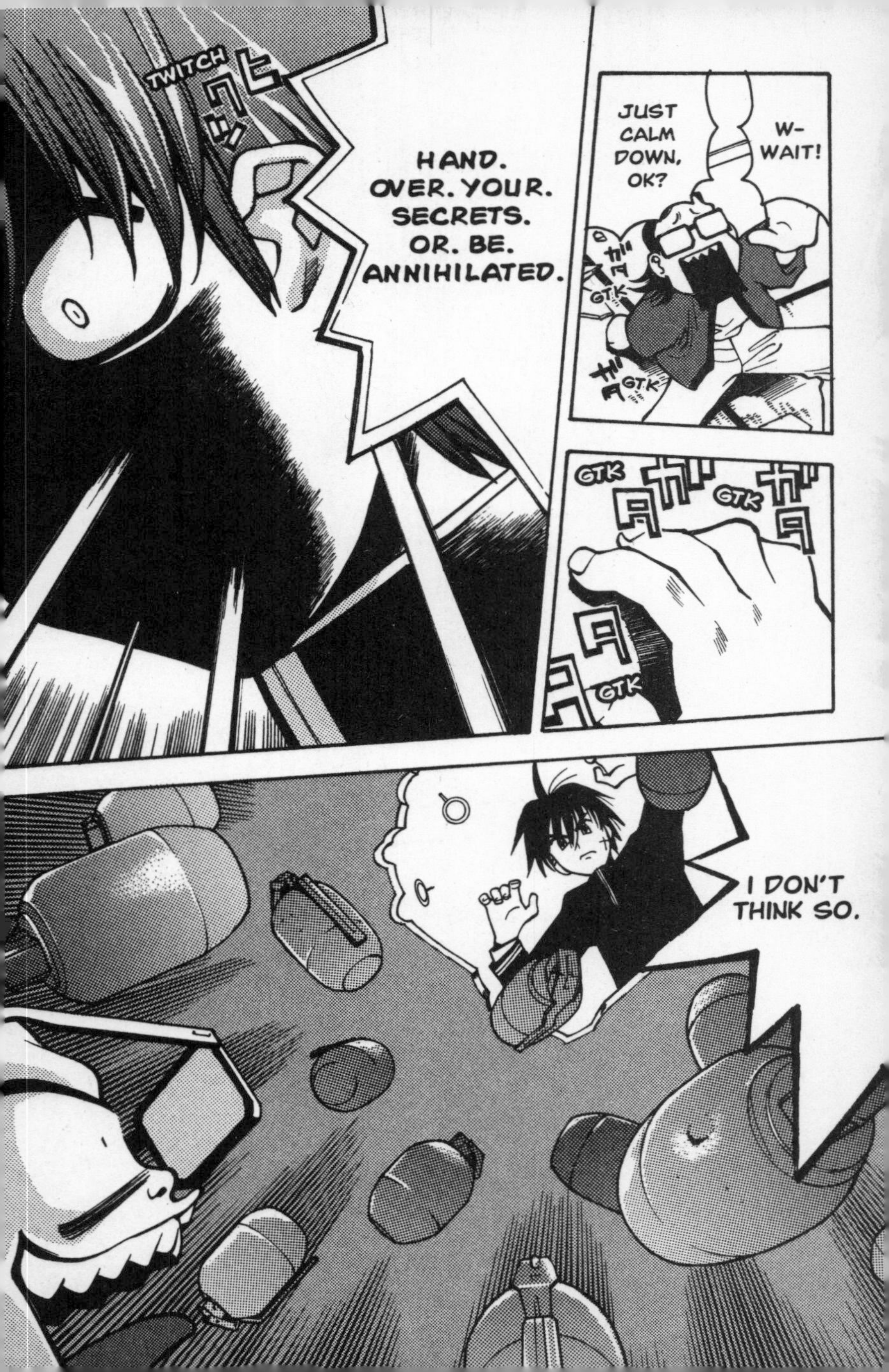

W-WAIT!
JUST CALM DOWN, OK?
GTK
GTK
GTK
GTK
GTK
TWITCH
HAND. OVER. YOUR. SECRETS. OR. BE. ANNIHILATED.
I DON'T THINK SO.

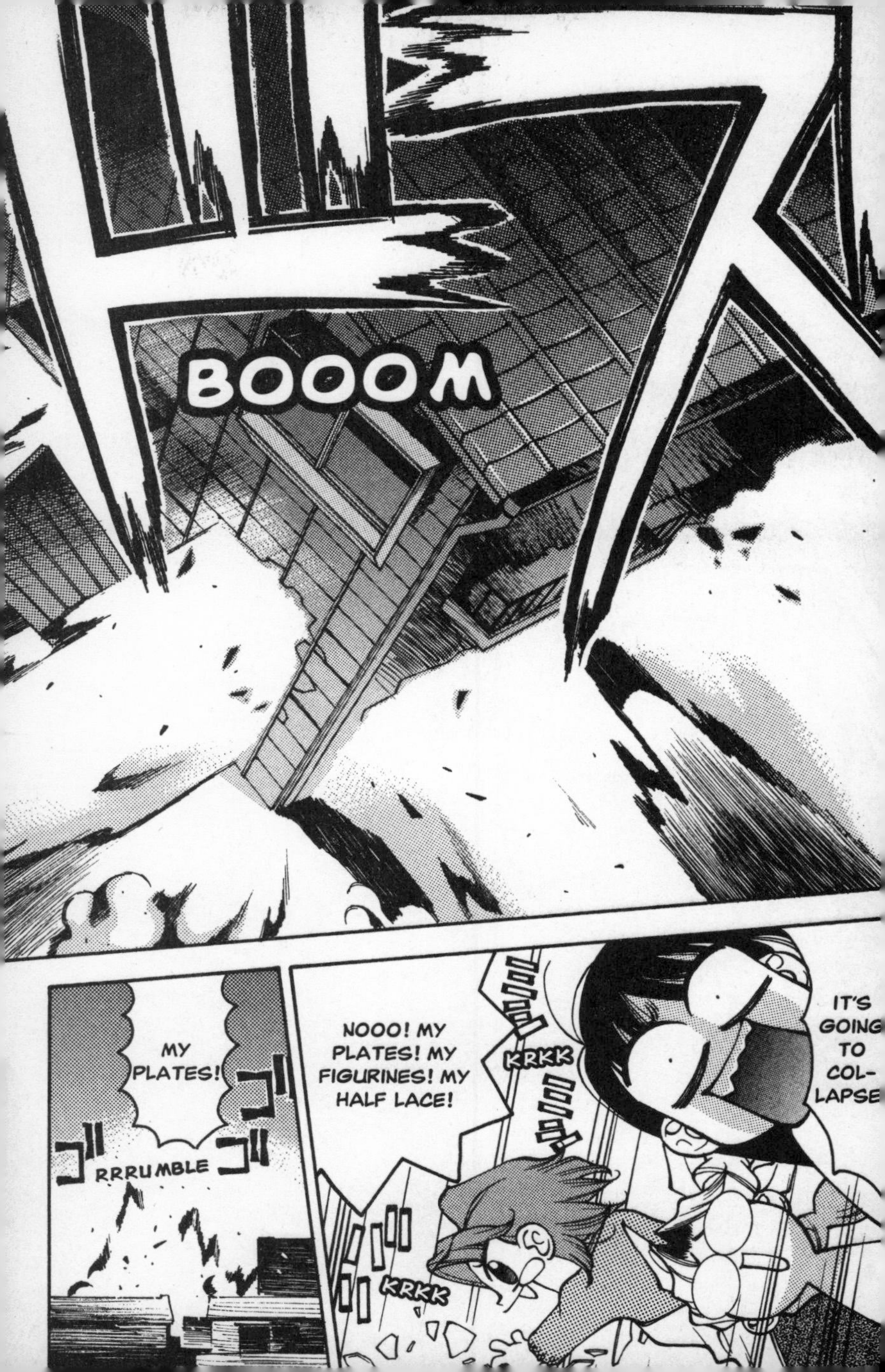

BOOOM
IT'S GOING TO COL-LAPSE
KRKK
NOOO! MY PLATES! MY FIGURINES! MY HALF LACE!
KRKK
MY PLATES!
RRRUMBLE

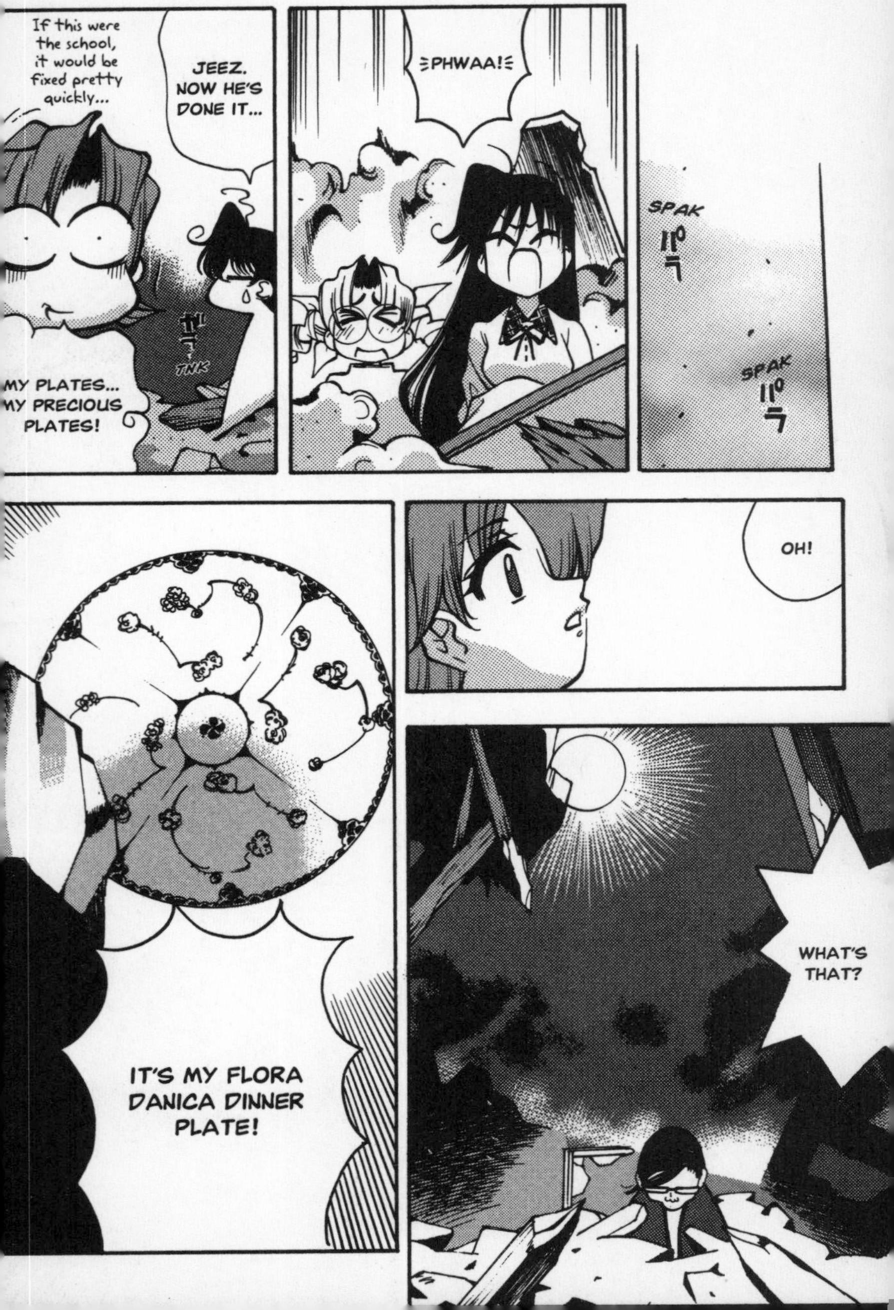
SPAK
パラ
SPAK
パラ
≡PHWAA!≡
JEEZ. NOW HE'S DONE IT...
If this were the school, it would be fixed pretty quickly...
TNK
MY PLATES... MY PRECIOUS PLATES!
OH!
IT'S MY FLORA DANICA DINNER PLATE!
WHAT'S THAT?

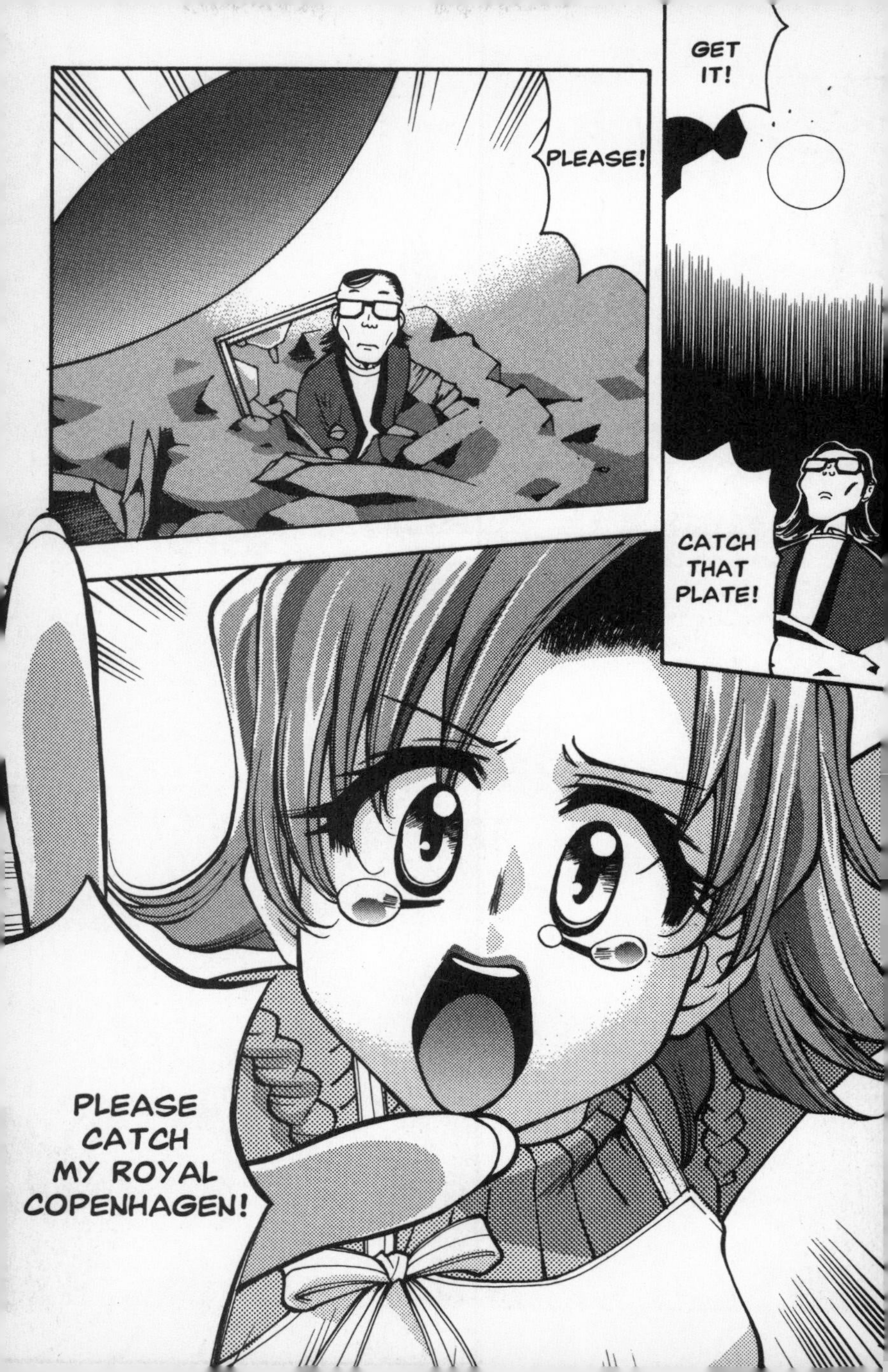
GET IT!
CATCH THAT PLATE!
PLEASE!
PLEASE CATCH MY ROYAL COPENHAGEN!

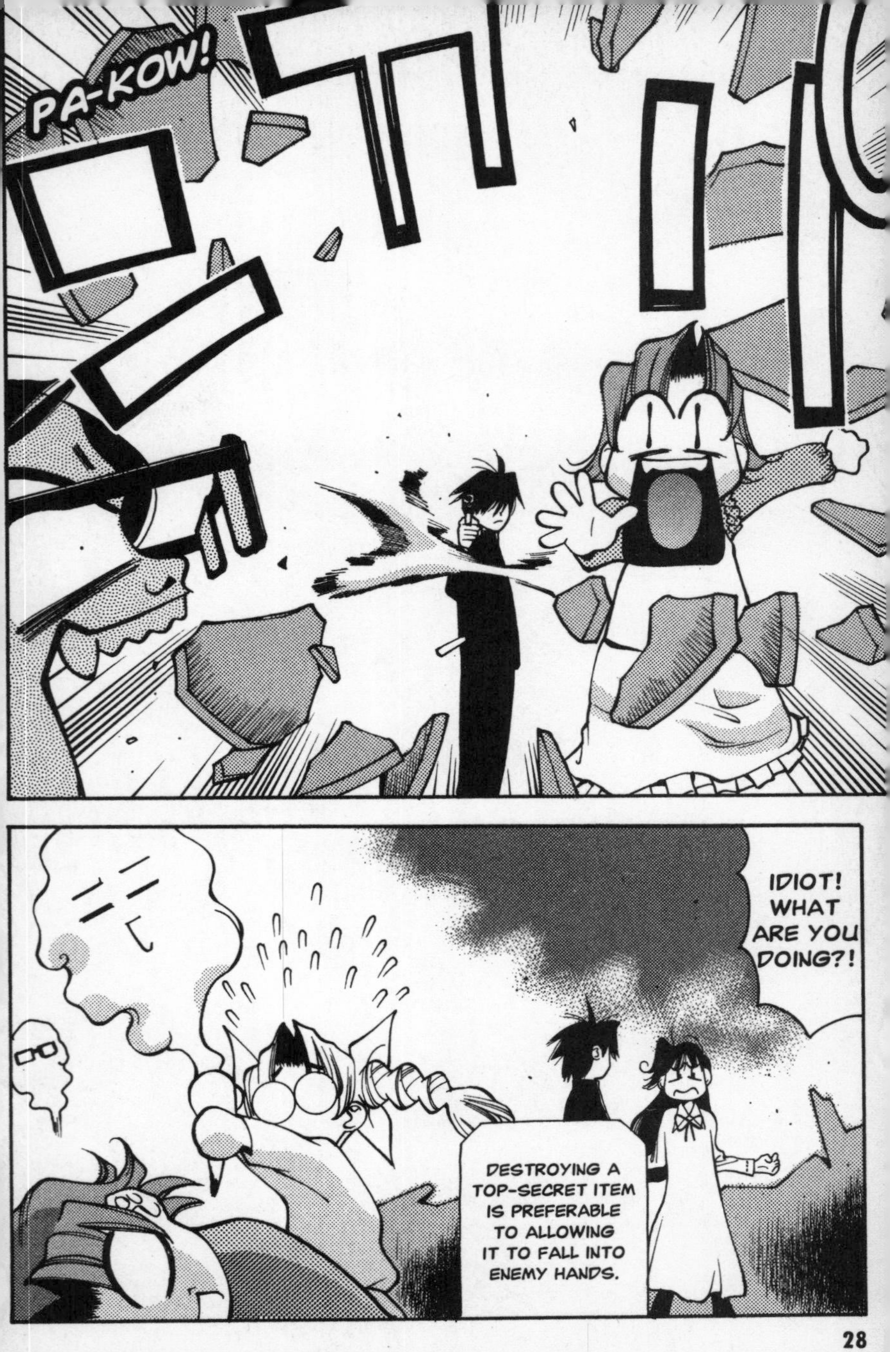
PA-KOW!
IDIOT! WHAT ARE YOU DOING?!
DESTROYING A TOP-SECRET ITEM IS PREFERABLE TO ALLOWING IT TO FALL INTO ENEMY HANDS.

BOMB 25 LOVE'S LIGHT—KYONCHIN, MY LOVE ♥

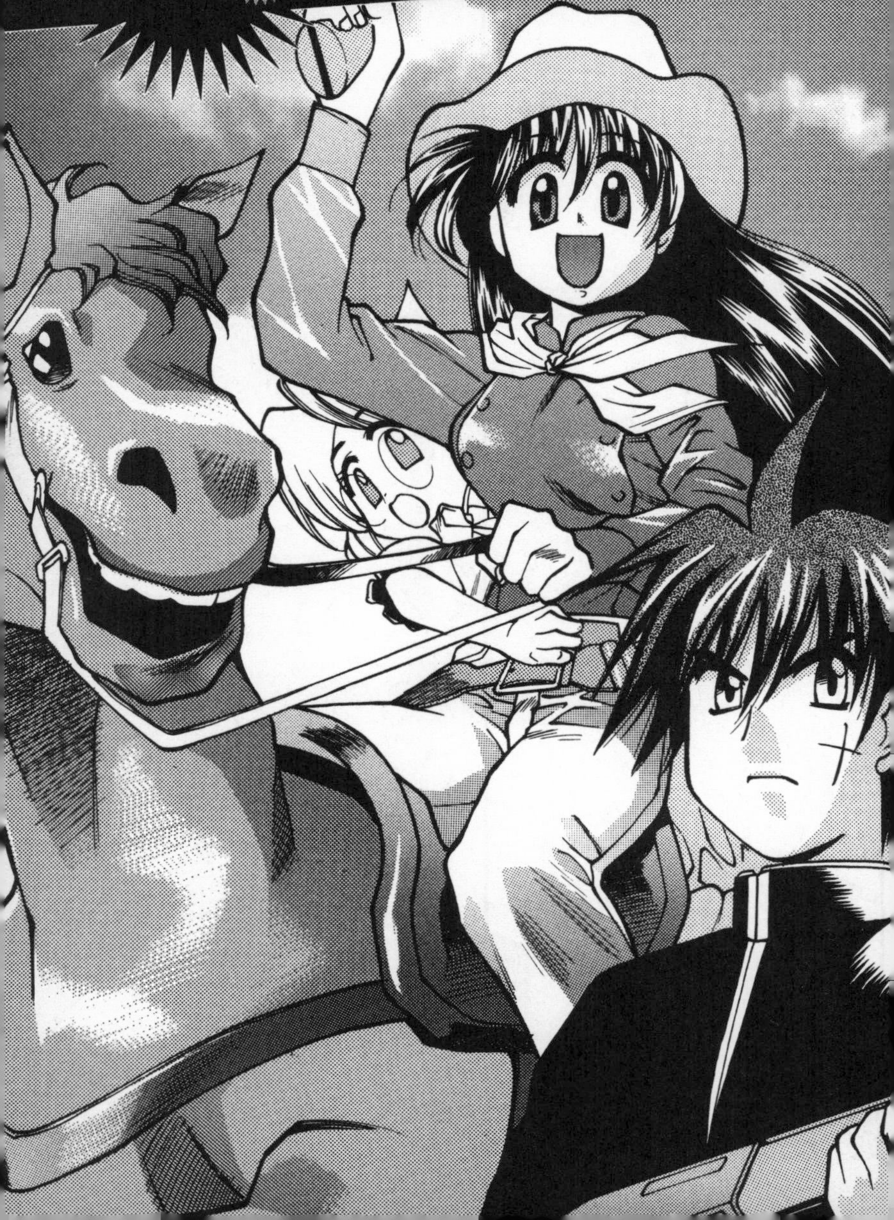

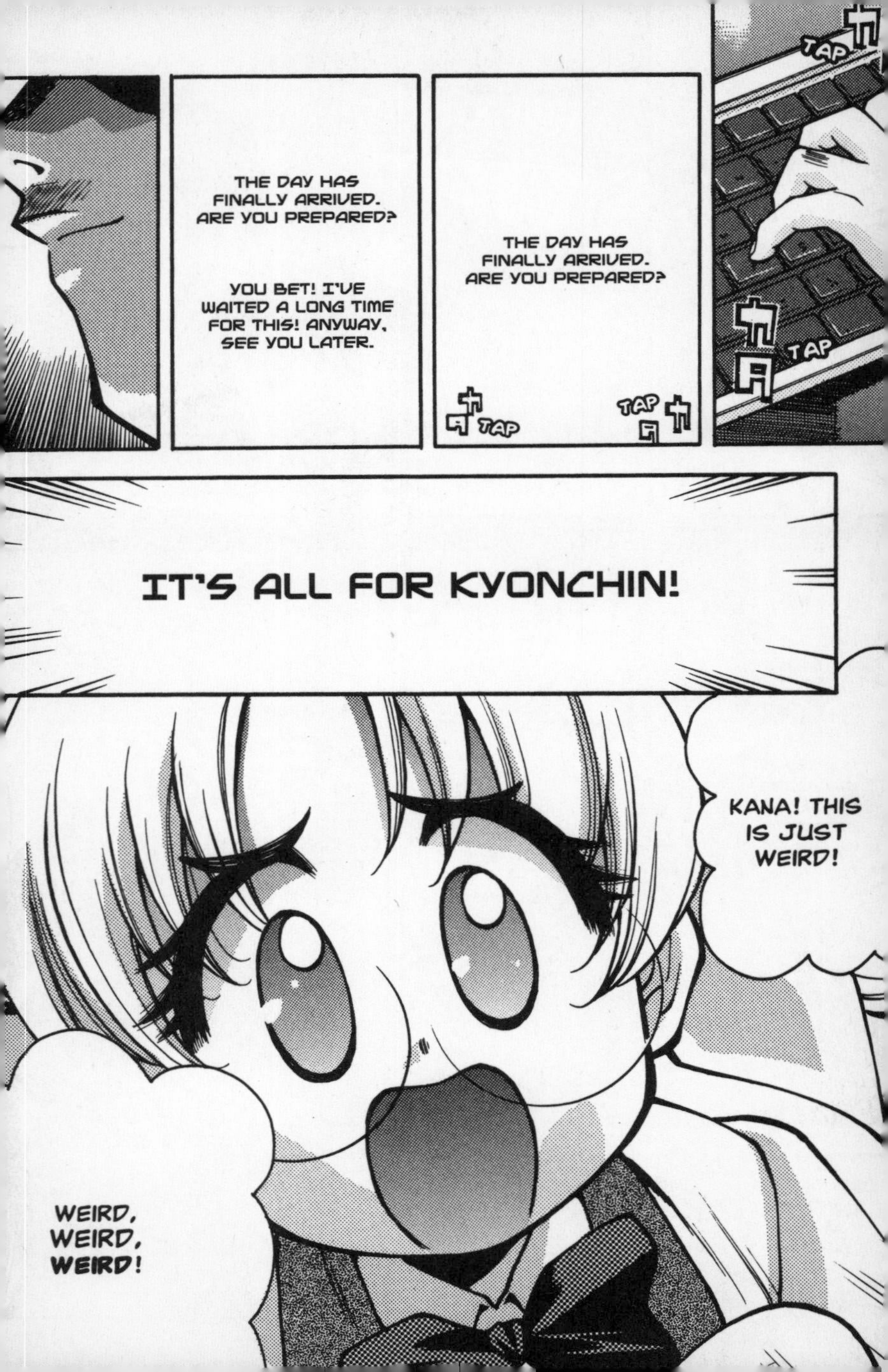
TAP
TAP
TAP
TAP
THE DAY HAS FINALLY ARRIVED. ARE YOU PREPARED?
THE DAY HAS FINALLY ARRIVED. ARE YOU PREPARED?
YOU BET! I'VE WAITED A LONG TIME FOR THIS! ANYWAY, SEE YOU LATER.
IT'S ALL FOR KYONCHIN!
KANA! THIS IS JUST WEIRD!
WEIRD, WEIRD, WEIRD!

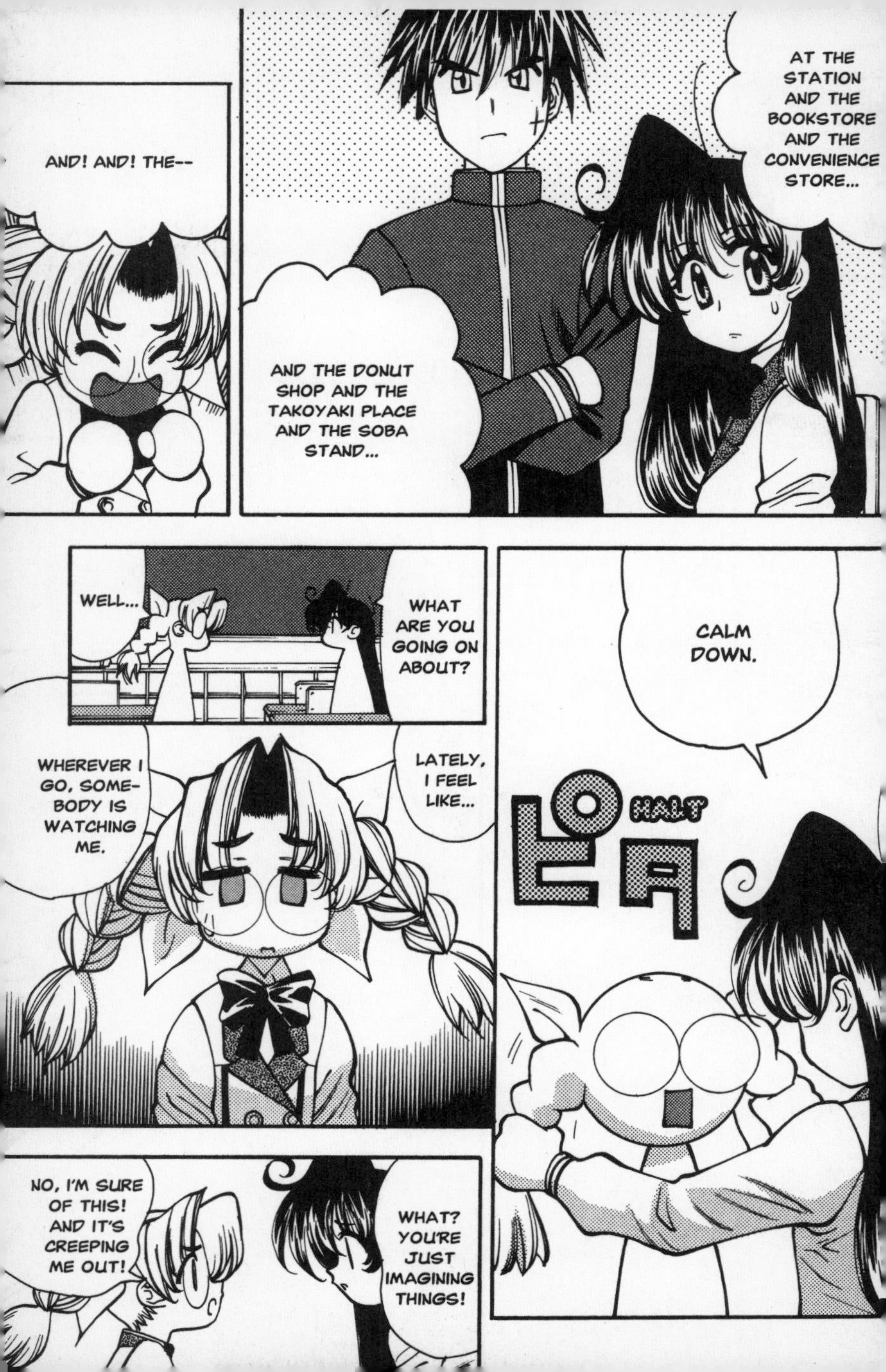
AT THE STATION AND THE BOOKSTORE AND THE CONVENIENCE STORE...
AND THE DONUT SHOP AND THE TAKOYAKI PLACE AND THE SOBA STAND...
AND! AND! THE--
CALM DOWN.
HALT
WHAT ARE YOU GOING ON ABOUT?
WELL...
LATELY, I FEEL LIKE...
WHEREVER I GO, SOME-BODY IS WATCHING ME.
WHAT? YOU'RE JUST IMAGINING THINGS!
NO, I'M SURE OF THIS! AND IT'S CREEPING ME OUT!

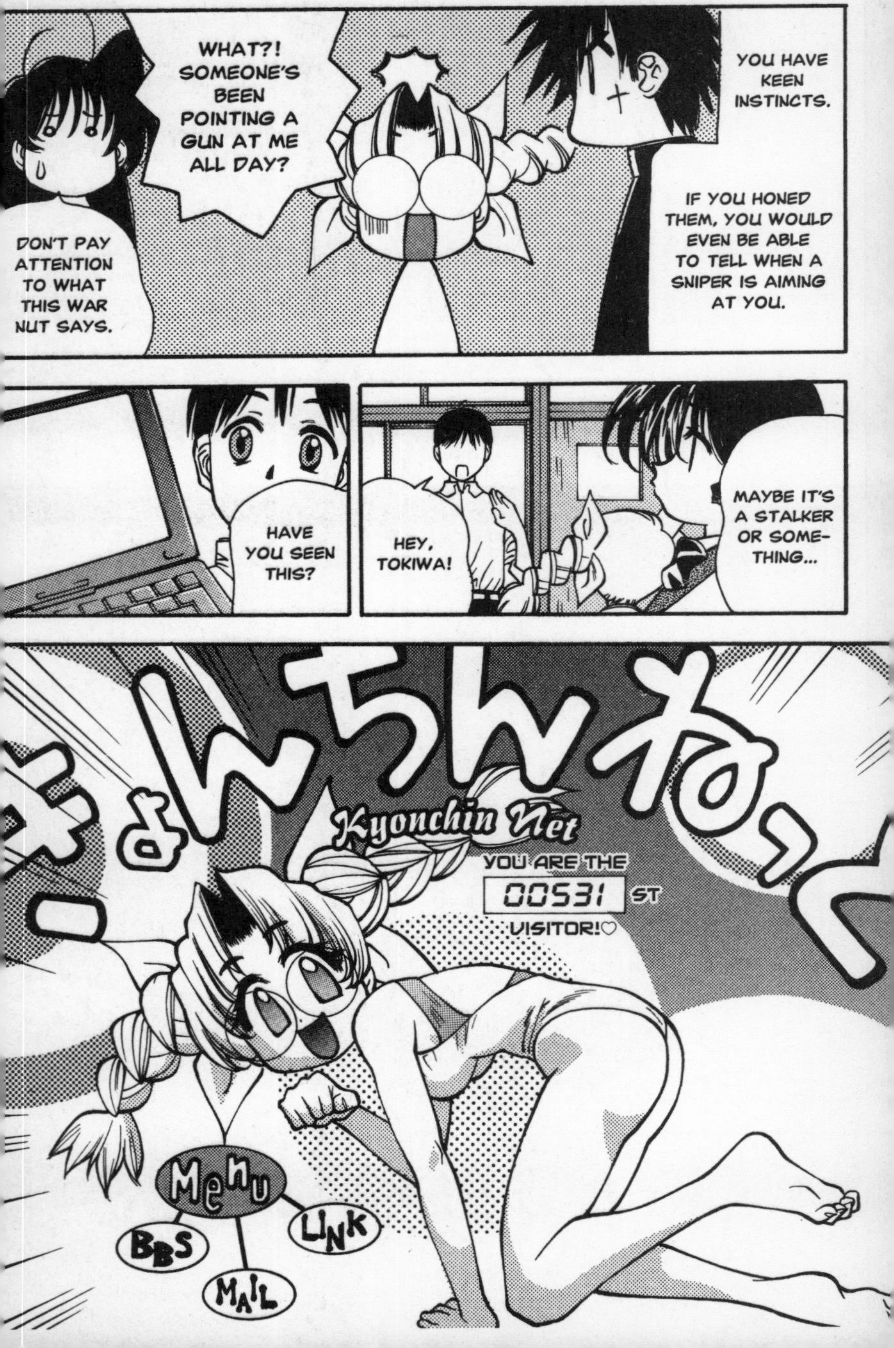
YOU HAVE KEEN INSTINCTS.
IF YOU HONED THEM, YOU WOULD EVEN BE ABLE TO TELL WHEN A SNIPER IS AIMING AT YOU.
WHAT?! SOMEONE'S BEEN POINTING A GUN AT ME ALL DAY?
DON'T PAY ATTENTION TO WHAT THIS WAR NUT SAYS.
MAYBE IT'S A STALKER OR SOME-THING...
HEY, TOKIWA!
HAVE YOU SEEN THIS?
Kyonchin Net
YOU ARE THE
00531 ST
VISITOR!♡
Menu
LINK
BBS
MAIL

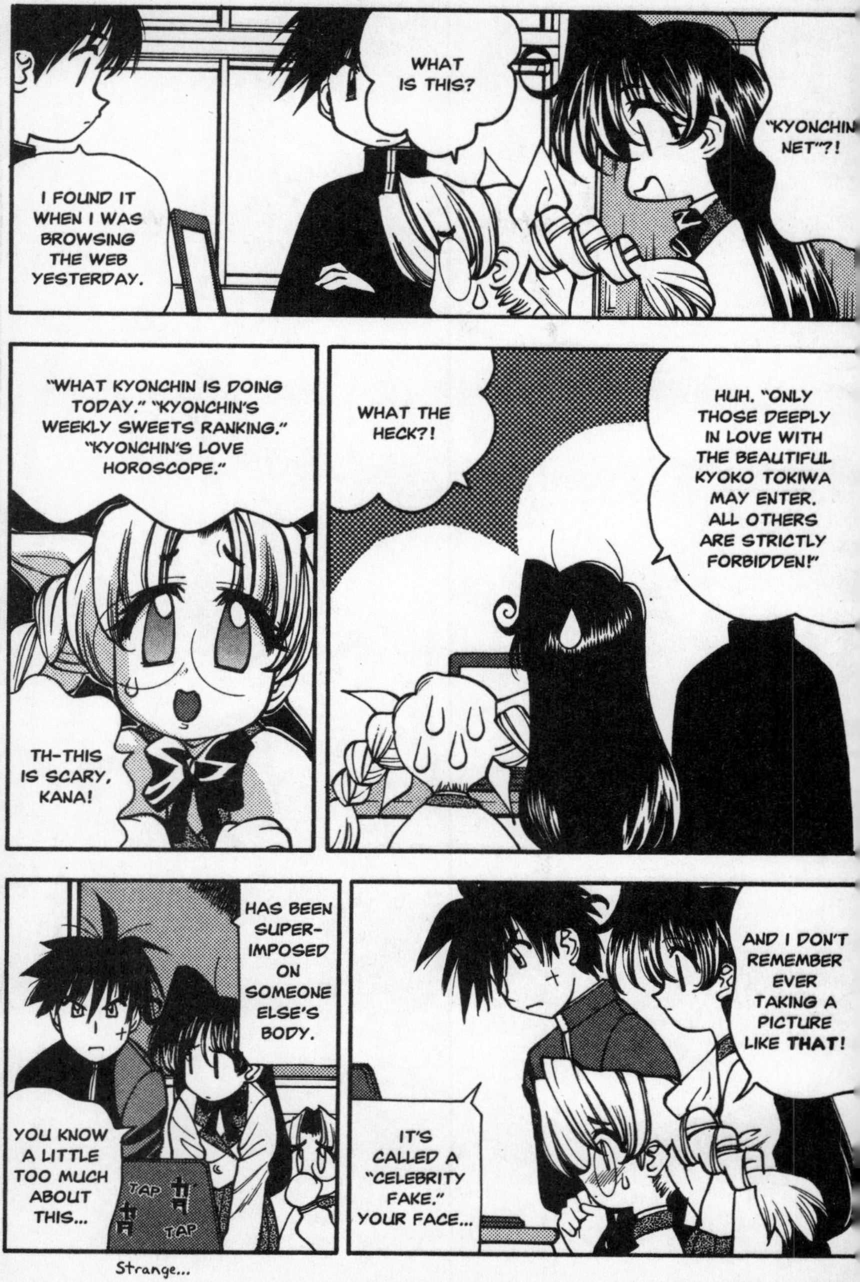
WHAT IS THIS?
"KYONCHIN NET"?!
I FOUND IT WHEN I WAS BROWSING THE WEB YESTERDAY.
HUH. "ONLY THOSE DEEPLY IN LOVE WITH THE BEAUTIFUL KYOKO TOKIWA MAY ENTER. ALL OTHERS ARE STRICTLY FORBIDDEN!"
WHAT THE HECK?!
"WHAT KYONCHIN IS DOING TODAY." "KYONCHIN'S WEEKLY SWEETS RANKING." "KYONCHIN'S LOVE HOROSCOPE."
TH-THIS IS SCARY, KANA!
AND I DON'T REMEMBER EVER TAKING A PICTURE LIKE **THAT**!
IT'S CALLED A "CELEBRITY FAKE." YOUR FACE...
HAS BEEN SUPER-IMPOSED ON SOMEONE ELSE'S BODY.
YOU KNOW A LITTLE TOO MUCH ABOUT THIS...
TAP
TAP

Strange...

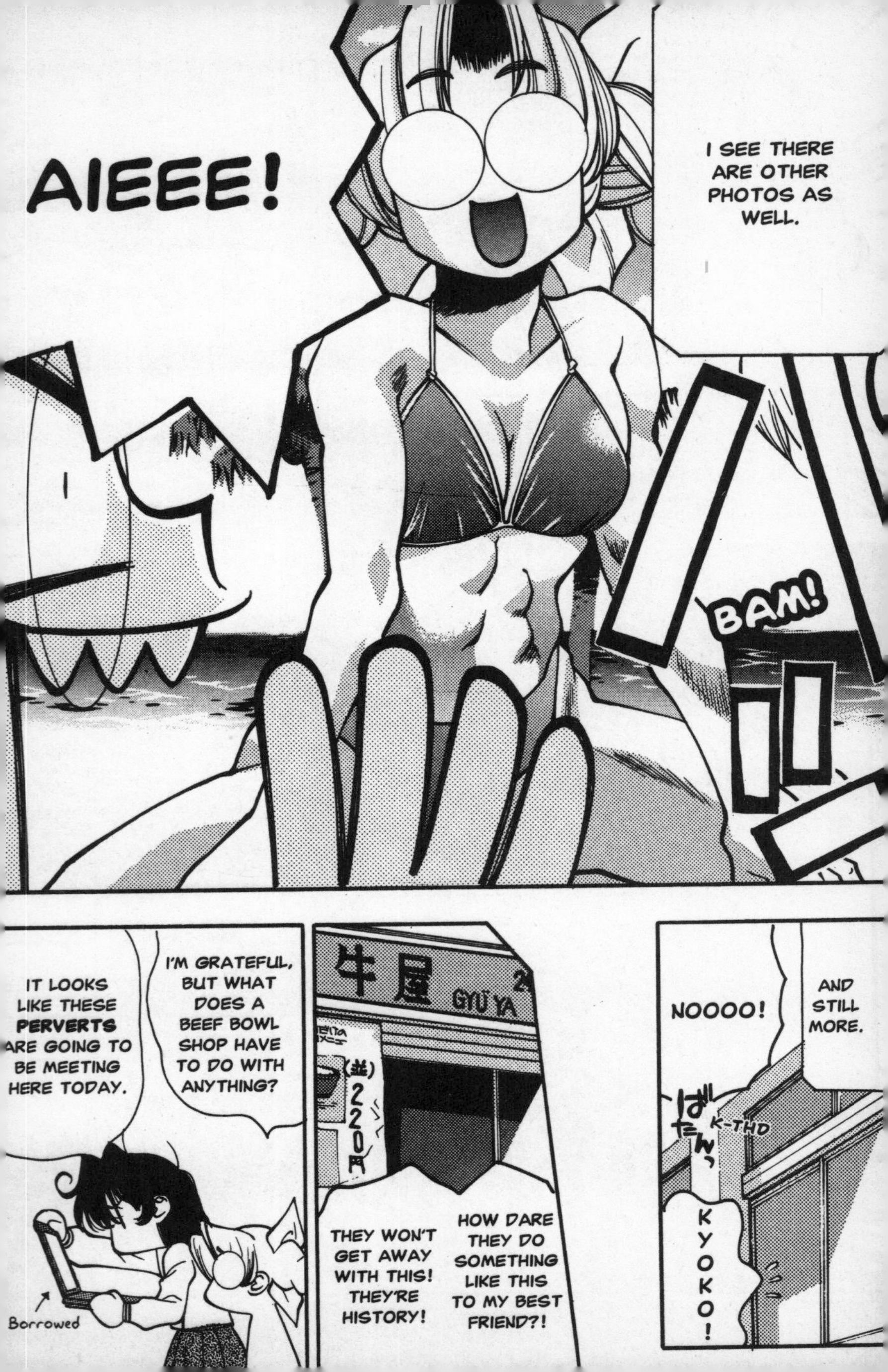
I SEE THERE ARE OTHER PHOTOS AS WELL.
AIEEE!
BAM!
AND STILL MORE.
NOOOO!
ばたんっ
K-THD
KYOKO!
牛屋
GYU YA
220円
HOW DARE THEY DO SOMETHING LIKE THIS TO MY BEST FRIEND?!
THEY WON'T GET AWAY WITH THIS! THEY'RE HISTORY!
I'M GRATEFUL, BUT WHAT DOES A BEEF BOWL SHOP HAVE TO DO WITH ANYTHING?
IT LOOKS LIKE THESE PERVERTS ARE GOING TO BE MEETING HERE TODAY.
Borrowed

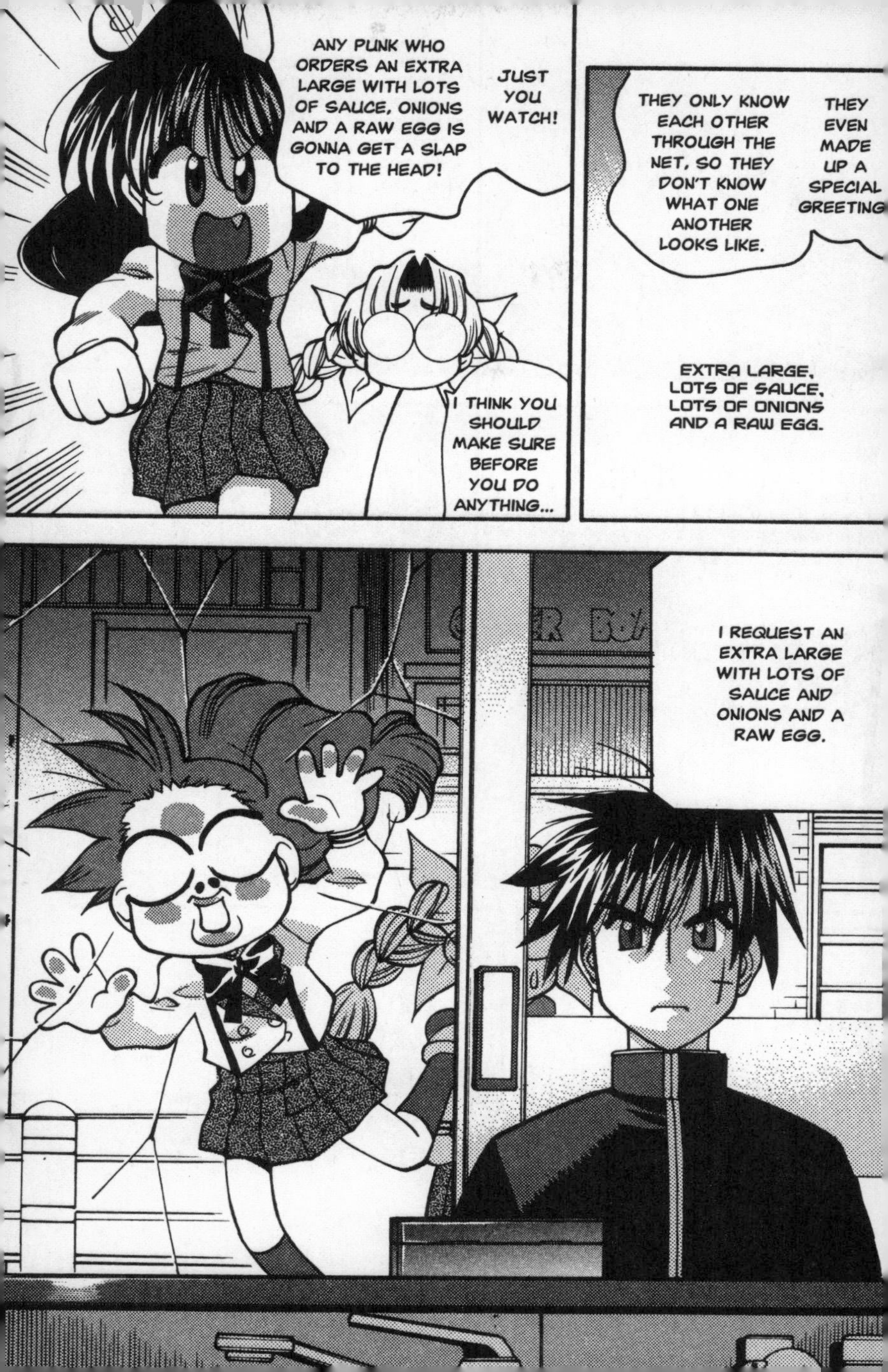

THEY EVEN MADE UP A SPECIAL GREETING
THEY ONLY KNOW EACH OTHER THROUGH THE NET, SO THEY DON'T KNOW WHAT ONE ANOTHER LOOKS LIKE.
EXTRA LARGE, LOTS OF SAUCE, LOTS OF ONIONS AND A RAW EGG.
ANY PUNK WHO ORDERS AN EXTRA LARGE WITH LOTS OF SAUCE, ONIONS AND A RAW EGG IS GONNA GET A SLAP TO THE HEAD!
JUST YOU WATCH!
I THINK YOU SHOULD MAKE SURE BEFORE YOU DO ANYTHING...
I REQUEST AN EXTRA LARGE WITH LOTS OF SAUCE AND ONIONS AND A RAW EGG.

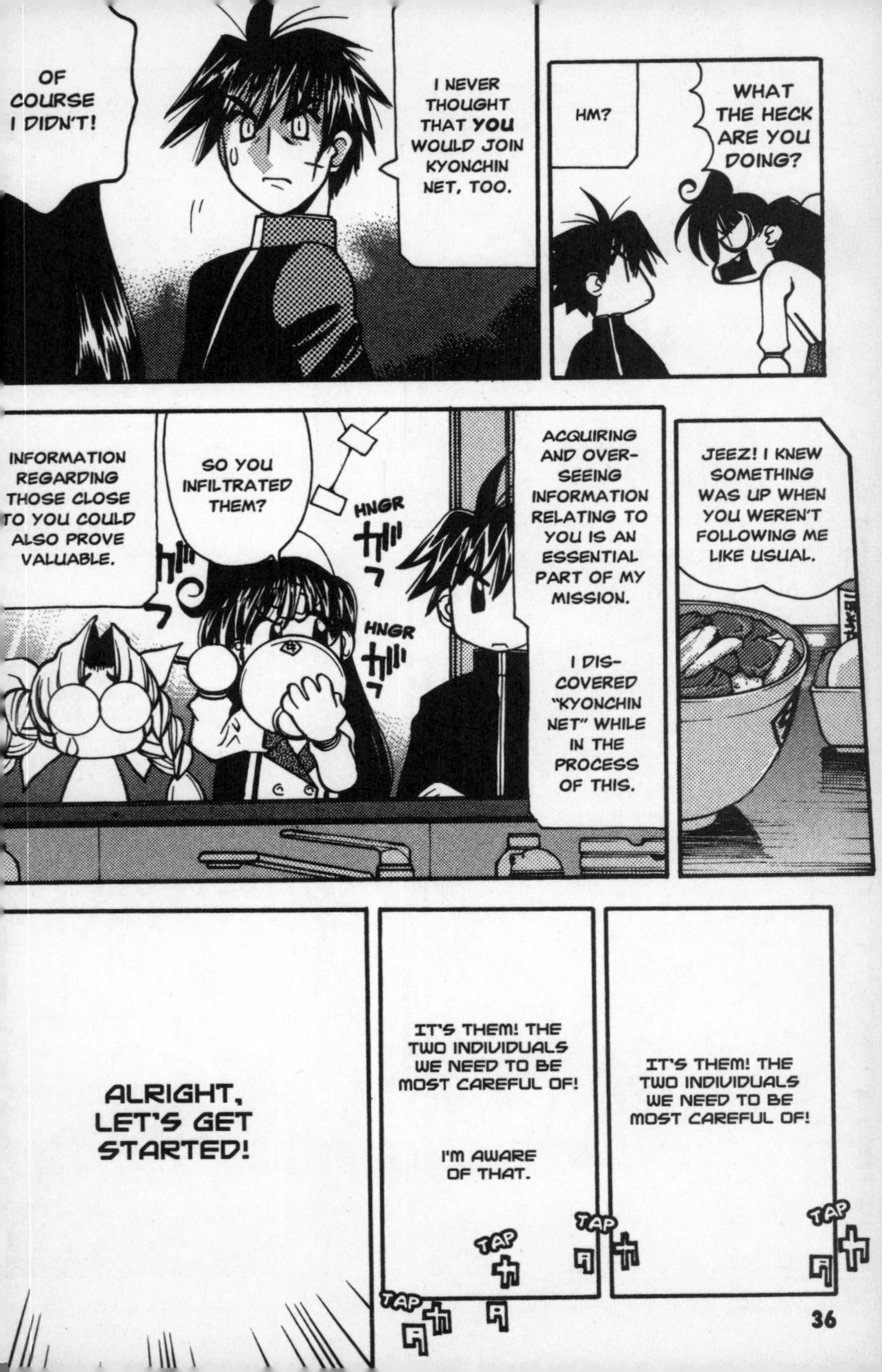
WHAT THE HECK ARE YOU DOING?
HM?
I NEVER THOUGHT THAT YOU WOULD JOIN KYONCHIN NET, TOO.
OF COURSE I DIDN'T!
JEEZ! I KNEW SOMETHING WAS UP WHEN YOU WEREN'T FOLLOWING ME LIKE USUAL.
ACQUIRING AND OVER-SEEING INFORMATION RELATING TO YOU IS AN ESSENTIAL PART OF MY MISSION.
I DIS-COVERED "KYONCHIN NET" WHILE IN THE PROCESS OF THIS.
HNGR
HNGR
SO YOU INFILTRATED THEM?
INFORMATION REGARDING THOSE CLOSE TO YOU COULD ALSO PROVE VALUABLE.
IT'S THEM! THE TWO INDIVIDUALS WE NEED TO BE MOST CAREFUL OF!
TAP
IT'S THEM! THE TWO INDIVIDUALS WE NEED TO BE MOST CAREFUL OF!
I'M AWARE OF THAT.
TAP
TAP
TAP
ALRIGHT, LET'S GET STARTED!

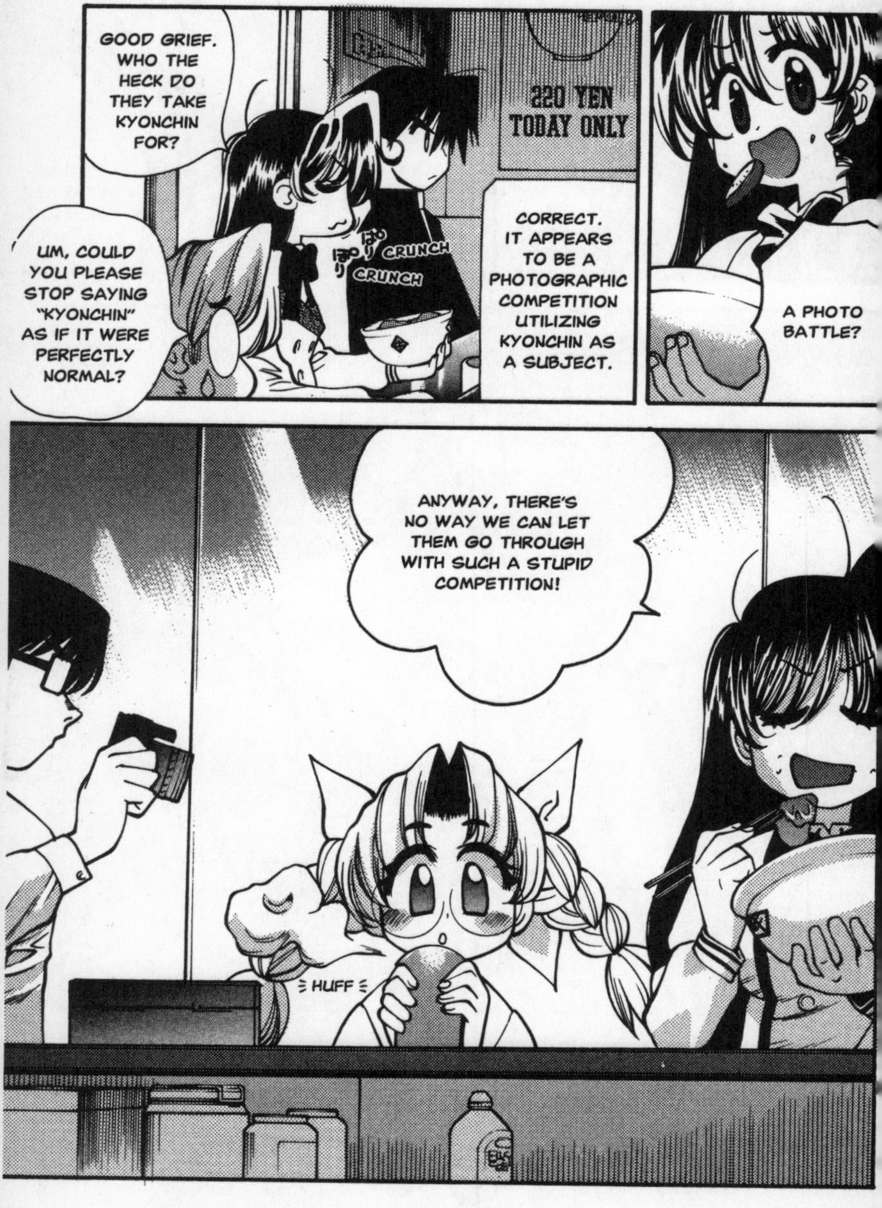
A PHOTO BATTLE?
220 YEN TODAY ONLY
CORRECT. IT APPEARS TO BE A PHOTOGRAPHIC COMPETITION UTILIZING KYONCHIN AS A SUBJECT.
GOOD GRIEF. WHO THE HECK DO THEY TAKE KYONCHIN FOR?
ぽり ぽり CRUNCH CRUNCH
UM, COULD YOU PLEASE STOP SAYING "KYONCHIN" AS IF IT WERE PERFECTLY NORMAL?
ANYWAY, THERE'S NO WAY WE CAN LET THEM GO THROUGH WITH SUCH A STUPID COMPETITION!
HUFF

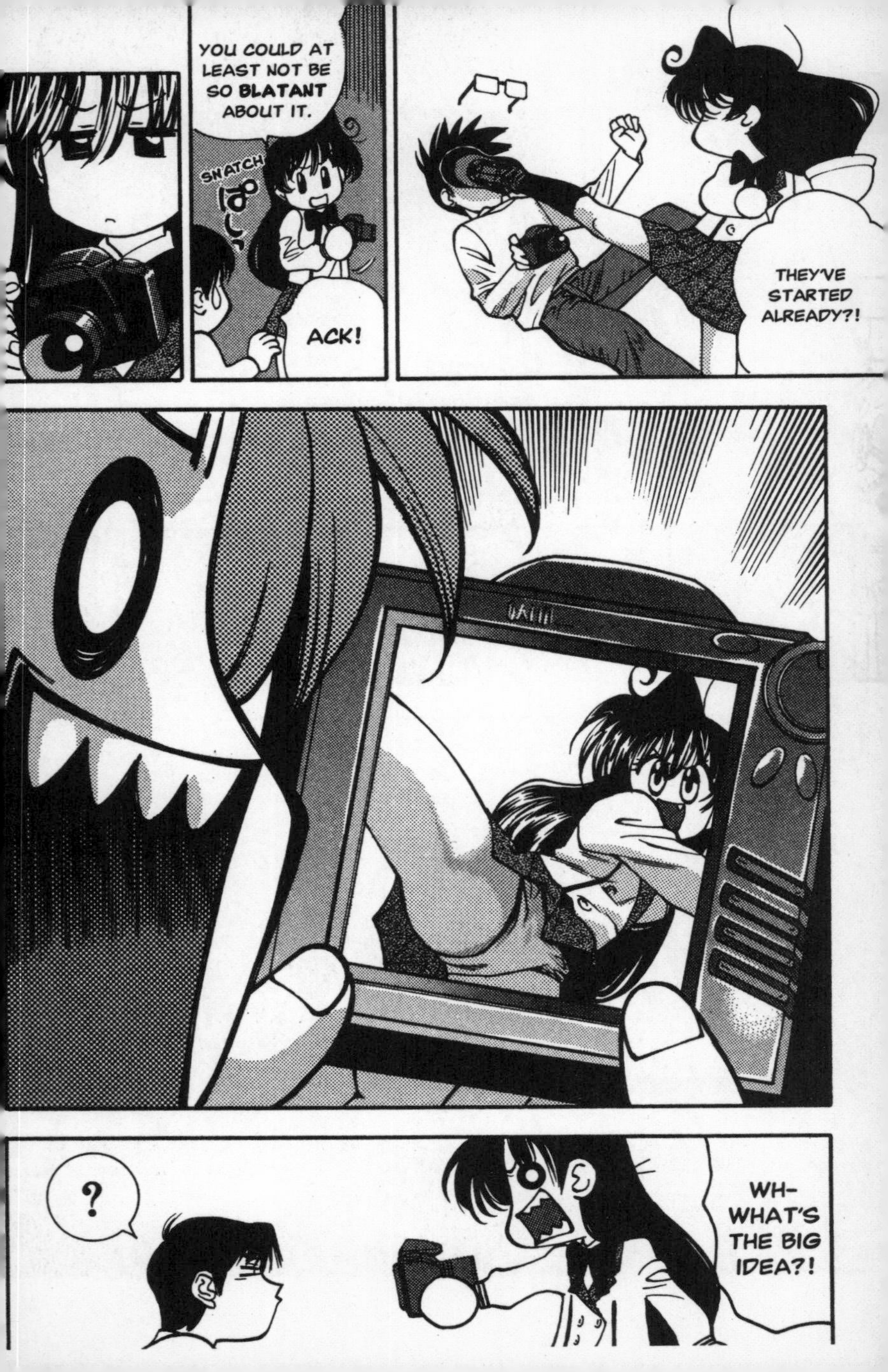

THEY'VE STARTED ALREADY?!
YOU COULD AT LEAST NOT BE SO BLATANT ABOUT IT.
SNATCH
ぱしっ
ACK!
WH- WHAT'S THE BIG IDEA?!
?

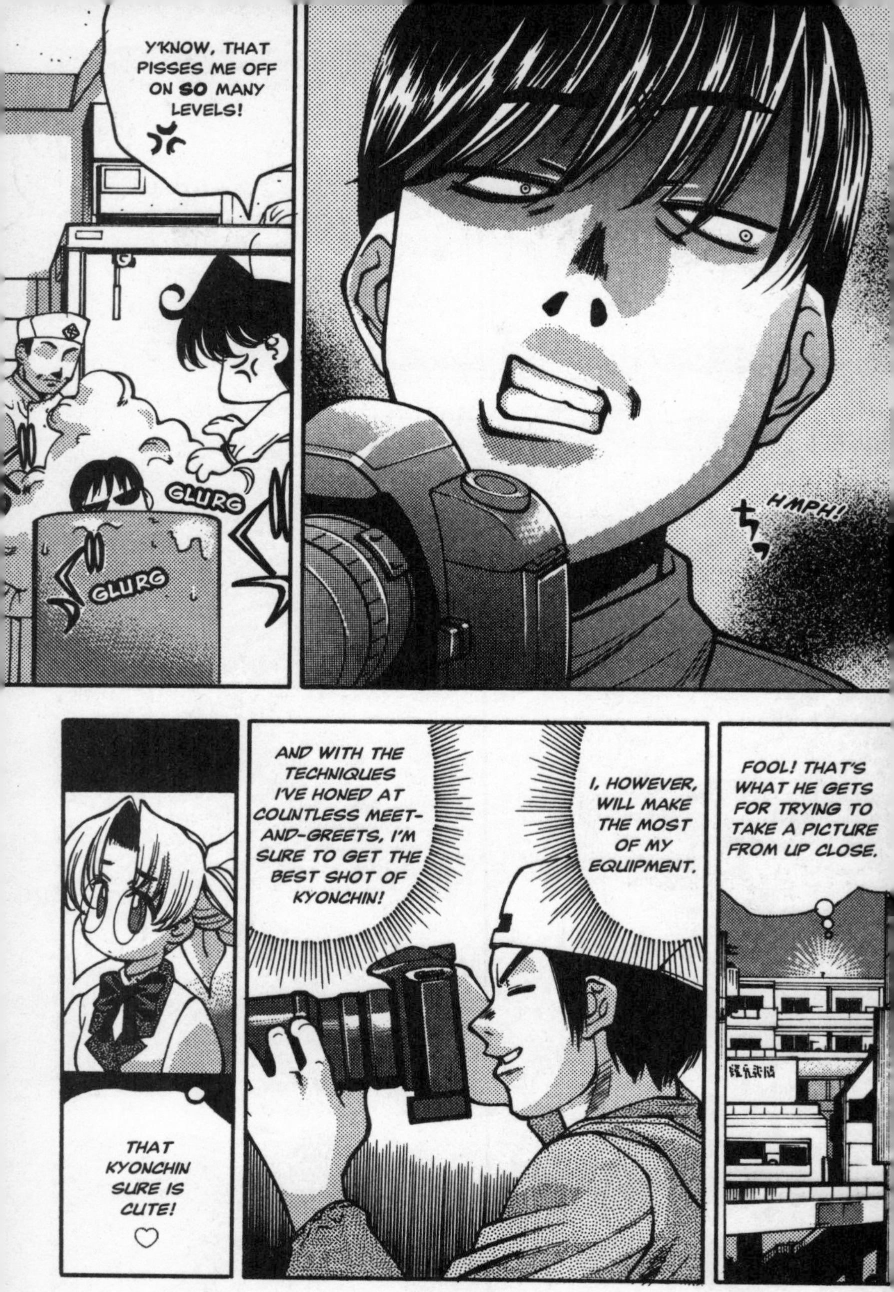
HMPH!
Y'KNOW, THAT PISSES ME OFF ON SO MANY LEVELS!
GLURG
GLURG
FOOL! THAT'S WHAT HE GETS FOR TRYING TO TAKE A PICTURE FROM UP CLOSE.
I, HOWEVER, WILL MAKE THE MOST OF MY EQUIPMENT.
AND WITH THE TECHNIQUES I'VE HONED AT COUNTLESS MEET-AND-GREETS, I'M SURE TO GET THE BEST SHOT OF KYONCHIN!
THAT KYONCHIN SURE IS CUTE!

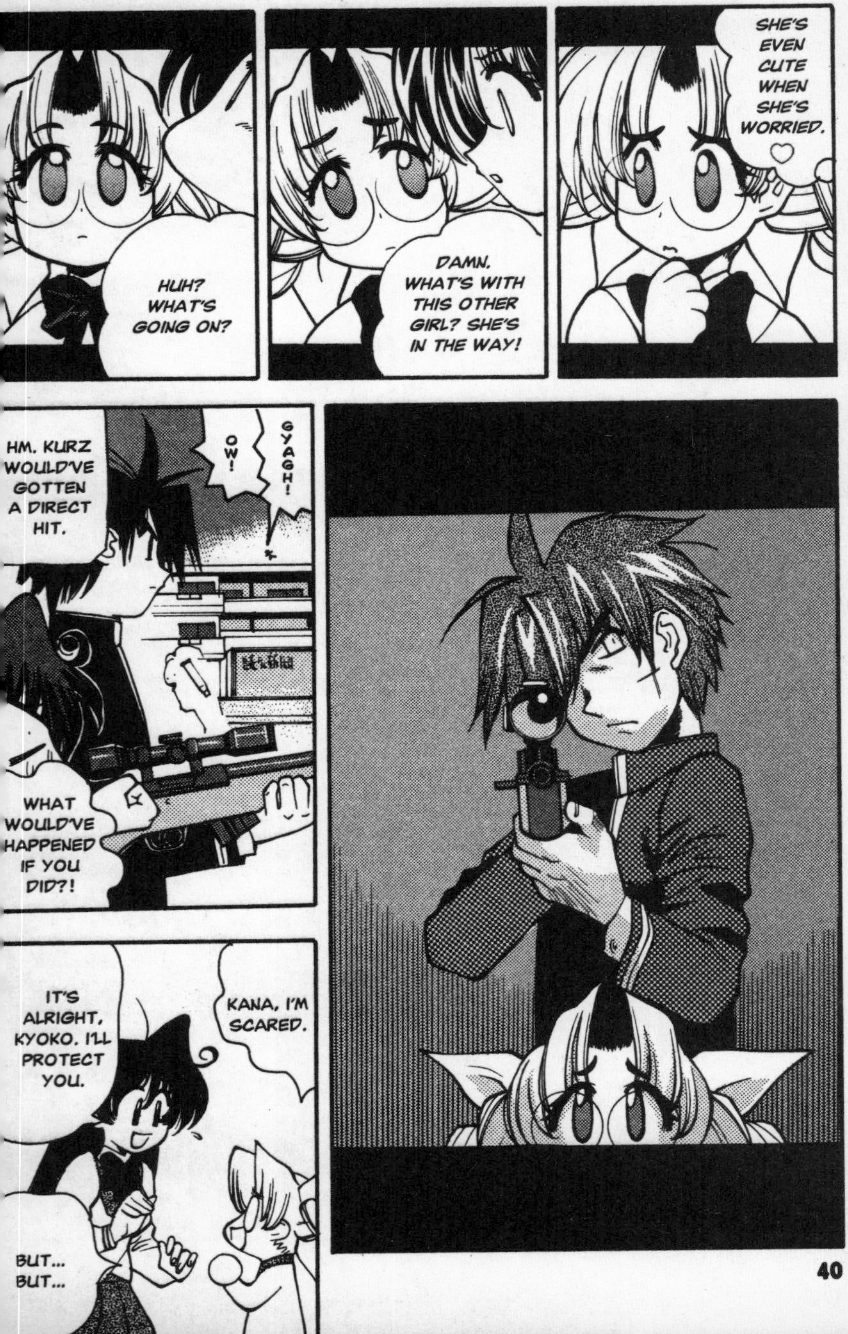
HUH? WHAT'S GOING ON?
DAMN. WHAT'S WITH THIS OTHER GIRL? SHE'S IN THE WAY!
SHE'S EVEN CUTE WHEN SHE'S WORRIED.
HM. KURZ WOULD'VE GOTTEN A DIRECT HIT.
GYAGH!
OW!
WHAT WOULD'VE HAPPENED IF YOU DID?!
KANA, I'M SCARED.
IT'S ALRIGHT, KYOKO. I'LL PROTECT YOU.
BUT... BUT...

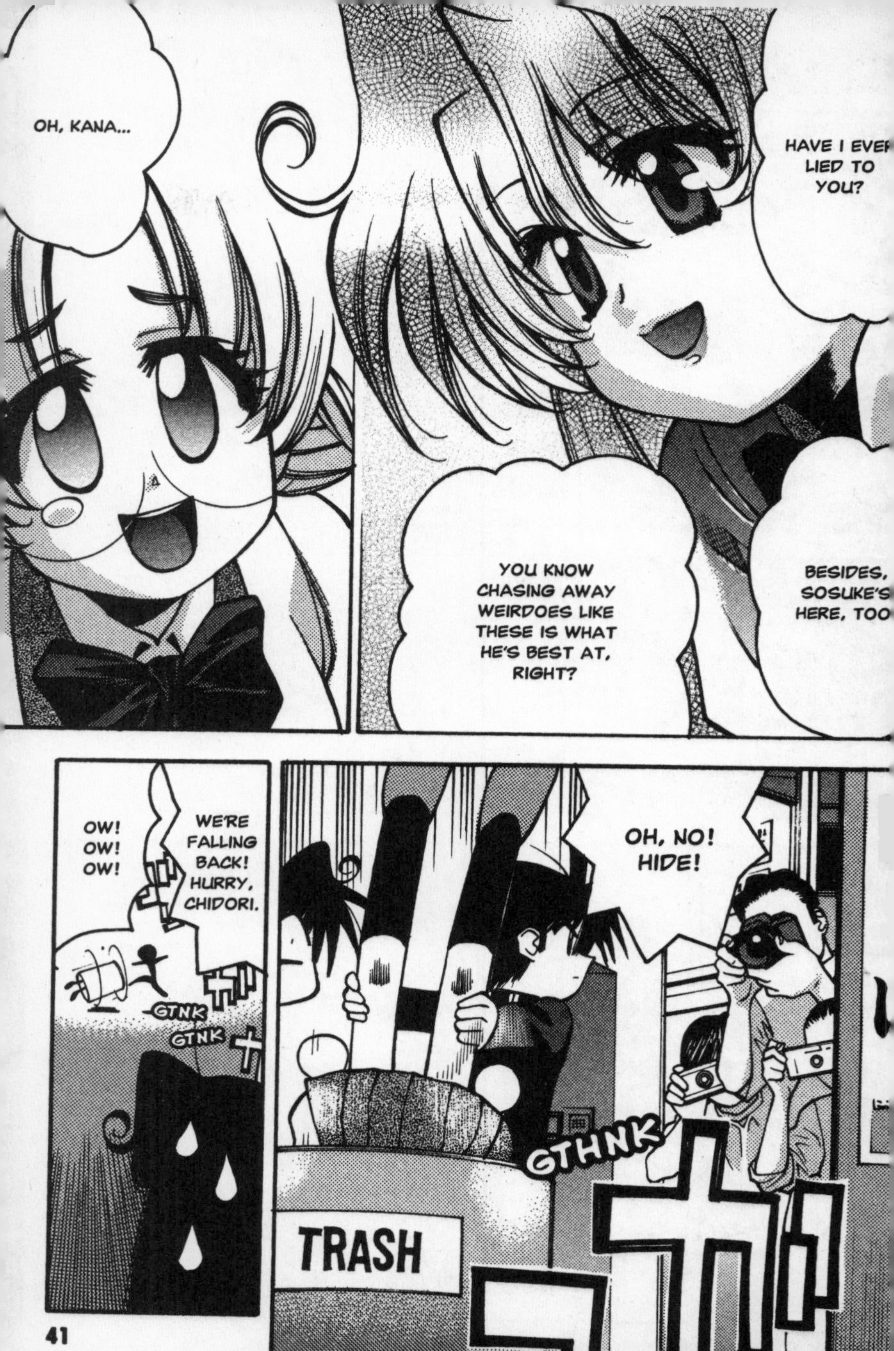
HAVE I EVER LIED TO YOU?
BESIDES, SOSUKE'S HERE, TOO
YOU KNOW CHASING AWAY WEIRDOES LIKE THESE IS WHAT HE'S BEST AT, RIGHT?
OH, KANA...
OH, NO! HIDE!
GTHNK
TRASH
WE'RE FALLING BACK! HURRY, CHIDORI.
OW! OW! OW!
GTNK
GTNK

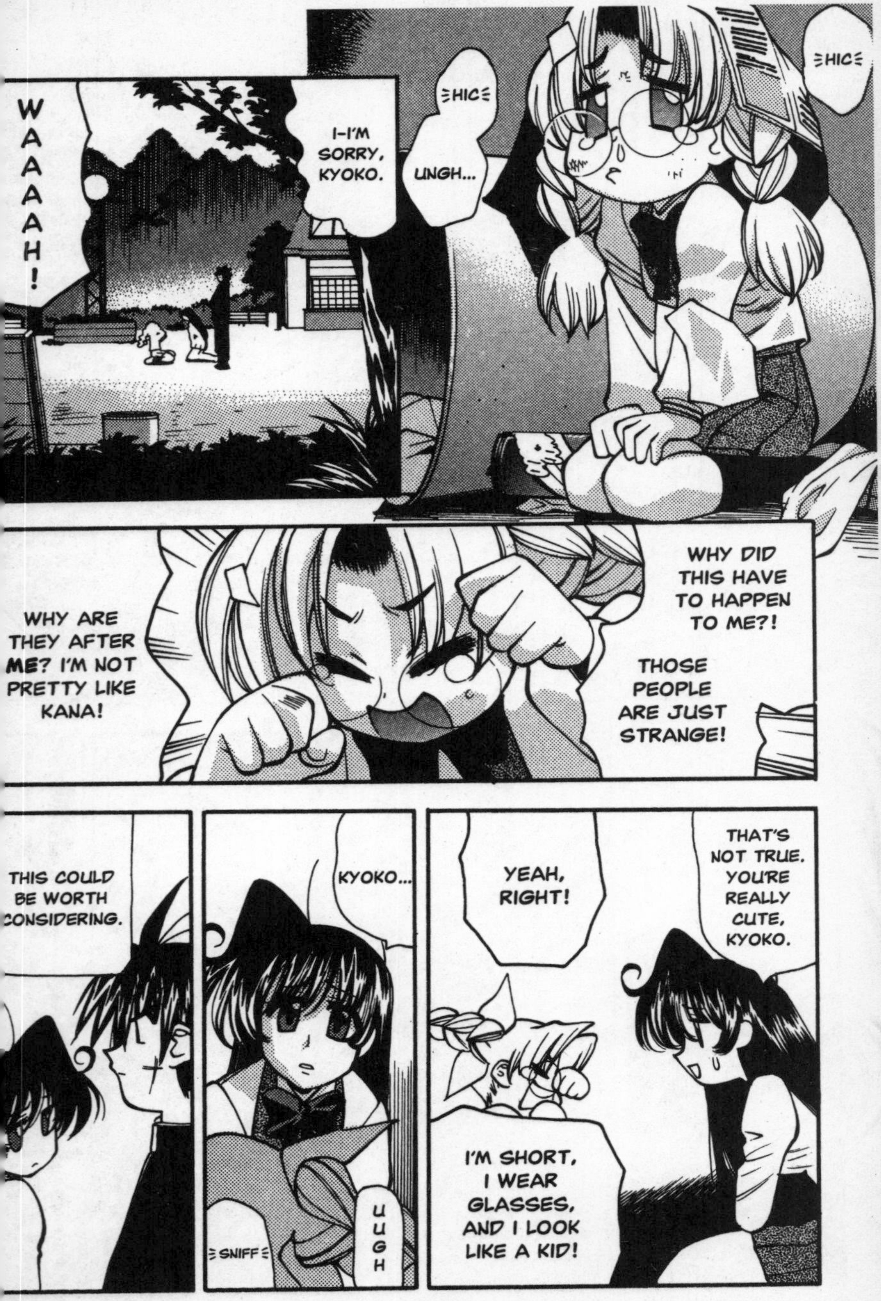
HIC
HIC
UNGH...
I-I'M SORRY, KYOKO.
WAAAAAH!
WHY DID THIS HAVE TO HAPPEN TO ME?!
THOSE PEOPLE ARE JUST STRANGE!
WHY ARE THEY AFTER ME? I'M NOT PRETTY LIKE KANA!
THAT'S NOT TRUE. YOU'RE REALLY CUTE, KYOKO.
YEAH, RIGHT!
I'M SHORT, I WEAR GLASSES, AND I LOOK LIKE A KID!
KYOKO...
UUGH
SNIFF
THIS COULD BE WORTH CONSIDERING.

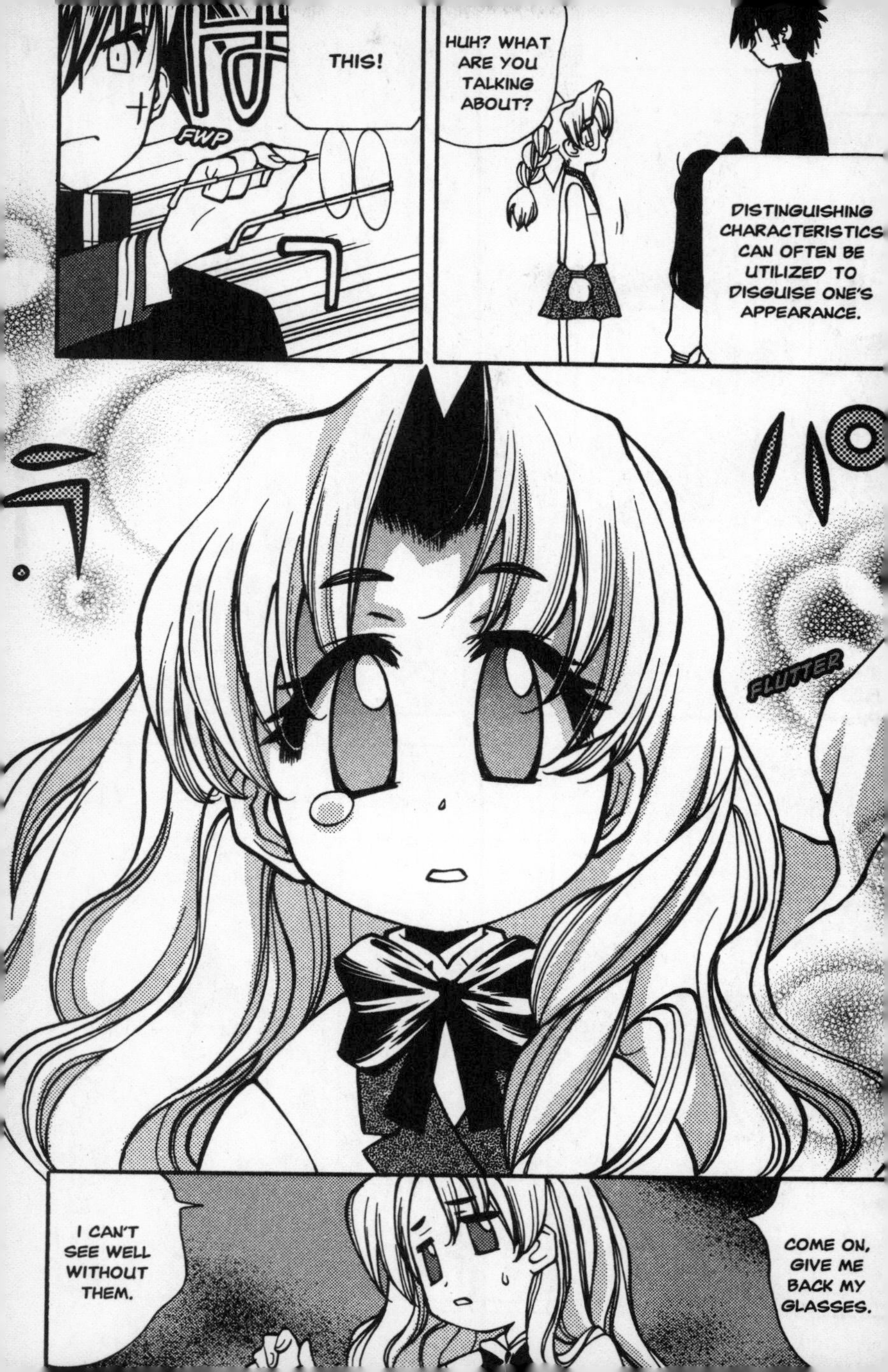

DISTINGUISHING CHARACTERISTICS CAN OFTEN BE UTILIZED TO DISGUISE ONE'S APPEARANCE.
HUH? WHAT ARE YOU TALKING ABOUT?
THIS!
FWP
FLUTTER
COME ON, GIVE ME BACK MY GLASSES.
I CAN'T SEE WELL WITHOUT THEM.

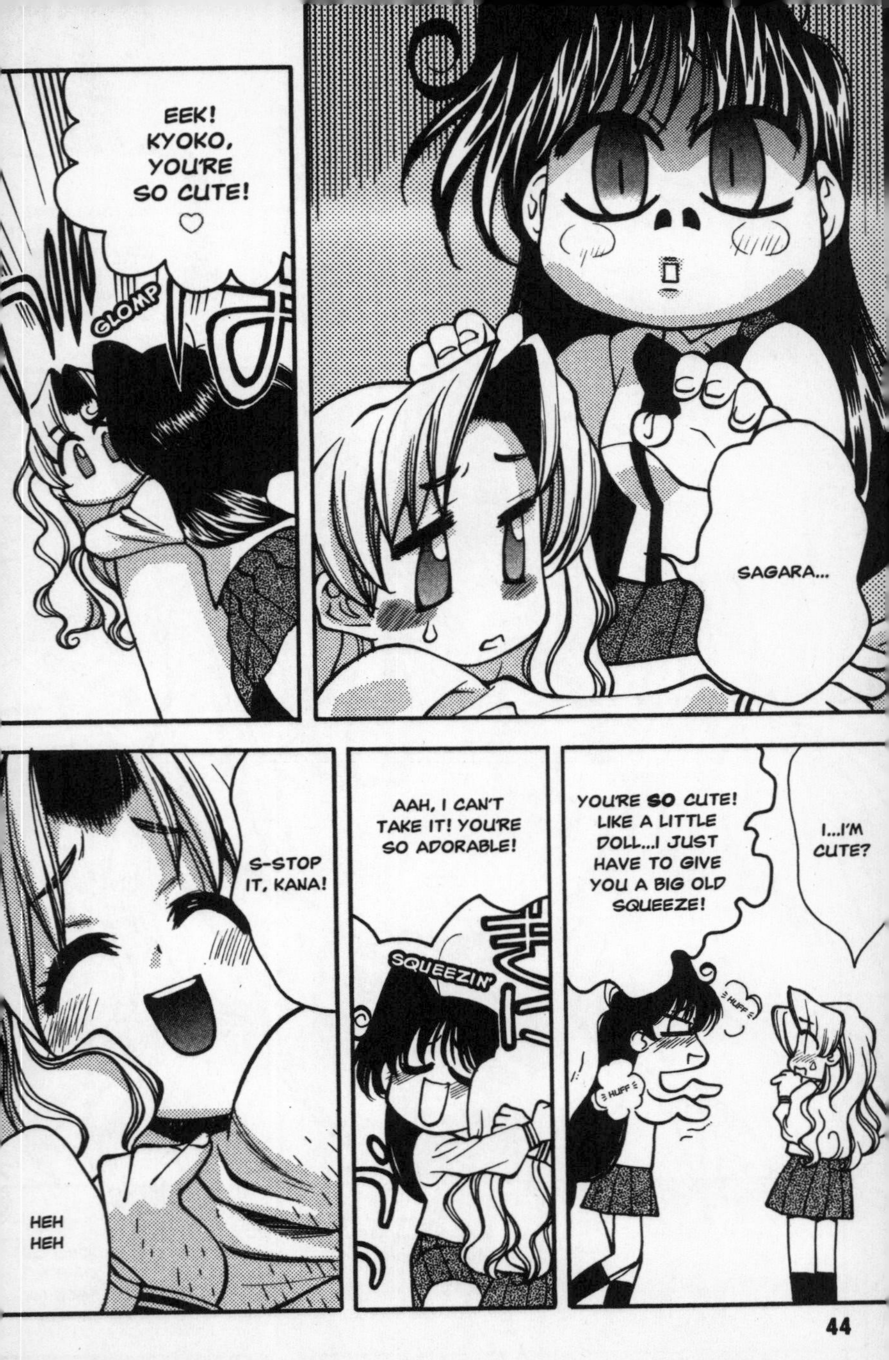
SAGARA...
EEK! KYOKO, YOU'RE SO CUTE! ♡
GLOMP
I...I'M CUTE?
HUFF
HUFF
YOU'RE SO CUTE! LIKE A LITTLE DOLL...I JUST HAVE TO GIVE YOU A BIG OLD SQUEEZE!
AAH, I CAN'T TAKE IT! YOU'RE SO ADORABLE!
SQUEEZIN'
S-STOP IT, KANA!
HEH HEH

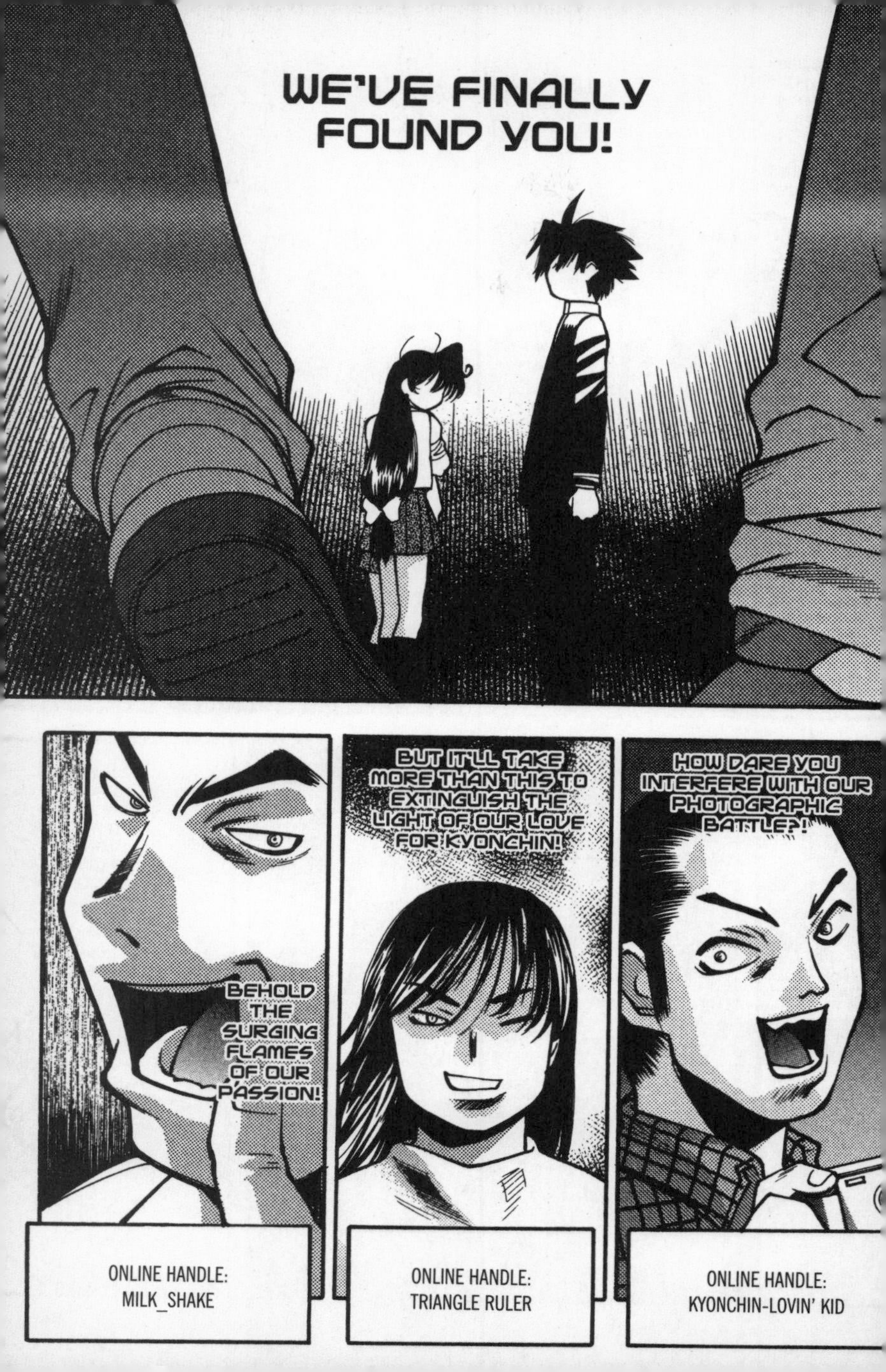
WE'VE FINALLY FOUND YOU!
HOW DARE YOU INTERFERE WITH OUR PHOTOGRAPHIC BATTLE?!
ONLINE HANDLE: KYONCHIN-LOVIN' KID
BUT IT'LL TAKE MORE THAN THIS TO EXTINGUISH THE LIGHT OF OUR LOVE FOR KYONCHIN!
ONLINE HANDLE: TRIANGLE RULER
BEHOLD THE SURGING FLAMES OF OUR PASSION!
ONLINE HANDLE: MILK_SHAKE

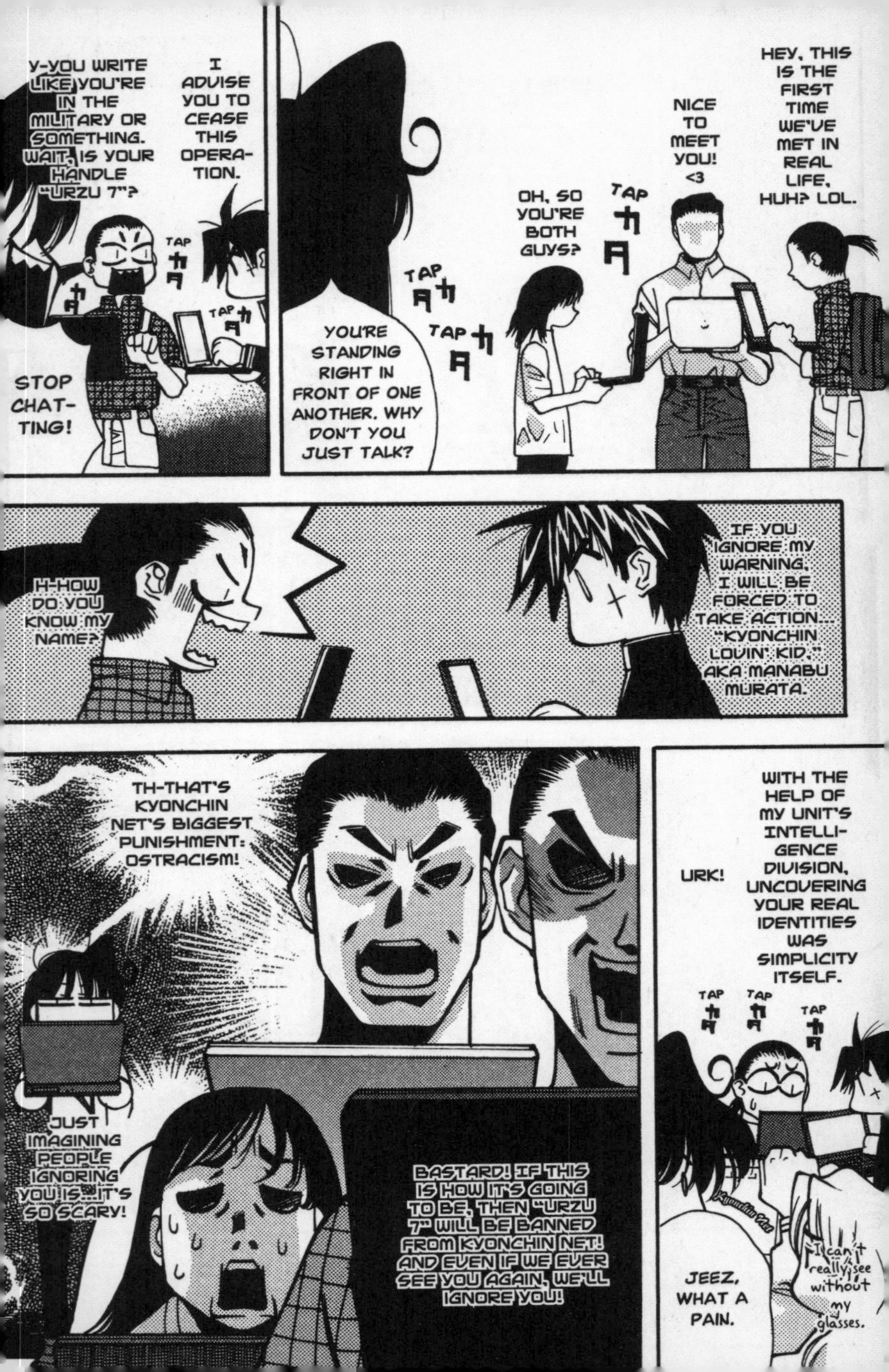
HEY, THIS IS THE FIRST TIME WE'VE MET IN REAL LIFE, HUH? LOL.
NICE TO MEET YOU! <3
TAP カタ
OH, SO YOU'RE BOTH GUYS?
TAP カタ
TAP カタ
YOU'RE STANDING RIGHT IN FRONT OF ONE ANOTHER. WHY DON'T YOU JUST TALK?
I ADVISE YOU TO CEASE THIS OPERATION.
Y-YOU WRITE LIKE YOU'RE IN THE MILITARY OR SOMETHING. WAIT, IS YOUR HANDLE "URZU 7"?
TAP カタ
TAP カタ
STOP CHATTING!
IF YOU IGNORE MY WARNING, I WILL BE FORCED TO TAKE ACTION... "KYONCHIN LOVIN' KID," AKA MANABU MURATA.
H-HOW DO YOU KNOW MY NAME?
WITH THE HELP OF MY UNIT'S INTELLIGENCE DIVISION, UNCOVERING YOUR REAL IDENTITIES WAS SIMPLICITY ITSELF.
URK!
TAP カタ
TAP カタ
TAP カタ
JEEZ, WHAT A PAIN.
I can't really see without my glasses.
BASTARD! IF THIS IS HOW IT'S GOING TO BE, THEN "URZU 7" WILL BE BANNED FROM KYONCHIN NET! AND EVEN IF WE EVER SEE YOU AGAIN, WE'LL IGNORE YOU!
TH-THAT'S KYONCHIN NET'S BIGGEST PUNISHMENT: OSTRACISM!
JUST IMAGINING PEOPLE IGNORING YOU IS...IT'S SO SCARY!

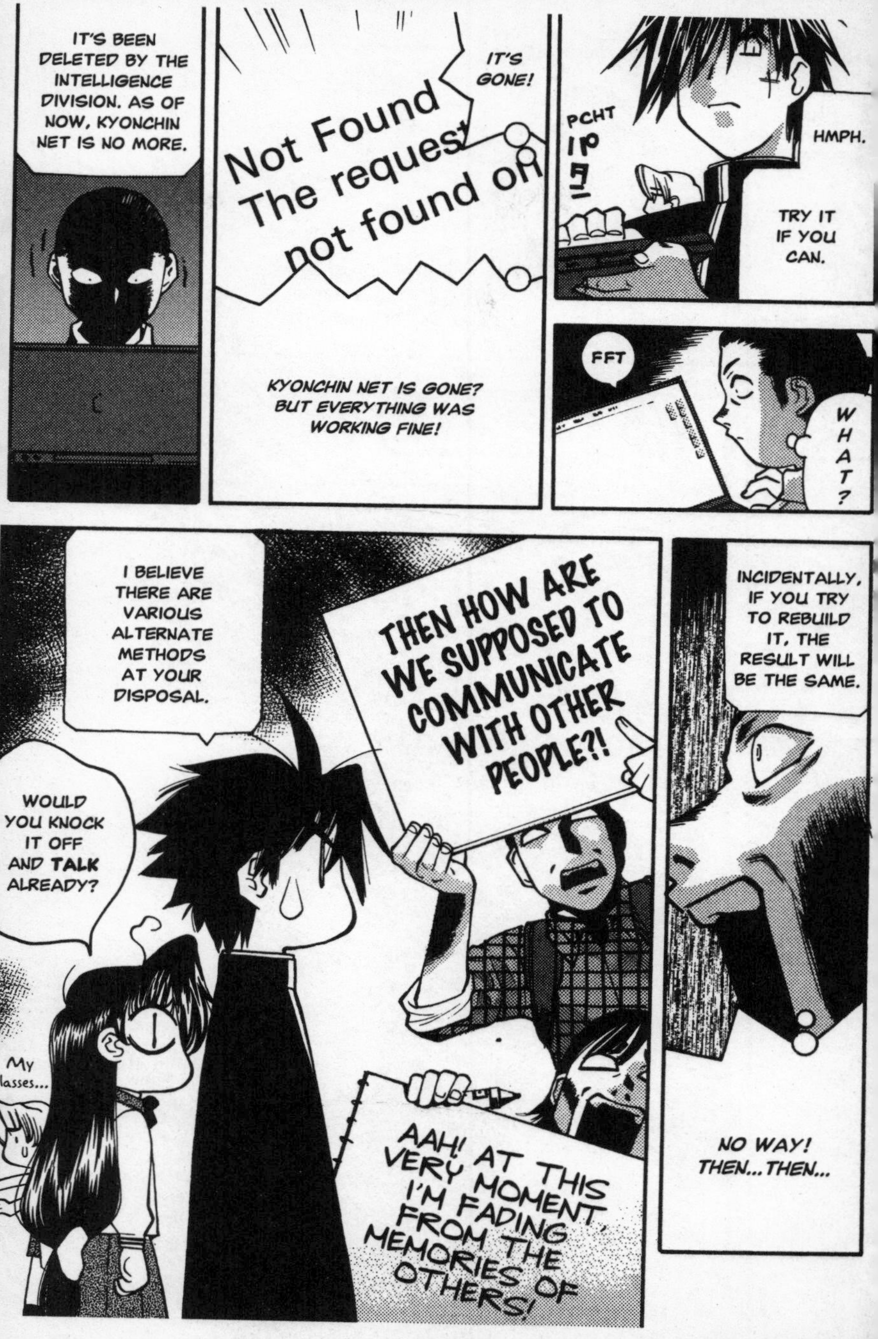

PCHT
HMPH.
TRY IT IF YOU CAN.
FFT
WHAT?
IT'S GONE!
Not Found
The reques
not found on
KYONCHIN NET IS GONE? BUT EVERYTHING WAS WORKING FINE!
IT'S BEEN DELETED BY THE INTELLIGENCE DIVISION. AS OF NOW, KYONCHIN NET IS NO MORE.
INCIDENTALLY, IF YOU TRY TO REBUILD IT, THE RESULT WILL BE THE SAME.
NO WAY! THEN...THEN...
THEN HOW ARE WE SUPPOSED TO COMMUNICATE WITH OTHER PEOPLE?!
I BELIEVE THERE ARE VARIOUS ALTERNATE METHODS AT YOUR DISPOSAL.
WOULD YOU KNOCK IT OFF AND TALK ALREADY?
AAH! AT THIS VERY MOMENT, I'M FADING FROM THE MEMORIES OF OTHERS!
My glasses...

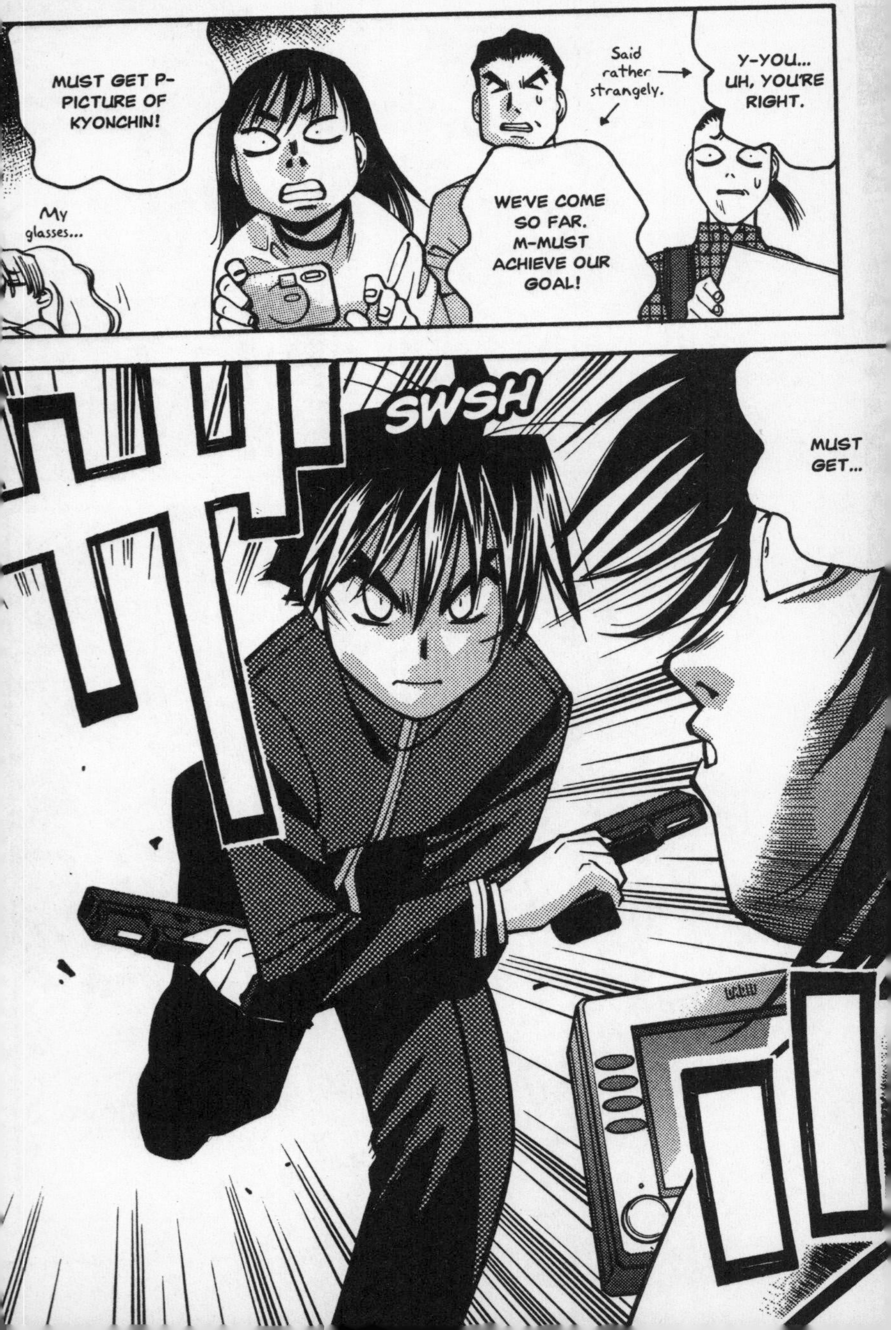
Y-YOU... UH, YOU'RE RIGHT.
Said rather strangely.
WE'VE COME SO FAR. M-MUST ACHIEVE OUR GOAL!
MUST GET P-PICTURE OF KYONCHIN!
My glasses...
MUST GET...
SWSH

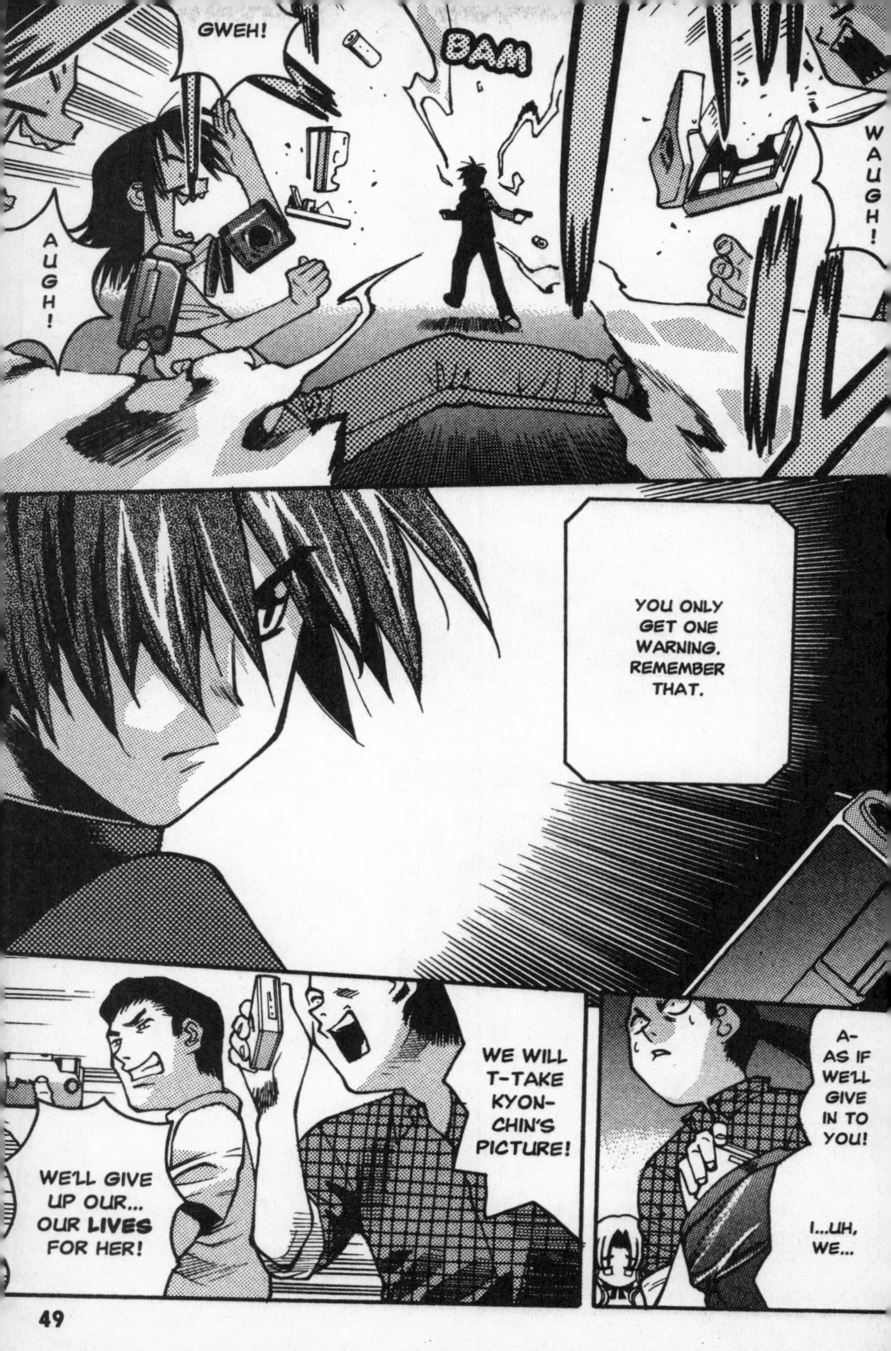
WAUGH!
BAM
GWEH!
AUGH!
YOU ONLY GET ONE WARNING. REMEMBER THAT.
A- AS IF WE'LL GIVE IN TO YOU!
I...UH, WE...
WE WILL T-TAKE KYON-CHIN'S PICTURE!
WE'LL GIVE UP OUR... OUR LIVES FOR HER!

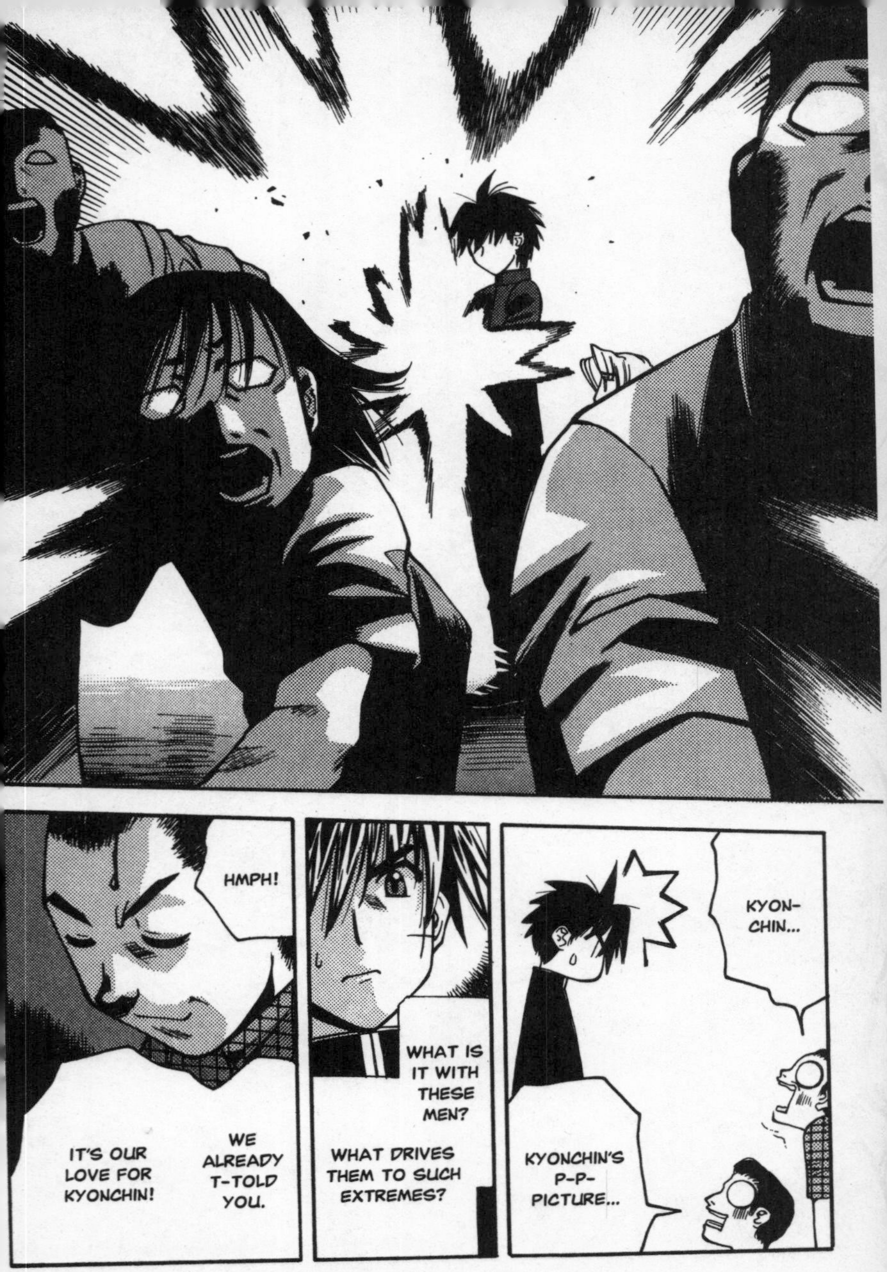
KYON-CHIN...
KYONCHIN'S P-P-PICTURE...
WHAT IS IT WITH THESE MEN?
WHAT DRIVES THEM TO SUCH EXTREMES?
HMPH!
WE ALREADY T-TOLD YOU.
IT'S OUR LOVE FOR KYONCHIN!

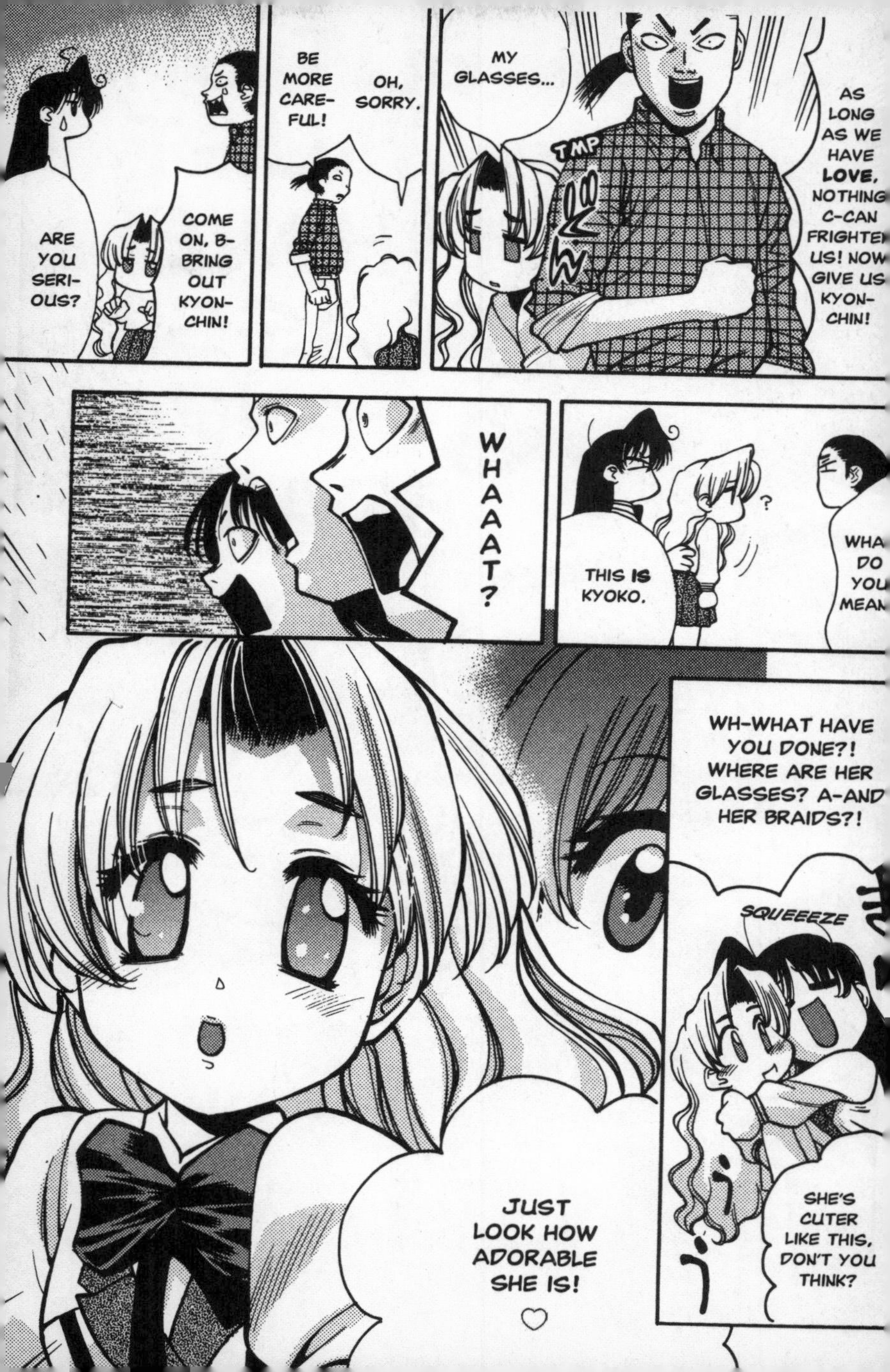
AS LONG AS WE HAVE LOVE, NOTHING C-CAN FRIGHTEN US! NOW GIVE US KYON-CHIN!
TMP
MY GLASSES...
OH, SORRY.
BE MORE CARE-FUL!
COME ON, B-BRING OUT KYON-CHIN!
ARE YOU SERI-OUS?
WHA DO YOU MEAN
THIS IS KYOKO.
WHAAAAT?
WH-WHAT HAVE YOU DONE?! WHERE ARE HER GLASSES? A-AND HER BRAIDS?!
SQUEEEZE
SHE'S CUTER LIKE THIS, DON'T YOU THINK?
JUST LOOK HOW ADORABLE SHE IS! ♡

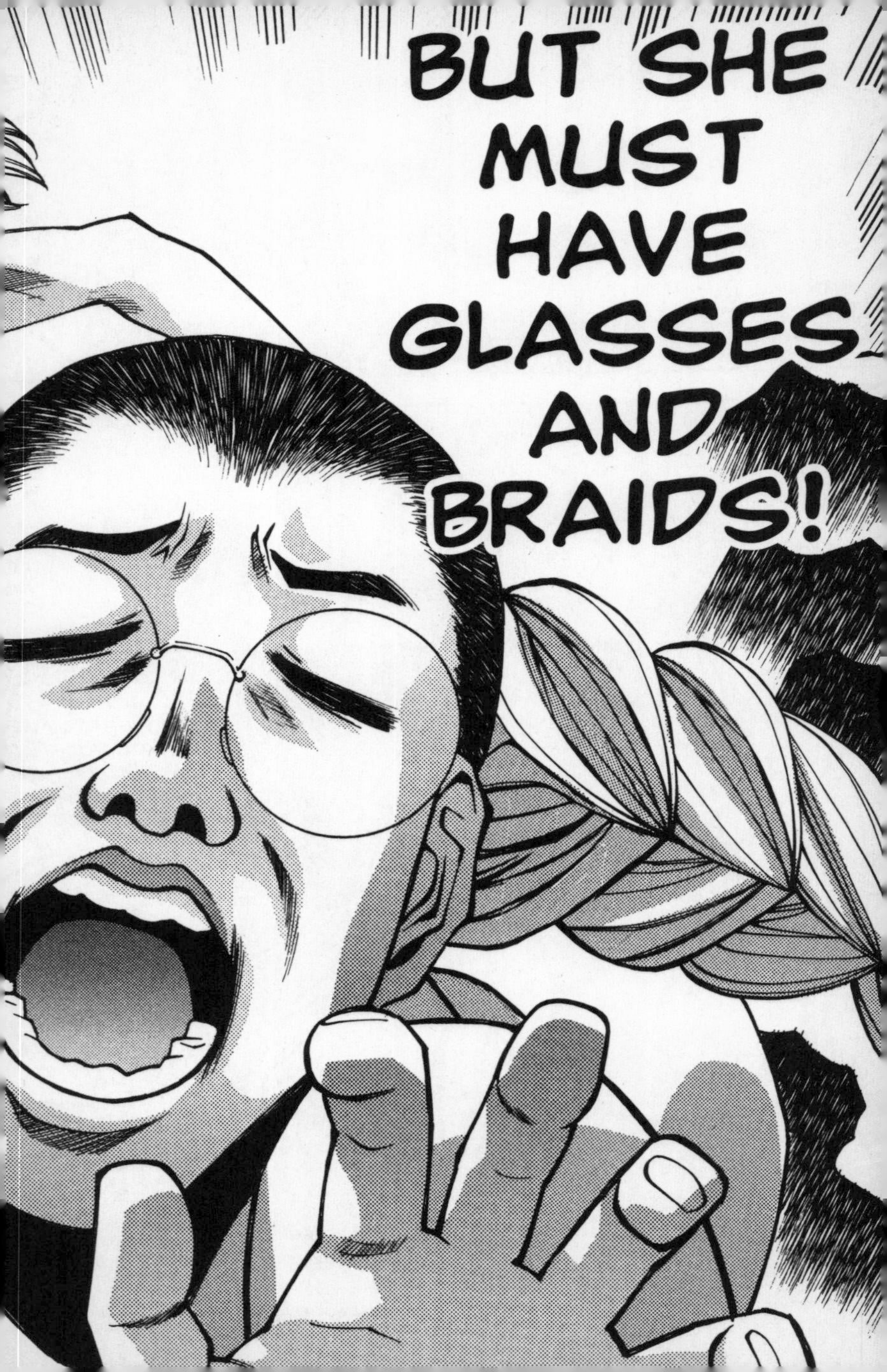
BUT SHE MUST HAVE GLASSES AND BRAIDS!

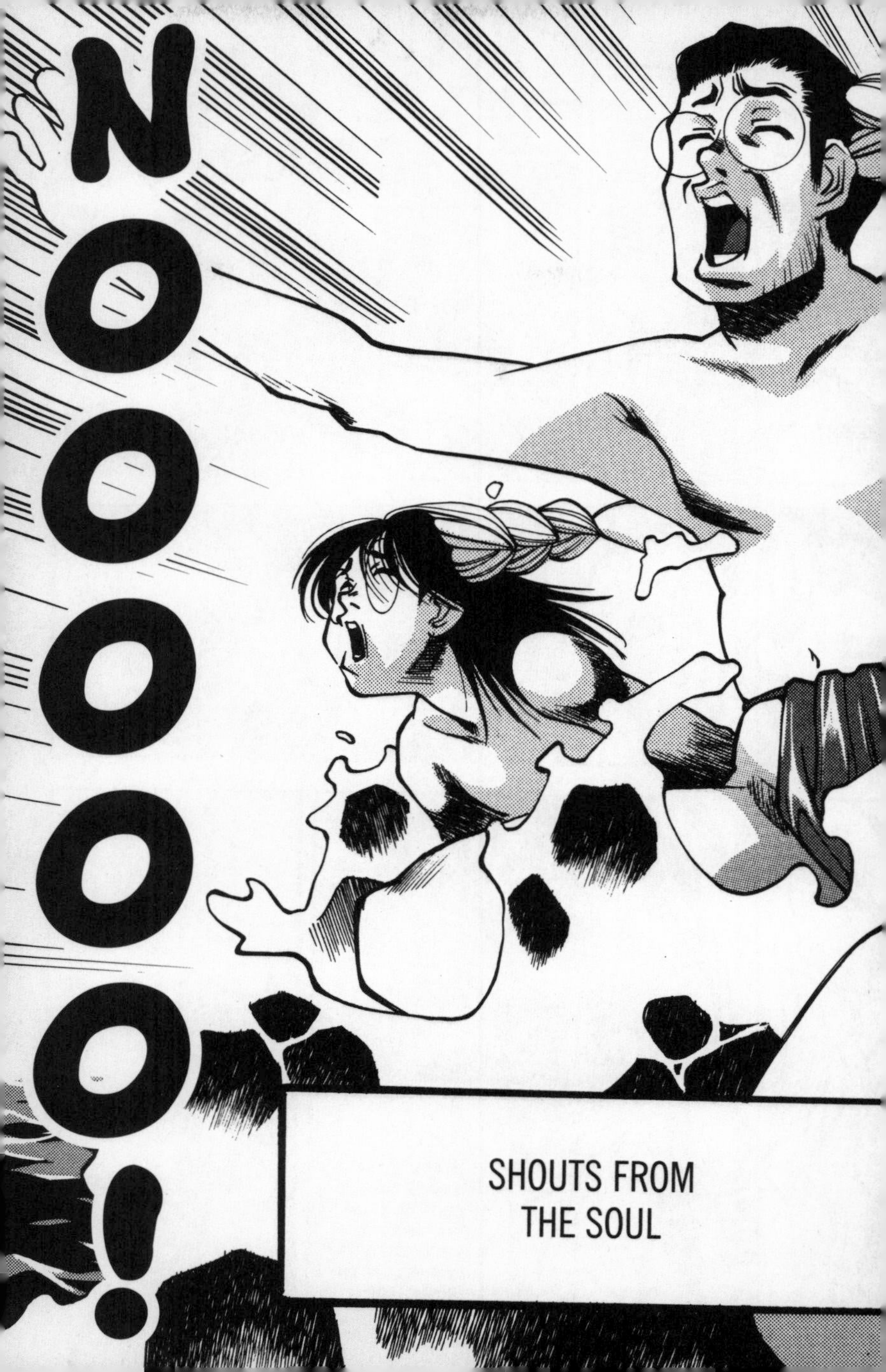
NOOOOO!
SHOUTS FROM
THE SOUL

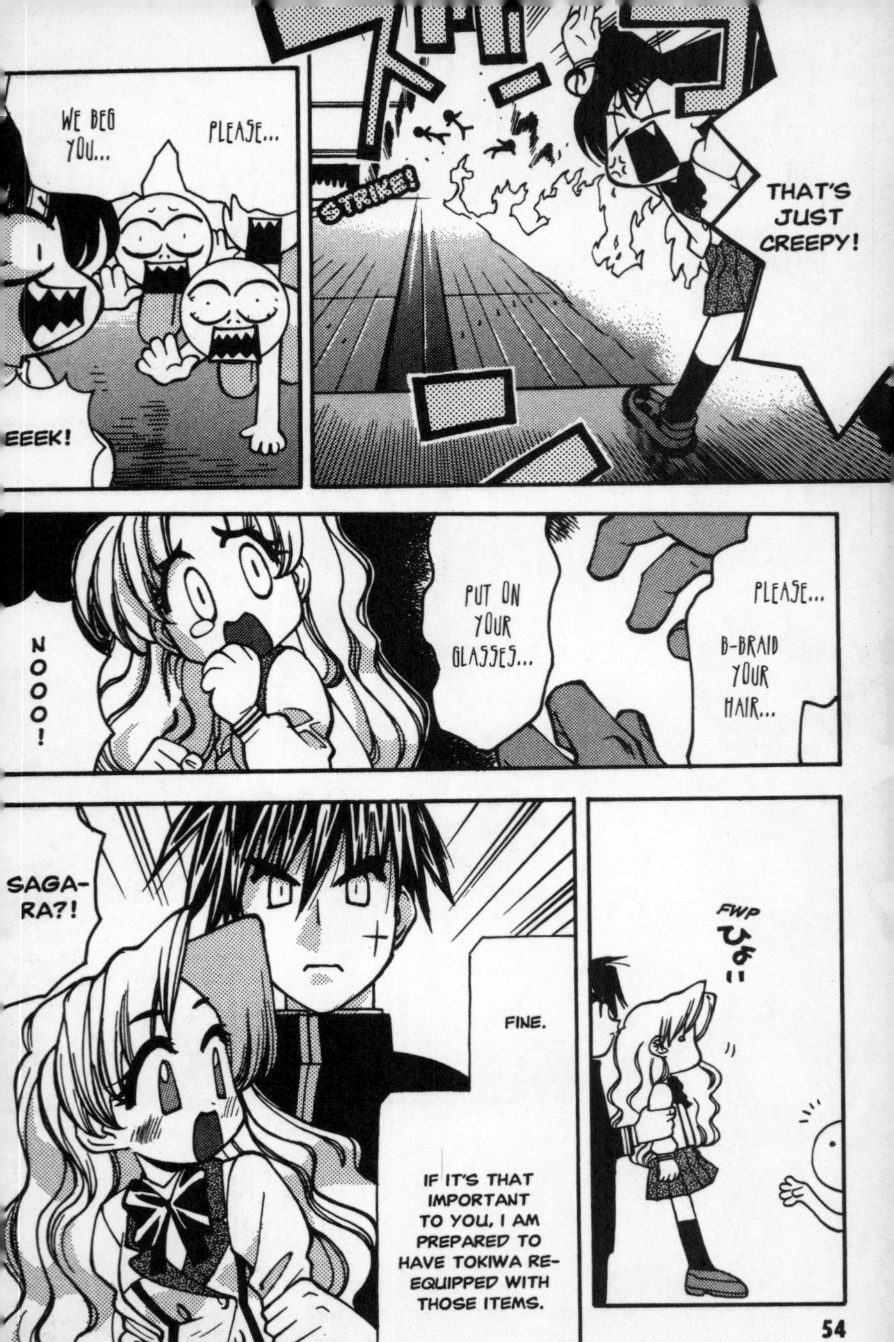
THAT'S JUST CREEPY!
STRIKE!
PLEASE...
WE BEG YOU...
EEEK!
PLEASE...
B-BRAID YOUR HAIR...
PUT ON YOUR GLASSES...
NOOOO!
FWP
SAGARA?!
FINE.
IF IT'S THAT IMPORTANT TO YOU, I AM PREPARED TO HAVE TOKIWA RE-EQUIPPED WITH THOSE ITEMS.

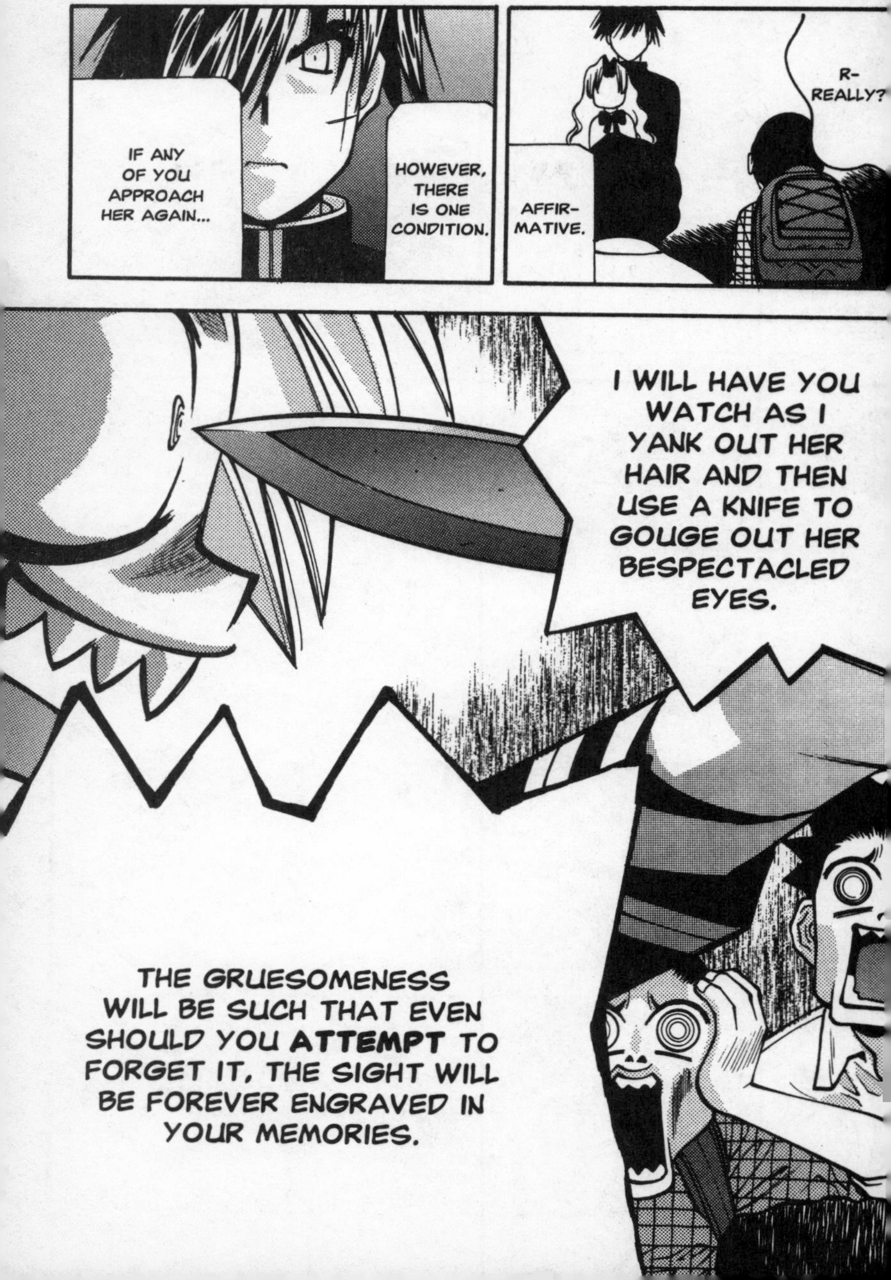
R-
REALLY?
AFFIR-
MATIVE.
HOWEVER, THERE IS ONE CONDITION.
IF ANY OF YOU APPROACH HER AGAIN...
I WILL HAVE YOU WATCH AS I YANK OUT HER HAIR AND THEN USE A KNIFE TO GOUGE OUT HER BESPECTACLED EYES.
THE GRUESOMENESS WILL BE SUCH THAT EVEN SHOULD YOU **ATTEMPT** TO FORGET IT, THE SIGHT WILL BE FOREVER ENGRAVED IN YOUR MEMORIES.

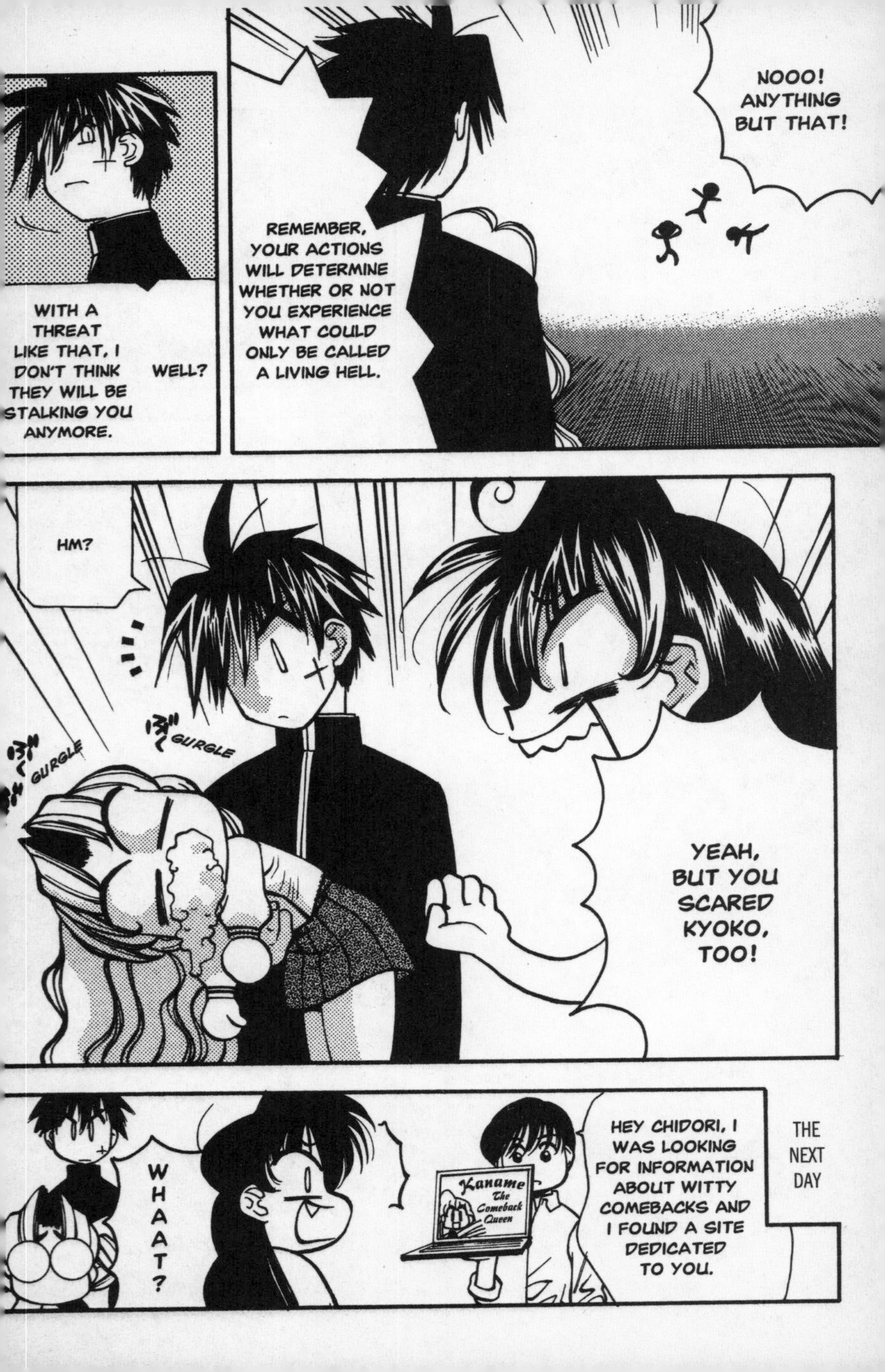
NOOO! ANYTHING BUT THAT!
REMEMBER, YOUR ACTIONS WILL DETERMINE WHETHER OR NOT YOU EXPERIENCE WHAT COULD ONLY BE CALLED A LIVING HELL.
WELL?
WITH A THREAT LIKE THAT, I DON'T THINK THEY WILL BE STALKING YOU ANYMORE.
YEAH, BUT YOU SCARED KYOKO, TOO!
HM?
GURGLE
GURGLE
THE NEXT DAY
HEY CHIDORI, I WAS LOOKING FOR INFORMATION ABOUT WITTY COMEBACKS AND I FOUND A SITE DEDICATED TO YOU.
Kaname The Comeback Queen
WHAAT?

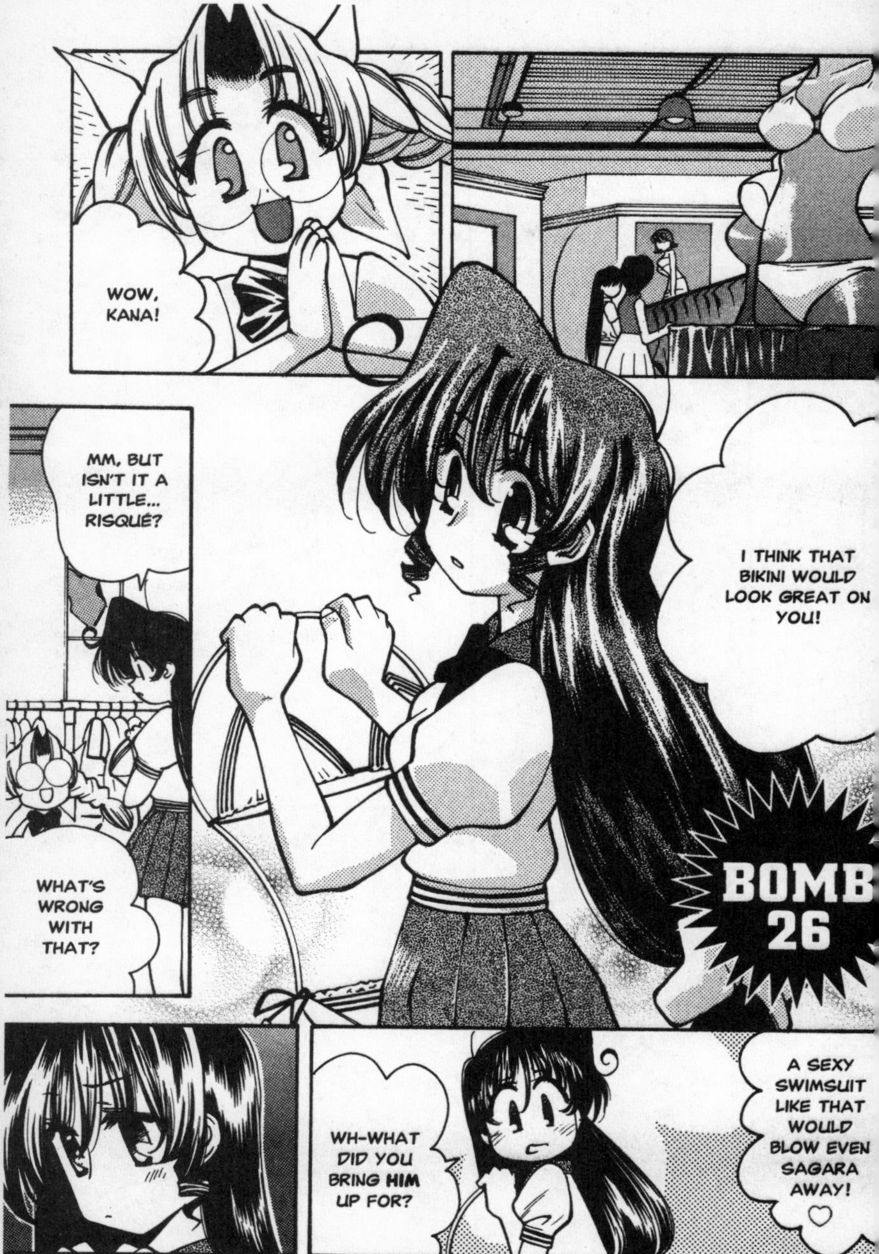
WOW, KANA!
I THINK THAT BIKINI WOULD LOOK GREAT ON YOU!
BOMB 26
MM, BUT ISN'T IT A LITTLE... RISQUÉ?
WHAT'S WRONG WITH THAT?
A SEXY SWIMSUIT LIKE THAT WOULD BLOW EVEN SAGARA AWAY! ♡
WH-WHAT DID YOU BRING HIM UP FOR?

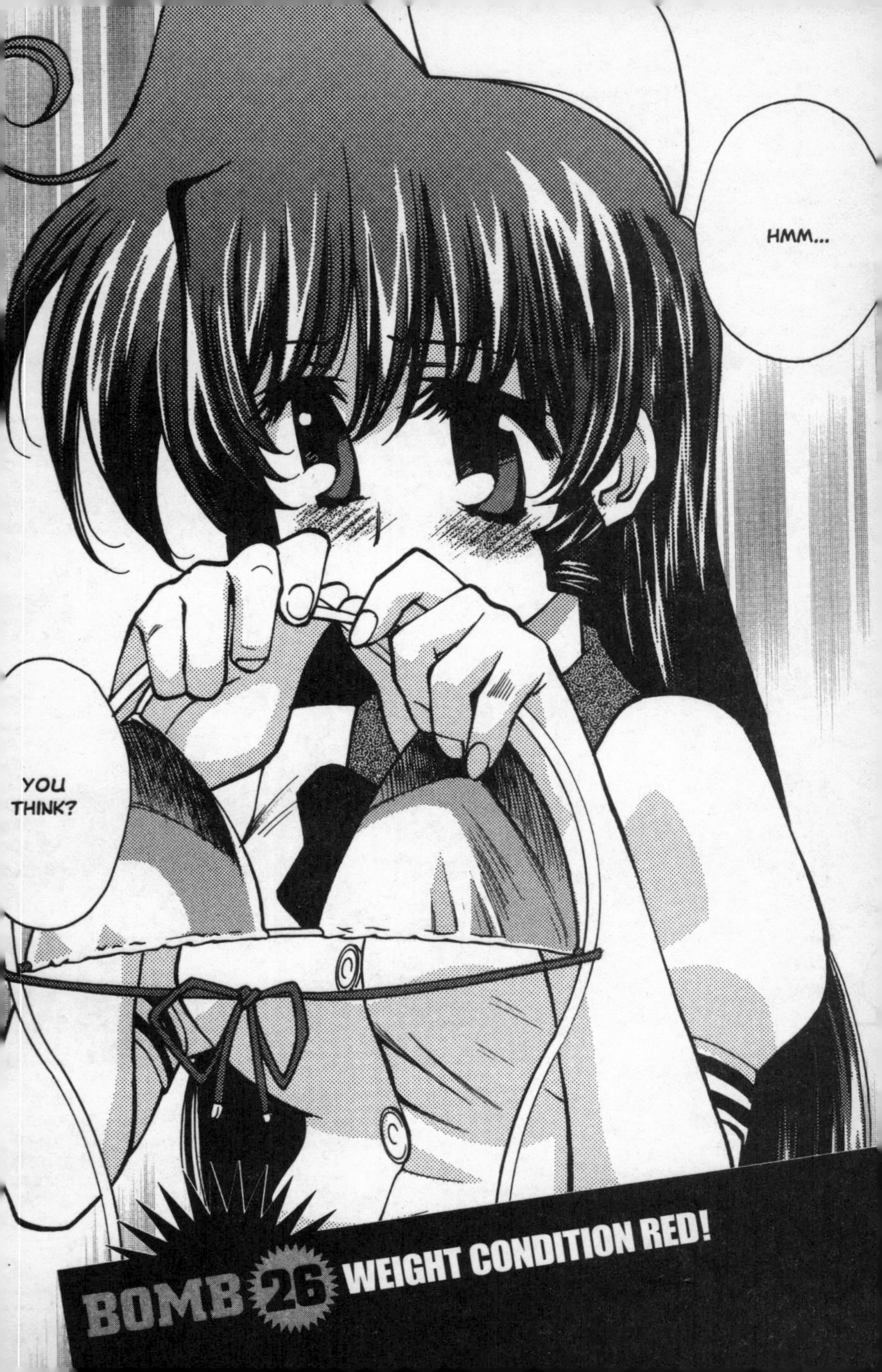
HMM...
YOU THINK?
BOMB 26 WEIGHT CONDITION RED!

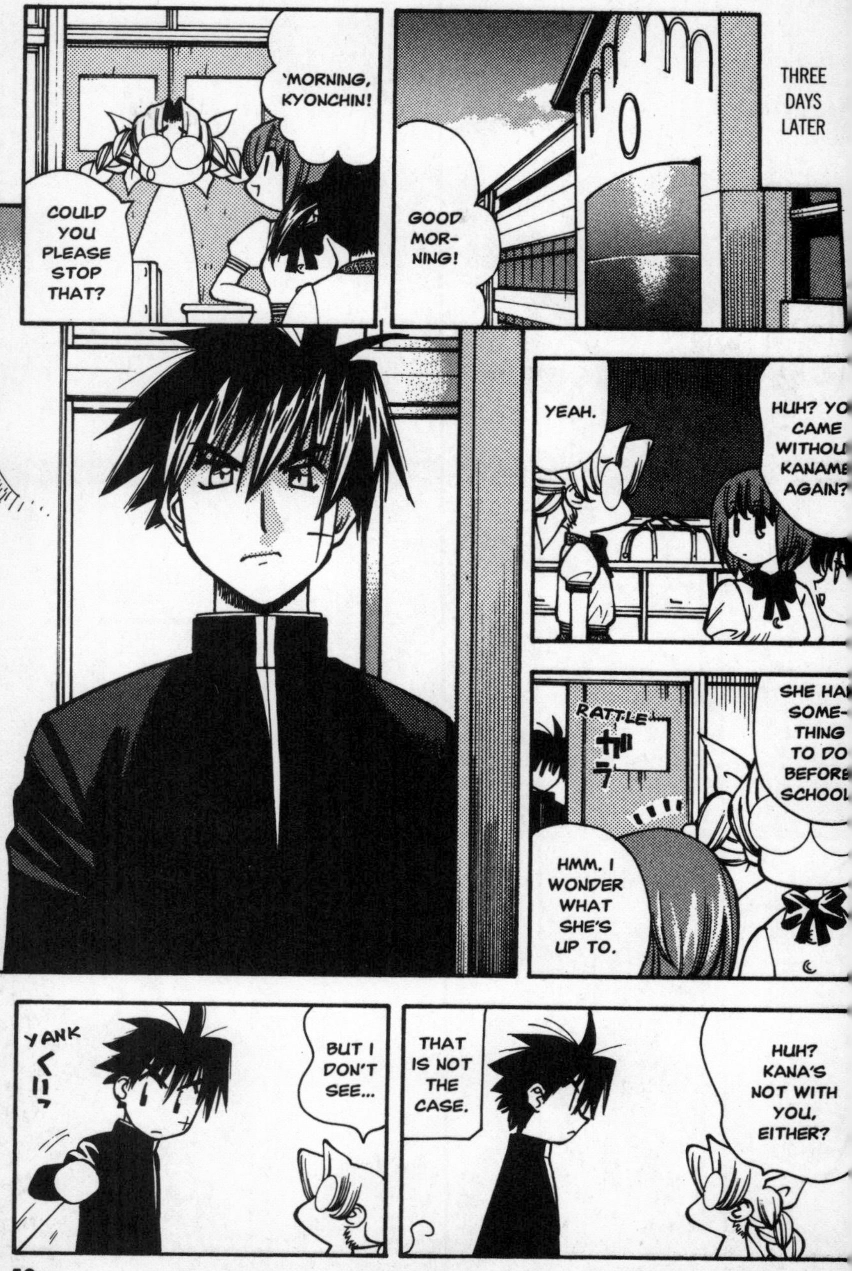
THREE DAYS LATER
GOOD MOR-NING!
'MORNING, KYONCHIN!
COULD YOU PLEASE STOP THAT?
HUH? YO CAME WITHOU KANAME AGAIN?
YEAH.
SHE HA SOME-THING TO DO BEFORE SCHOOL
RATTLE
HMM. I WONDER WHAT SHE'S UP TO.
HUH? KANA'S NOT WITH YOU, EITHER?
THAT IS NOT THE CASE.
BUT I DON'T SEE...
YANK

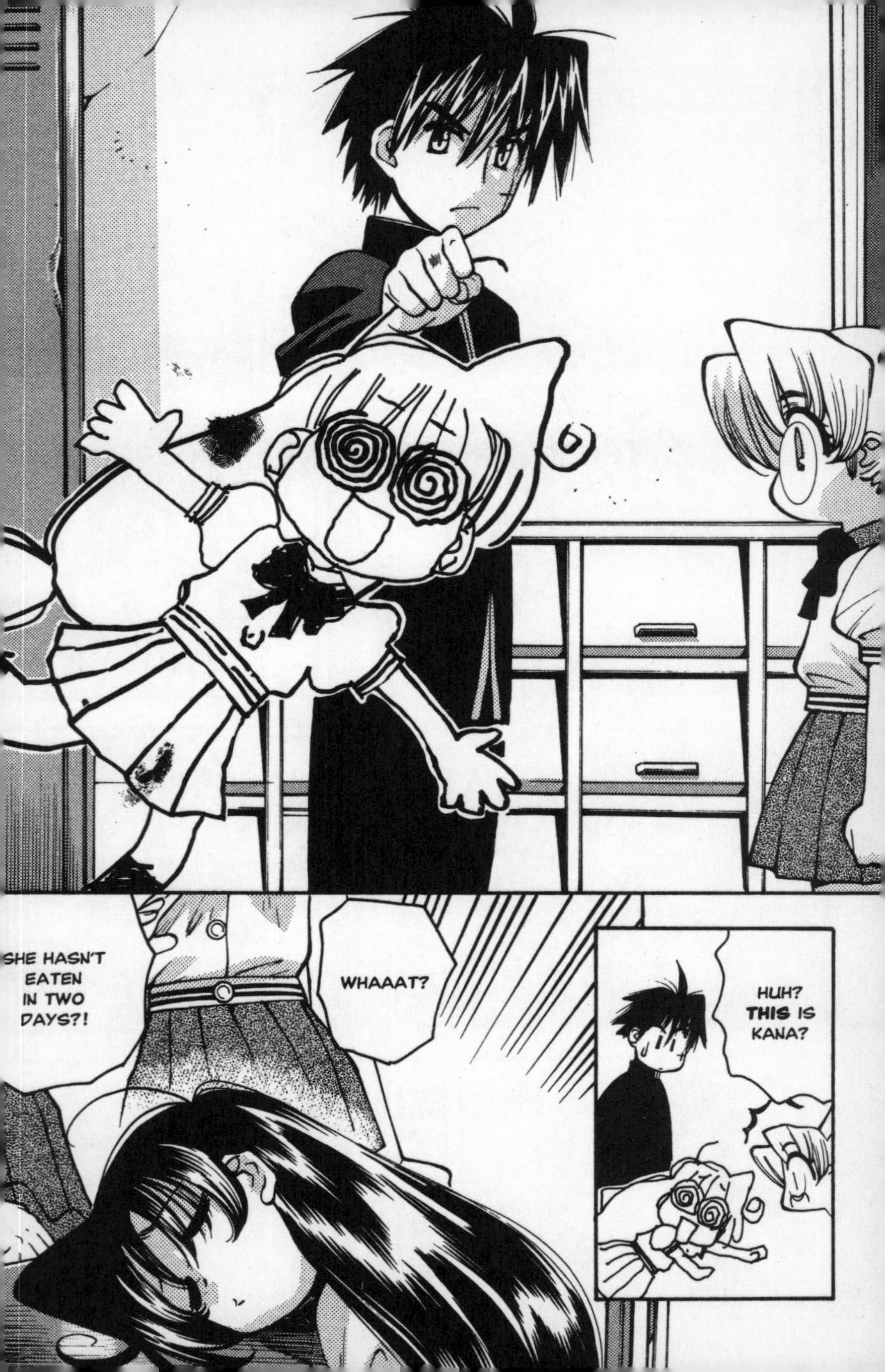
HUH? THIS IS KANA?
WHAAAT?
SHE HASN'T EATEN IN TWO DAYS?!

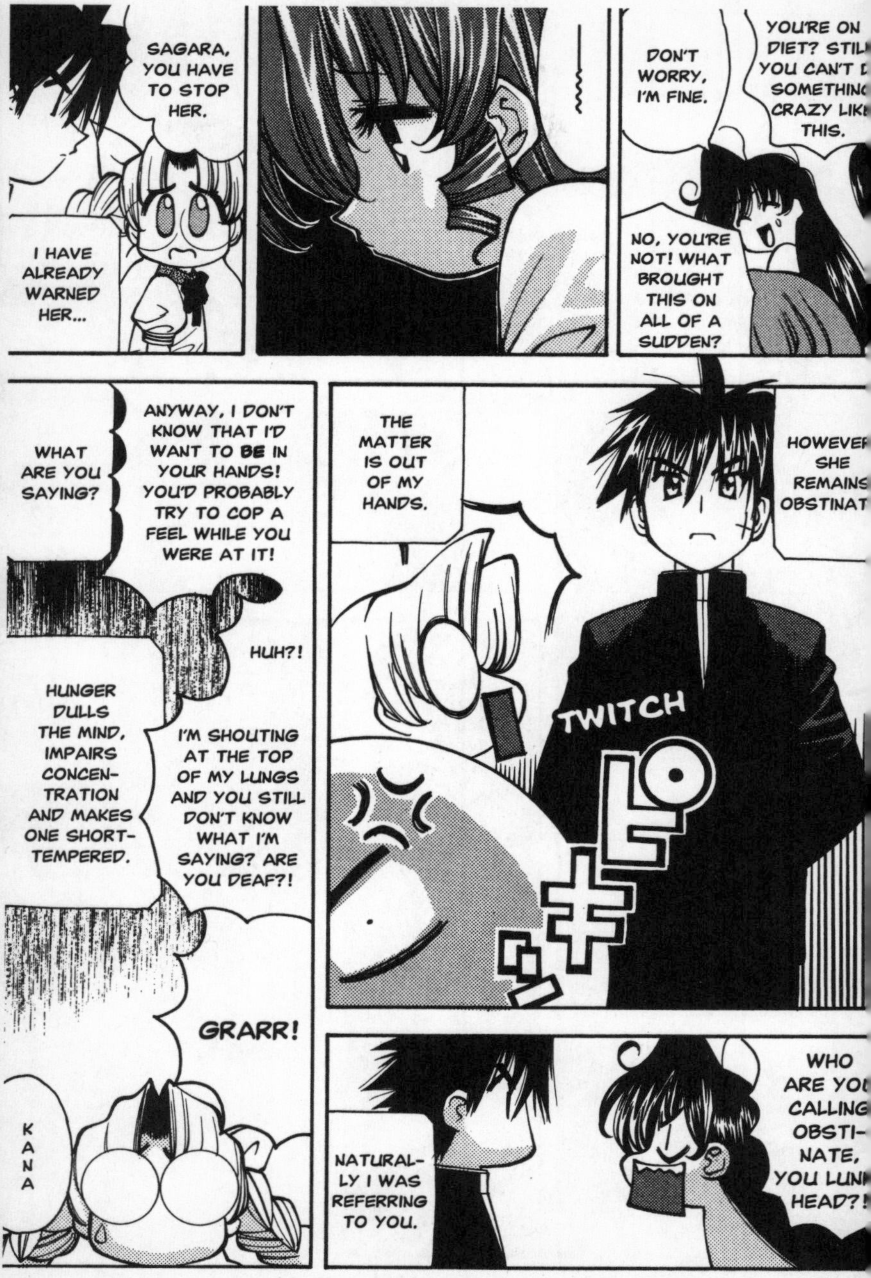
YOU'RE ON DIET? STIL YOU CAN'T D SOMETHIN CRAZY LIK THIS.
DON'T WORRY, I'M FINE.
NO, YOU'RE NOT! WHAT BROUGHT THIS ON ALL OF A SUDDEN?
......
SAGARA, YOU HAVE TO STOP HER.
I HAVE ALREADY WARNED HER...
HOWEVE SHE REMAINS OBSTINAT
THE MATTER IS OUT OF MY HANDS.
TWITCH
WHAT ARE YOU SAYING?
ANYWAY, I DON'T KNOW THAT I'D WANT TO BE IN YOUR HANDS! YOU'D PROBABLY TRY TO COP A FEEL WHILE YOU WERE AT IT!
HUH?!
I'M SHOUTING AT THE TOP OF MY LUNGS AND YOU STILL DON'T KNOW WHAT I'M SAYING? ARE YOU DEAF?!
HUNGER DULLS THE MIND, IMPAIRS CONCEN-TRATION AND MAKES ONE SHORT-TEMPERED.
GRARR!
WHO ARE YO CALLING OBSTI-NATE, YOU LUN HEAD?!
NATURAL-LY I WAS REFERRING TO YOU.
KANA

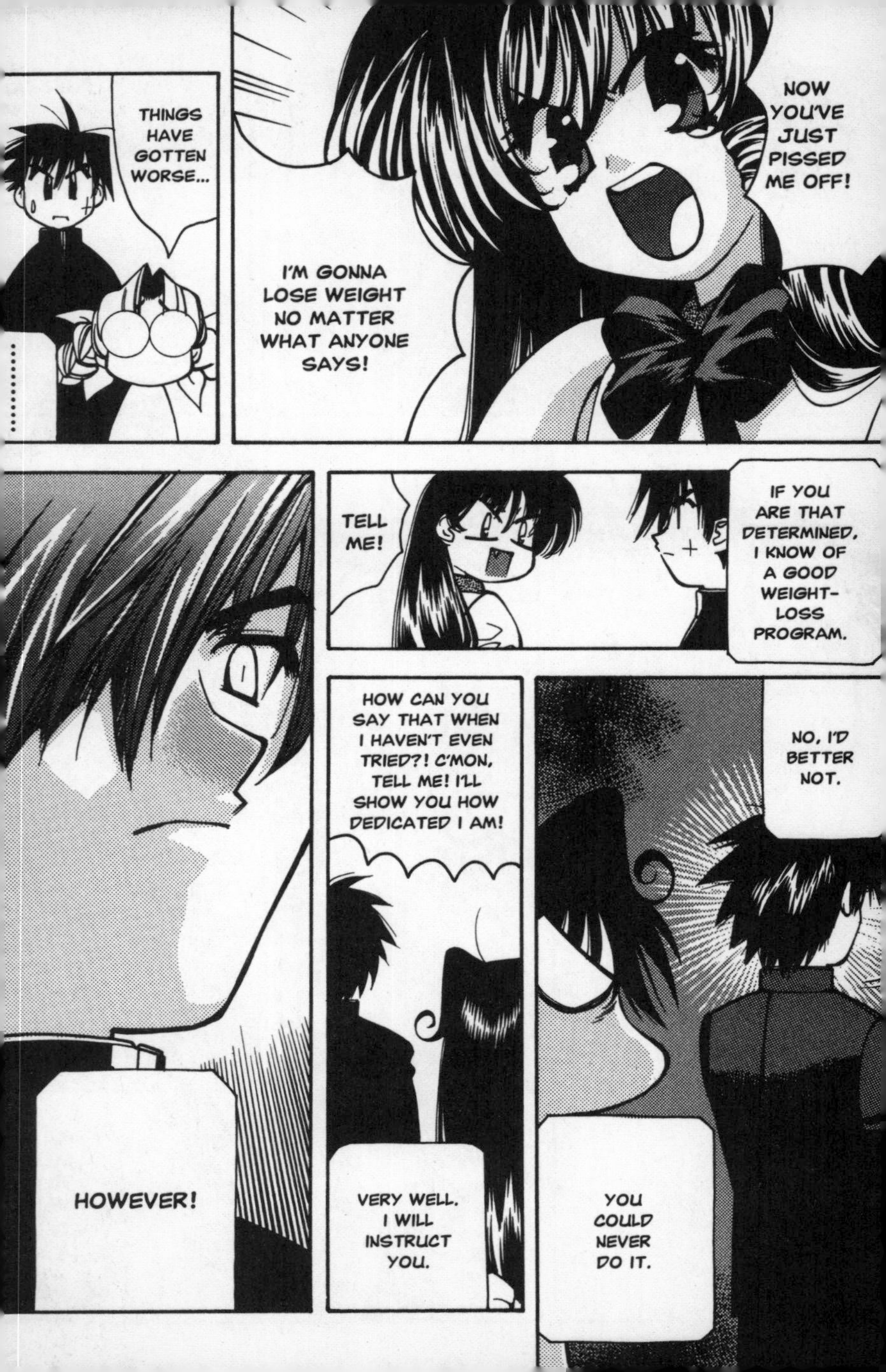
NOW YOU'VE JUST PISSED ME OFF!
I'M GONNA LOSE WEIGHT NO MATTER WHAT ANYONE SAYS!
THINGS HAVE GOTTEN WORSE...
IF YOU ARE THAT DETERMINED, I KNOW OF A GOOD WEIGHT-LOSS PROGRAM.
TELL ME!
NO, I'D BETTER NOT.
YOU COULD NEVER DO IT.
HOW CAN YOU SAY THAT WHEN I HAVEN'T EVEN TRIED?! C'MON, TELL ME! I'LL SHOW YOU HOW DEDICATED I AM!
VERY WELL. I WILL INSTRUCT YOU.
HOWEVER!

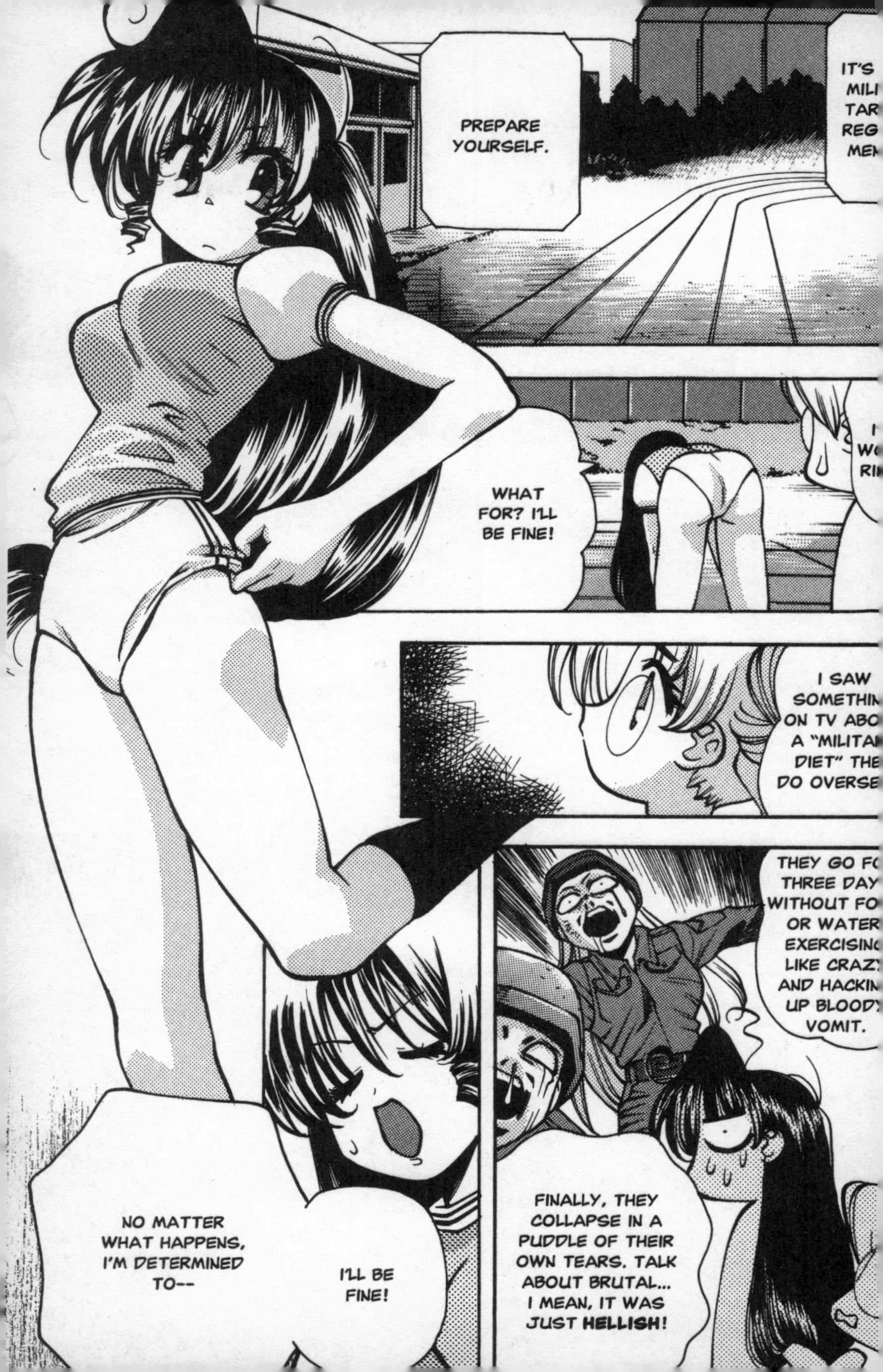
IT'S MILI TAR REG MEN
PREPARE YOURSELF.
WHAT FOR? I'LL BE FINE!
I SAW SOMETHIN ON TV ABO A "MILITA DIET" THE DO OVERSE
THEY GO FO THREE DAY WITHOUT FO OR WATER EXERCISING LIKE CRAZY AND HACKIN UP BLOODY VOMIT.
FINALLY, THEY COLLAPSE IN A PUDDLE OF THEIR OWN TEARS. TALK ABOUT BRUTAL... I MEAN, IT WAS JUST **HELLISH**!
I'LL BE FINE!
NO MATTER WHAT HAPPENS, I'M DETERMINED TO--

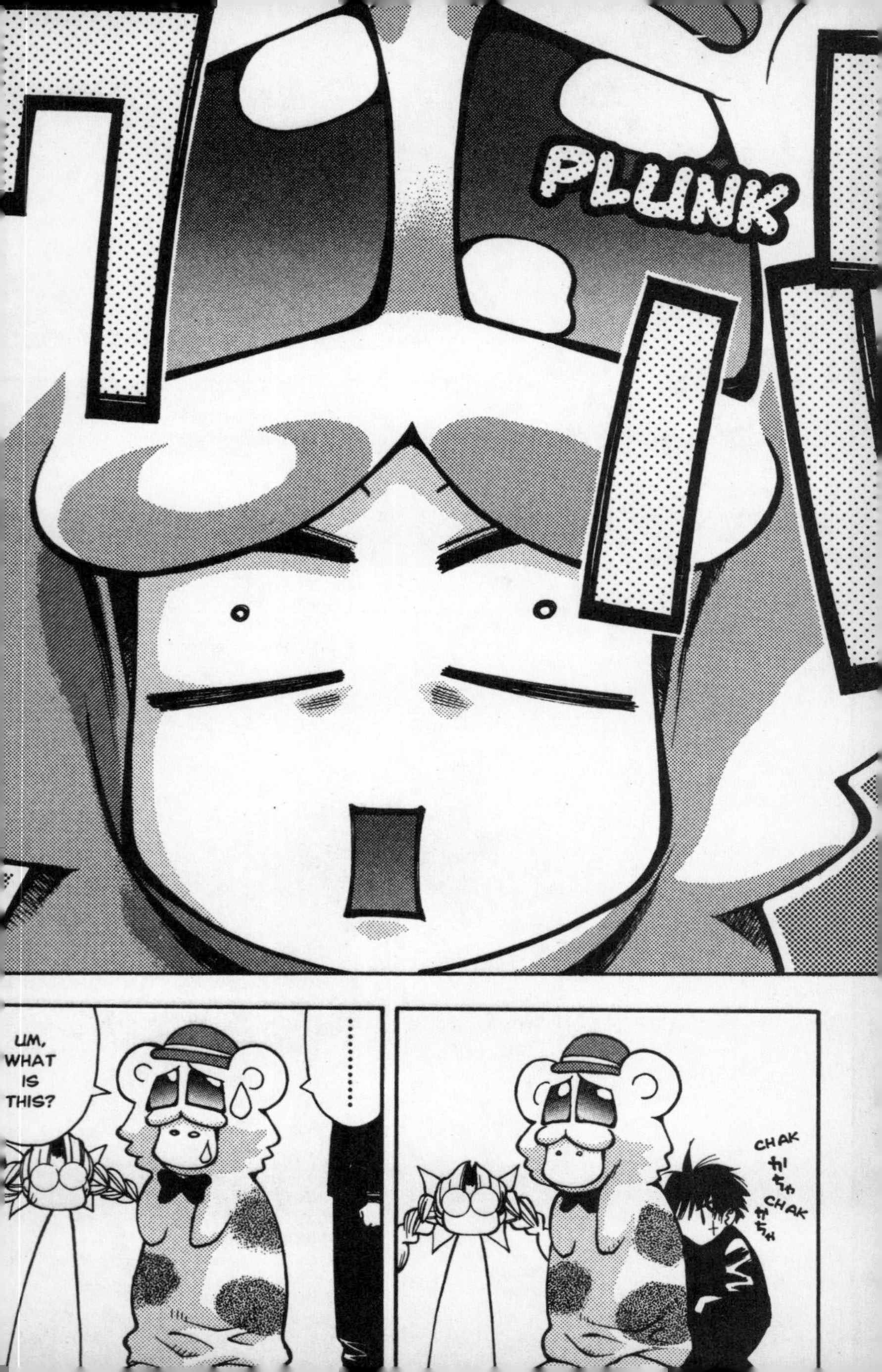
PLUNK
CHAK かちゃ CHAK かちゃ
......
UM, WHAT IS THIS?

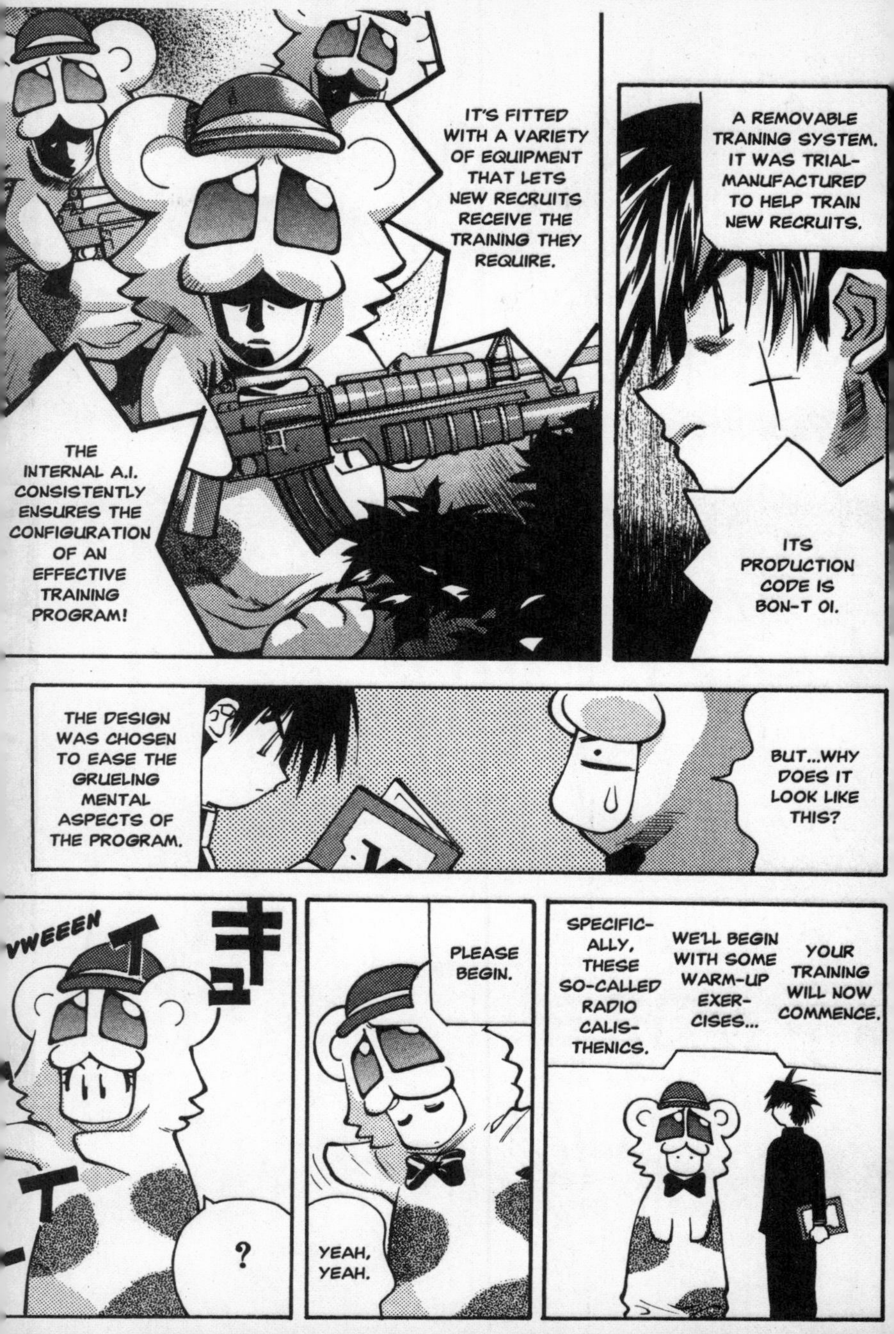
A REMOVABLE TRAINING SYSTEM. IT WAS TRIAL-MANUFACTURED TO HELP TRAIN NEW RECRUITS.
ITS PRODUCTION CODE IS BON-T 01.
IT'S FITTED WITH A VARIETY OF EQUIPMENT THAT LETS NEW RECRUITS RECEIVE THE TRAINING THEY REQUIRE.
THE INTERNAL A.I. CONSISTENTLY ENSURES THE CONFIGURATION OF AN EFFECTIVE TRAINING PROGRAM!
BUT...WHY DOES IT LOOK LIKE THIS?
THE DESIGN WAS CHOSEN TO EASE THE GRUELING MENTAL ASPECTS OF THE PROGRAM.
YOUR TRAINING WILL NOW COMMENCE.
WE'LL BEGIN WITH SOME WARM-UP EXER-CISES...
SPECIFIC-ALLY, THESE SO-CALLED RADIO CALIS-THENICS.
PLEASE BEGIN.
YEAH, YEAH.
VWEEEN
?

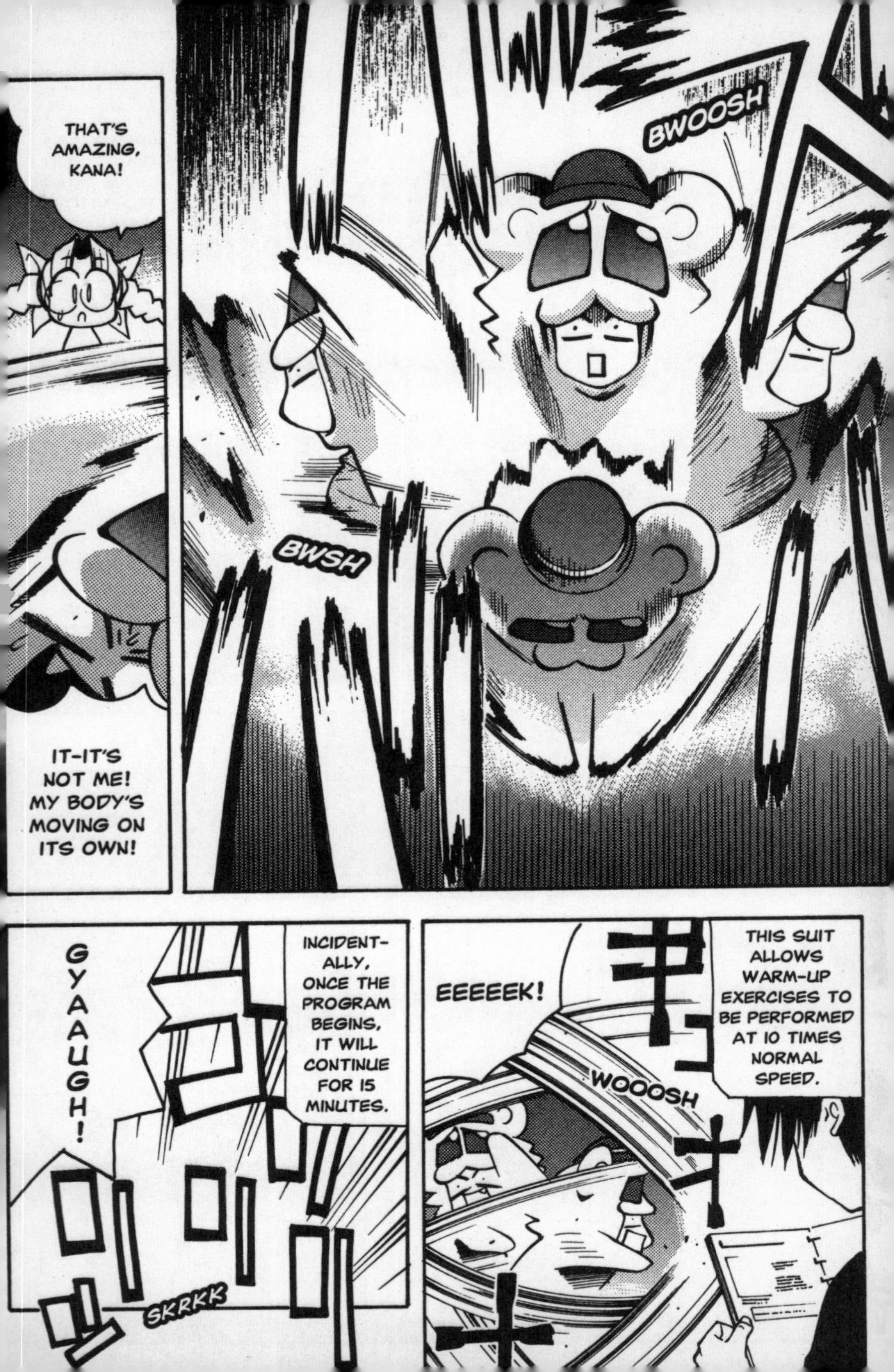
BWOOSH
BWSH
THAT'S AMAZING, KANA!
IT-IT'S NOT ME! MY BODY'S MOVING ON ITS OWN!
THIS SUIT ALLOWS WARM-UP EXERCISES TO BE PERFORMED AT 10 TIMES NORMAL SPEED.
EEEEEK!
WOOOSH
INCIDENT-ALLY, ONCE THE PROGRAM BEGINS, IT WILL CONTINUE FOR 15 MINUTES.
GYAAUGH!
SKRKK

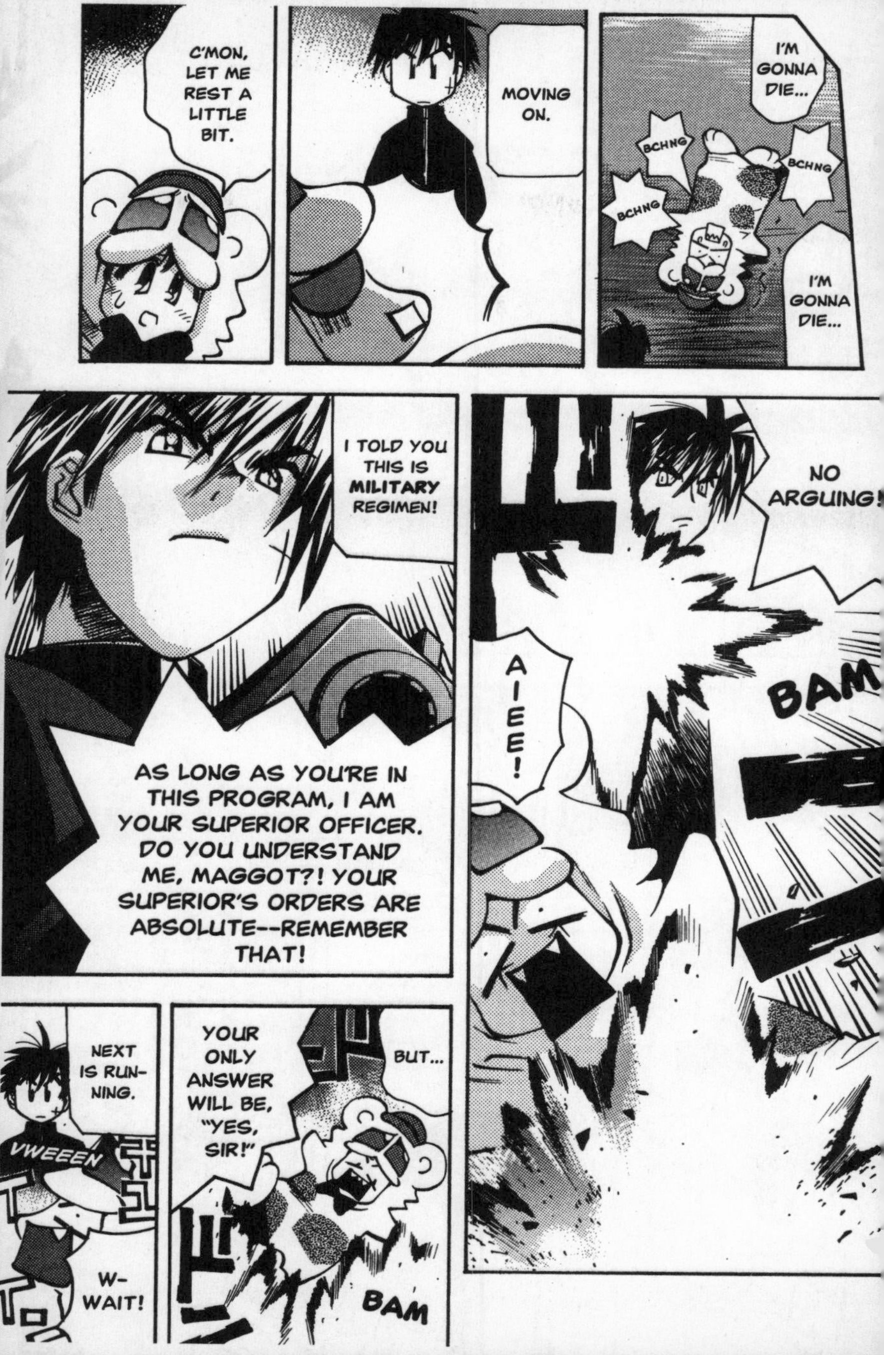
C'MON, LET ME REST A LITTLE BIT.
MOVING ON.
I'M GONNA DIE...
BCHNG
BCHNG
BCHNG
I'M GONNA DIE...
I TOLD YOU THIS IS MILITARY REGIMEN!
AS LONG AS YOU'RE IN THIS PROGRAM, I AM YOUR SUPERIOR OFFICER. DO YOU UNDERSTAND ME, MAGGOT?! YOUR SUPERIOR'S ORDERS ARE ABSOLUTE--REMEMBER THAT!
NO ARGUING!
AIEE!
BAM
NEXT IS RUN-NING.
VWEEEN
W-WAIT!
YOUR ONLY ANSWER WILL BE, "YES, SIR!"
BUT...
BAM

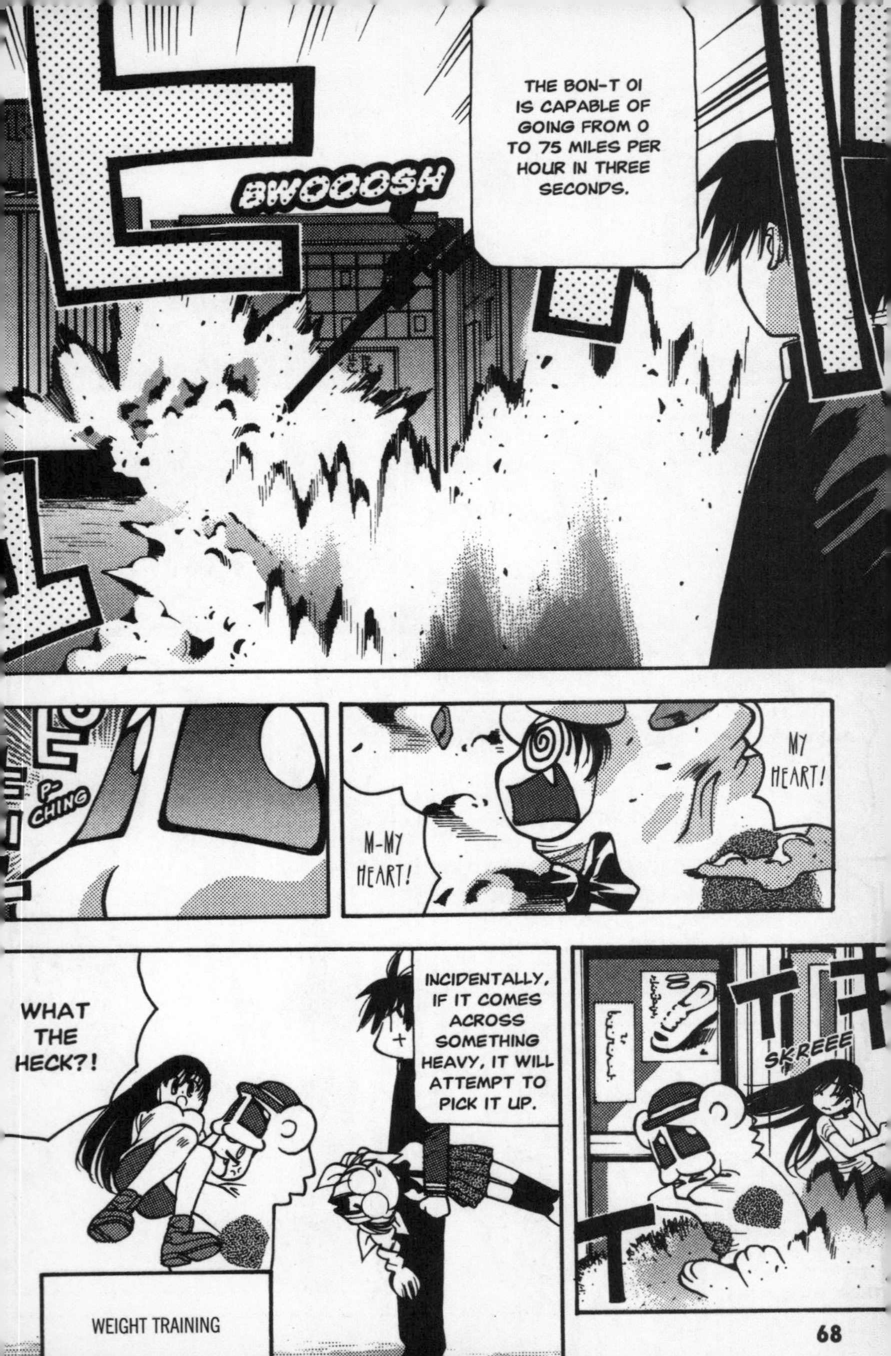
BWOOOSH
THE BON-T 01 IS CAPABLE OF GOING FROM 0 TO 75 MILES PER HOUR IN THREE SECONDS.
MY HEART!
M-MY HEART!
P-CHING
SKREEE
INCIDENTALLY, IF IT COMES ACROSS SOMETHING HEAVY, IT WILL ATTEMPT TO PICK IT UP.
WHAT THE HECK?!
WEIGHT TRAINING

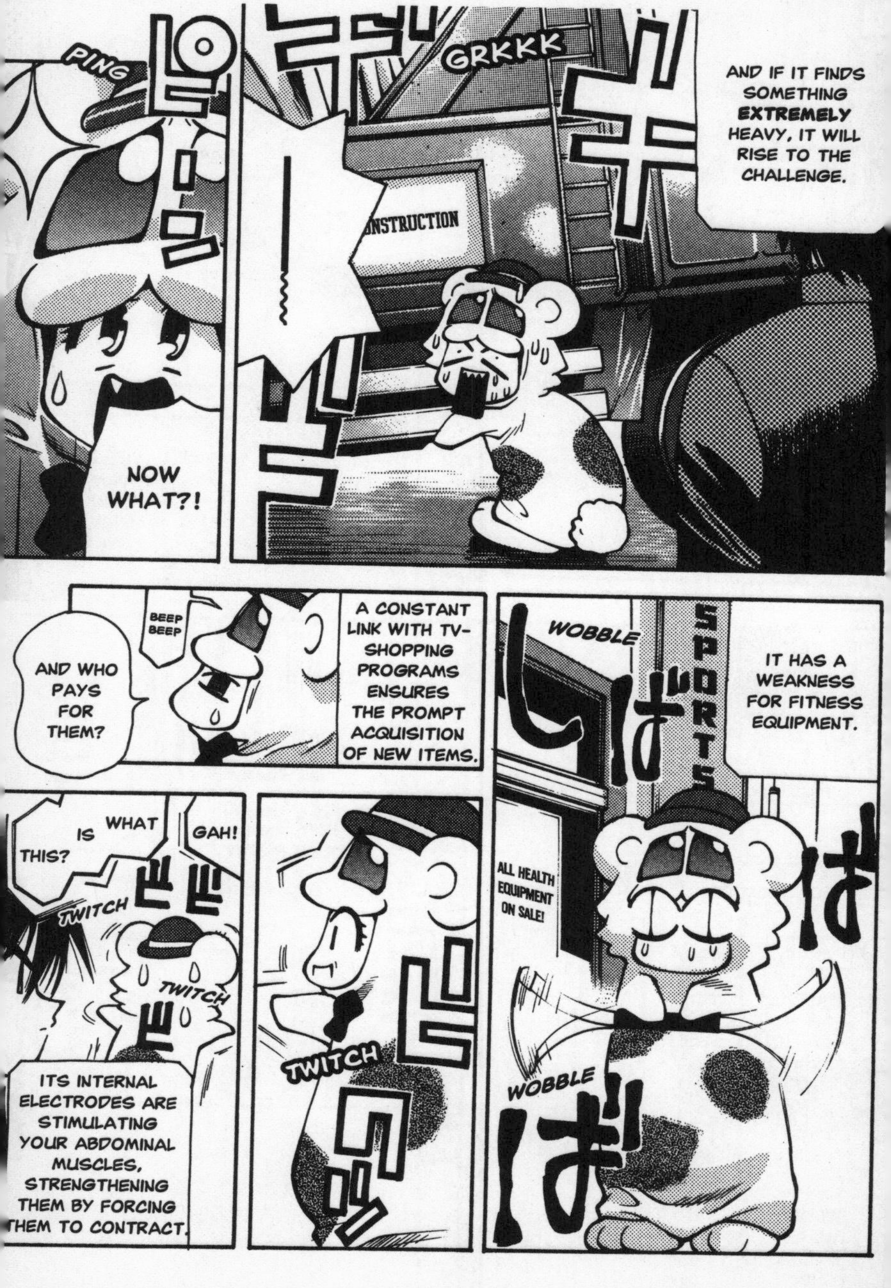

AND IF IT FINDS SOMETHING **EXTREMELY** HEAVY, IT WILL RISE TO THE CHALLENGE.
GRKKK
CONSTRUCTION
PING
NOW WHAT?!
A CONSTANT LINK WITH TV-SHOPPING PROGRAMS ENSURES THE PROMPT ACQUISITION OF NEW ITEMS.
BEEP BEEP
AND WHO PAYS FOR THEM?
IT HAS A WEAKNESS FOR FITNESS EQUIPMENT.
SPORTS
WOBBLE
ALL HEALTH EQUIPMENT ON SALE!
WOBBLE
GAH!
WHAT IS THIS?
TWITCH
TWITCH
TWITCH
ITS INTERNAL ELECTRODES ARE STIMULATING YOUR ABDOMINAL MUSCLES, STRENGTHENING THEM BY FORCING THEM TO CONTRACT.

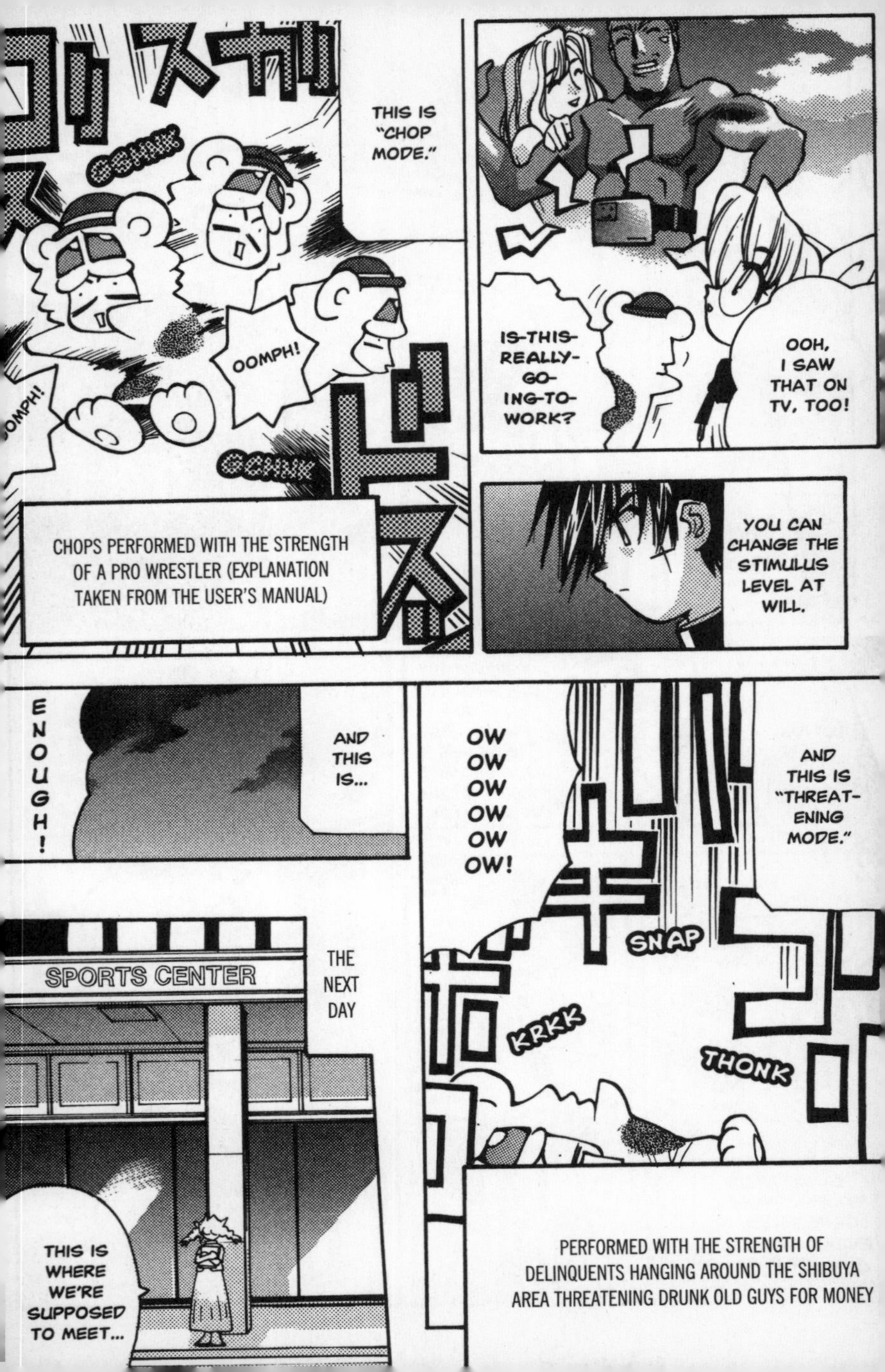

OOH, I SAW THAT ON TV, TOO!
IS-THIS-REALLY-GO-ING-TO-WORK?
YOU CAN CHANGE THE STIMULUS LEVEL AT WILL.
THIS IS "CHOP MODE."
GGHIK
OOMPH!
OOMPH!
GGHIK
CHOPS PERFORMED WITH THE STRENGTH OF A PRO WRESTLER (EXPLANATION TAKEN FROM THE USER'S MANUAL)
AND THIS IS "THREAT-ENING MODE."
OW OW OW OW OW OW!
SNAP
KRKK
THONK
PERFORMED WITH THE STRENGTH OF DELINQUENTS HANGING AROUND THE SHIBUYA AREA THREATENING DRUNK OLD GUYS FOR MONEY
AND THIS IS...
ENOUGH!
THE NEXT DAY
SPORTS CENTER
THIS IS WHERE WE'RE SUPPOSED TO MEET...

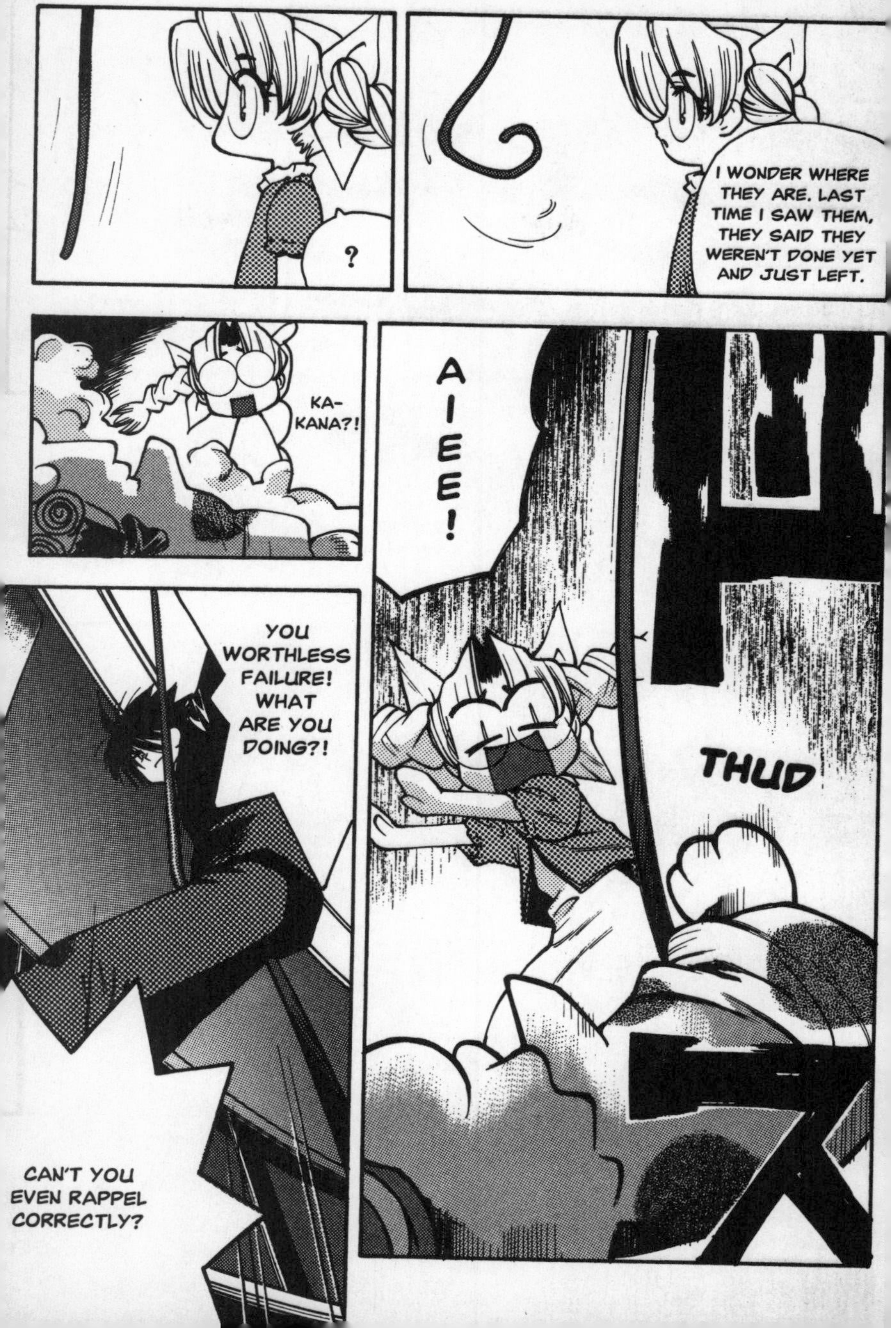
?
I WONDER WHERE THEY ARE. LAST TIME I SAW THEM, THEY SAID THEY WEREN'T DONE YET AND JUST LEFT.
KA-KANA?!
AIEE!
THUD
YOU WORTHLESS FAILURE! WHAT ARE YOU DOING?!
CAN'T YOU EVEN RAPPEL CORRECTLY?

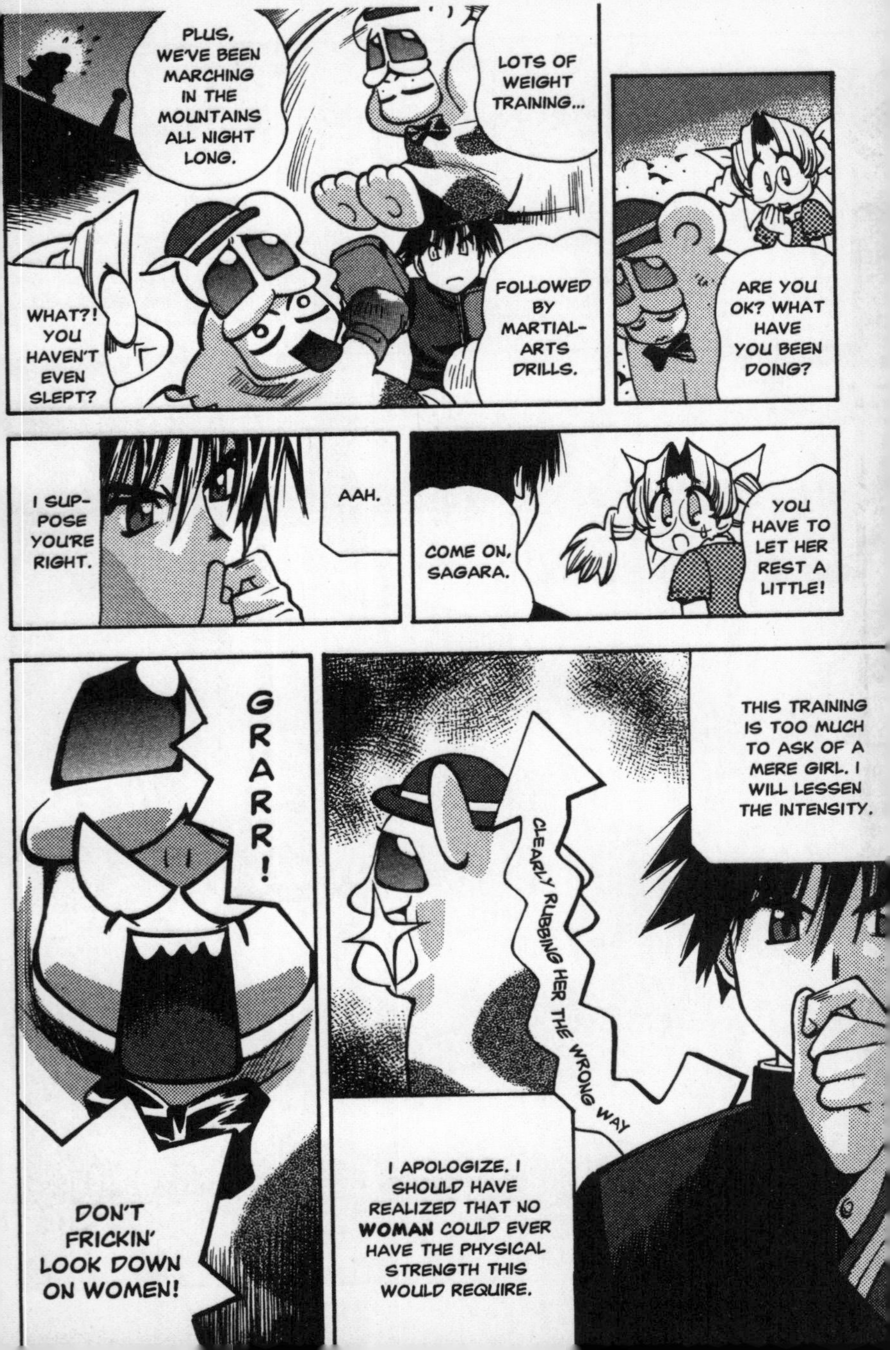

ARE YOU OK? WHAT HAVE YOU BEEN DOING?
LOTS OF WEIGHT TRAINING...
FOLLOWED BY MARTIAL-ARTS DRILLS.
PLUS, WE'VE BEEN MARCHING IN THE MOUNTAINS ALL NIGHT LONG.
WHAT?! YOU HAVEN'T EVEN SLEPT?
YOU HAVE TO LET HER REST A LITTLE!
COME ON, SAGARA.
AAH.
I SUPPOSE YOU'RE RIGHT.
THIS TRAINING IS TOO MUCH TO ASK OF A MERE GIRL. I WILL LESSEN THE INTENSITY.
CLEARLY RUBBING HER THE WRONG WAY
I APOLOGIZE. I SHOULD HAVE REALIZED THAT NO **WOMAN** COULD EVER HAVE THE PHYSICAL STRENGTH THIS WOULD REQUIRE.
GRARR!
DON'T FRICKIN' LOOK DOWN ON WOMEN!

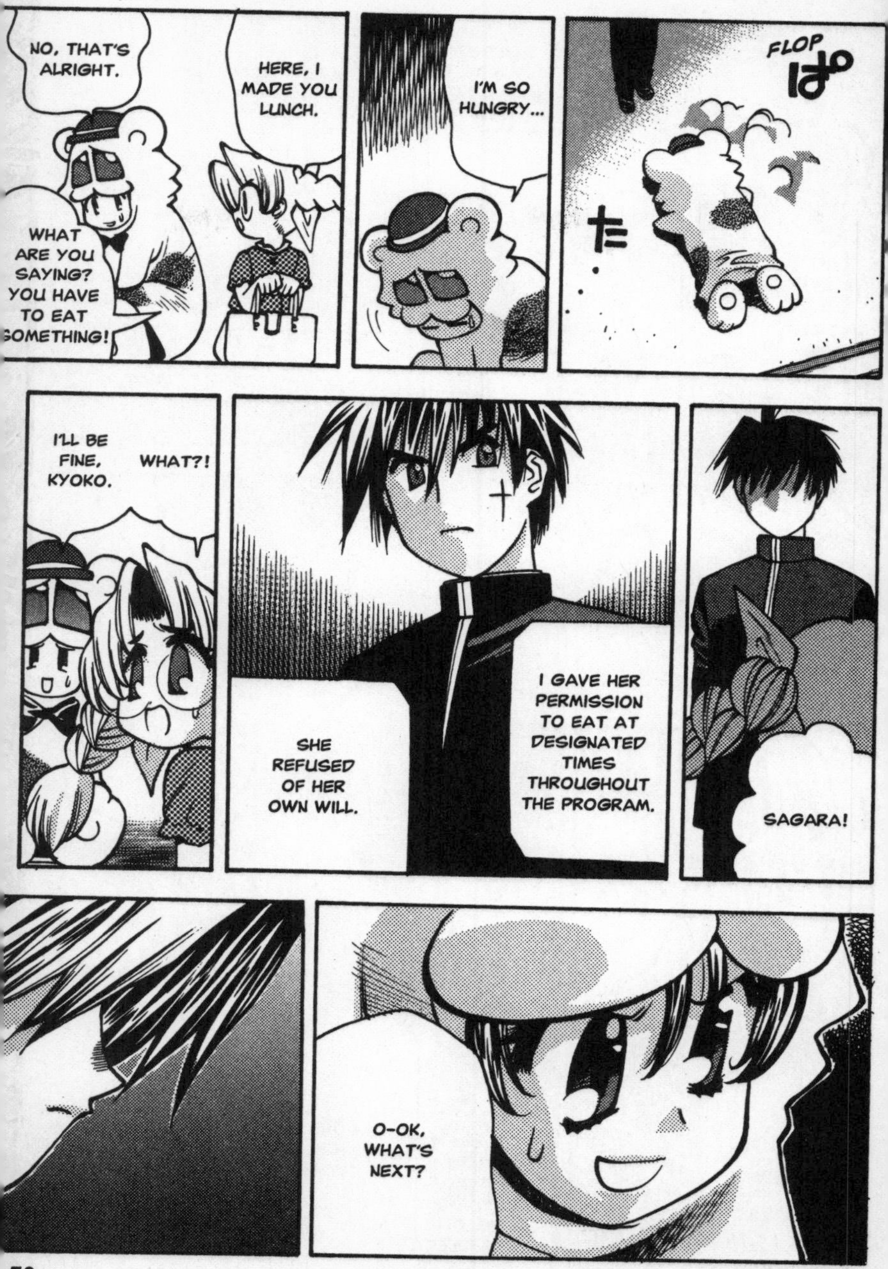
FLOP
ぱ
た
I'M SO HUNGRY...
HERE, I MADE YOU LUNCH.
NO, THAT'S ALRIGHT.
WHAT ARE YOU SAYING? YOU HAVE TO EAT SOMETHING!
SAGARA!
I GAVE HER PERMISSION TO EAT AT DESIGNATED TIMES THROUGHOUT THE PROGRAM.
SHE REFUSED OF HER OWN WILL.
WHAT?!
I'LL BE FINE, KYOKO.
O-OK, WHAT'S NEXT?

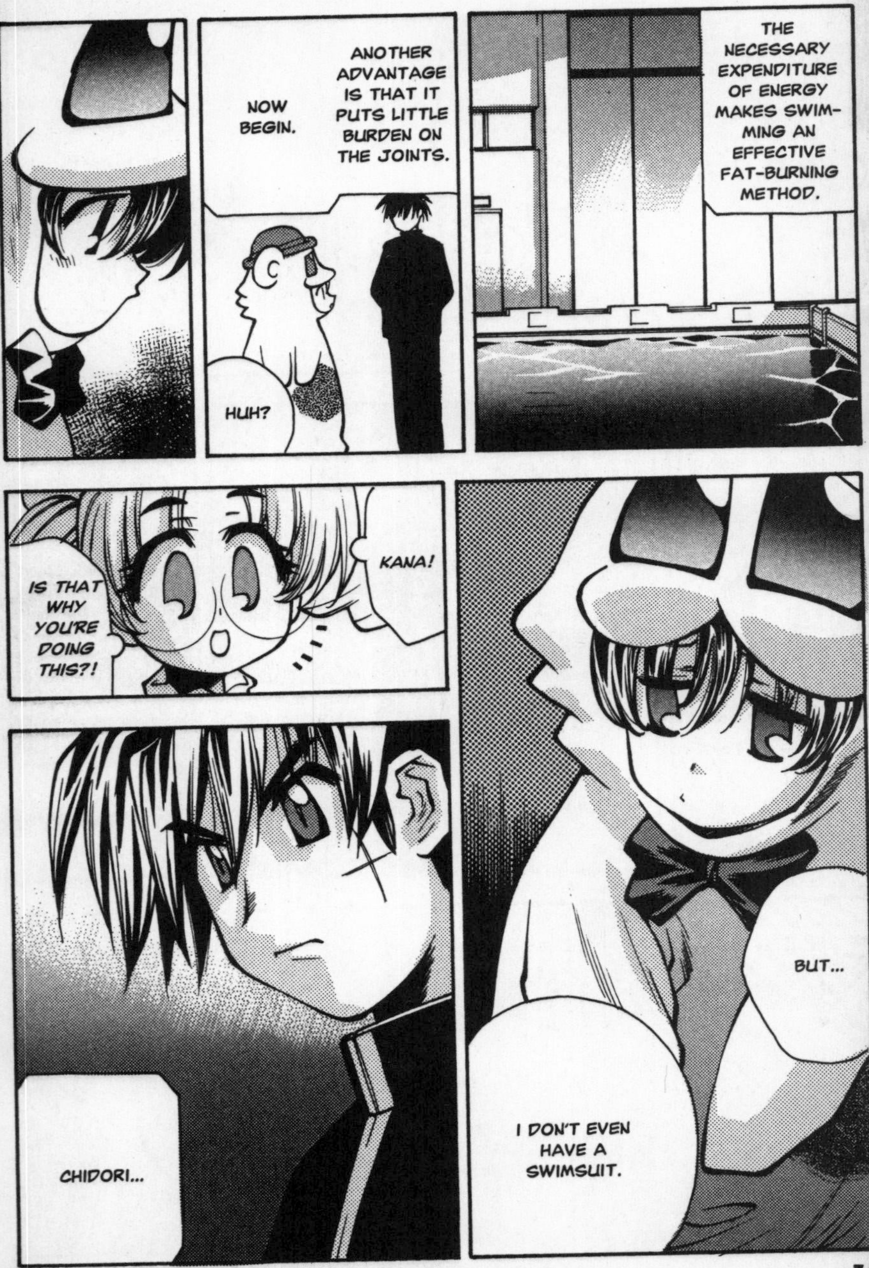
THE NECESSARY EXPENDITURE OF ENERGY MAKES SWIMMING AN EFFECTIVE FAT-BURNING METHOD.
ANOTHER ADVANTAGE IS THAT IT PUTS LITTLE BURDEN ON THE JOINTS.
NOW BEGIN.
HUH?
KANA!
IS THAT WHY YOU'RE DOING THIS?!
BUT...
I DON'T EVEN HAVE A SWIMSUIT.
CHIDORI...

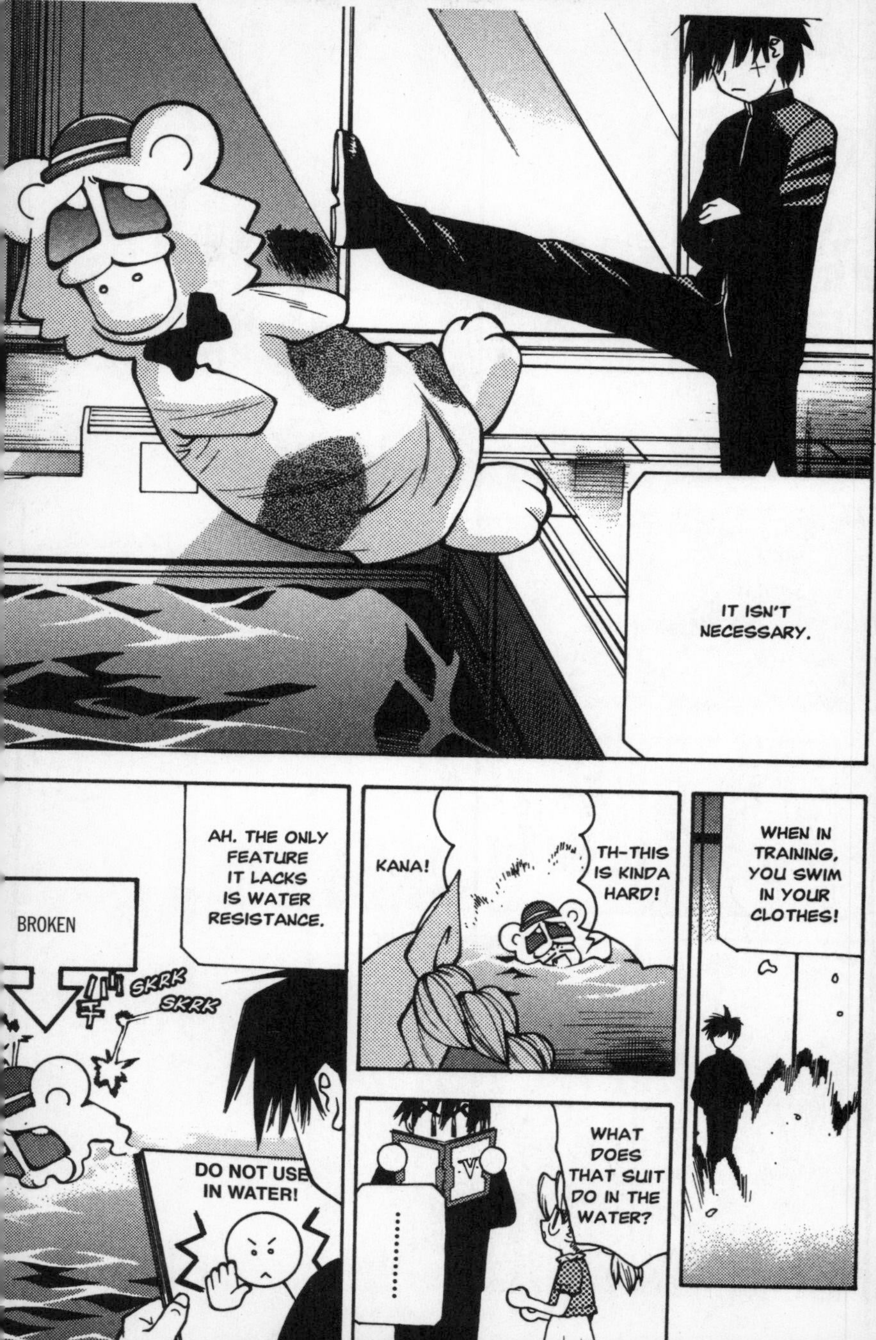
IT ISN'T NECESSARY.
WHEN IN TRAINING, YOU SWIM IN YOUR CLOTHES!
TH-THIS IS KINDA HARD!
KANA!
WHAT DOES THAT SUIT DO IN THE WATER?
AH. THE ONLY FEATURE IT LACKS IS WATER RESISTANCE.
BROKEN
SKRK
SKRK
DO NOT USE IN WATER!

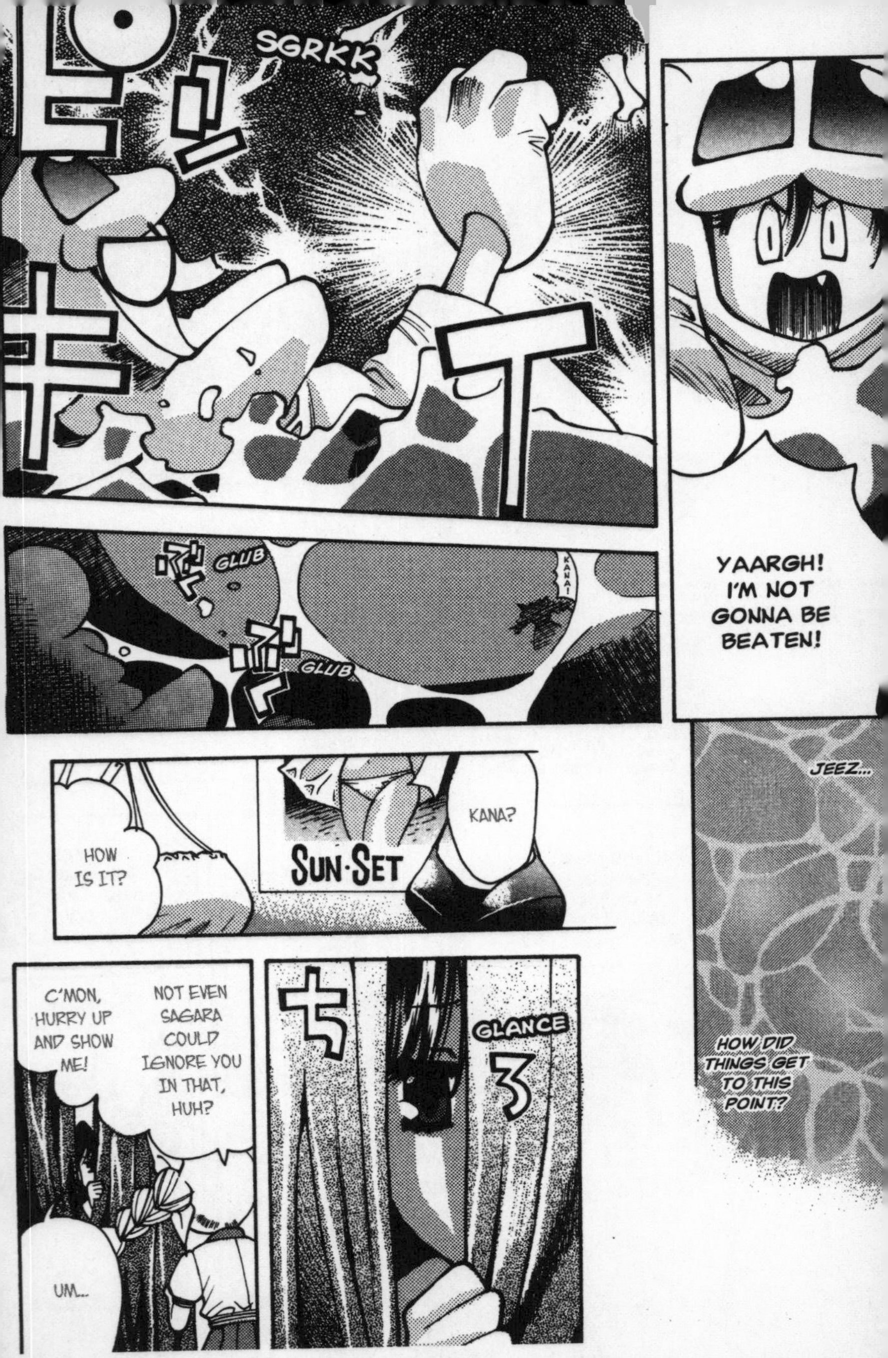
YAARGH! I'M NOT GONNA BE BEATEN!
SGRKK
GLUB
GLUB
KANA!
JEEZ...
HOW DID THINGS GET TO THIS POINT?
KANA?
SUN·SET
HOW IS IT?
GLANCE
NOT EVEN SAGARA COULD IGNORE YOU IN THAT, HUH?
C'MON, HURRY UP AND SHOW ME!
UM...

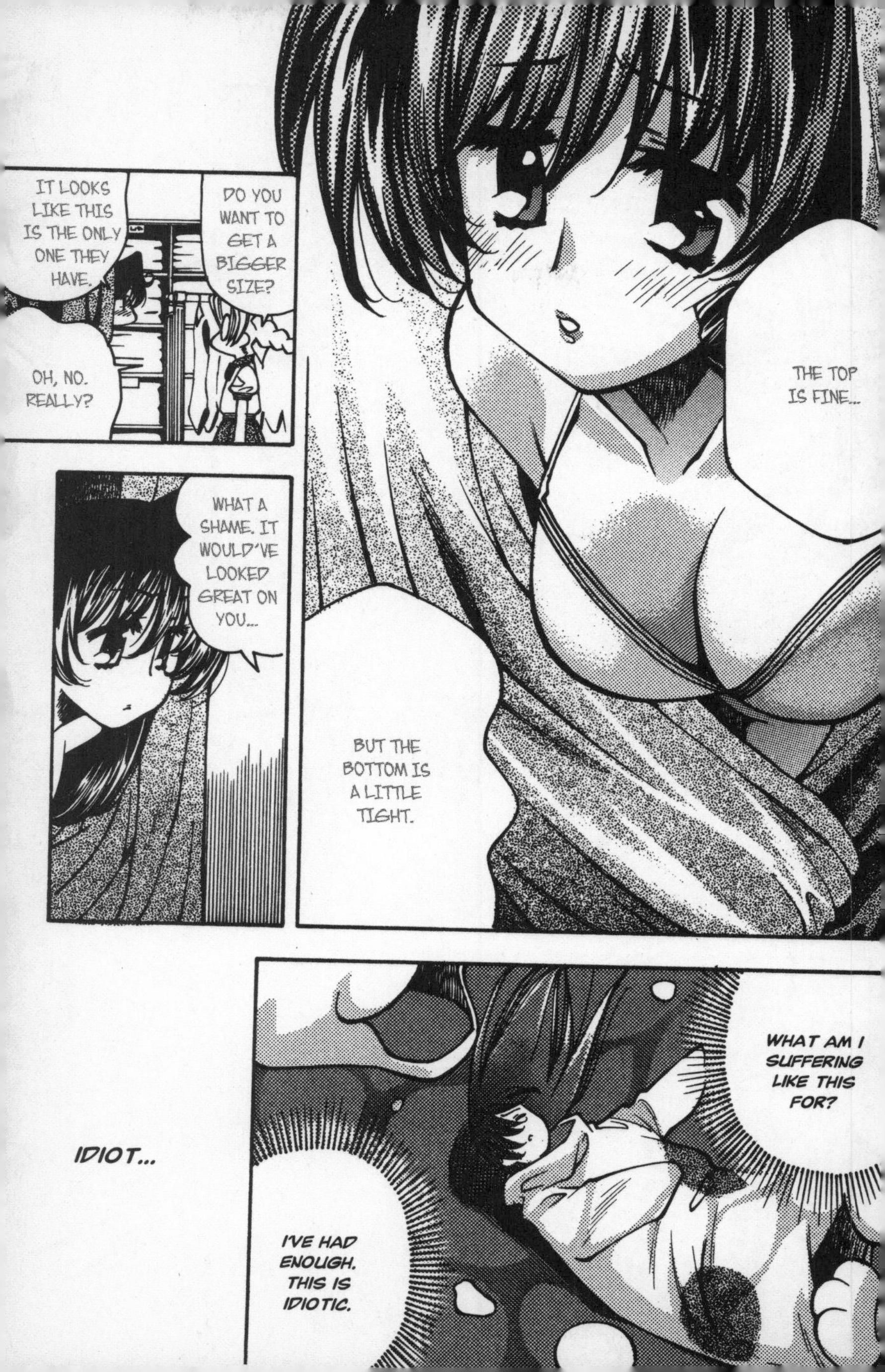
THE TOP IS FINE...
BUT THE BOTTOM IS A LITTLE TIGHT.
DO YOU WANT TO GET A BIGGER SIZE?
IT LOOKS LIKE THIS IS THE ONLY ONE THEY HAVE.
OH, NO. REALLY?
WHAT A SHAME. IT WOULD'VE LOOKED GREAT ON YOU...
WHAT AM I SUFFERING LIKE THIS FOR?
I'VE HAD ENOUGH. THIS IS IDIOTIC.
IDIOT...

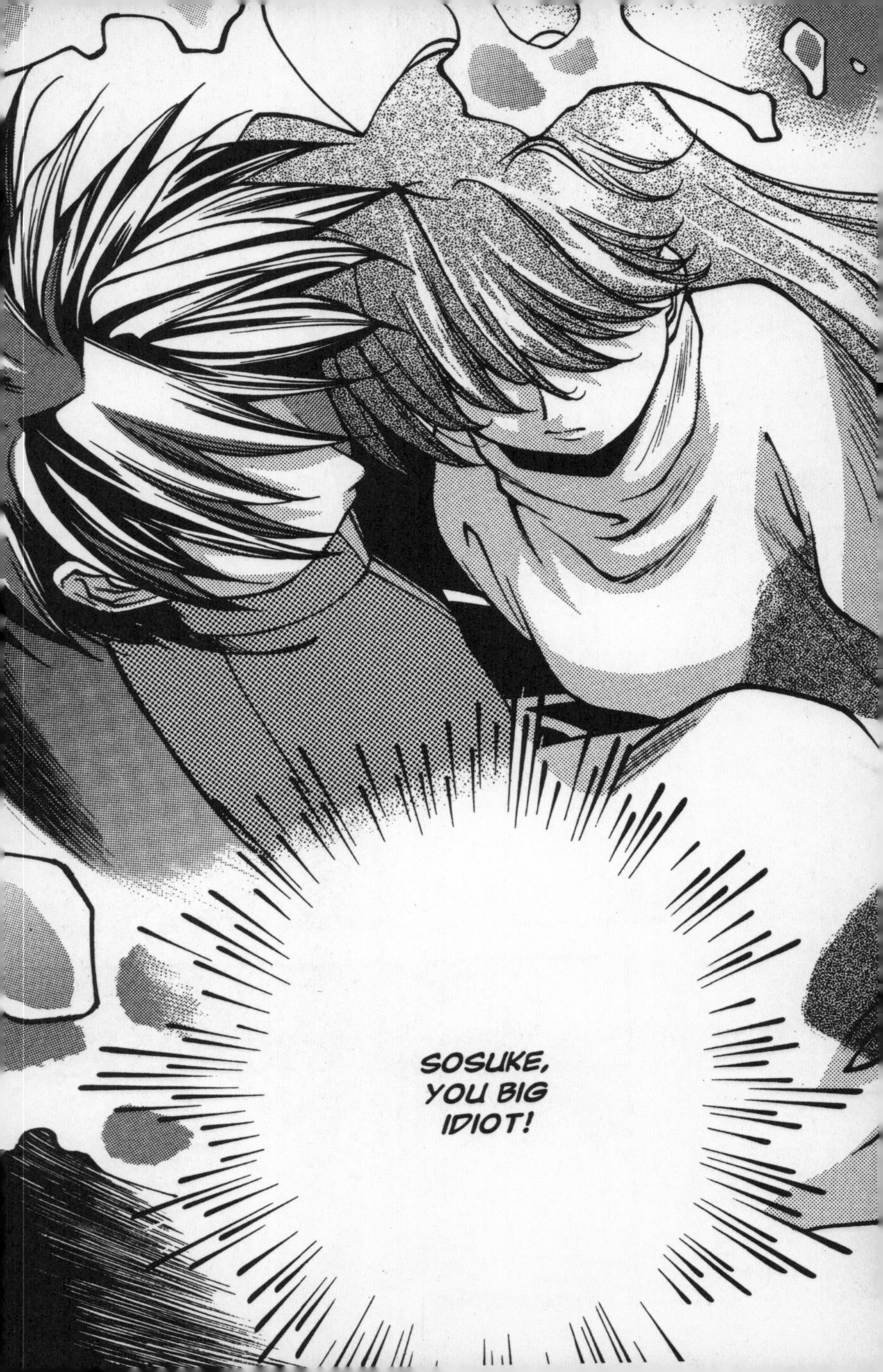
SOSUKE, YOU BIG IDIOT!

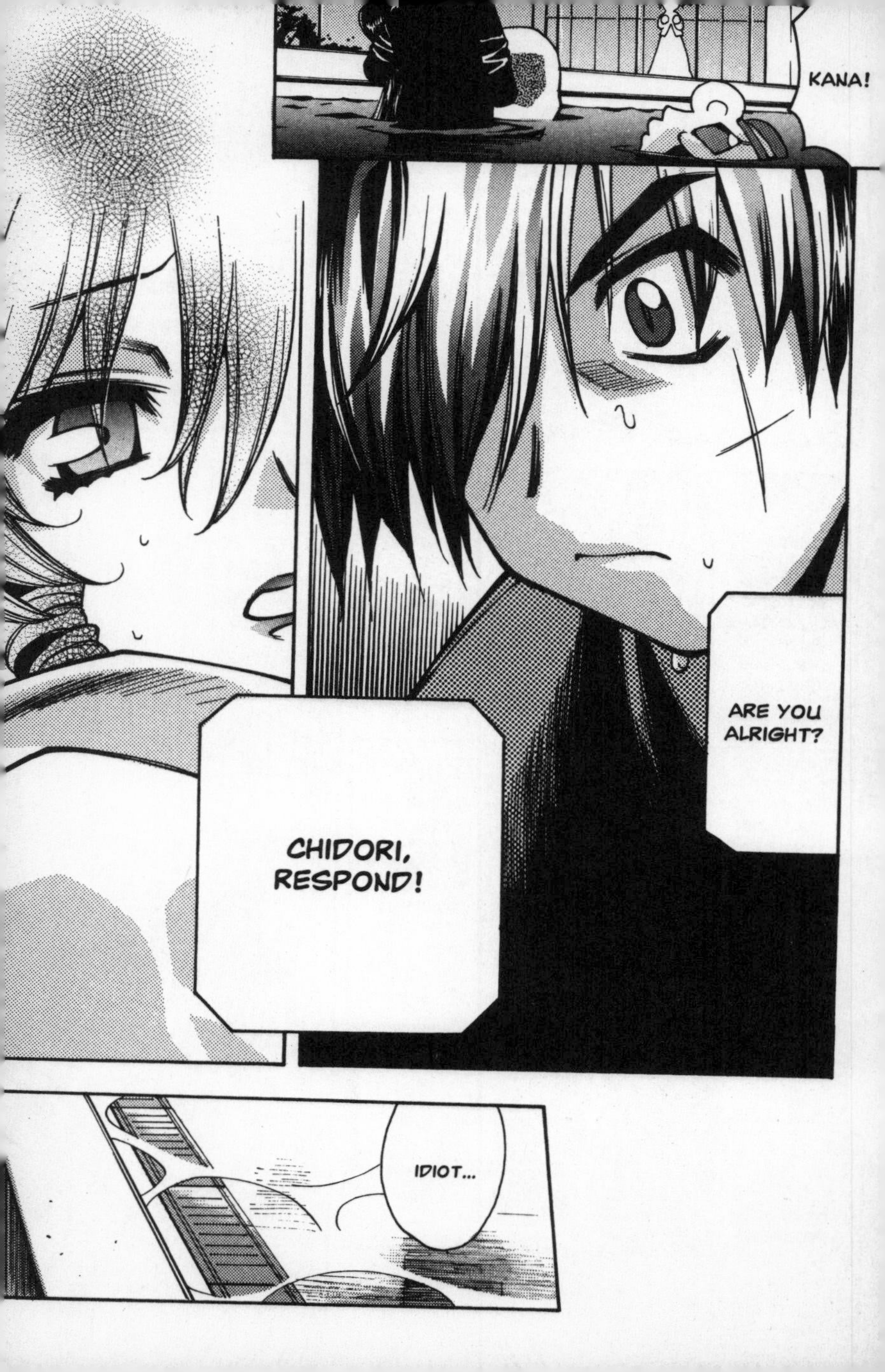
KANA!
ARE YOU ALRIGHT?
CHIDORI, RESPOND!
IDIOT...

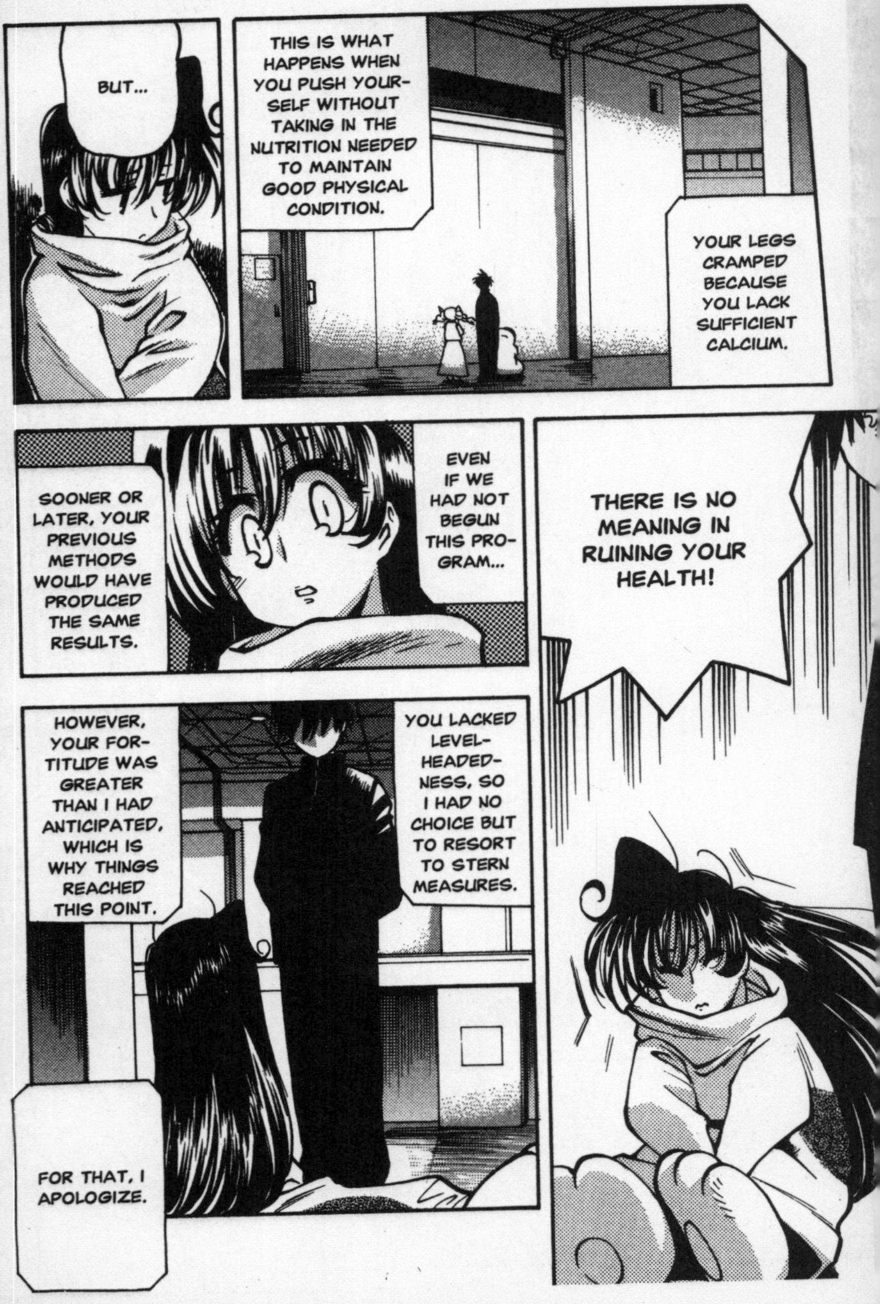
YOUR LEGS CRAMPED BECAUSE YOU LACK SUFFICIENT CALCIUM.
THIS IS WHAT HAPPENS WHEN YOU PUSH YOURSELF WITHOUT TAKING IN THE NUTRITION NEEDED TO MAINTAIN GOOD PHYSICAL CONDITION.
BUT...
THERE IS NO MEANING IN RUINING YOUR HEALTH!
EVEN IF WE HAD NOT BEGUN THIS PROGRAM...
SOONER OR LATER, YOUR PREVIOUS METHODS WOULD HAVE PRODUCED THE SAME RESULTS.
YOU LACKED LEVEL-HEADEDNESS, SO I HAD NO CHOICE BUT TO RESORT TO STERN MEASURES.
HOWEVER, YOUR FORTITUDE WAS GREATER THAN I HAD ANTICIPATED, WHICH IS WHY THINGS REACHED THIS POINT.
FOR THAT, I APOLOGIZE.

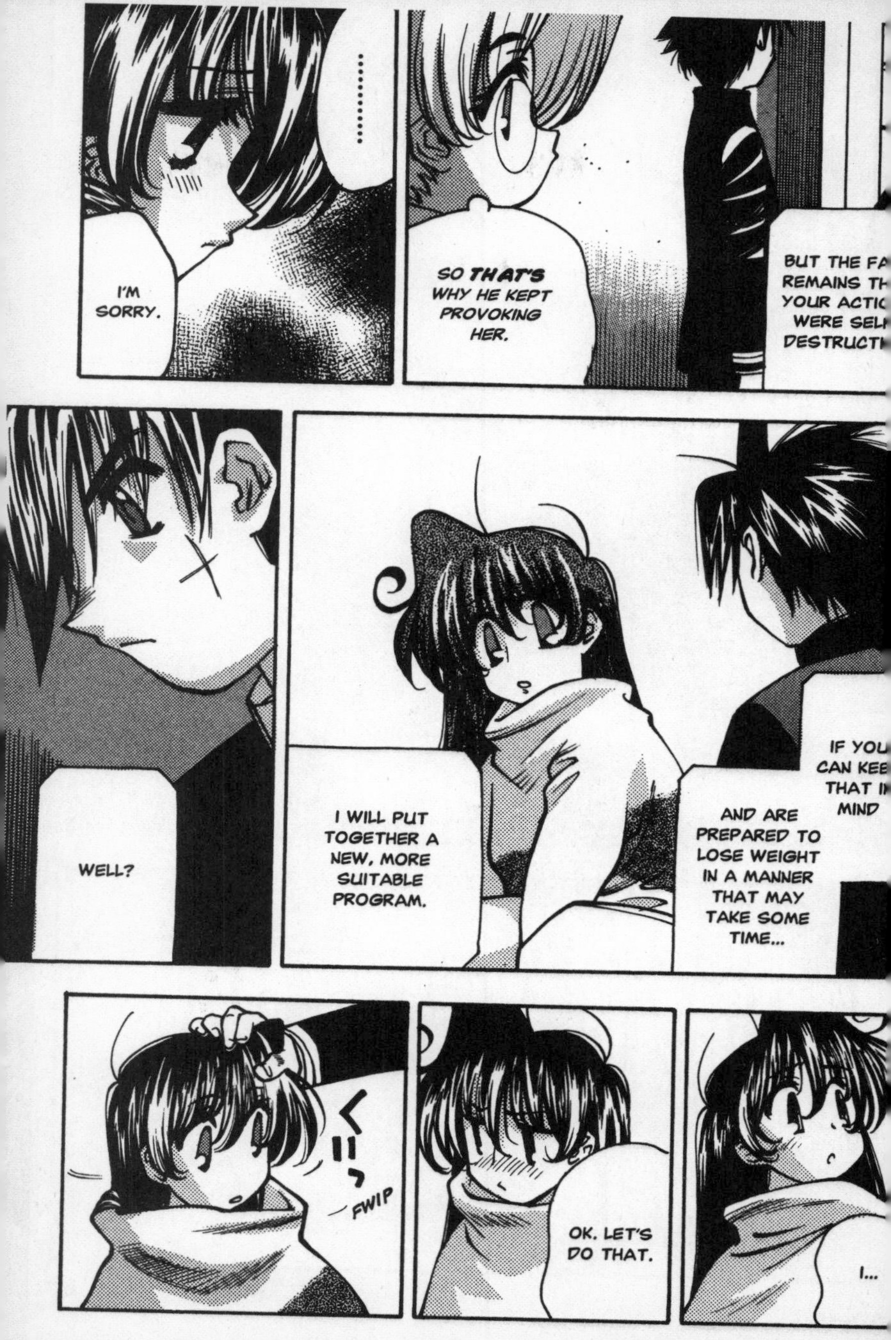
BUT THE FA
REMAINS TH
YOUR ACTI
WERE SEL
DESTRUCT
SO THAT'S WHY HE KEPT PROVOKING HER.
......
I'M SORRY.
IF YOU CAN KEE THAT I MIND
AND ARE PREPARED TO LOSE WEIGHT IN A MANNER THAT MAY TAKE SOME TIME...
I WILL PUT TOGETHER A NEW, MORE SUITABLE PROGRAM.
WELL?
I...
OK. LET'S DO THAT.
FWIP

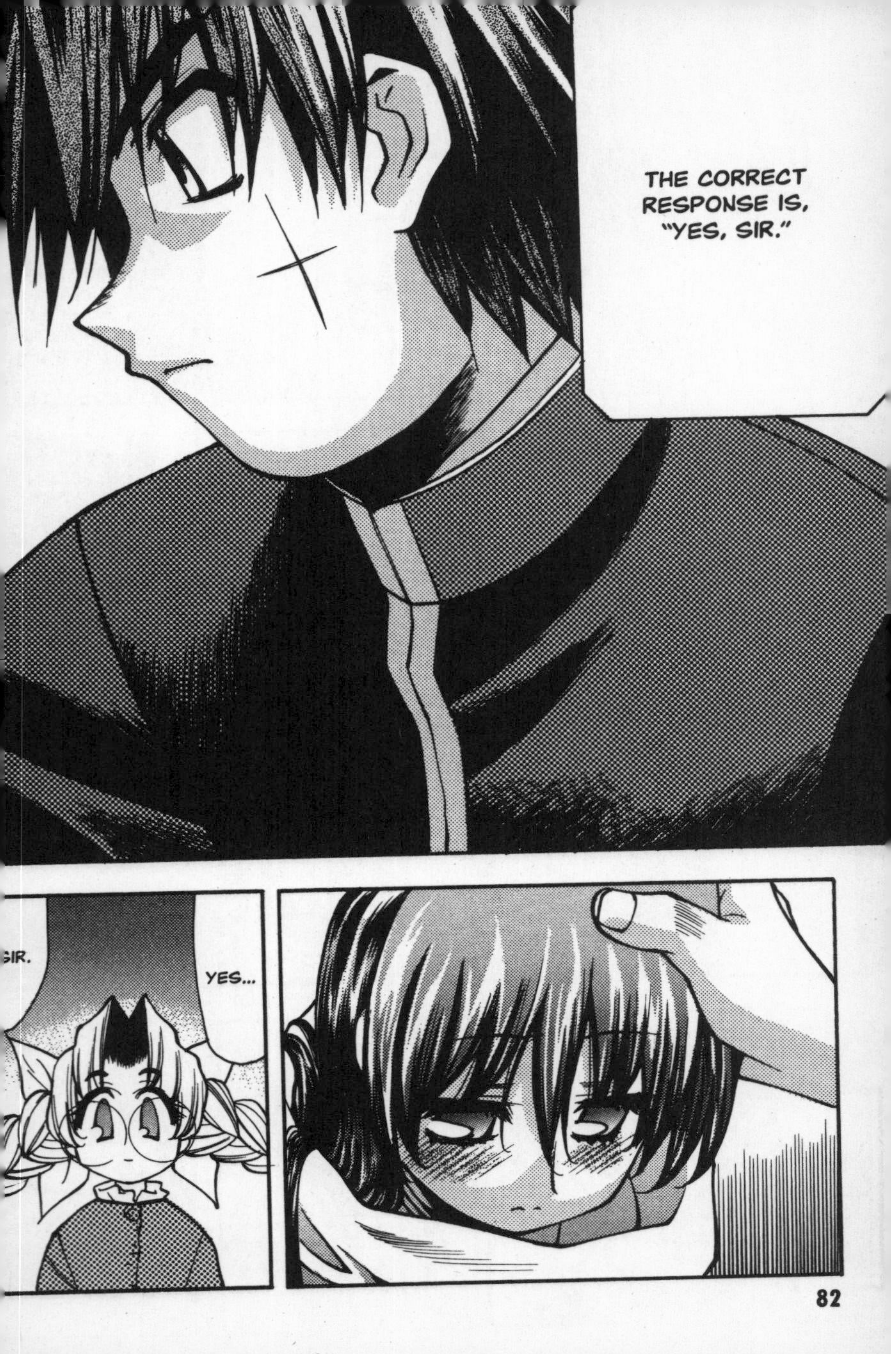
THE CORRECT RESPONSE IS, "YES, SIR."
YES...
SIR.

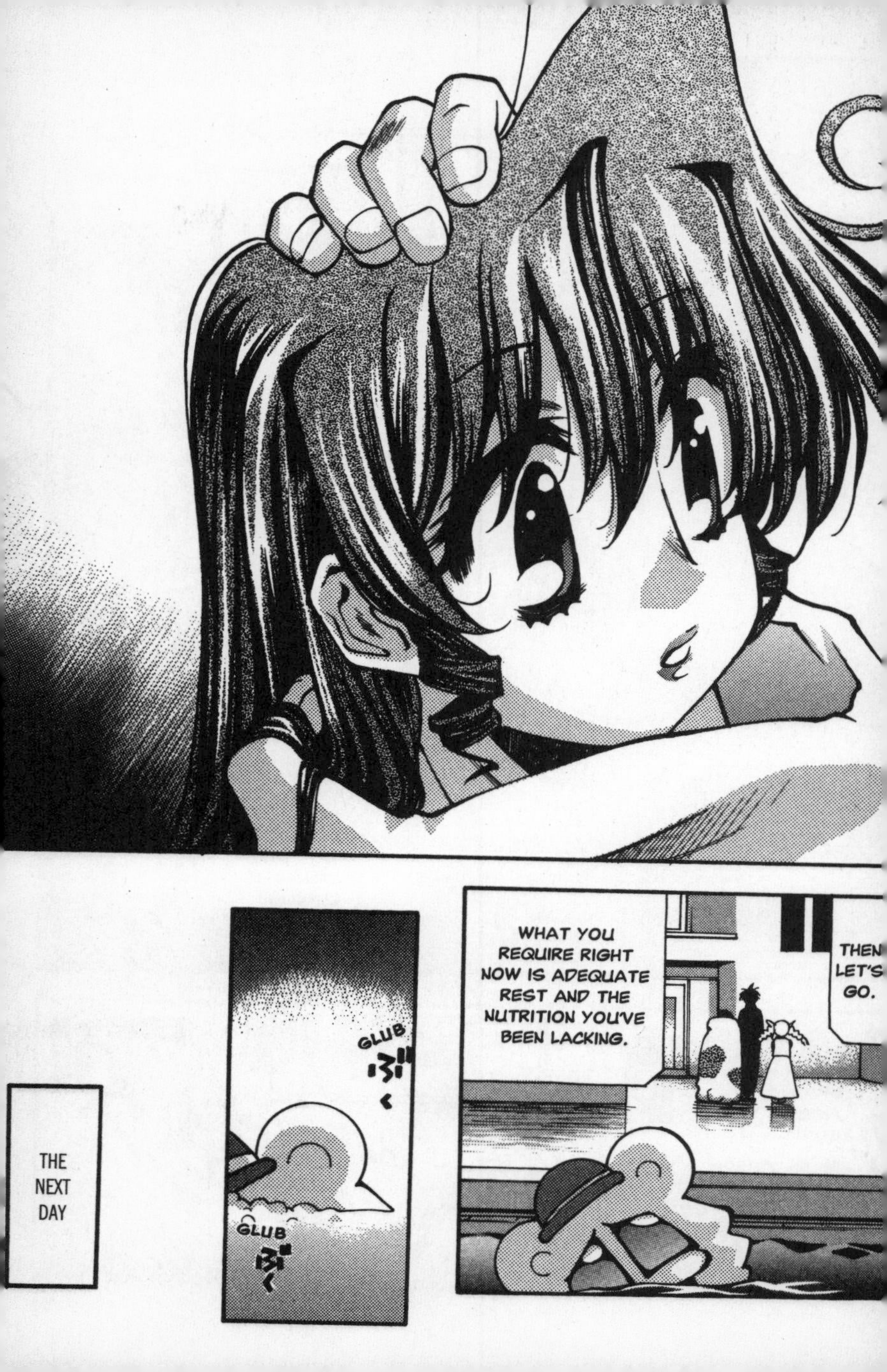
THEN LET'S GO.
WHAT YOU REQUIRE RIGHT NOW IS ADEQUATE REST AND THE NUTRITION YOU'VE BEEN LACKING.
GLUB
ぶく
GLUB
ぶく
THE NEXT DAY

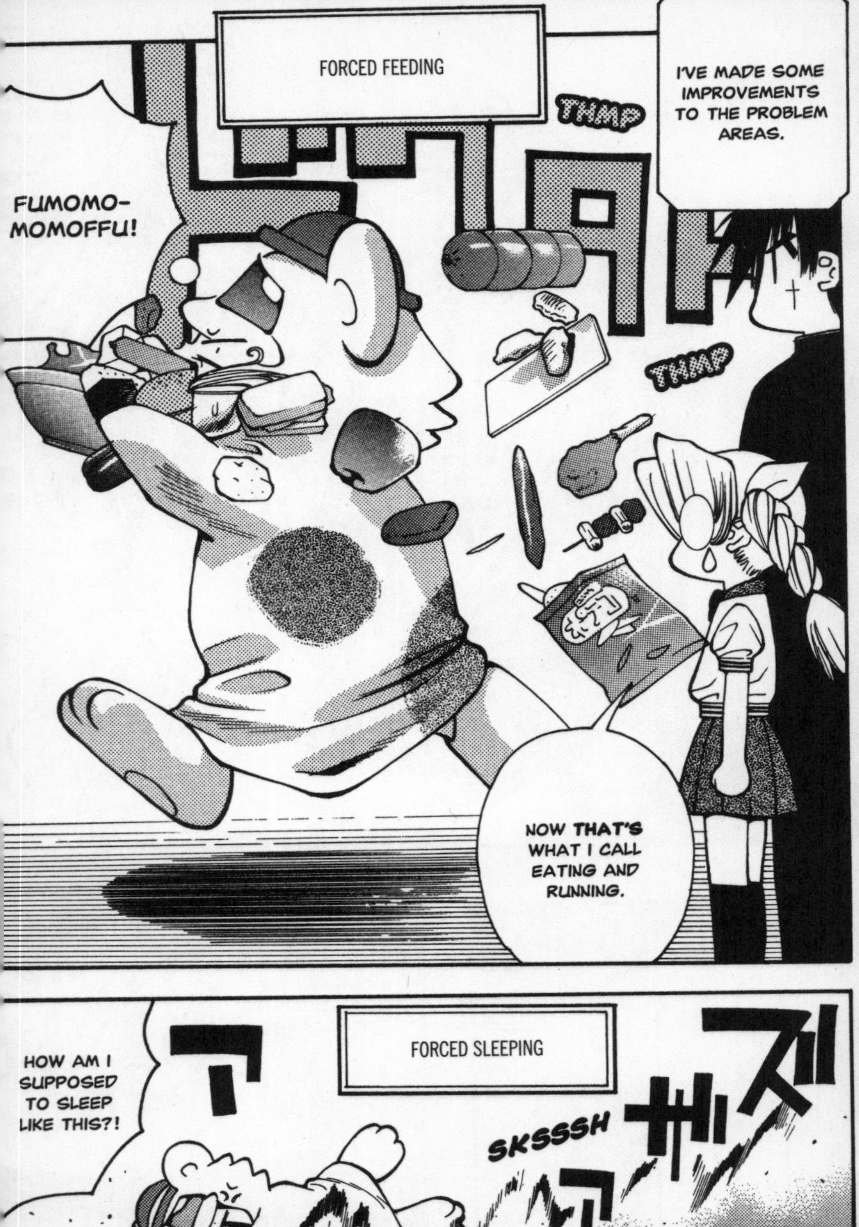
FORCED FEEDING
I'VE MADE SOME IMPROVEMENTS TO THE PROBLEM AREAS.
THMP
THMP
FUMOMO-MOMOFFU!
NOW THAT'S WHAT I CALL EATING AND RUNNING.
FORCED SLEEPING
SKSSSH
HOW AM I SUPPOSED TO SLEEP LIKE THIS?!

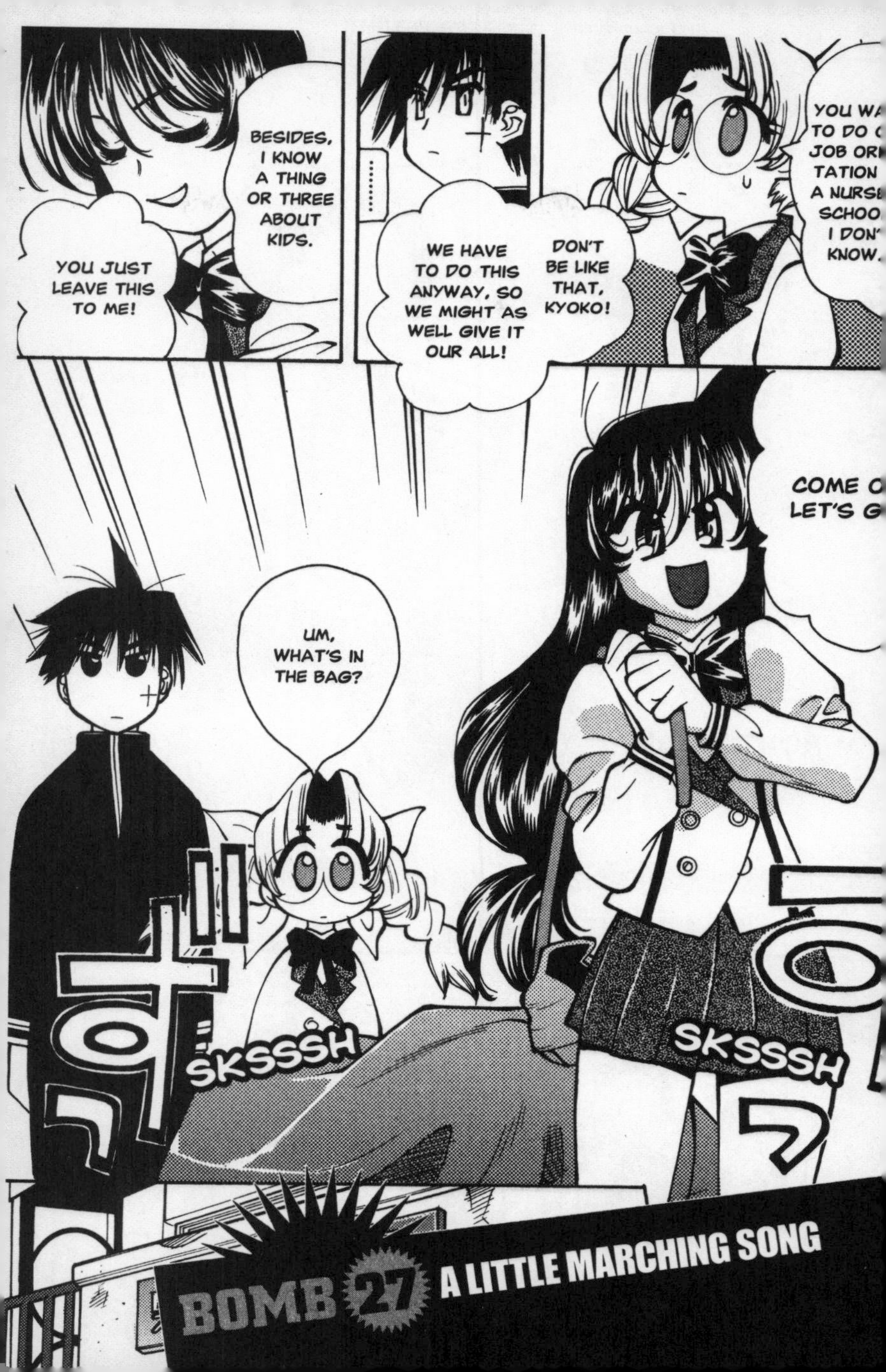
YOU WA TO DO C JOB ORI TATION A NURSE SCHOO I DON'T KNOW.
DON'T BE LIKE THAT, KYOKO!
WE HAVE TO DO THIS ANYWAY, SO WE MIGHT AS WELL GIVE IT OUR ALL!
......
BESIDES, I KNOW A THING OR THREE ABOUT KIDS.
YOU JUST LEAVE THIS TO ME!
COME O LET'S G
UM, WHAT'S IN THE BAG?
SKSSSH
SKSSSH
BOMB 27 A LITTLE MARCHING SONG

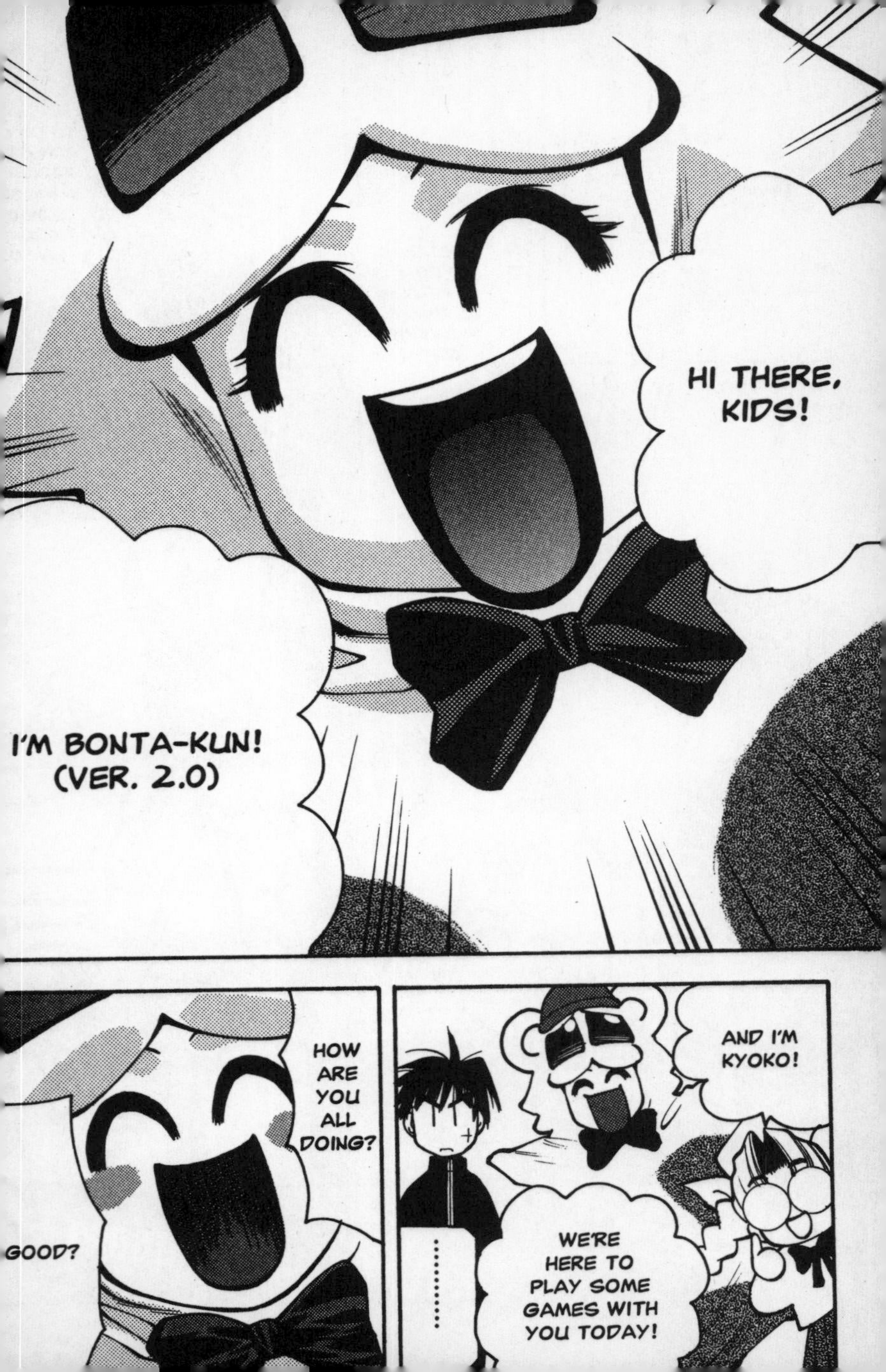
HI THERE, KIDS!
I'M BONTA-KUN! (VER. 2.0)
AND I'M KYOKO!
WE'RE HERE TO PLAY SOME GAMES WITH YOU TODAY!
......
HOW ARE YOU ALL DOING?
GOOD?

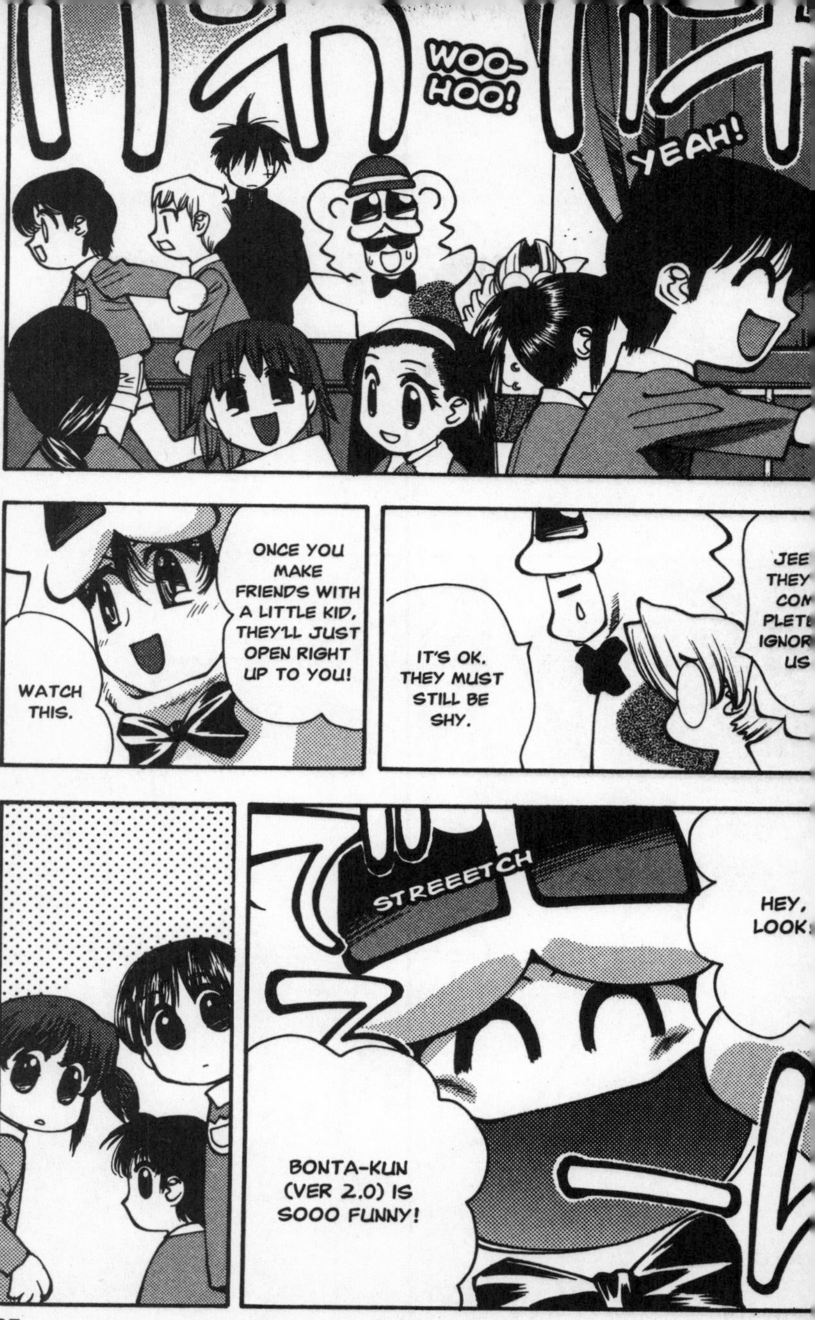
YEAH!
WOO-HOO!
JEE THEY COM PLETE IGNOR US
IT'S OK. THEY MUST STILL BE SHY.
ONCE YOU MAKE FRIENDS WITH A LITTLE KID, THEY'LL JUST OPEN RIGHT UP TO YOU!
WATCH THIS.
HEY, LOOK.
STREEETCH
BONTA-KUN (VER 2.0) IS SOOO FUNNY!

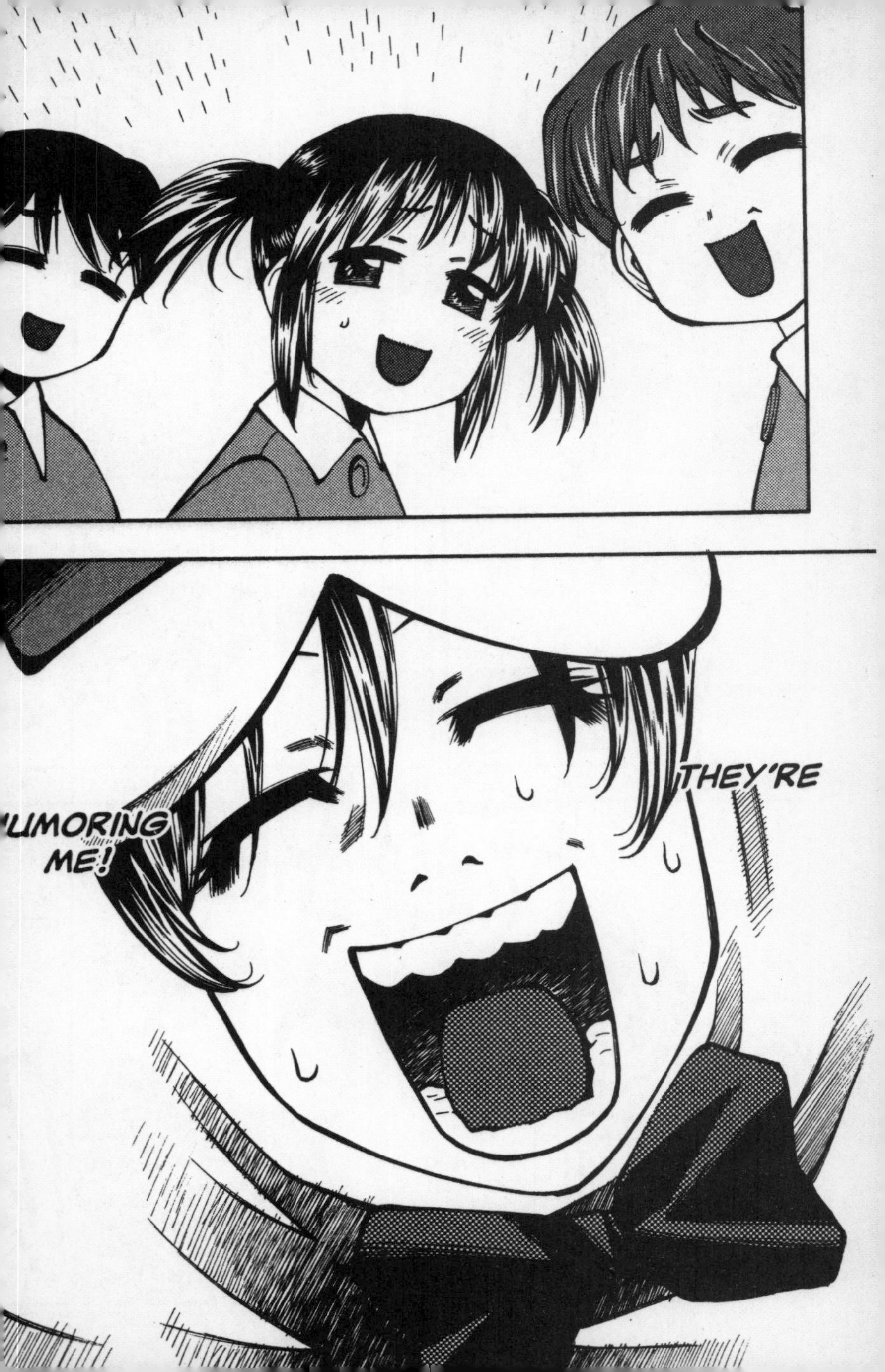
THEY'RE
'UMORING ME!

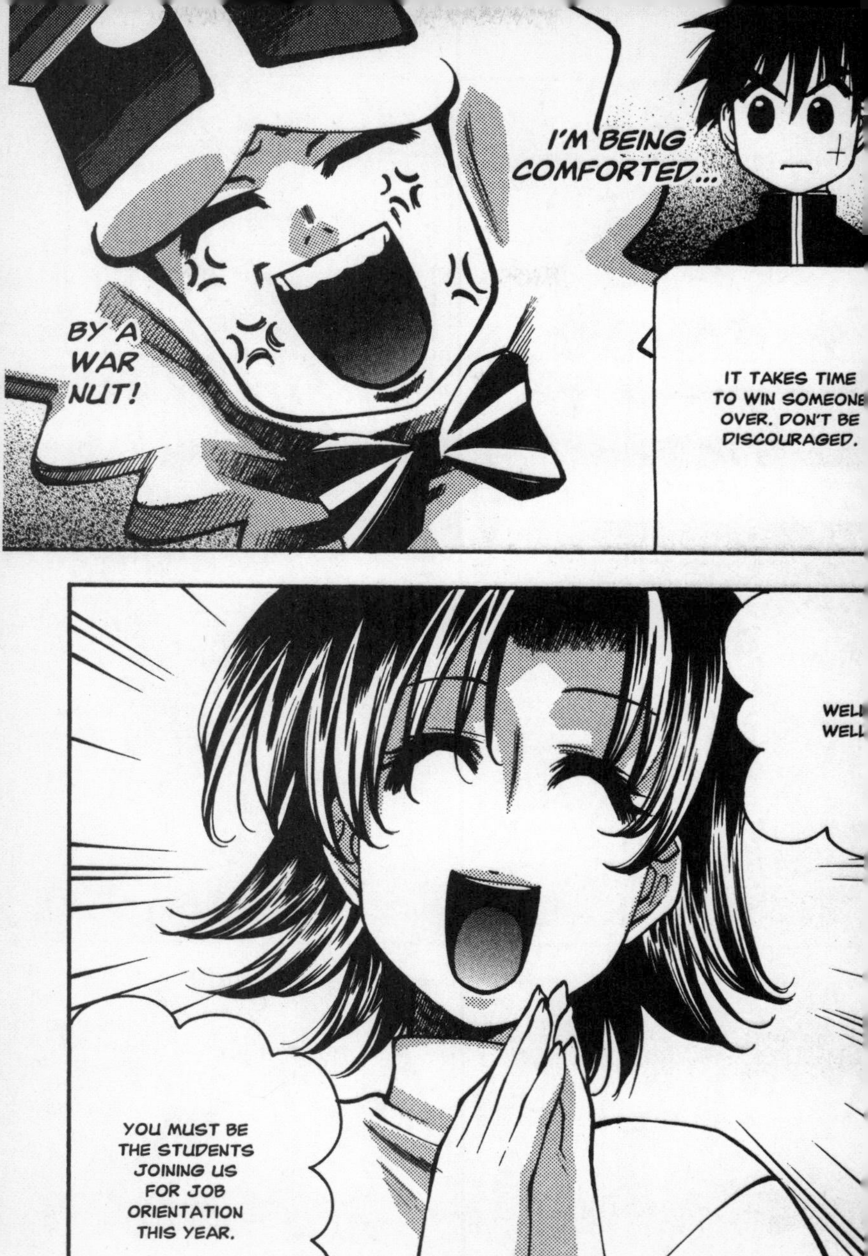
I'M BEING COMFORTED...
BY A WAR NUT!
IT TAKES TIME TO WIN SOMEONE OVER. DON'T BE DISCOURAGED.
WELL WELL
YOU MUST BE THE STUDENTS JOINING US FOR JOB ORIENTATION THIS YEAR.

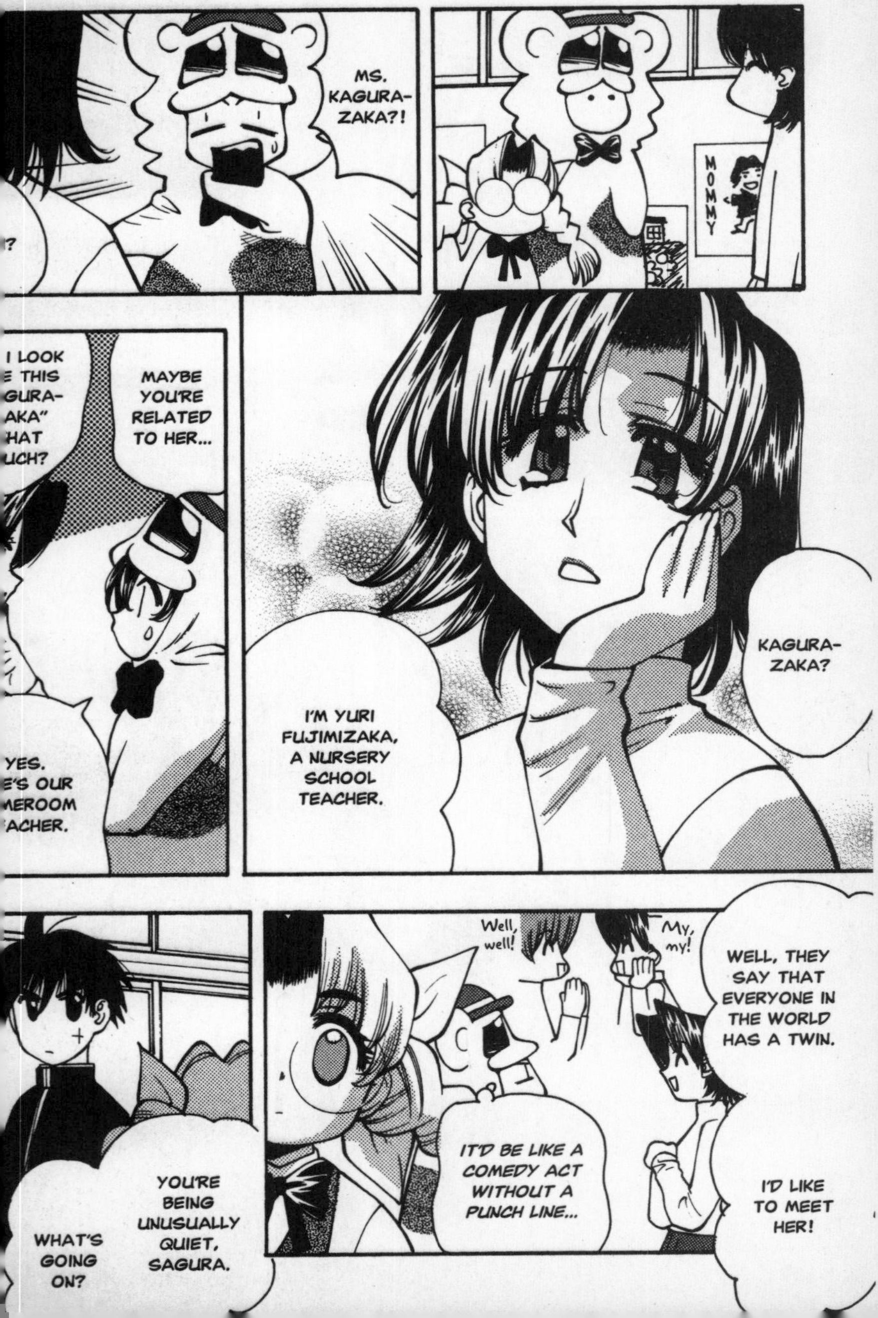

?
MS. KAGURA-ZAKA?!
MOMMY
KAGURA-ZAKA?
I'M YURI FUJIMIZAKA, A NURSERY SCHOOL TEACHER.
I LOOK E THIS GURA-AKA" HAT UCH?
MAYBE YOU'RE RELATED TO HER...
YES. E'S OUR MEROOM ACHER.
Well, well!
My, my!
WELL, THEY SAY THAT EVERYONE IN THE WORLD HAS A TWIN.
I'D LIKE TO MEET HER!
IT'D BE LIKE A COMEDY ACT WITHOUT A PUNCH LINE...
YOU'RE BEING UNUSUALLY QUIET, SAGURA.
WHAT'S GOING ON?

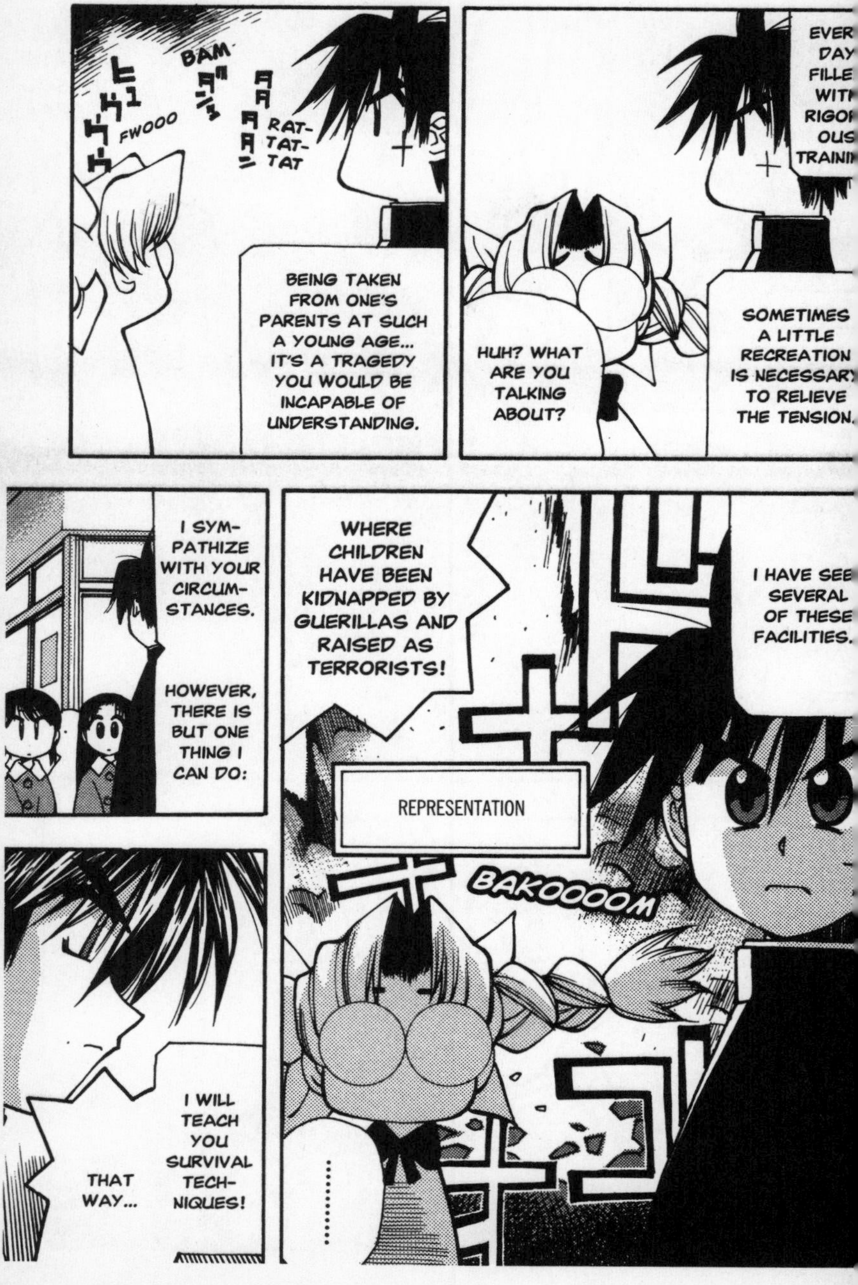
EVER
DAY
FILLE
WITH
RIGOR
OUS
TRAINI
SOMETIMES A LITTLE RECREATION IS NECESSARY TO RELIEVE THE TENSION.
HUH? WHAT ARE YOU TALKING ABOUT?
BAM
RAT-TAT-TAT
FWOOO
BEING TAKEN FROM ONE'S PARENTS AT SUCH A YOUNG AGE... IT'S A TRAGEDY YOU WOULD BE INCAPABLE OF UNDERSTANDING.
I HAVE SEE SEVERAL OF THESE FACILITIES.
WHERE CHILDREN HAVE BEEN KIDNAPPED BY GUERILLAS AND RAISED AS TERRORISTS!
REPRESENTATION
BAKOOOOM
I SYMPATHIZE WITH YOUR CIRCUMSTANCES.
HOWEVER, THERE IS BUT ONE THING I CAN DO:
I WILL TEACH YOU SURVIVAL TECHNIQUES!
THAT WAY...
......

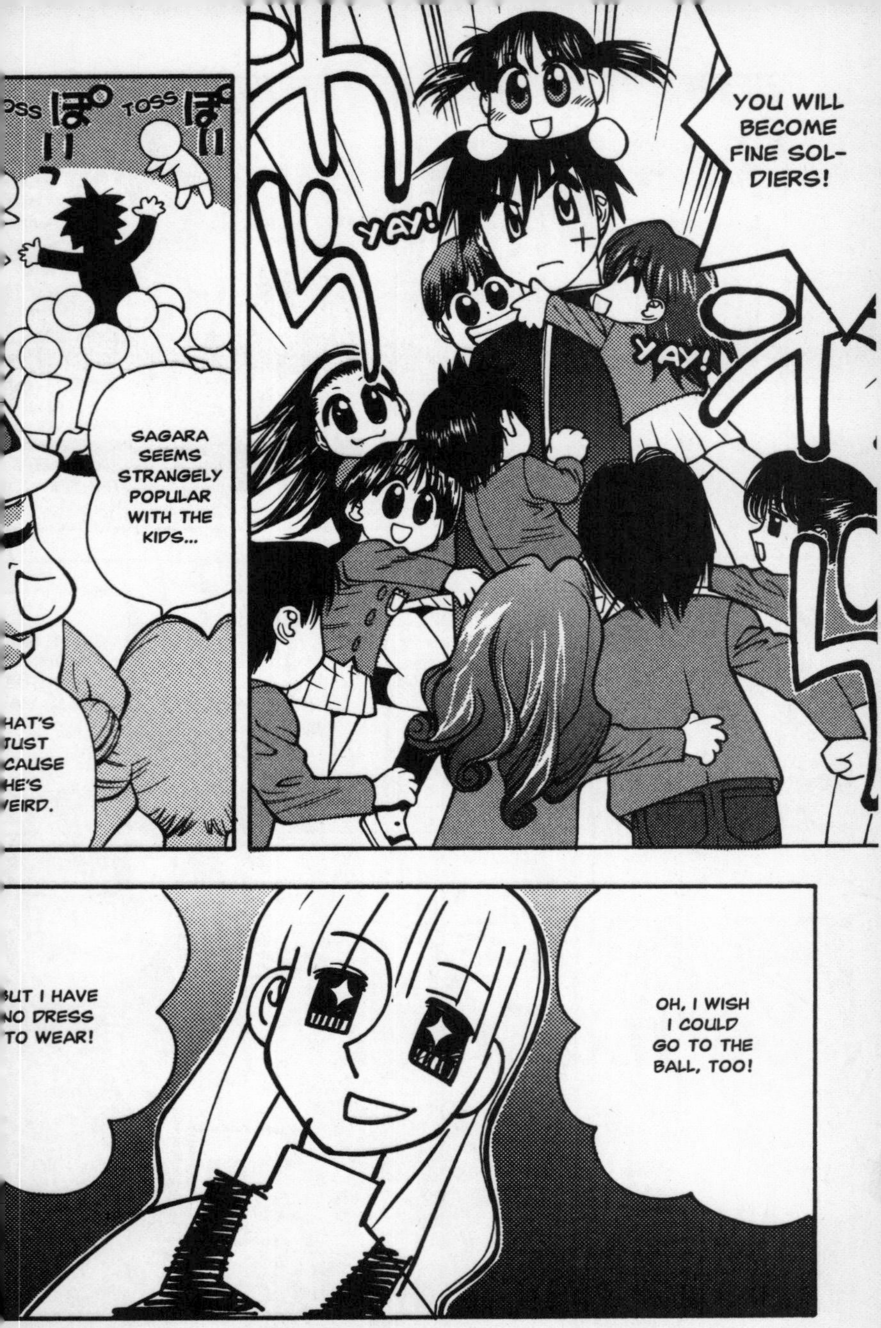
YOU WILL BECOME FINE SOL-DIERS!
YAY!
YAY!
TOSS
OSS
SAGARA SEEMS STRANGELY POPULAR WITH THE KIDS...
HAT'S JUST CAUSE HE'S VEIRD.
OH, I WISH I COULD GO TO THE BALL, TOO!
UT I HAVE NO DRESS TO WEAR!

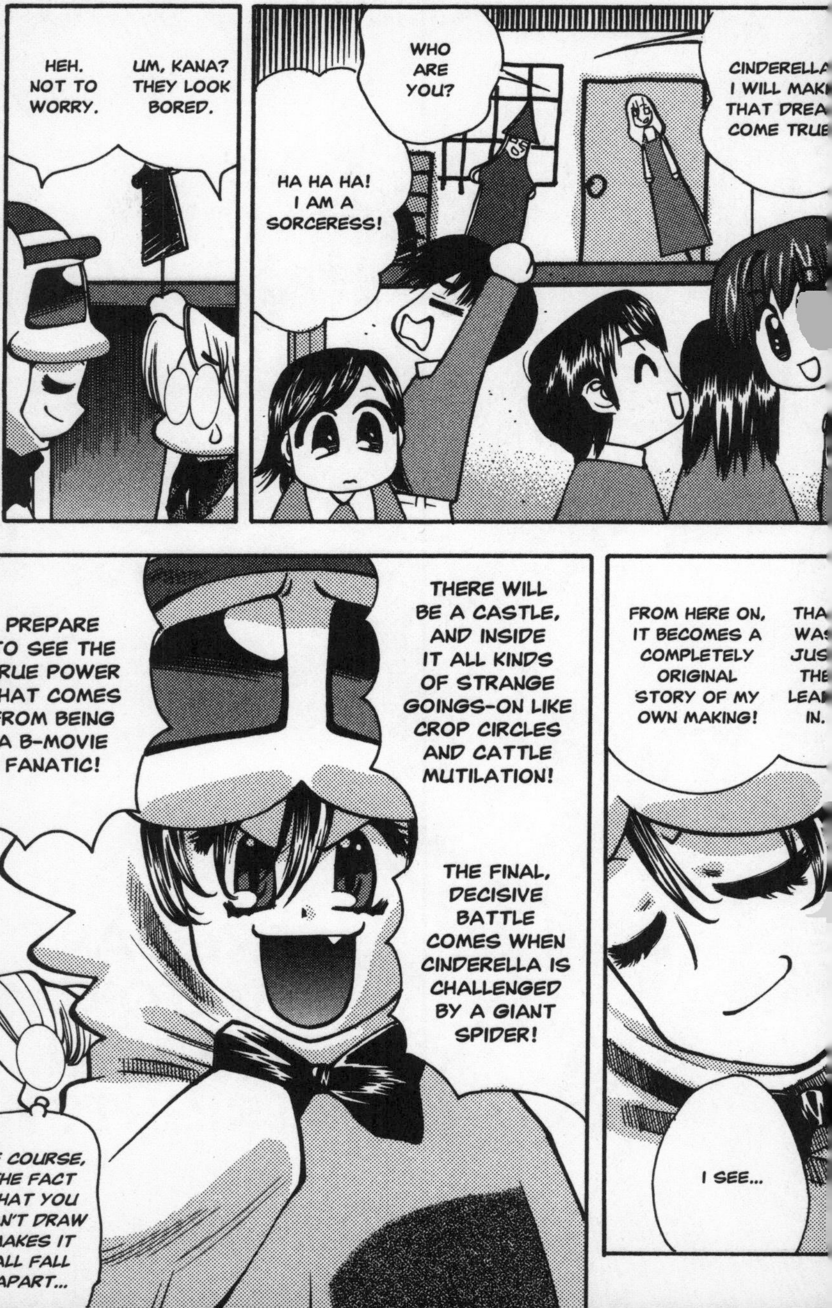
CINDERELLA I WILL MAK THAT DREA COME TRUE
WHO ARE YOU?
HA HA HA! I AM A SORCERESS!
UM, KANA? THEY LOOK BORED.
HEH. NOT TO WORRY.
THA WAS JUS THE LEA IN.
FROM HERE ON, IT BECOMES A COMPLETELY ORIGINAL STORY OF MY OWN MAKING!
I SEE...
THERE WILL BE A CASTLE, AND INSIDE IT ALL KINDS OF STRANGE GOINGS-ON LIKE CROP CIRCLES AND CATTLE MUTILATION!
THE FINAL, DECISIVE BATTLE COMES WHEN CINDERELLA IS CHALLENGED BY A GIANT SPIDER!
PREPARE TO SEE THE TRUE POWER THAT COMES FROM BEING A B-MOVIE FANATIC!
OF COURSE, THE FACT THAT YOU CAN'T DRAW MAKES IT ALL FALL APART...

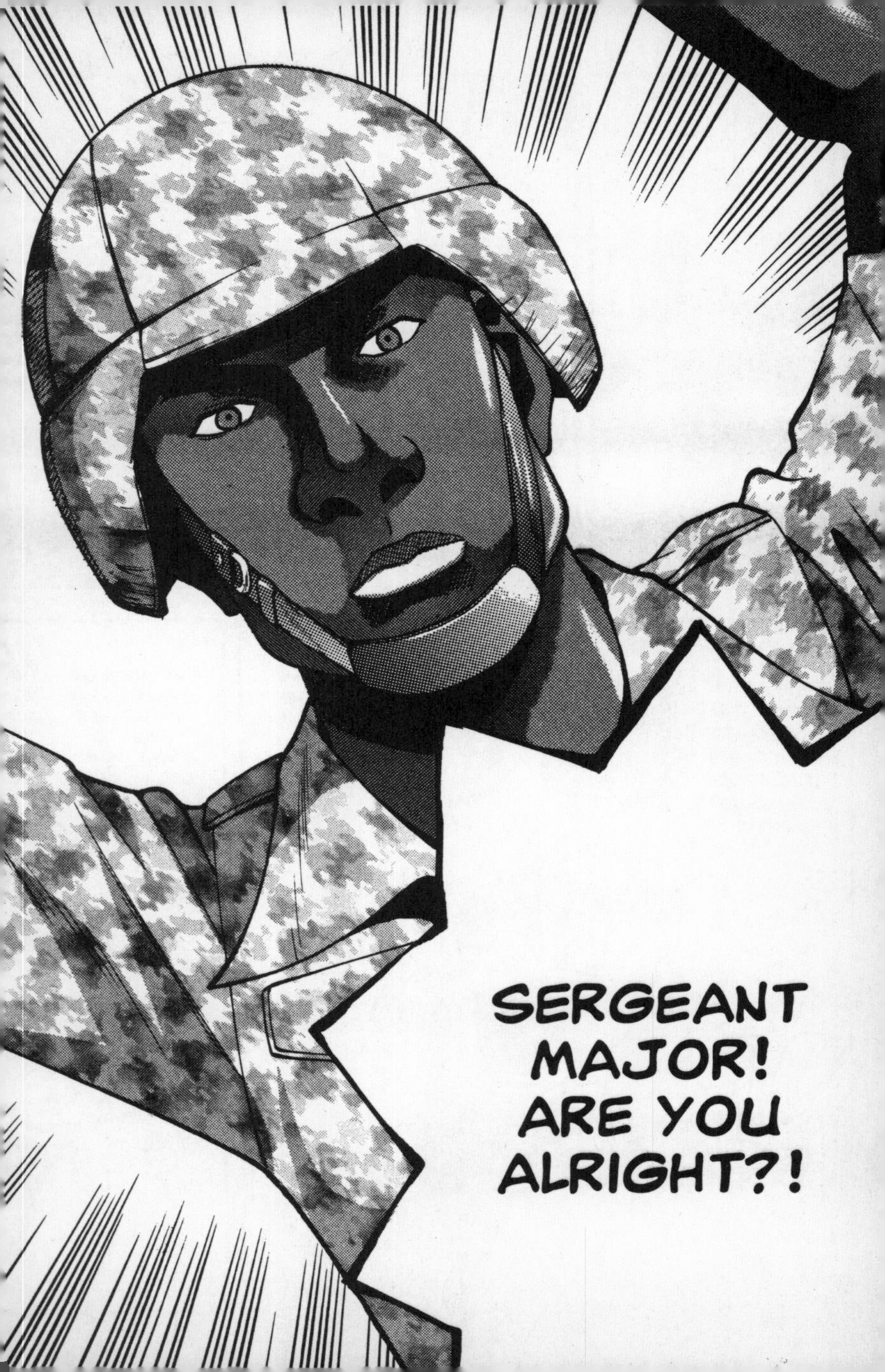
SERGEANT MAJOR! ARE YOU ALRIGHT?!

BUT I...

AS OF N
YOU'RE
COMMA
SERGEA

YO
FOO

YOUR ACTIONS WILL DETERMINE WHETHER THE MEN IN THIS UNIT LIVE OR DIE!

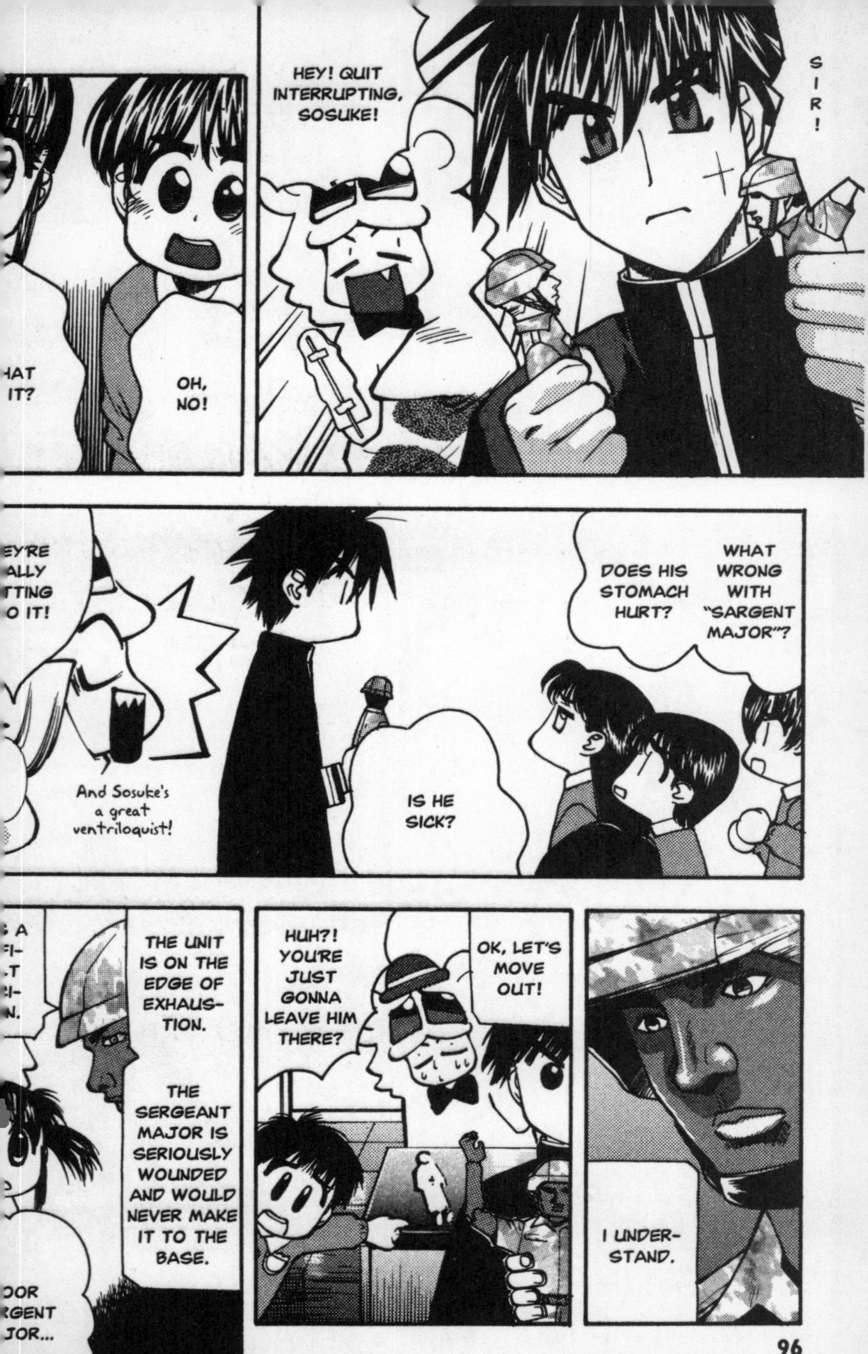
SIR!
HEY! QUIT INTERRUPTING, SOSUKE!
OH, NO!
WHAT WRONG WITH "SARGENT MAJOR"?
DOES HIS STOMACH HURT?
IS HE SICK?
And Sosuke's a great ventriloquist!
I UNDERSTAND.
OK, LET'S MOVE OUT!
HUH?! YOU'RE JUST GONNA LEAVE HIM THERE?
THE UNIT IS ON THE EDGE OF EXHAUSTION.
THE SERGEANT MAJOR IS SERIOUSLY WOUNDED AND WOULD NEVER MAKE IT TO THE BASE.

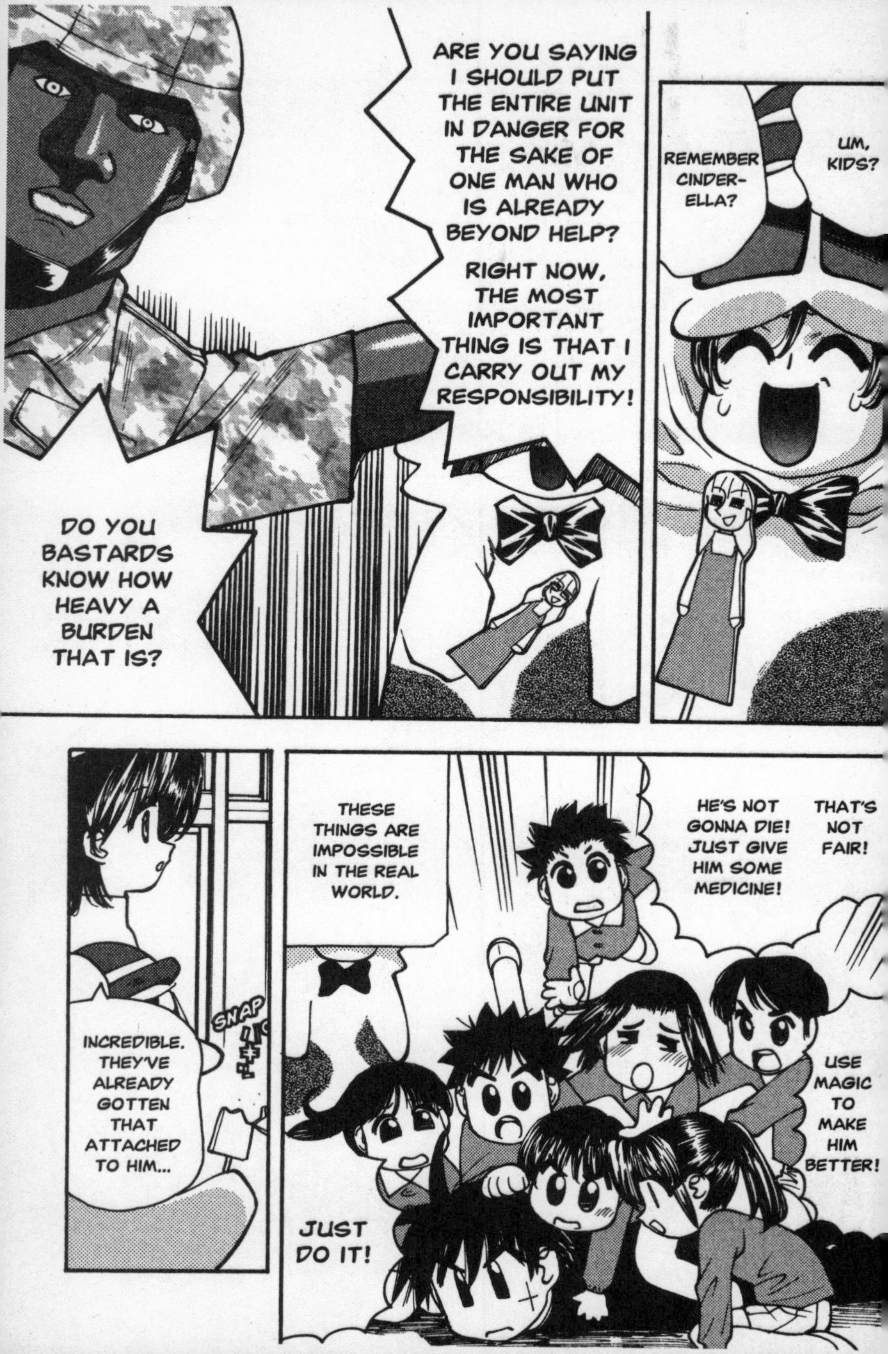

UM, KIDS?
REMEMBER CINDER-ELLA?
ARE YOU SAYING I SHOULD PUT THE ENTIRE UNIT IN DANGER FOR THE SAKE OF ONE MAN WHO IS ALREADY BEYOND HELP?
RIGHT NOW, THE MOST IMPORTANT THING IS THAT I CARRY OUT MY RESPONSIBILITY!
DO YOU BASTARDS KNOW HOW HEAVY A BURDEN THAT IS?
THAT'S NOT FAIR!
HE'S NOT GONNA DIE! JUST GIVE HIM SOME MEDICINE!
THESE THINGS ARE IMPOSSIBLE IN THE REAL WORLD.
USE MAGIC TO MAKE HIM BETTER!
JUST DO IT!
SNAP
INCREDIBLE. THEY'VE ALREADY GOTTEN THAT ATTACHED TO HIM...

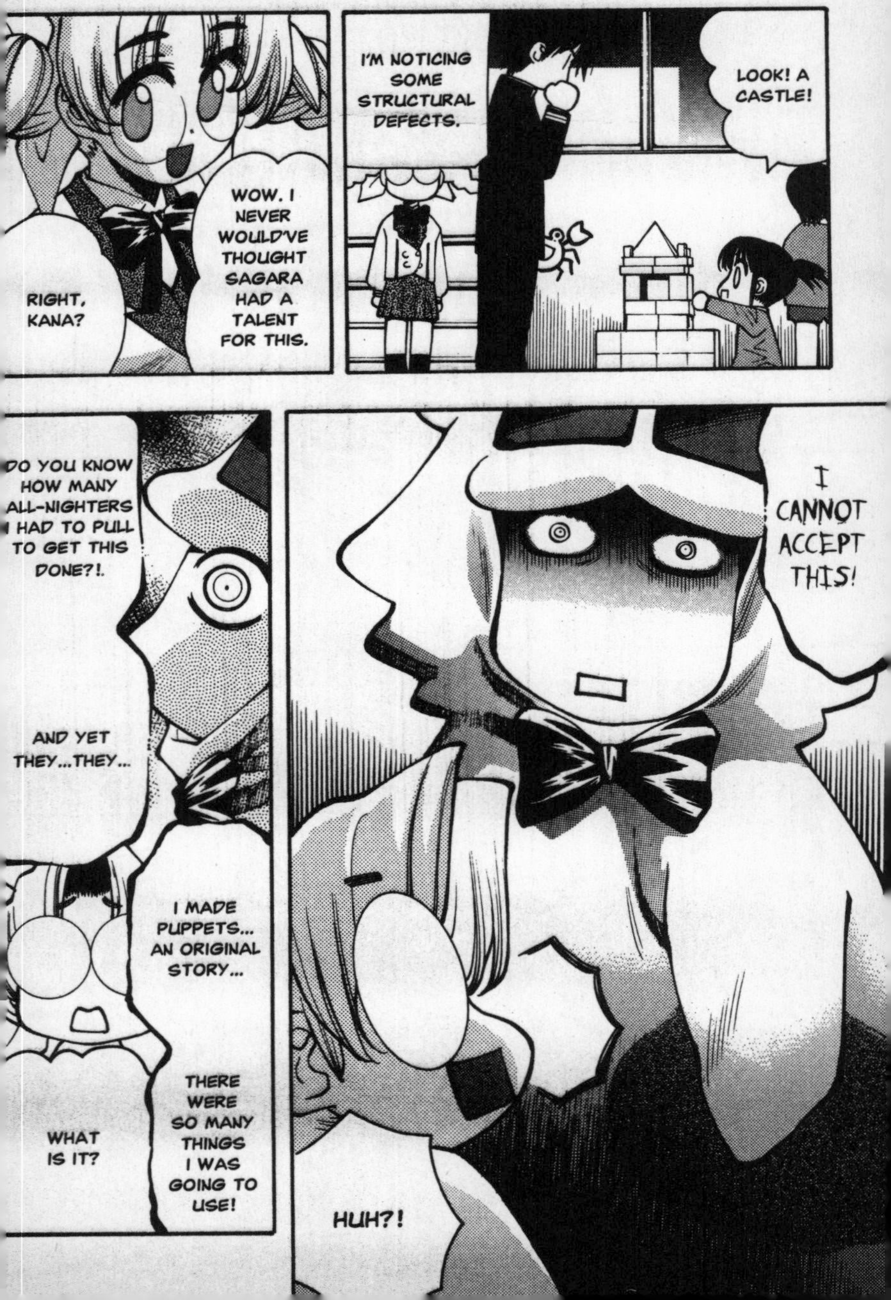
LOOK! A CASTLE!
I'M NOTICING SOME STRUCTURAL DEFECTS.
WOW. I NEVER WOULD'VE THOUGHT SAGARA HAD A TALENT FOR THIS.
RIGHT, KANA?
I CANNOT ACCEPT THIS!
DO YOU KNOW HOW MANY ALL-NIGHTERS I HAD TO PULL TO GET THIS DONE?!.
AND YET THEY...THEY...
I MADE PUPPETS... AN ORIGINAL STORY...
THERE WERE SO MANY THINGS I WAS GOING TO USE!
WHAT IS IT?
HUH?!

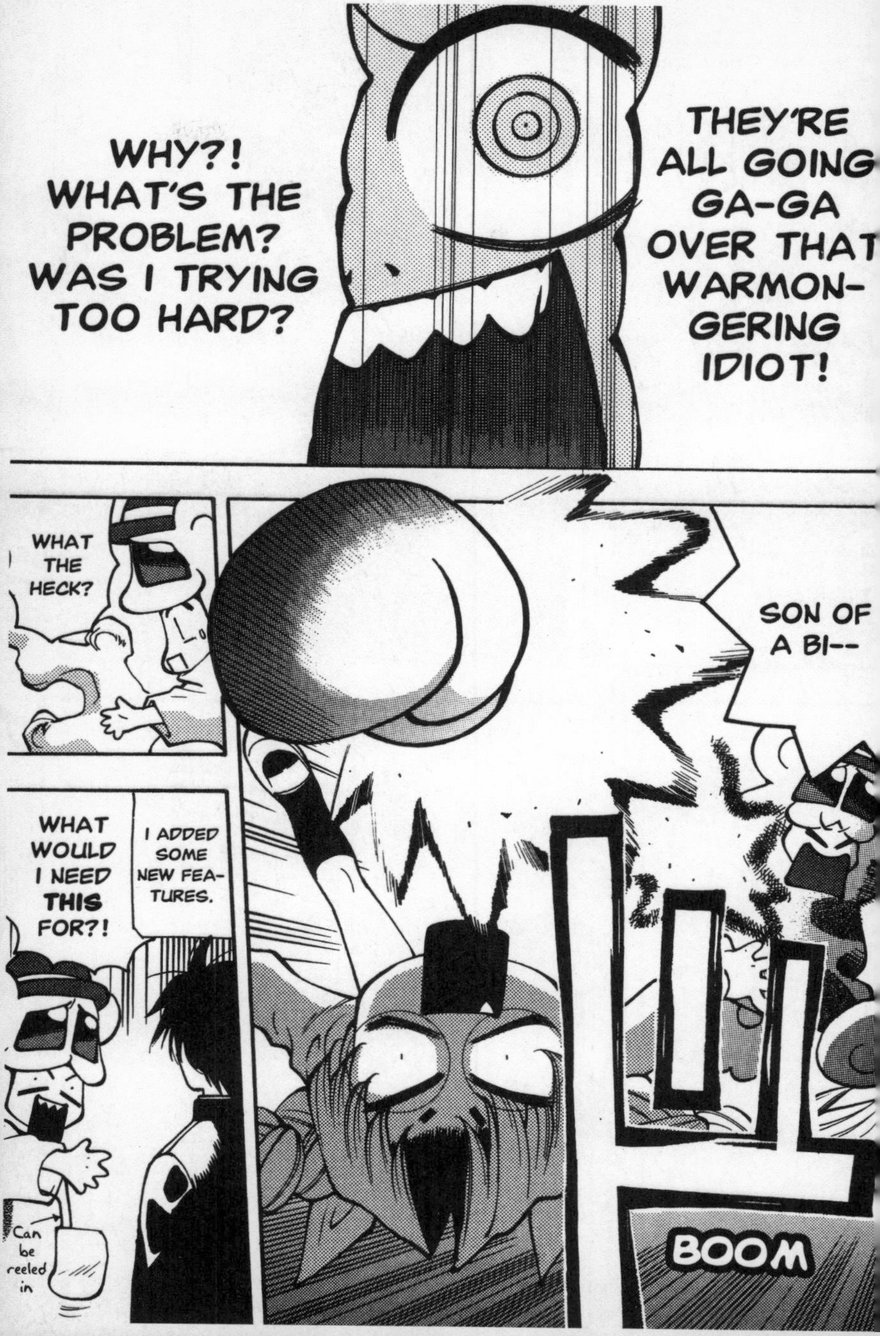
THEY'RE ALL GOING GA-GA OVER THAT WARMON-GERING IDIOT!
WHY?! WHAT'S THE PROBLEM? WAS I TRYING TOO HARD?
SON OF A BI--
BOOM
WHAT THE HECK?
I ADDED SOME NEW FEA-TURES.
WHAT WOULD I NEED **THIS** FOR?!
Can be reeled in

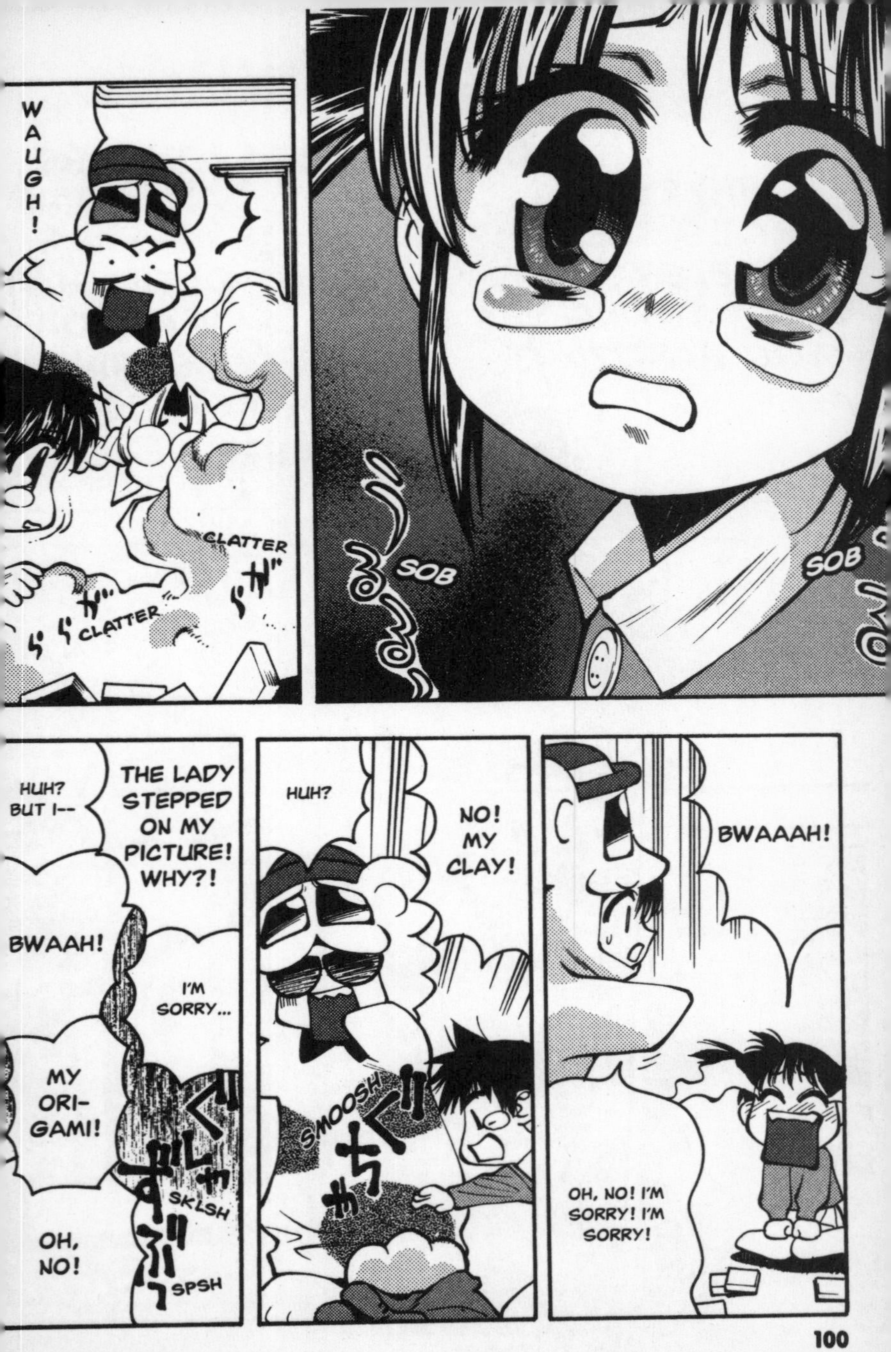
SOB
SOB
WAUGH!
CLATTER
CLATTER
BWAAAH!
OH, NO! I'M SORRY! I'M SORRY!
HUH?
NO! MY CLAY!
SMOOSH
THE LADY STEPPED ON MY PICTURE! WHY?!
HUH? BUT I--
BWAAH!
I'M SORRY...
MY ORI-GAMI!
SKLSH
SPSH
OH, NO!

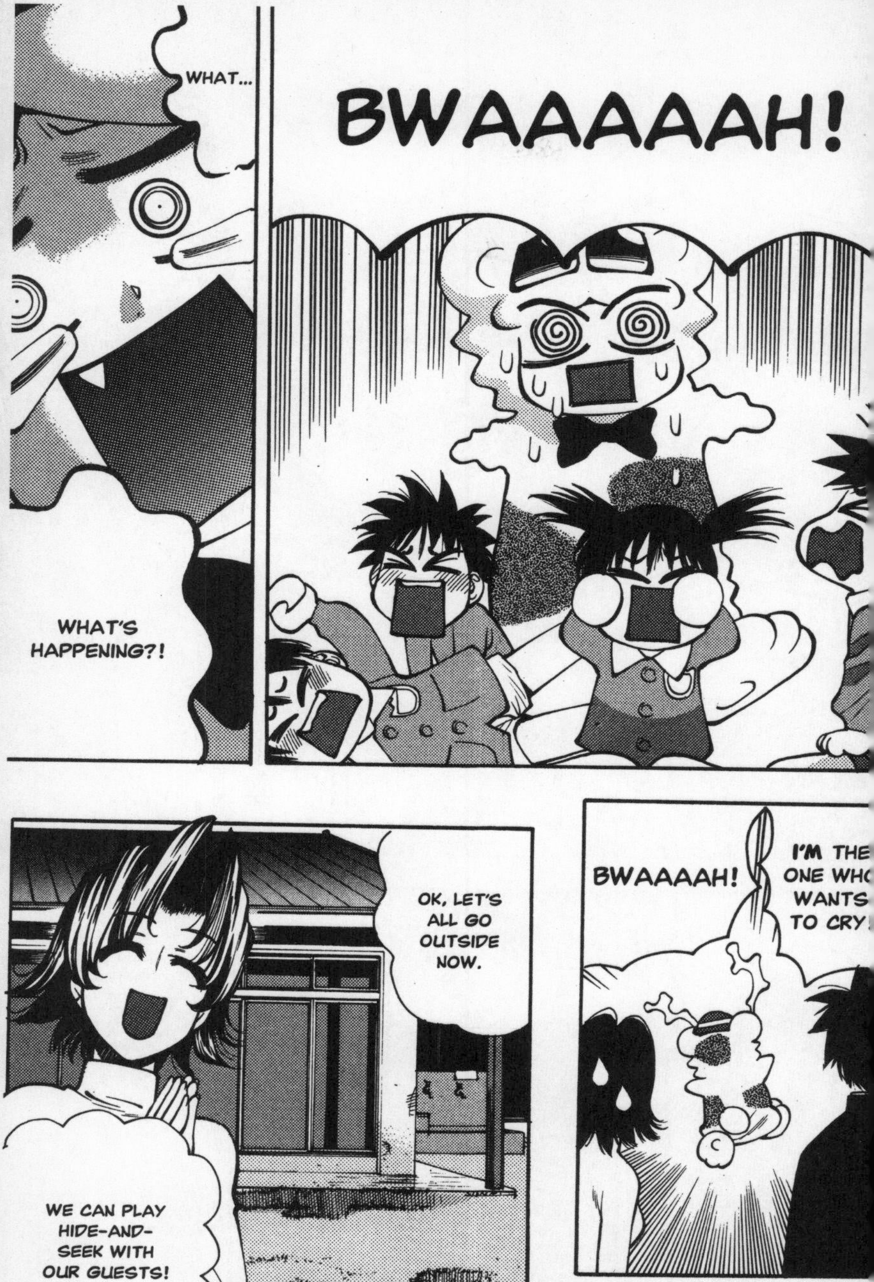
WHAT...
BWAAAAAAH!
WHAT'S HAPPENING?!
OK, LET'S ALL GO OUTSIDE NOW.
WE CAN PLAY HIDE-AND-SEEK WITH OUR GUESTS!
BWAAAAH!
I'M THE ONE WHO WANTS TO CRY!

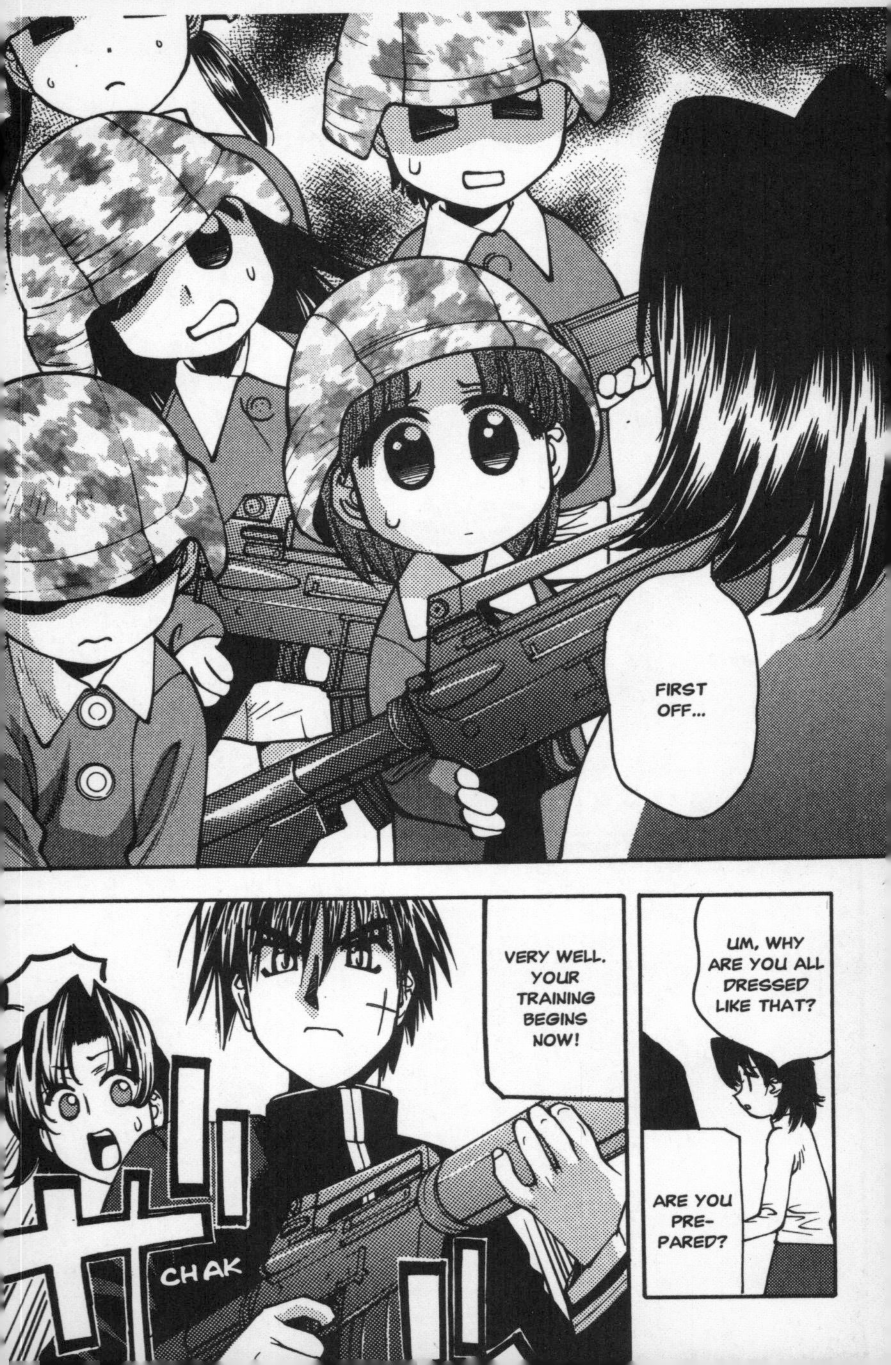
FIRST OFF...
UM, WHY ARE YOU ALL DRESSED LIKE THAT?
ARE YOU PRE-PARED?
VERY WELL. YOUR TRAINING BEGINS NOW!
CHAK

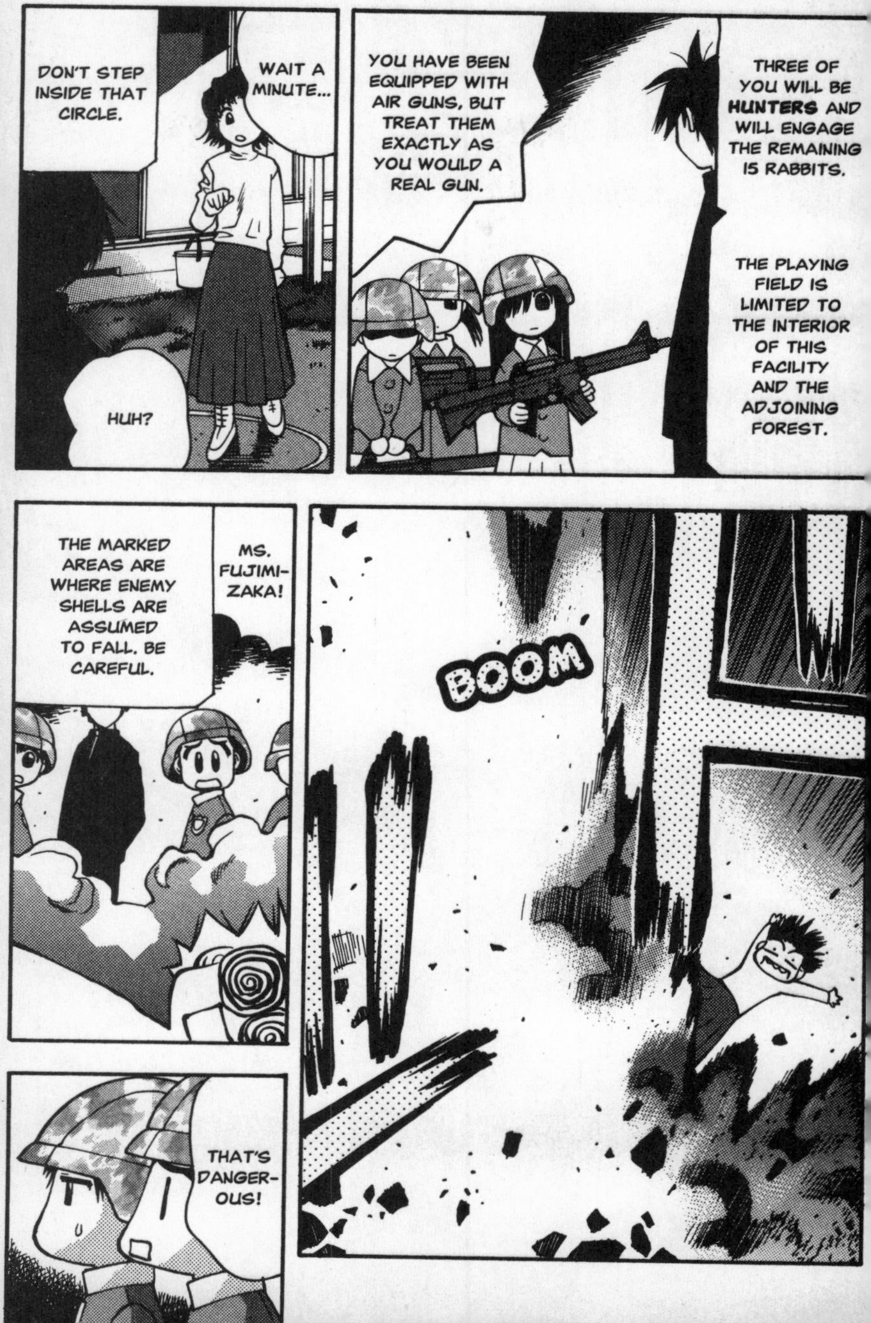

THREE OF YOU WILL BE **HUNTERS** AND WILL ENGAGE THE REMAINING 15 RABBITS.
THE PLAYING FIELD IS LIMITED TO THE INTERIOR OF THIS FACILITY AND THE ADJOINING FOREST.
YOU HAVE BEEN EQUIPPED WITH AIR GUNS, BUT TREAT THEM EXACTLY AS YOU WOULD A REAL GUN.
WAIT A MINUTE...
DON'T STEP INSIDE THAT CIRCLE.
HUH?
BOOM
MS. FUJIMI-ZAKA!
THE MARKED AREAS ARE WHERE ENEMY SHELLS ARE ASSUMED TO FALL. BE CAREFUL.
THAT'S DANGER-OUS!

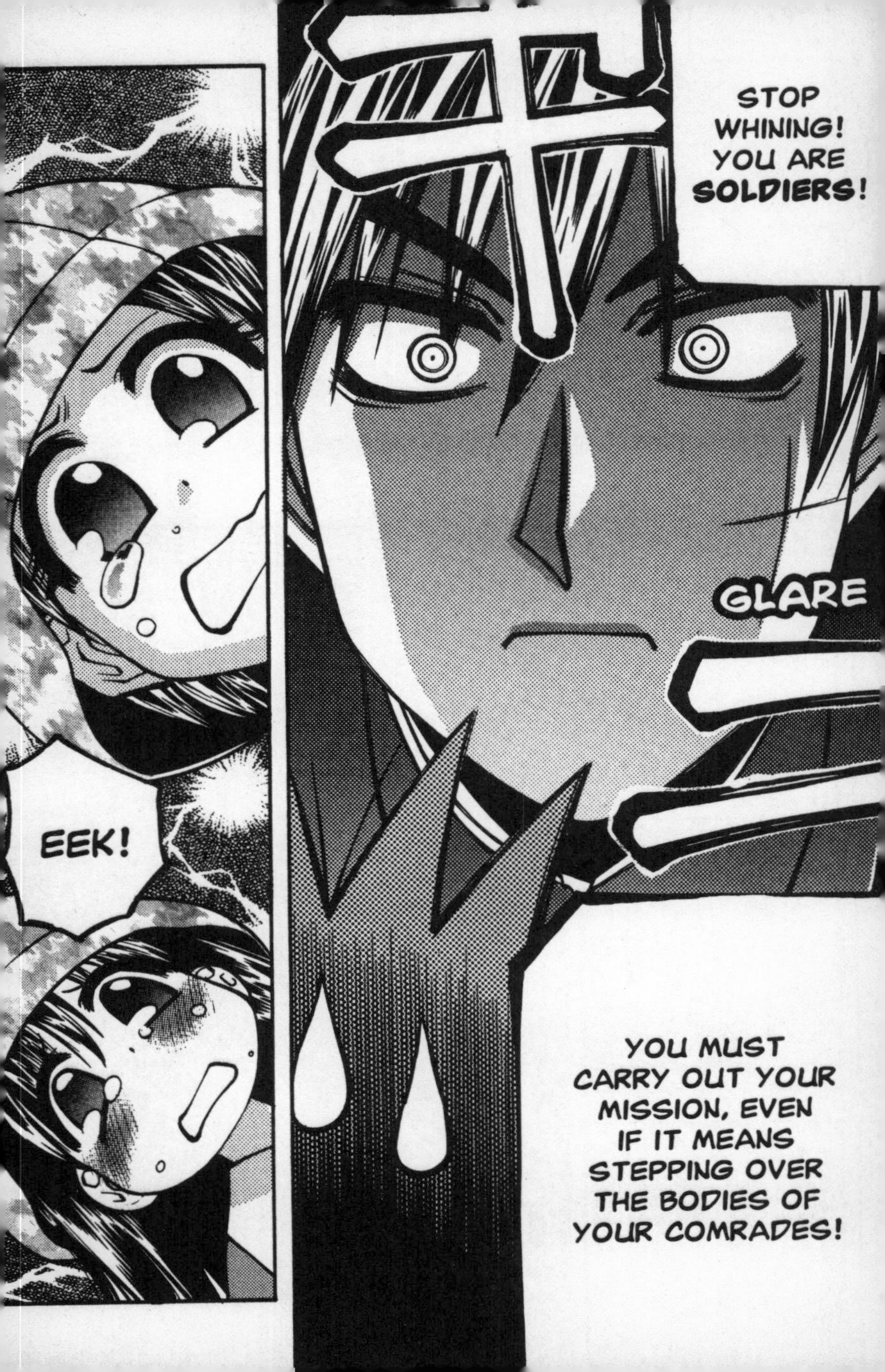
STOP WHINING! YOU ARE SOLDIERS!
GLARE
EEK!
YOU MUST CARRY OUT YOUR MISSION, EVEN IF IT MEANS STEPPING OVER THE BODIES OF YOUR COMRADES!

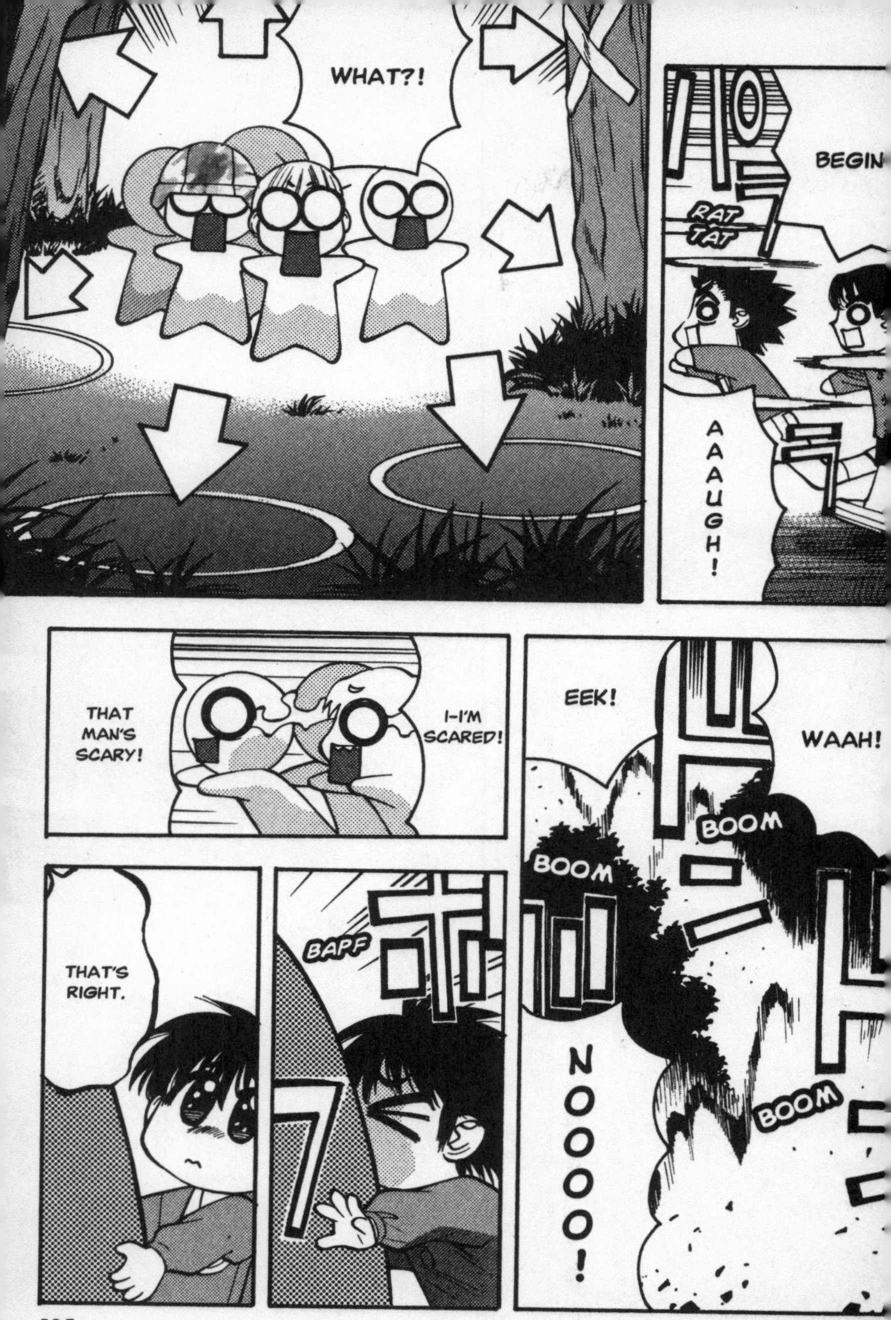
BEGIN
RAT TAT
AAAUGH!
WHAT?!
WAAH!
EEK!
BOOM
BOOM
BOOM
NOOOOO!
I-I'M SCARED!
THAT MAN'S SCARY!
BAPF
THAT'S RIGHT.

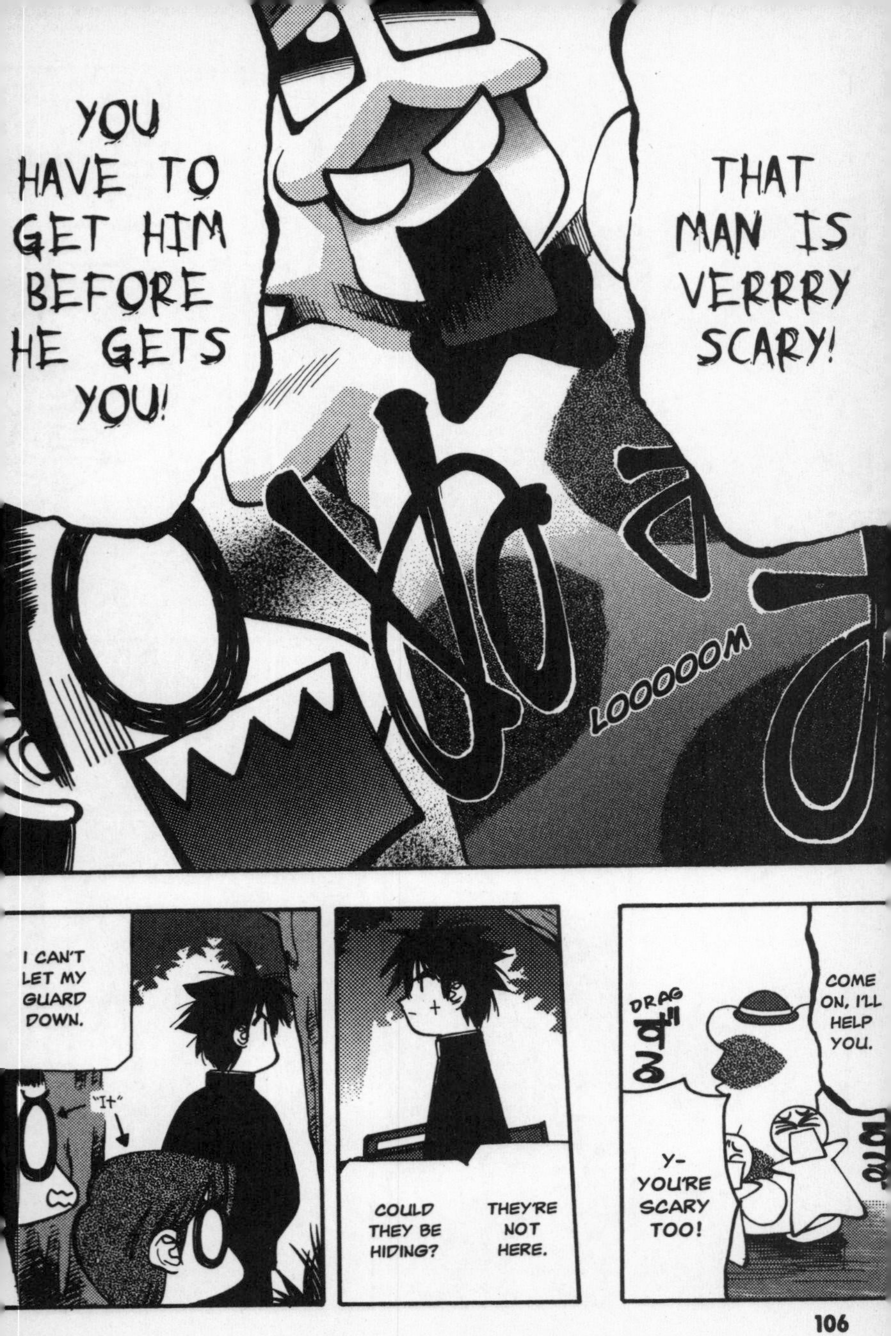
THAT MAN IS VERRRY SCARY!
YOU HAVE TO GET HIM BEFORE HE GETS YOU!
LOOOOOOM
I CAN'T LET MY GUARD DOWN.
"It"
THEY'RE NOT HERE.
COULD THEY BE HIDING?
COME ON, I'LL HELP YOU.
DRAG
Y-YOU'RE SCARY TOO!

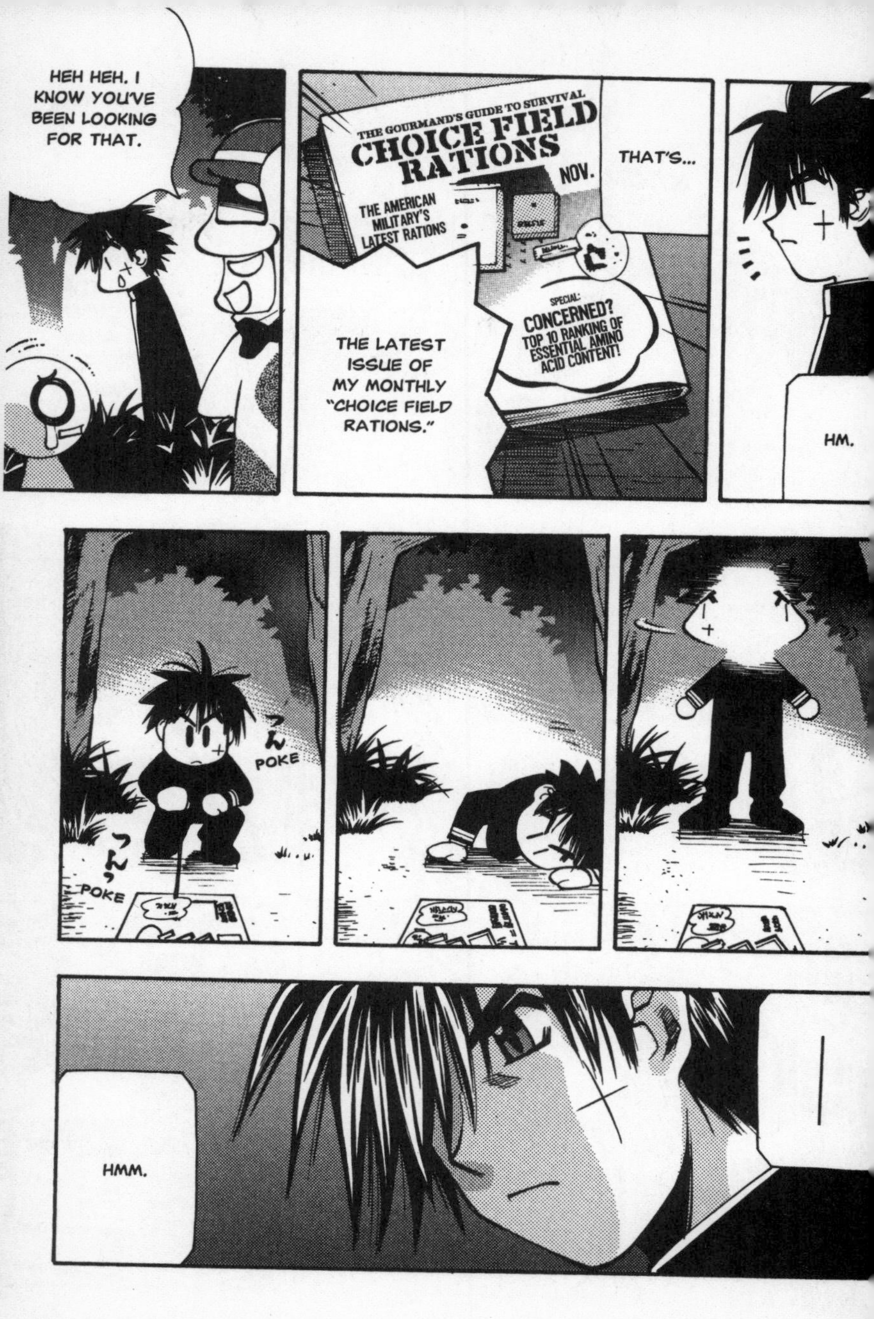
HEH HEH. I KNOW YOU'VE BEEN LOOKING FOR THAT.
THAT'S...
THE GOURMAND'S GUIDE TO SURVIVAL
CHOICE FIELD RATIONS
NOV.
THE AMERICAN MILITARY'S LATEST RATIONS
SPECIAL:
CONCERNED? TOP 10 RANKING OF ESSENTIAL AMINO ACID CONTENT!
THE LATEST ISSUE OF MY MONTHLY "CHOICE FIELD RATIONS."
HM.
POKE
POKE
HMM.

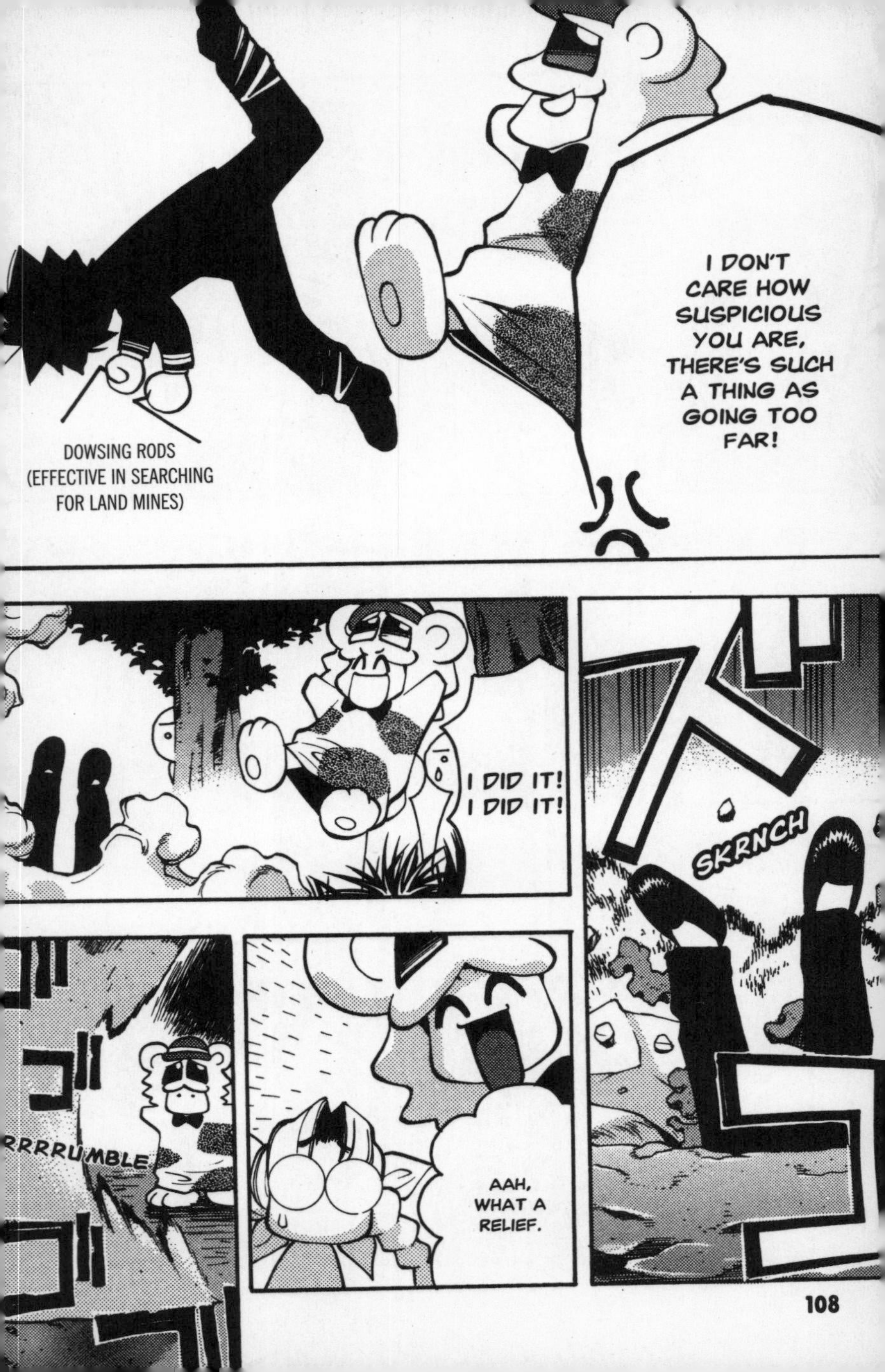
I DON'T CARE HOW SUSPICIOUS YOU ARE, THERE'S SUCH A THING AS GOING TOO FAR!
DOWSING RODS (EFFECTIVE IN SEARCHING FOR LAND MINES)
SKRNCH
I DID IT! I DID IT!
AAH, WHAT A RELIEF.
RRRRUMBLE

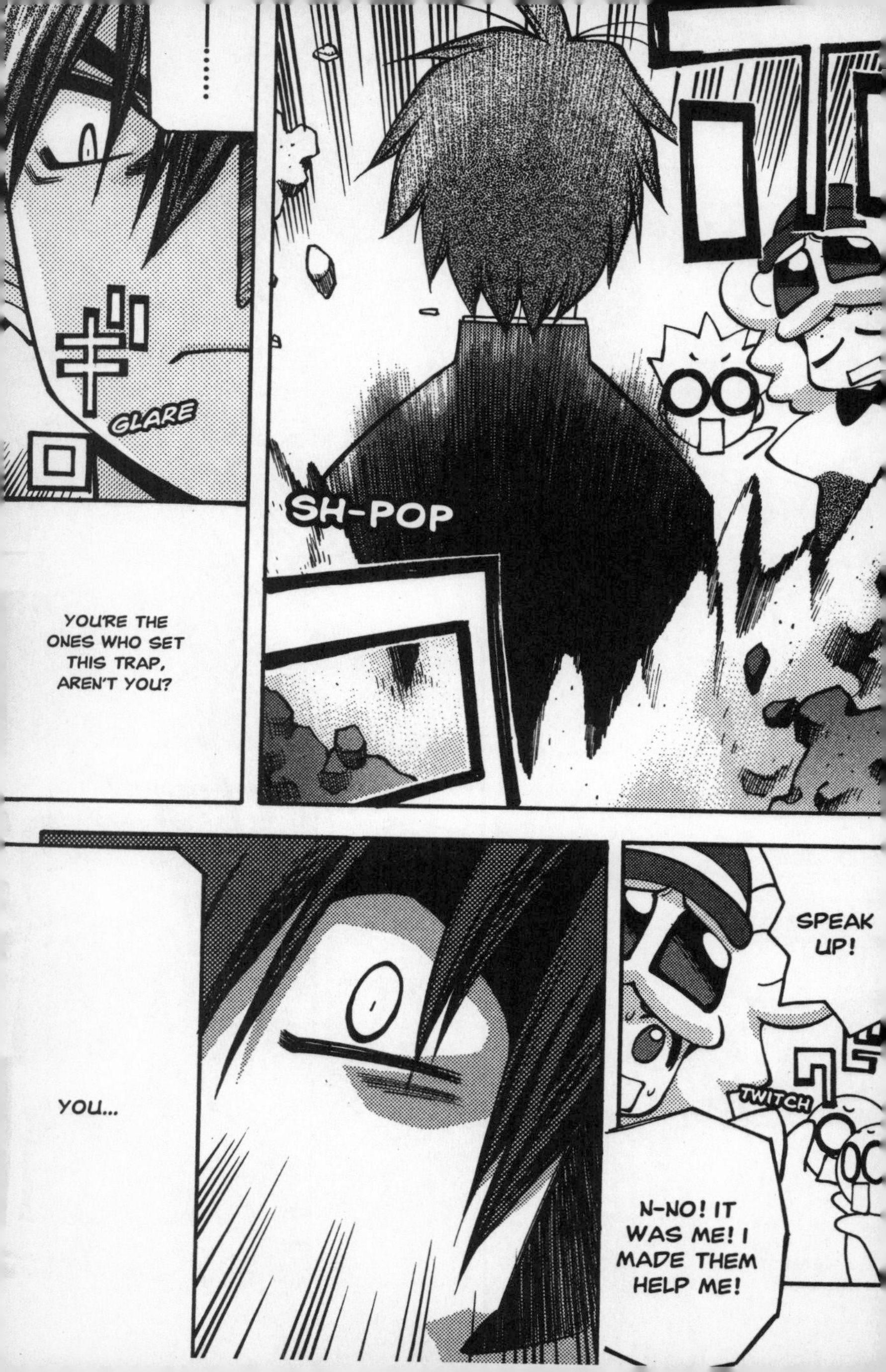
SH-POP
GLARE
YOU'RE THE ONES WHO SET THIS TRAP, AREN'T YOU?
SPEAK UP!
TWITCH
N-NO! IT WAS ME! I MADE THEM HELP ME!
YOU...

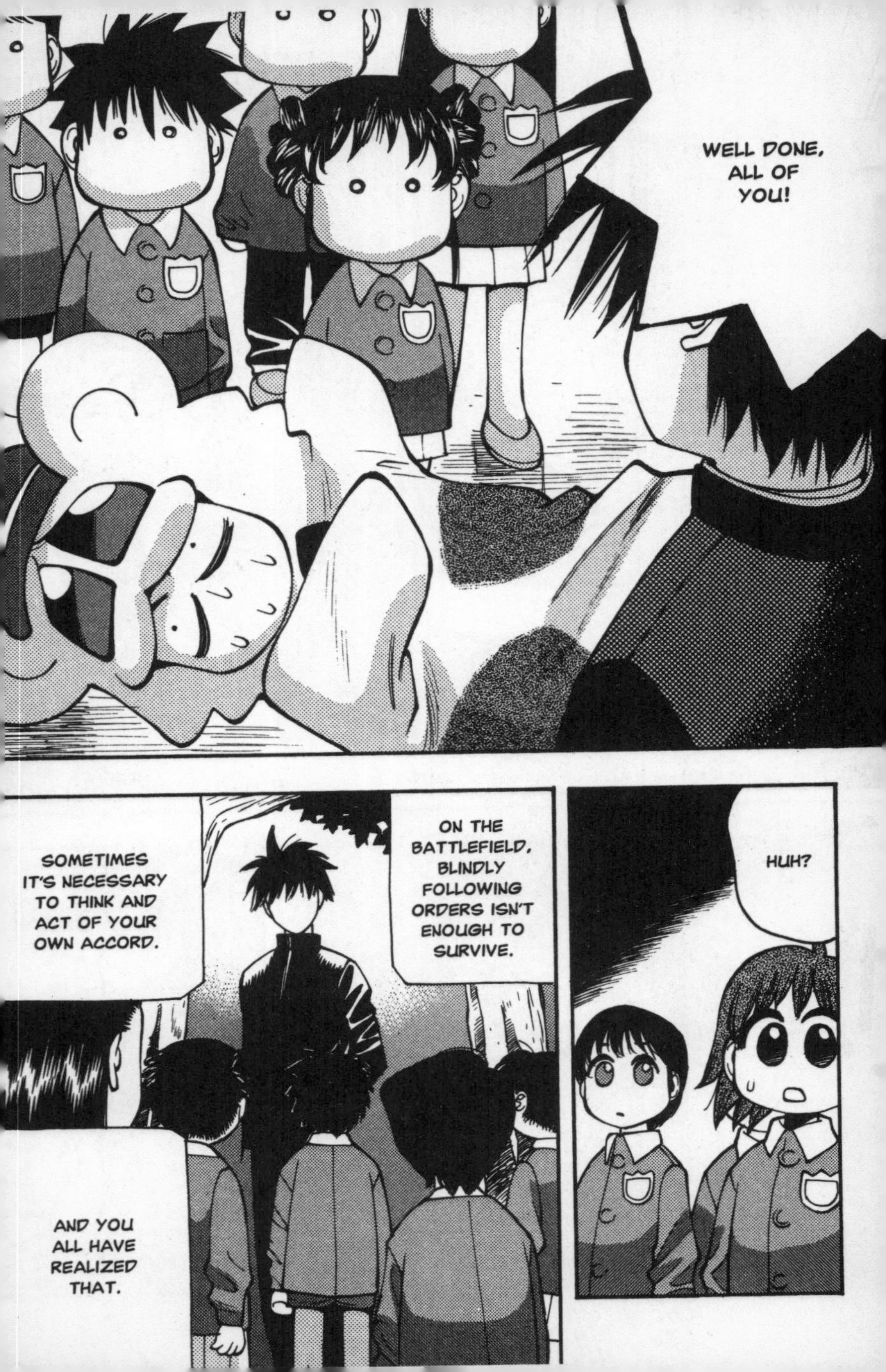
WELL DONE, ALL OF YOU!
HUH?
ON THE BATTLEFIELD, BLINDLY FOLLOWING ORDERS ISN'T ENOUGH TO SURVIVE.
SOMETIMES IT'S NECESSARY TO THINK AND ACT OF YOUR OWN ACCORD.
AND YOU ALL HAVE REALIZED THAT.

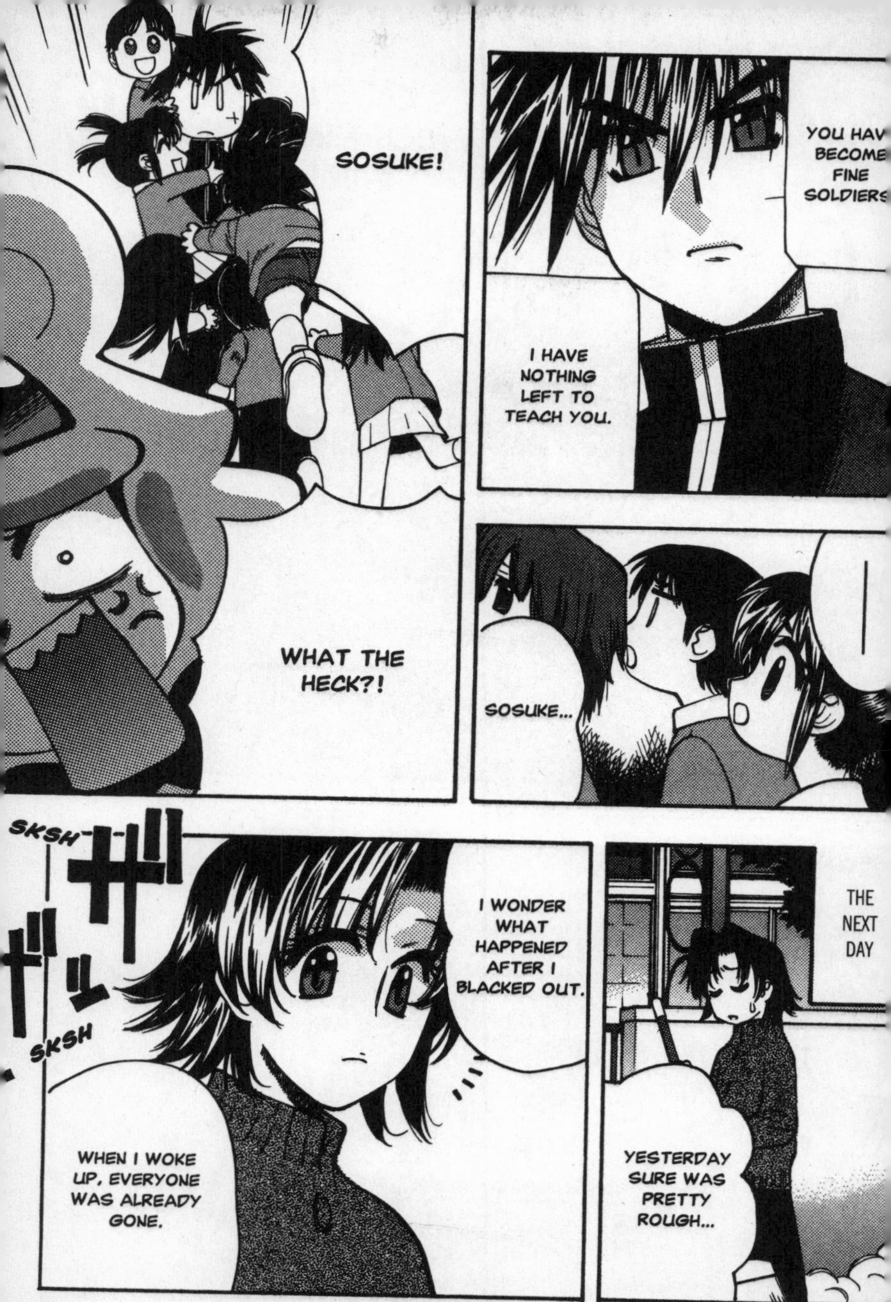
YOU HAV BECOME FINE SOLDIERS
I HAVE NOTHING LEFT TO TEACH YOU.
SOSUKE...
SOSUKE!
WHAT THE HECK?!
THE NEXT DAY
YESTERDAY SURE WAS PRETTY ROUGH...
I WONDER WHAT HAPPENED AFTER I BLACKED OUT.
WHEN I WOKE UP, EVERYONE WAS ALREADY GONE.
SKSH
SKSH

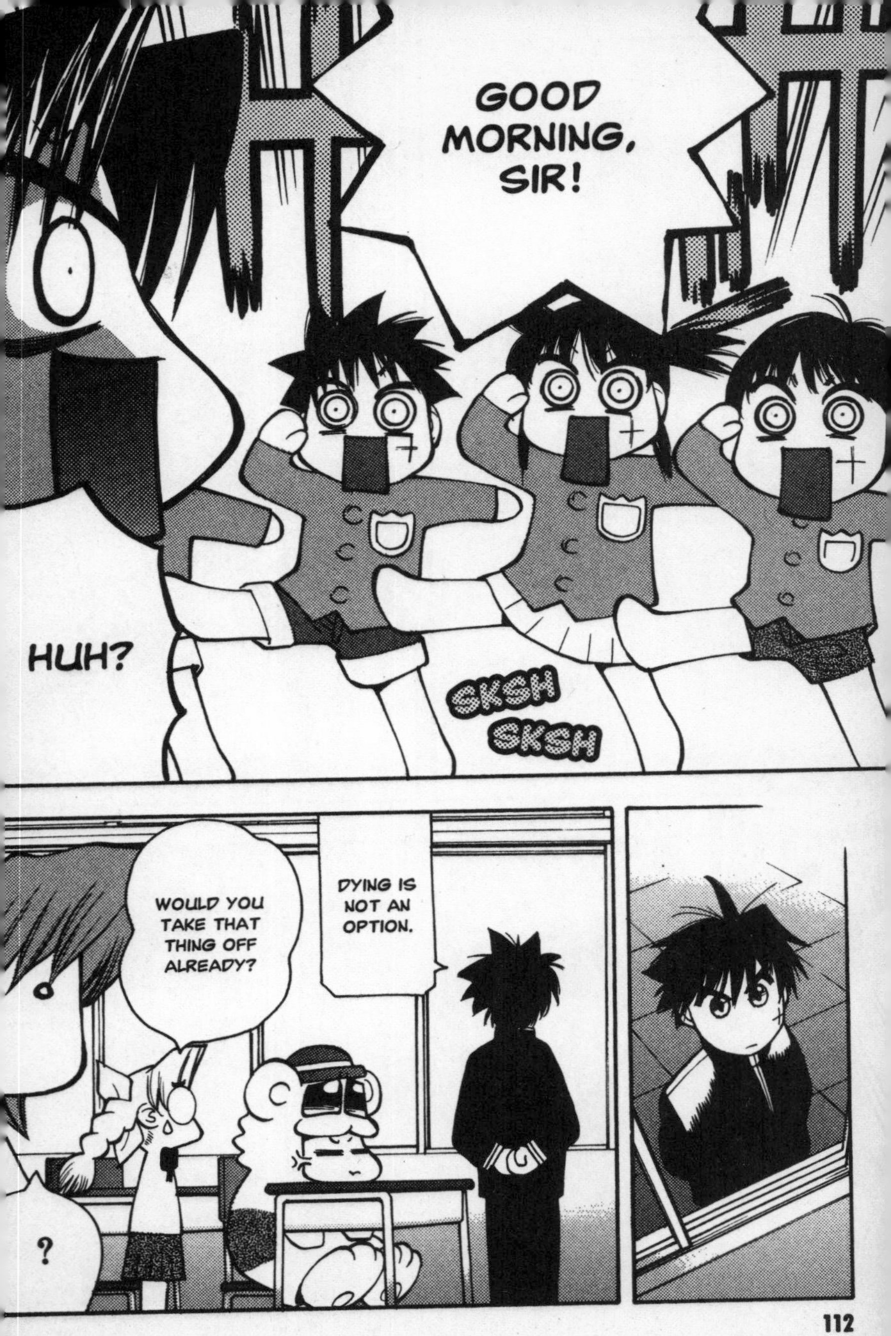
GOOD MORNING, SIR!
HUH?
SKSH SKSH
DYING IS NOT AN OPTION.
WOULD YOU TAKE THAT THING OFF ALREADY?
?

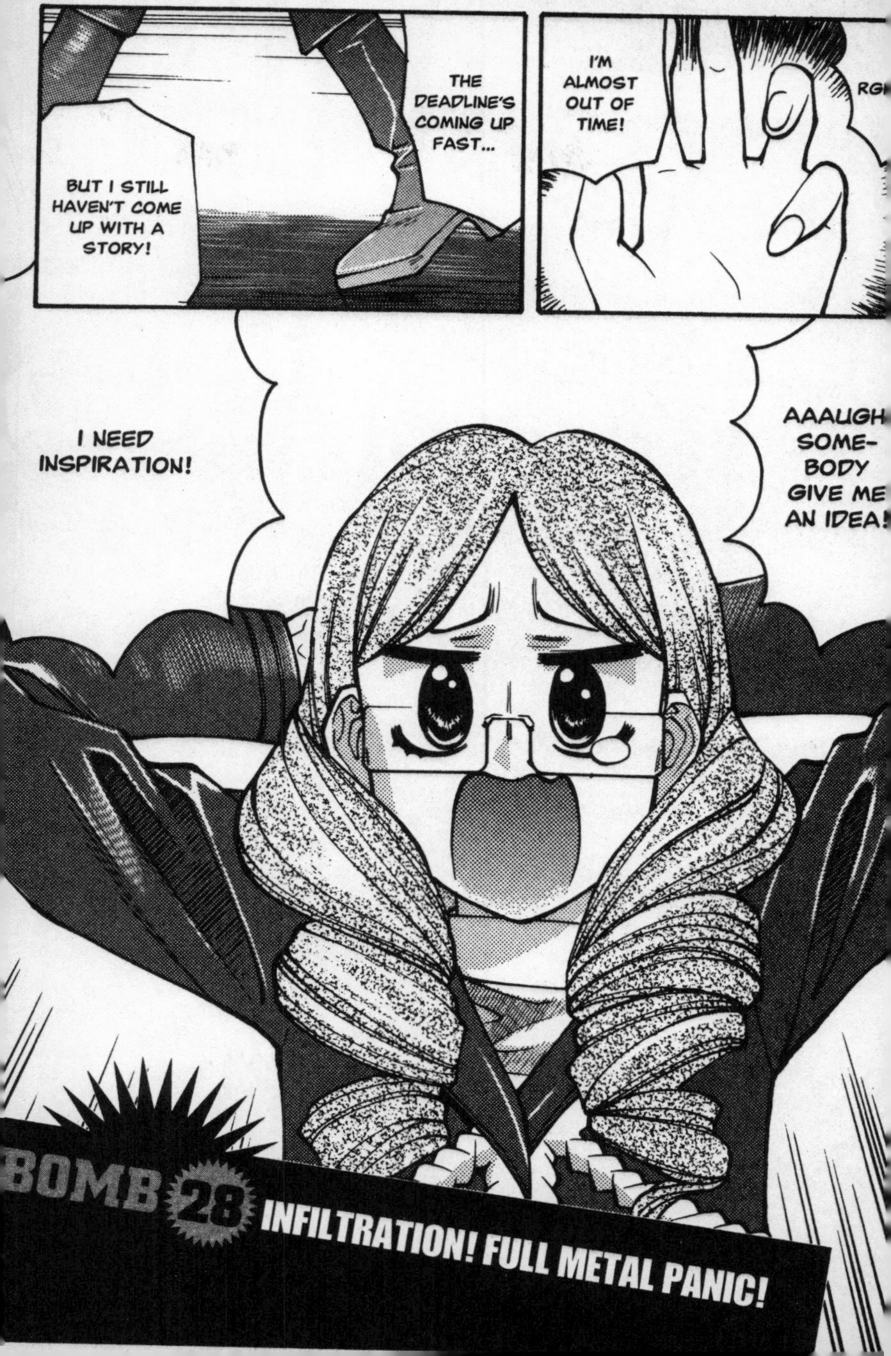

I'M ALMOST OUT OF TIME!
THE DEADLINE'S COMING UP FAST...
BUT I STILL HAVEN'T COME UP WITH A STORY!
AAAUGH SOME-BODY GIVE ME AN IDEA!
I NEED INSPIRATION!
BOMB 28
INFILTRATION! FULL METAL PANIC!

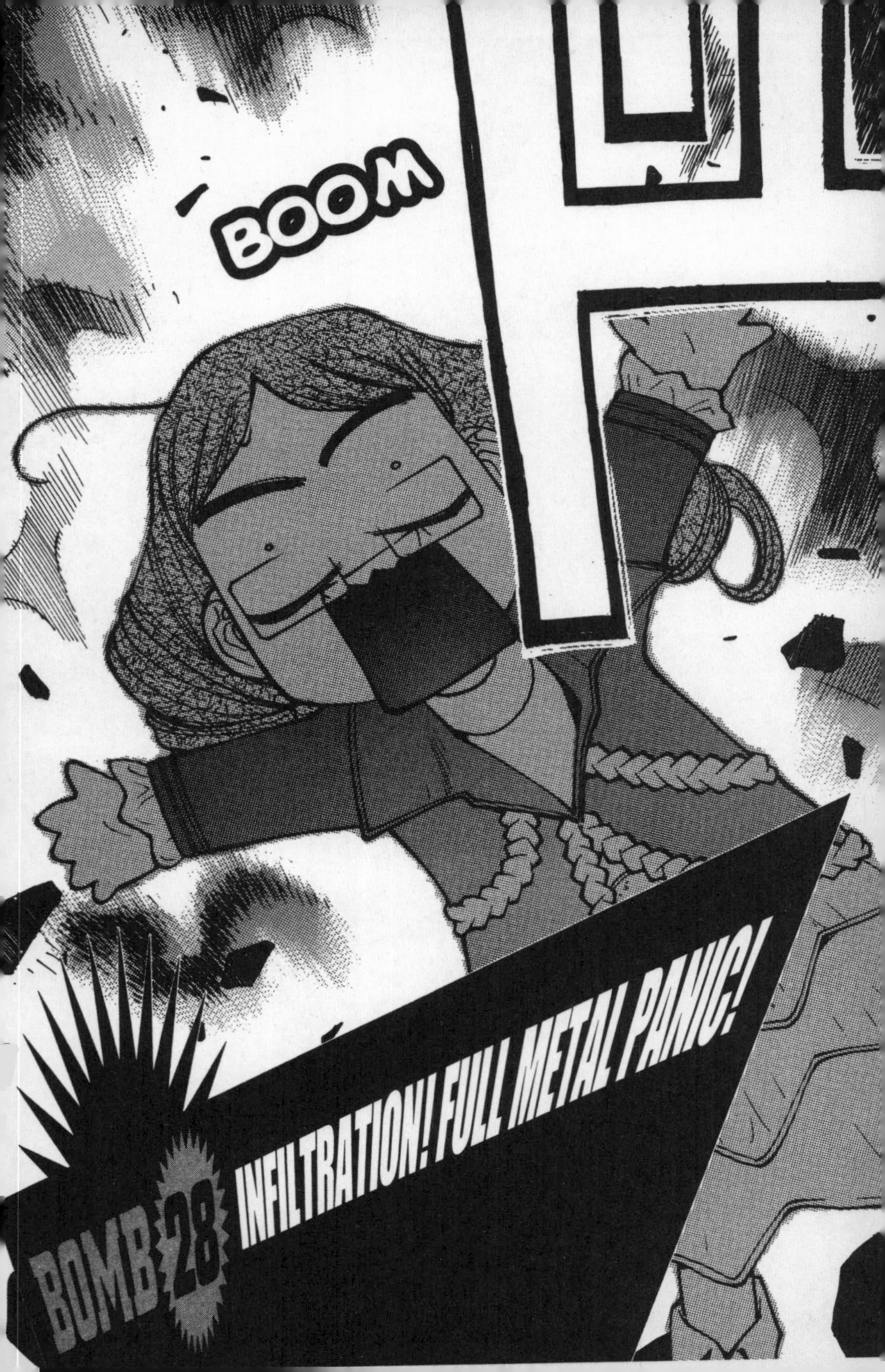
BOOM
BOMB 28
INFILTRATION! FULL METAL PANIC!

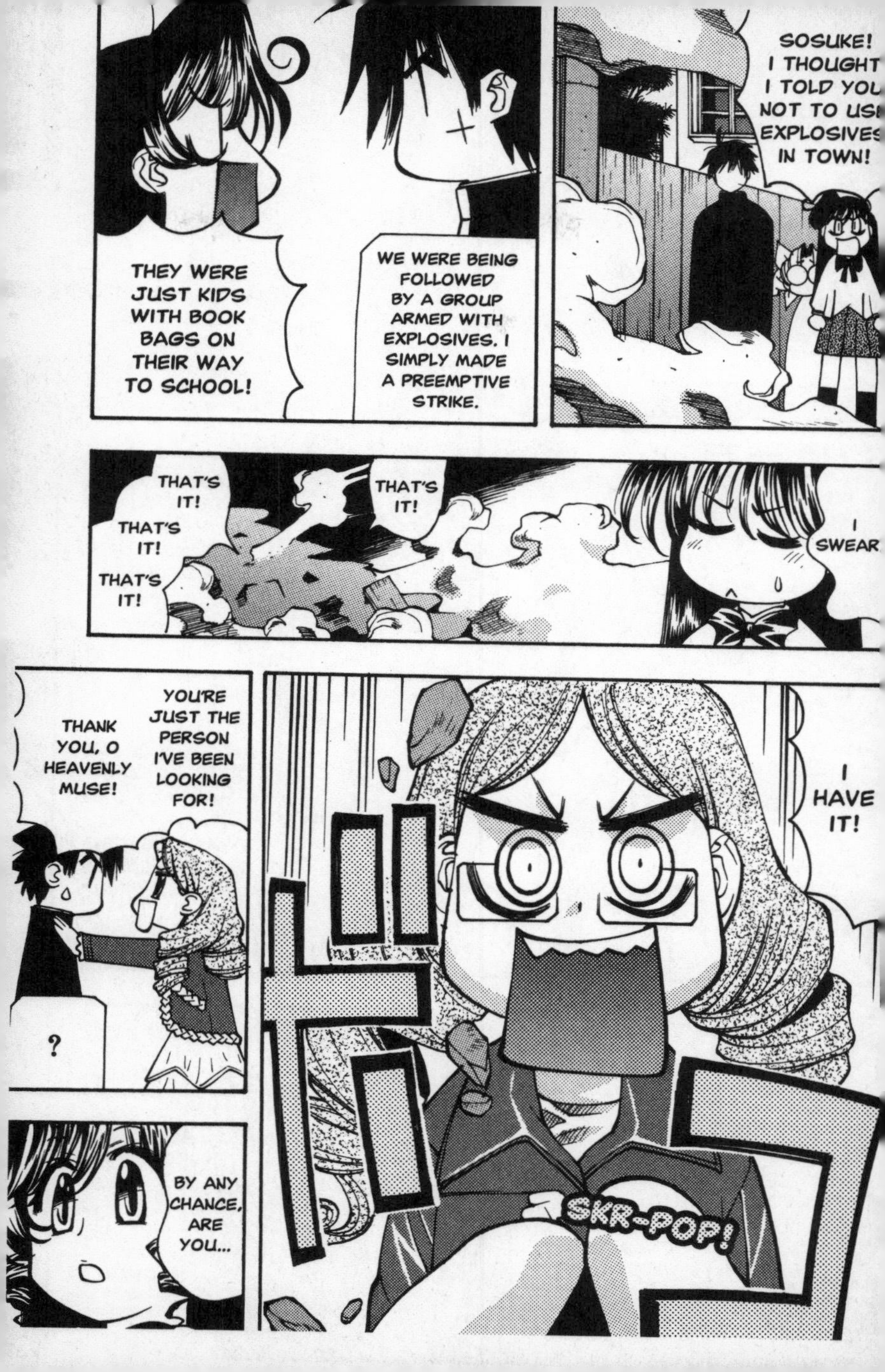
SOSUKE! I THOUGHT I TOLD YOU NOT TO USE EXPLOSIVES IN TOWN!
WE WERE BEING FOLLOWED BY A GROUP ARMED WITH EXPLOSIVES. I SIMPLY MADE A PREEMPTIVE STRIKE.
THEY WERE JUST KIDS WITH BOOK BAGS ON THEIR WAY TO SCHOOL!
I SWEAR...
THAT'S IT!
THAT'S IT!
THAT'S IT!
THAT'S IT!
I HAVE IT!
SKR-POP!
YOU'RE JUST THE PERSON I'VE BEEN LOOKING FOR!
THANK YOU, O HEAVENLY MUSE!
?
BY ANY CHANCE, ARE YOU...

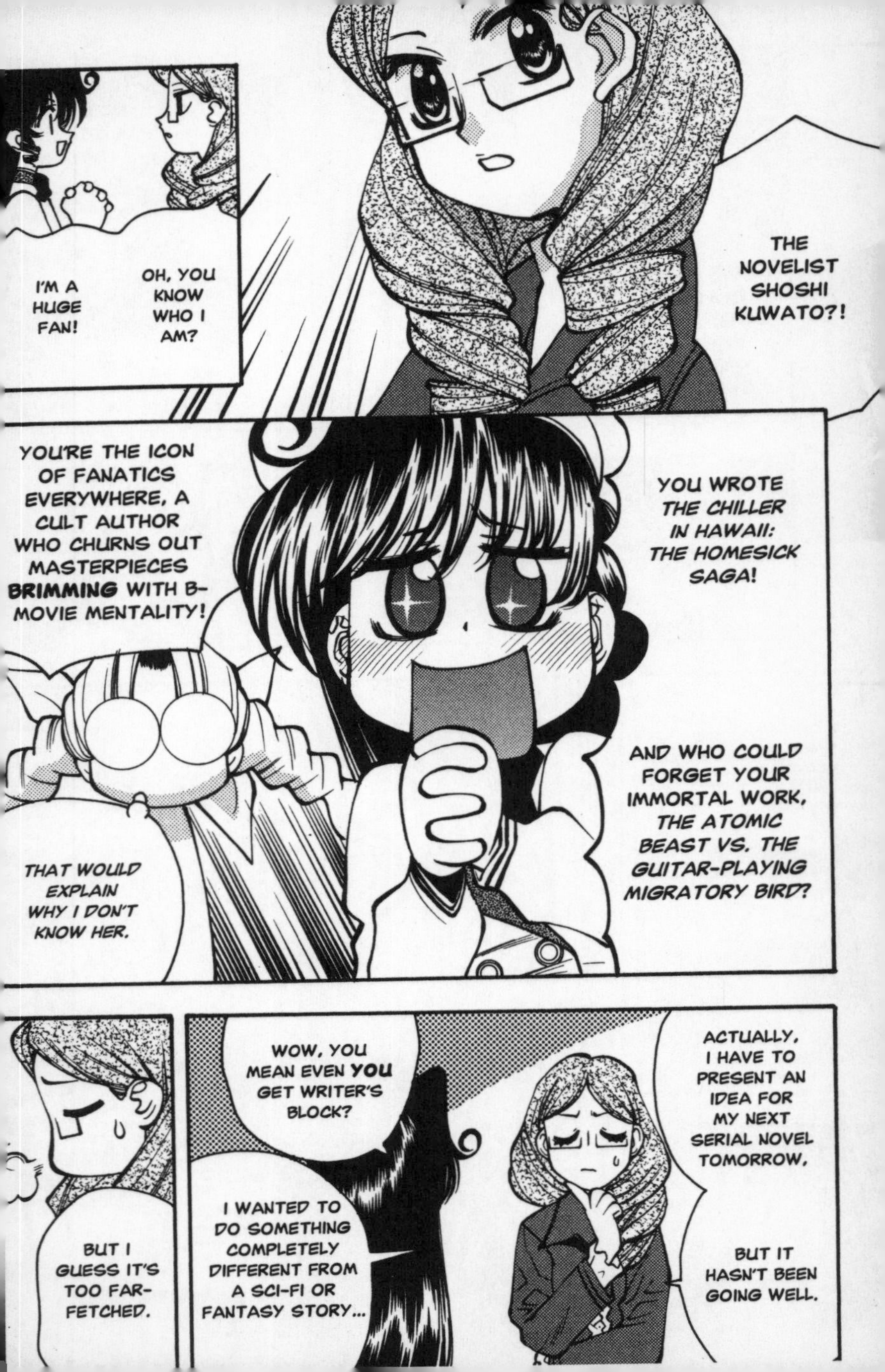
THE NOVELIST SHOSHI KUWATO?!
OH, YOU KNOW WHO I AM?
I'M A HUGE FAN!
YOU WROTE THE CHILLER IN HAWAII: THE HOMESICK SAGA!
AND WHO COULD FORGET YOUR IMMORTAL WORK, THE ATOMIC BEAST VS. THE GUITAR-PLAYING MIGRATORY BIRD?
YOU'RE THE ICON OF FANATICS EVERYWHERE, A CULT AUTHOR WHO CHURNS OUT MASTERPIECES BRIMMING WITH B-MOVIE MENTALITY!
THAT WOULD EXPLAIN WHY I DON'T KNOW HER.
ACTUALLY, I HAVE TO PRESENT AN IDEA FOR MY NEXT SERIAL NOVEL TOMORROW,
BUT IT HASN'T BEEN GOING WELL.
WOW, YOU MEAN EVEN YOU GET WRITER'S BLOCK?
I WANTED TO DO SOMETHING COMPLETELY DIFFERENT FROM A SCI-FI OR FANTASY STORY...
BUT I GUESS IT'S TOO FAR-FETCHED.

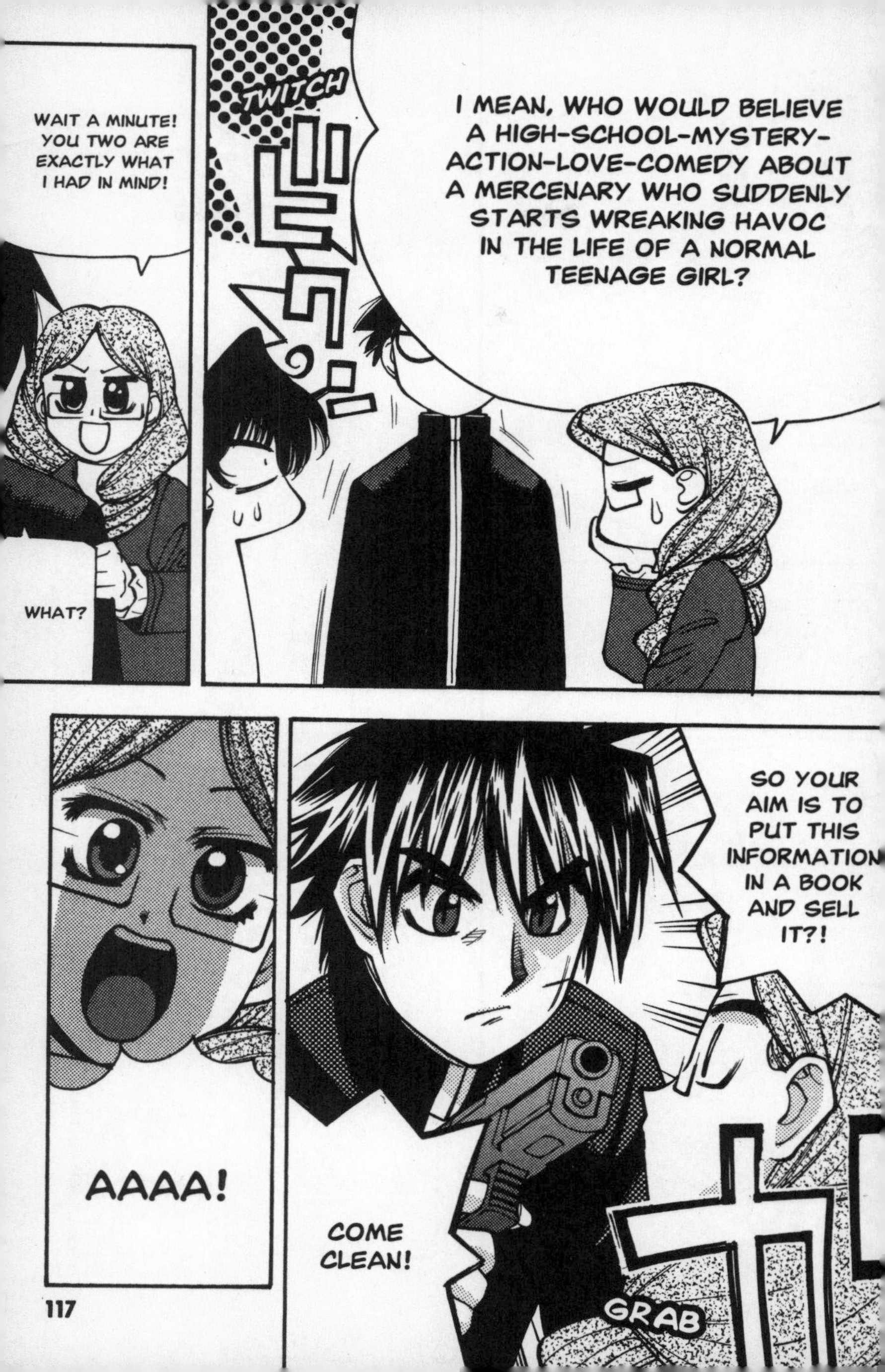
I MEAN, WHO WOULD BELIEVE A HIGH-SCHOOL-MYSTERY-ACTION-LOVE-COMEDY ABOUT A MERCENARY WHO SUDDENLY STARTS WREAKING HAVOC IN THE LIFE OF A NORMAL TEENAGE GIRL?
TWITCH
WAIT A MINUTE! YOU TWO ARE EXACTLY WHAT I HAD IN MIND!
WHAT?
SO YOUR AIM IS TO PUT THIS INFORMATION IN A BOOK AND SELL IT?!
COME CLEAN!
GRAB
AAAA!

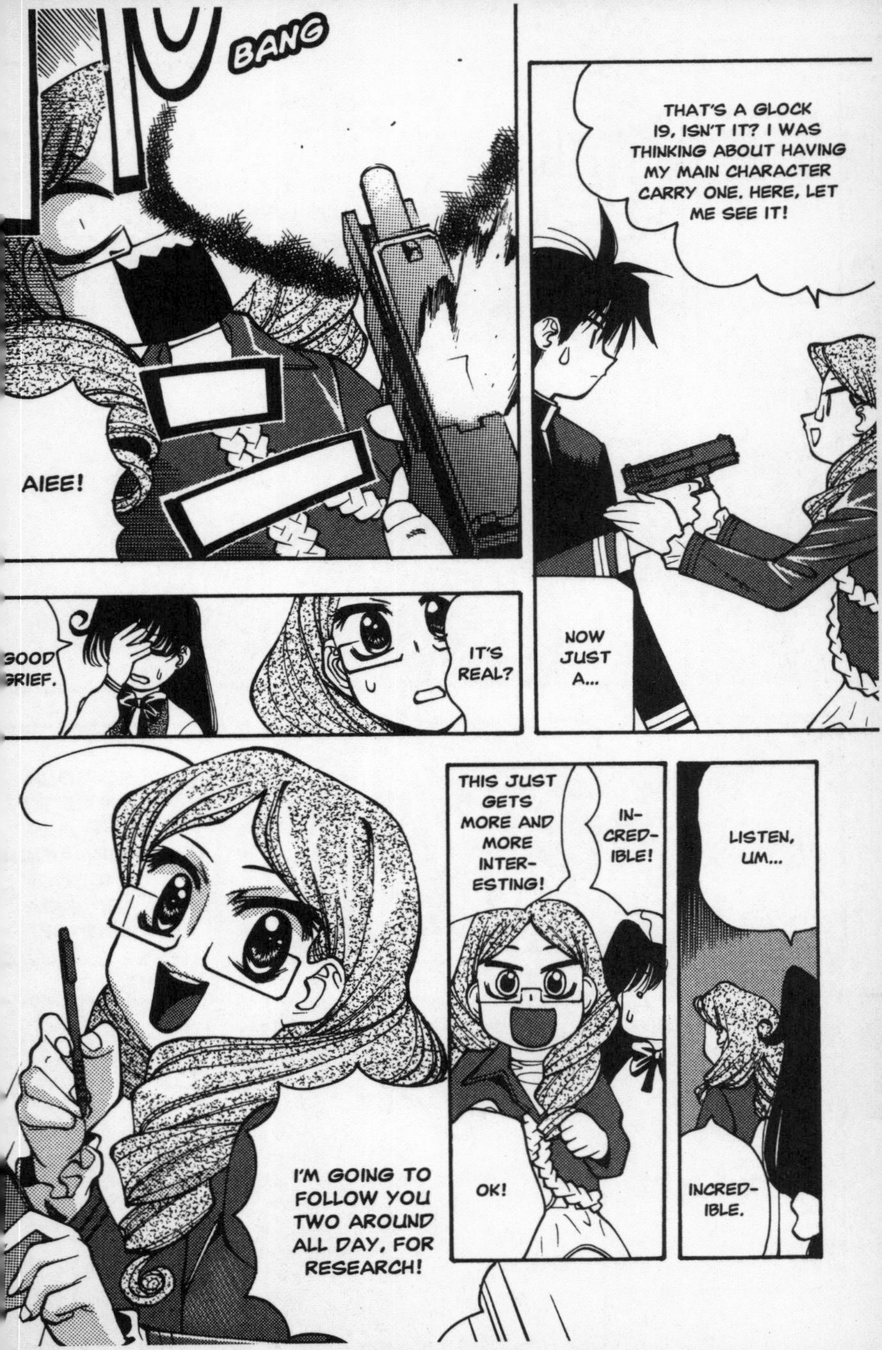
THAT'S A GLOCK 19, ISN'T IT? I WAS THINKING ABOUT HAVING MY MAIN CHARACTER CARRY ONE. HERE, LET ME SEE IT!
NOW JUST A...
BANG
AIEE!
IT'S REAL?
GOOD GRIEF.
LISTEN, UM...
INCREDIBLE.
IN-CRED-IBLE!
THIS JUST GETS MORE AND MORE INTER-ESTING!
OK!
I'M GOING TO FOLLOW YOU TWO AROUND ALL DAY, FOR RESEARCH!

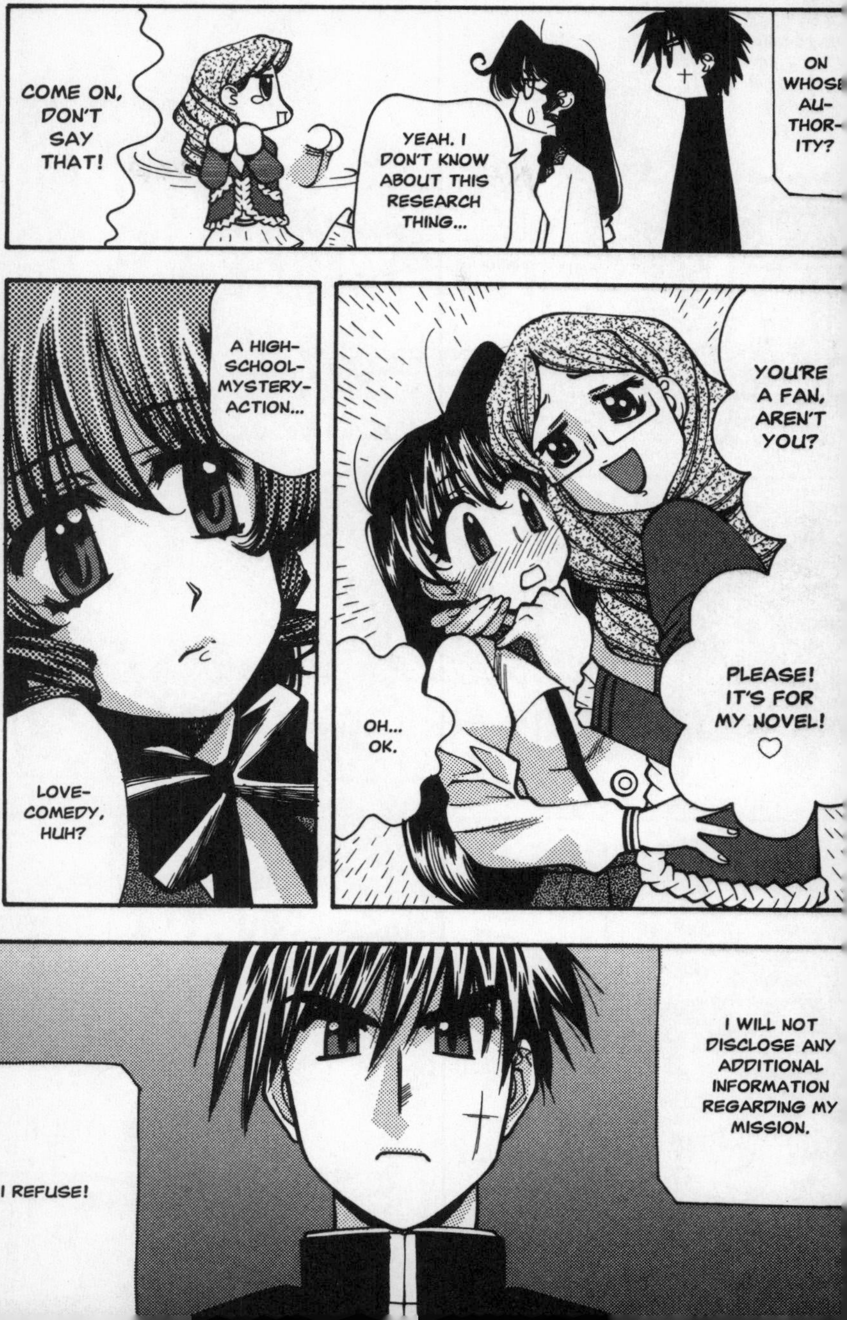
ON WHOSE AU- THOR- ITY?
YEAH. I DON'T KNOW ABOUT THIS RESEARCH THING...
COME ON, DON'T SAY THAT!
YOU'RE A FAN, AREN'T YOU?
PLEASE! IT'S FOR MY NOVEL! ♡
OH... OK.
A HIGH-SCHOOL-MYSTERY-ACTION...
LOVE-COMEDY, HUH?
I WILL NOT DISCLOSE ANY ADDITIONAL INFORMATION REGARDING MY MISSION.
I REFUSE!

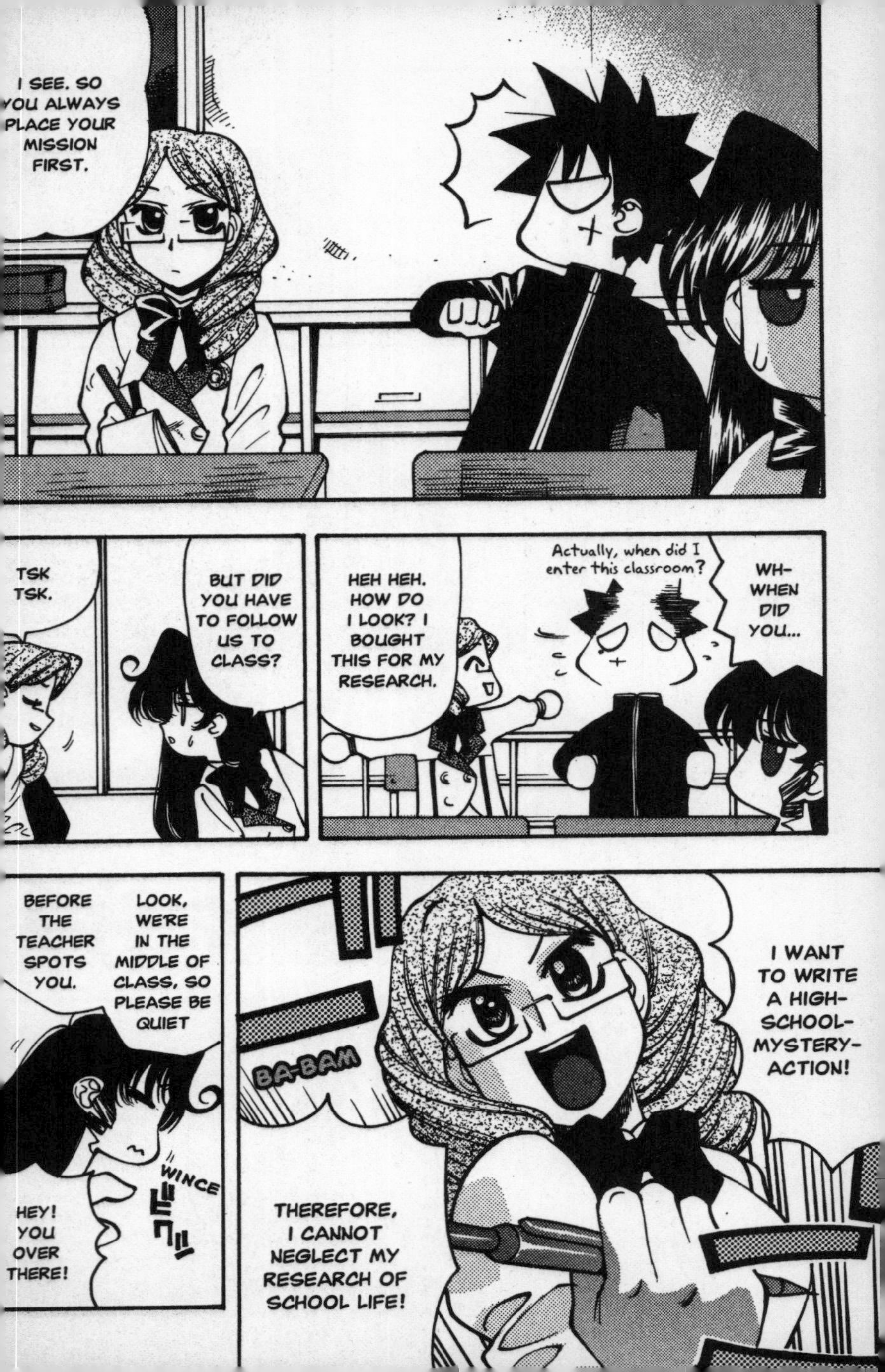
I SEE. SO YOU ALWAYS PLACE YOUR MISSION FIRST.
WH- WHEN DID YOU...
Actually, when did I enter this classroom?
HEH HEH. HOW DO I LOOK? I BOUGHT THIS FOR MY RESEARCH.
BUT DID YOU HAVE TO FOLLOW US TO CLASS?
TSK TSK.
I WANT TO WRITE A HIGH-SCHOOL-MYSTERY-ACTION!
BA-BAM
THEREFORE, I CANNOT NEGLECT MY RESEARCH OF SCHOOL LIFE!
LOOK, WE'RE IN THE MIDDLE OF CLASS, SO PLEASE BE QUIET
BEFORE THE TEACHER SPOTS YOU.
WINCE
HEY! YOU OVER THERE!

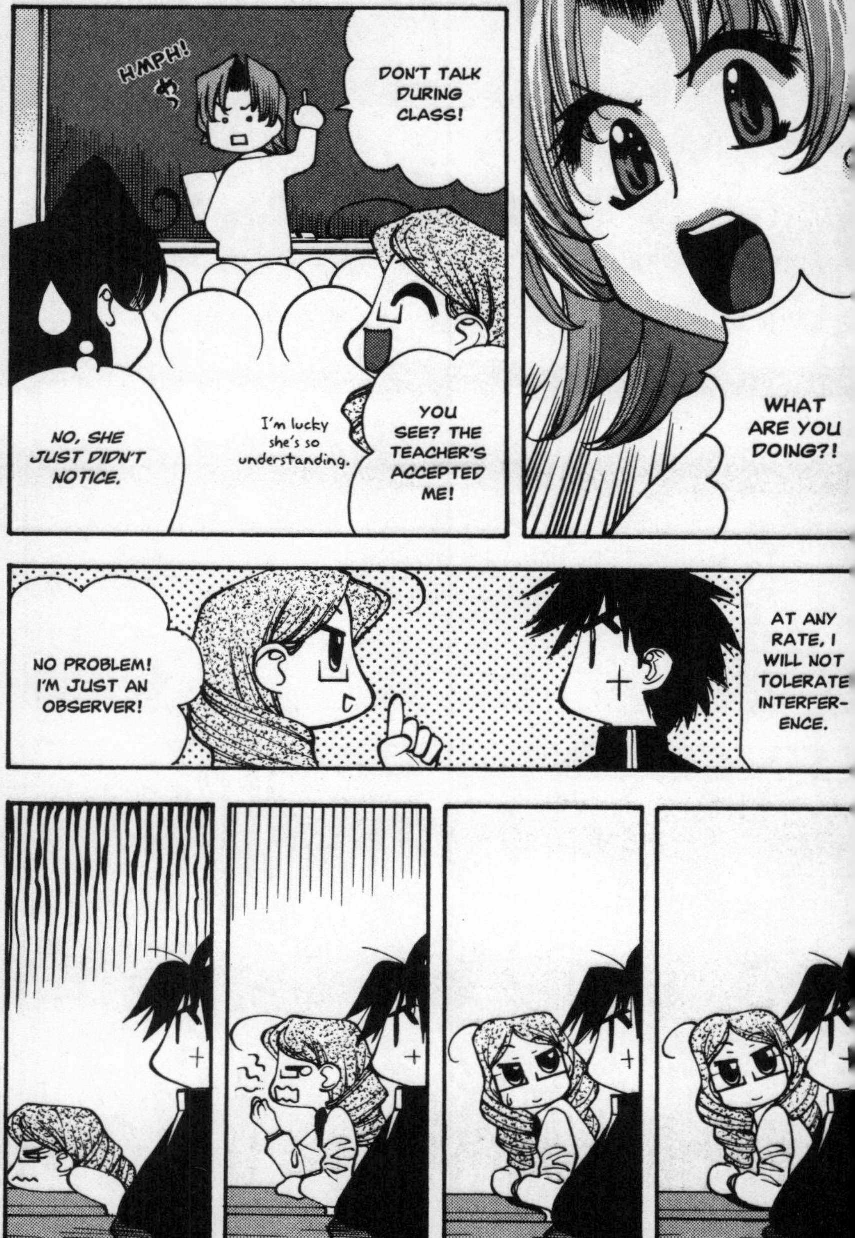
WHAT ARE YOU DOING?!
DON'T TALK DURING CLASS!
HMPH!
め
YOU SEE? THE TEACHER'S ACCEPTED ME!
I'm lucky she's so understanding.
NO, SHE JUST DIDN'T NOTICE.
AT ANY RATE, I WILL NOT TOLERATE INTERFERENCE.
NO PROBLEM! I'M JUST AN OBSERVER!

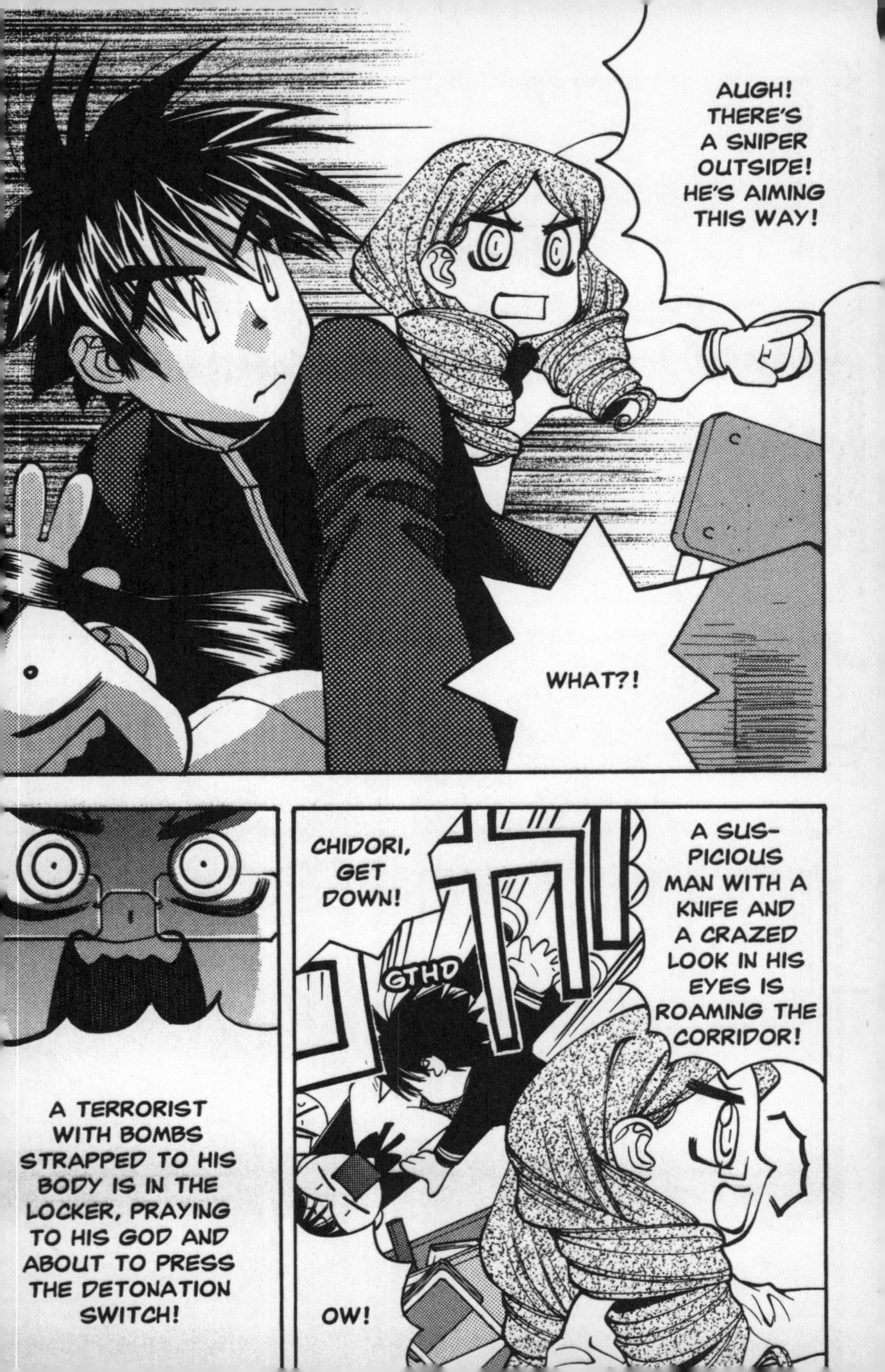
AUGH! THERE'S A SNIPER OUTSIDE! HE'S AIMING THIS WAY!
WHAT?!
A SUS-PICIOUS MAN WITH A KNIFE AND A CRAZED LOOK IN HIS EYES IS ROAMING THE CORRIDOR!
CHIDORI, GET DOWN!
GTHD
OW!
A TERRORIST WITH BOMBS STRAPPED TO HIS BODY IS IN THE LOCKER, PRAYING TO HIS GOD AND ABOUT TO PRESS THE DETONATION SWITCH!

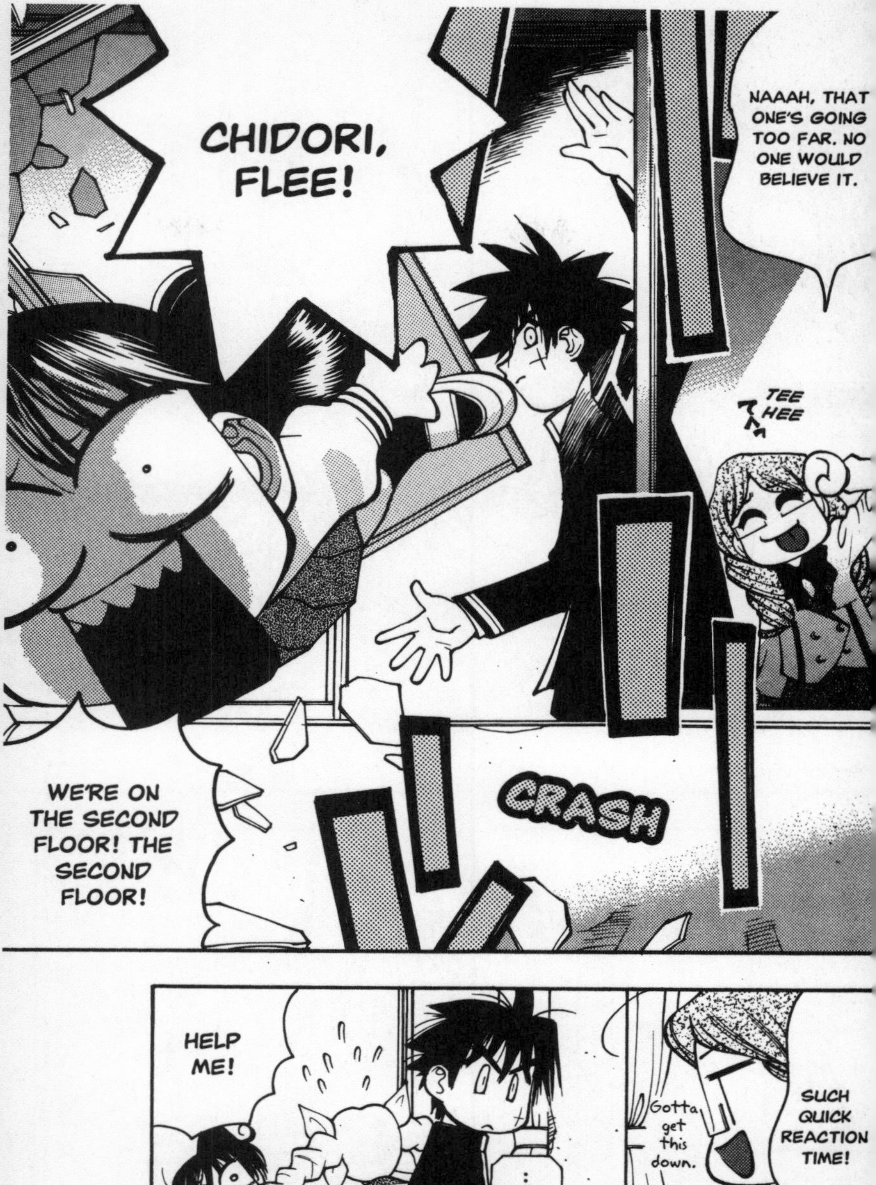
NAAAH, THAT ONE'S GOING TOO FAR. NO ONE WOULD BELIEVE IT.
CHIDORI, FLEE!
TEE HEE
CRASH
WE'RE ON THE SECOND FLOOR! THE SECOND FLOOR!
SUCH QUICK REACTION TIME!
Gotta get this down.
HELP ME!

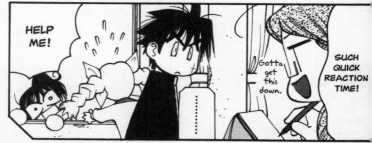

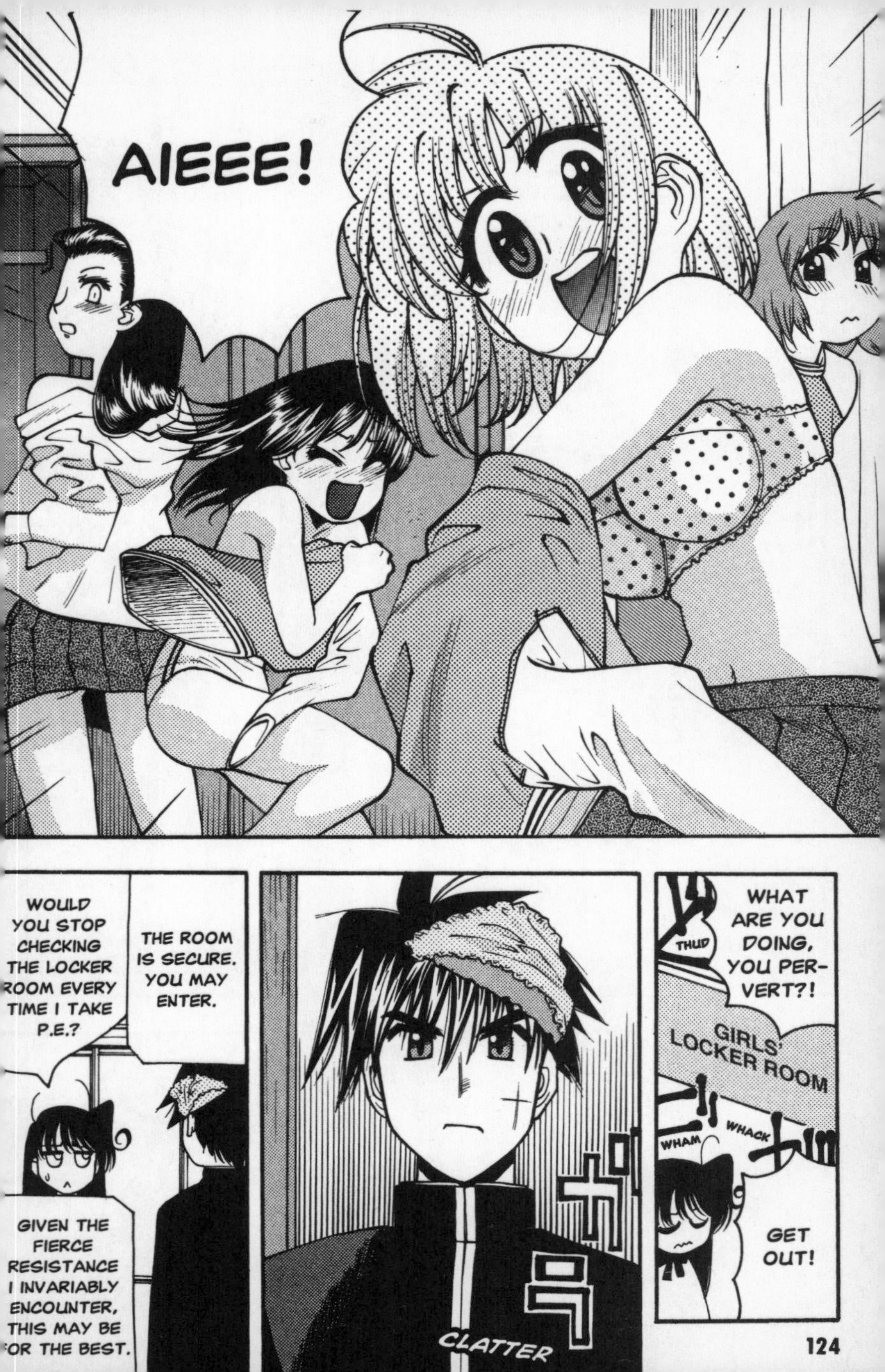
AIEEE!
WHAT ARE YOU DOING, YOU PER-VERT?!
THUD
GIRLS' LOCKER ROOM
WHAM
WHACK
GET OUT!
CLATTER
THE ROOM IS SECURE. YOU MAY ENTER.
WOULD YOU STOP CHECKING THE LOCKER ROOM EVERY TIME I TAKE P.E.?
GIVEN THE FIERCE RESISTANCE I INVARIABLY ENCOUNTER, THIS MAY BE FOR THE BEST.

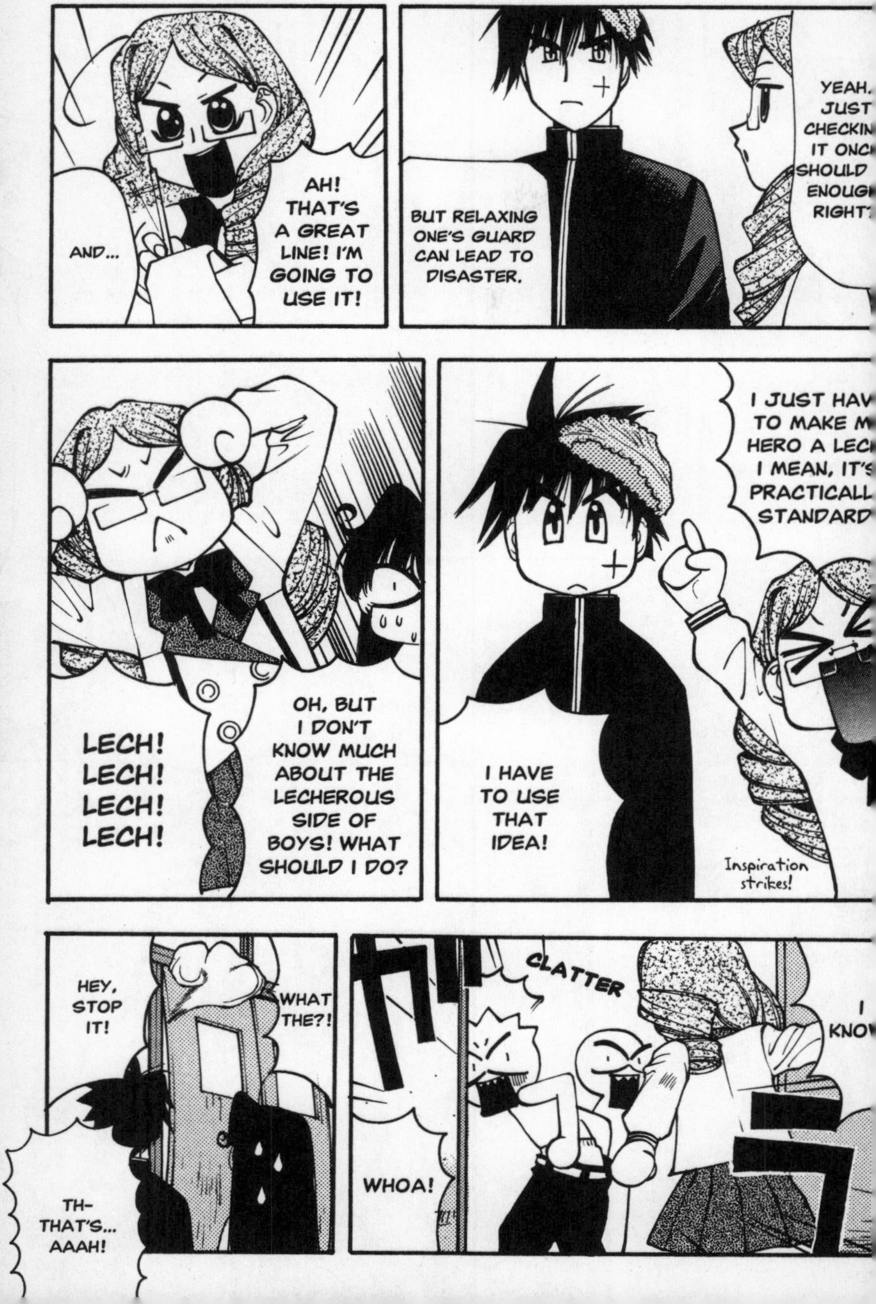
YEAH. JUST CHECKIN IT ONC SHOULD ENOUG RIGHT?
BUT RELAXING ONE'S GUARD CAN LEAD TO DISASTER.
AH! THAT'S A GREAT LINE! I'M GOING TO USE IT!
AND...
I JUST HAV TO MAKE M HERO A LEC I MEAN, IT'S PRACTICALL STANDARD
I HAVE TO USE THAT IDEA!
Inspiration strikes!
OH, BUT I DON'T KNOW MUCH ABOUT THE LECHEROUS SIDE OF BOYS! WHAT SHOULD I DO?
LECH! LECH! LECH! LECH!
I KNO
CLATTER
WHOA!
HEY, STOP IT!
WHAT THE?!
TH- THAT'S... AAAH!

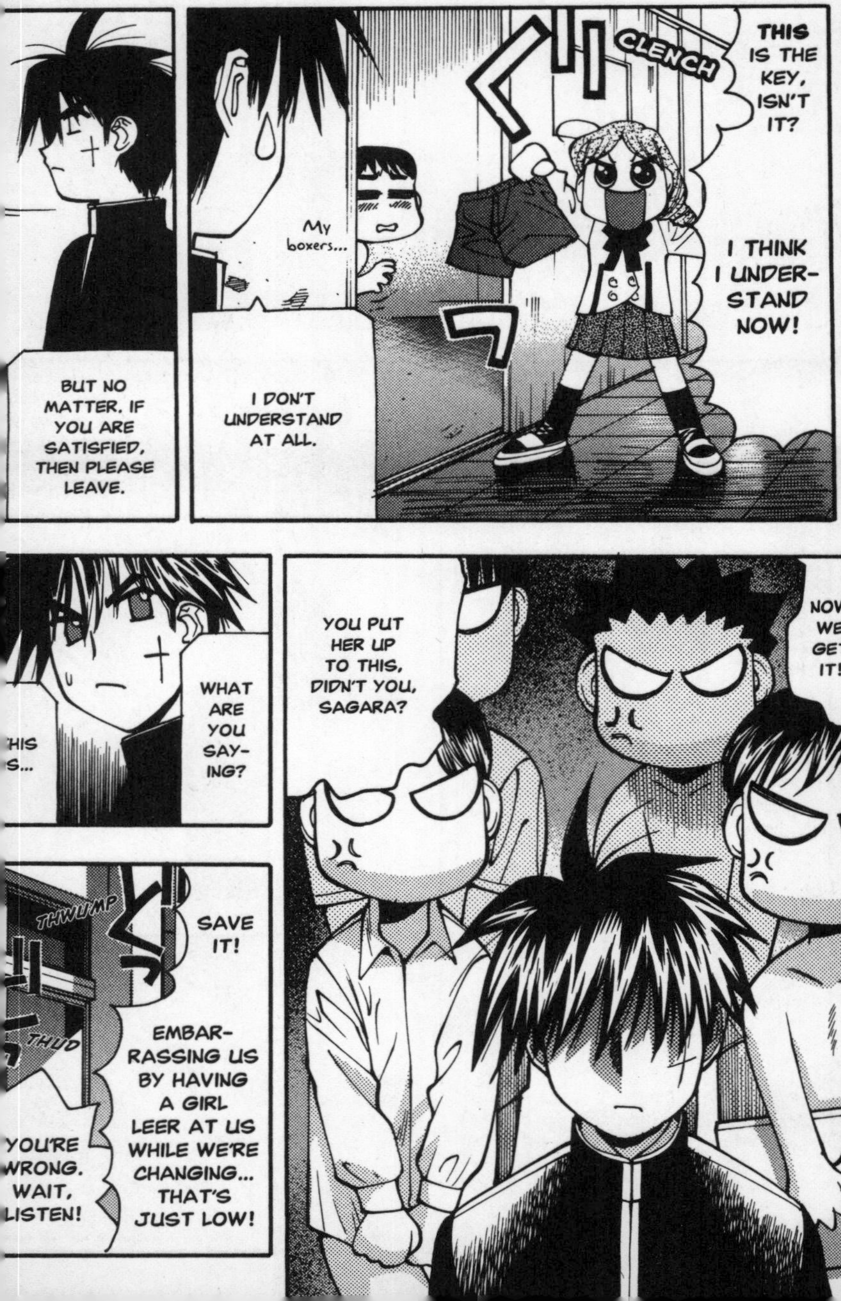
THIS IS THE KEY, ISN'T IT?
CLENCH
I THINK I UNDERSTAND NOW!
My boxers...
I DON'T UNDERSTAND AT ALL.
BUT NO MATTER. IF YOU ARE SATISFIED, THEN PLEASE LEAVE.
NOW WE GET IT!
YOU PUT HER UP TO THIS, DIDN'T YOU, SAGARA?
WHAT ARE YOU SAYING?
SAVE IT!
THWUMP
EMBARRASSING US BY HAVING A GIRL LEER AT US WHILE WE'RE CHANGING... THAT'S JUST LOW!
THUD
YOU'RE WRONG. WAIT, LISTEN!

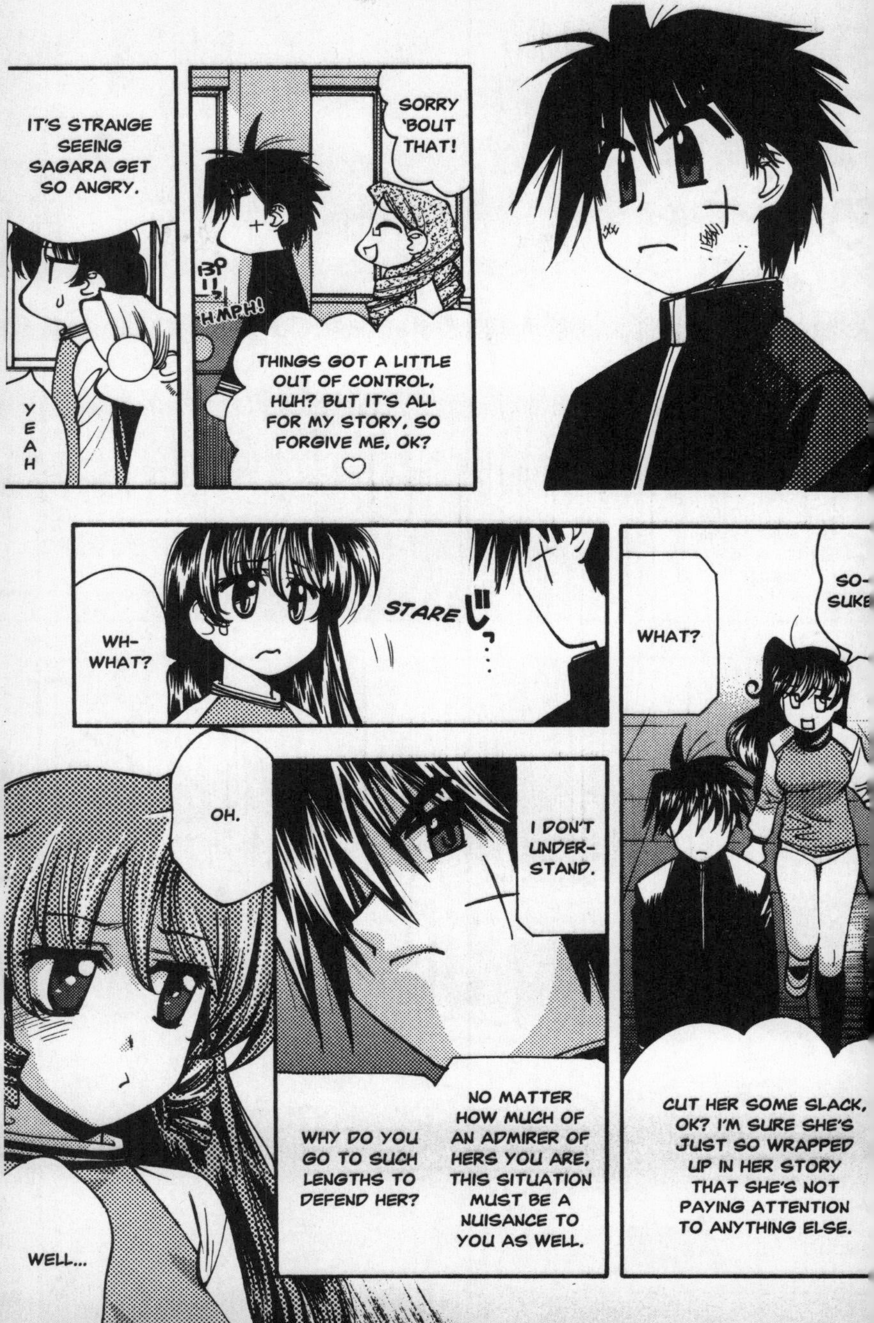
SORRY 'BOUT THAT!
HMPH!
THINGS GOT A LITTLE OUT OF CONTROL, HUH? BUT IT'S ALL FOR MY STORY, SO FORGIVE ME, OK? ♡
IT'S STRANGE SEEING SAGARA GET SO ANGRY.
YEAH
SO-SUKE
WHAT?
CUT HER SOME SLACK, OK? I'M SURE SHE'S JUST SO WRAPPED UP IN HER STORY THAT SHE'S NOT PAYING ATTENTION TO ANYTHING ELSE.
STARE
WH-WHAT?
I DON'T UNDER-STAND.
NO MATTER HOW MUCH OF AN ADMIRER OF HERS YOU ARE, THIS SITUATION MUST BE A NUISANCE TO YOU AS WELL.
WHY DO YOU GO TO SUCH LENGTHS TO DEFEND HER?
OH.
WELL...

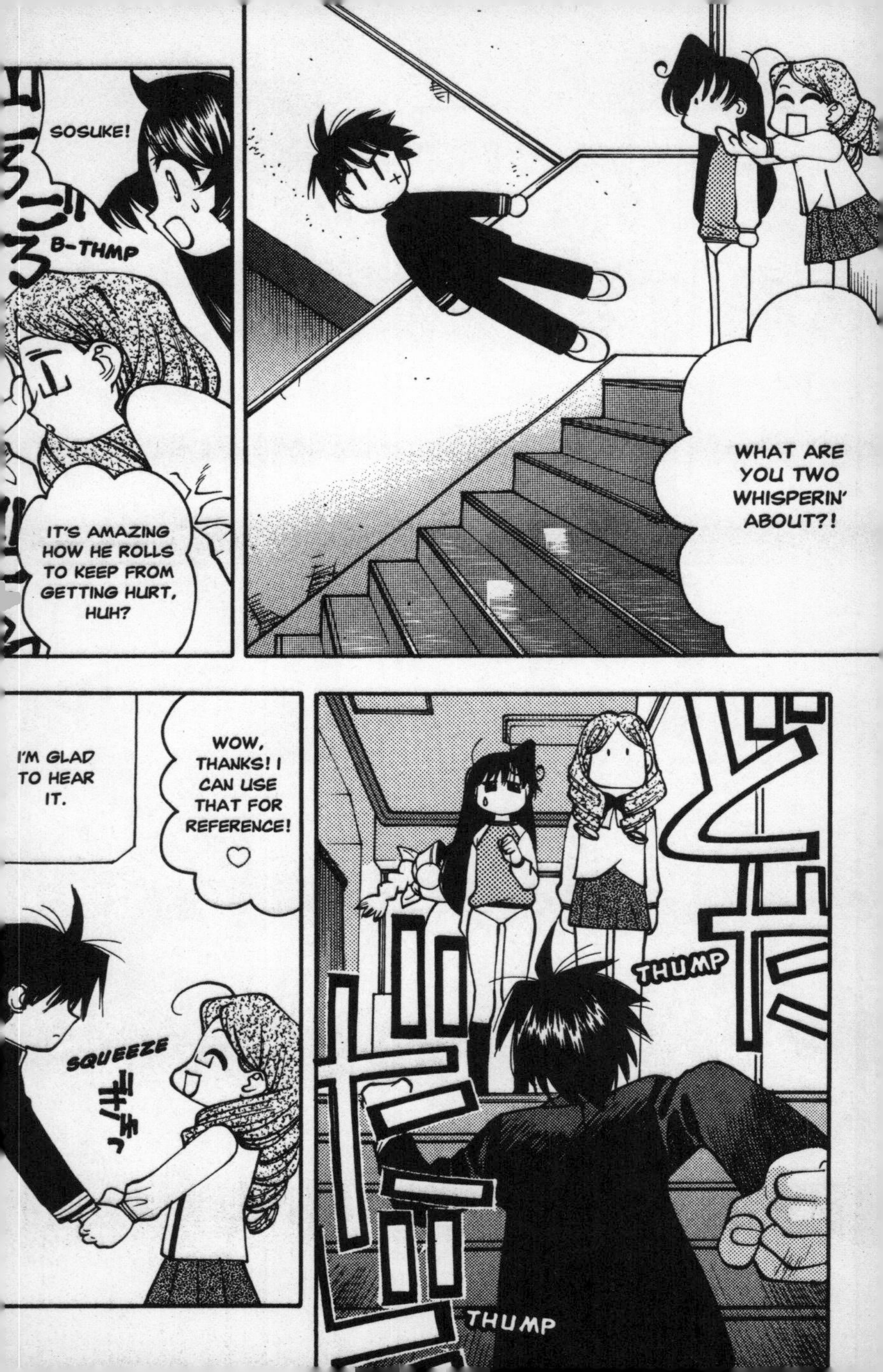

WHAT ARE YOU TWO WHISPERIN' ABOUT?!
SOSUKE!
B-THMP
IT'S AMAZING HOW HE ROLLS TO KEEP FROM GETTING HURT, HUH?
THUMP
THUMP
WOW, THANKS! I CAN USE THAT FOR REFERENCE! ♡
I'M GLAD TO HEAR IT.
SQUEEZE

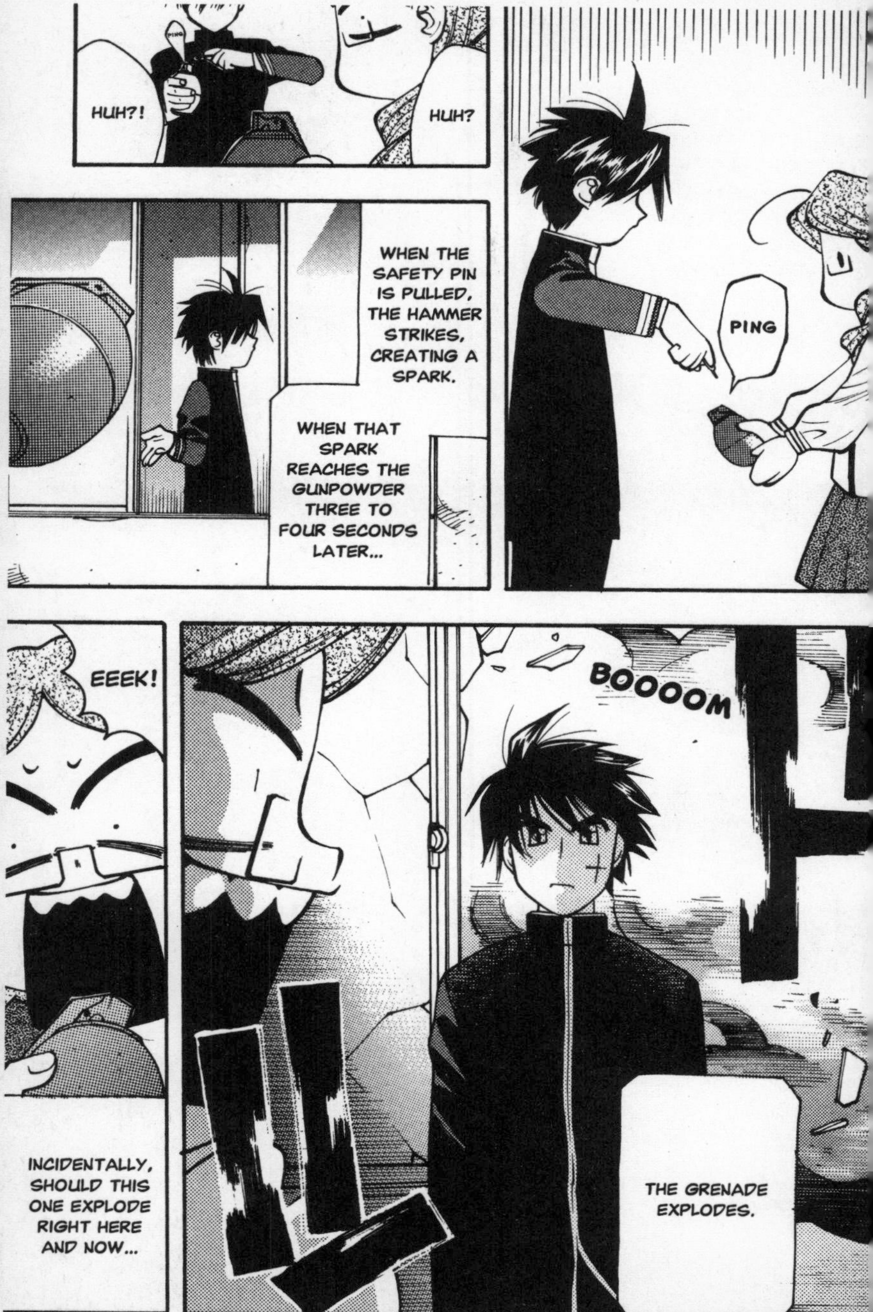
PING
HUH?
HUH?!
WHEN THE SAFETY PIN IS PULLED, THE HAMMER STRIKES, CREATING A SPARK.
WHEN THAT SPARK REACHES THE GUNPOWDER THREE TO FOUR SECONDS LATER...
BOOOOM
THE GRENADE EXPLODES.
EEEK!
INCIDENTALLY, SHOULD THIS ONE EXPLODE RIGHT HERE AND NOW...

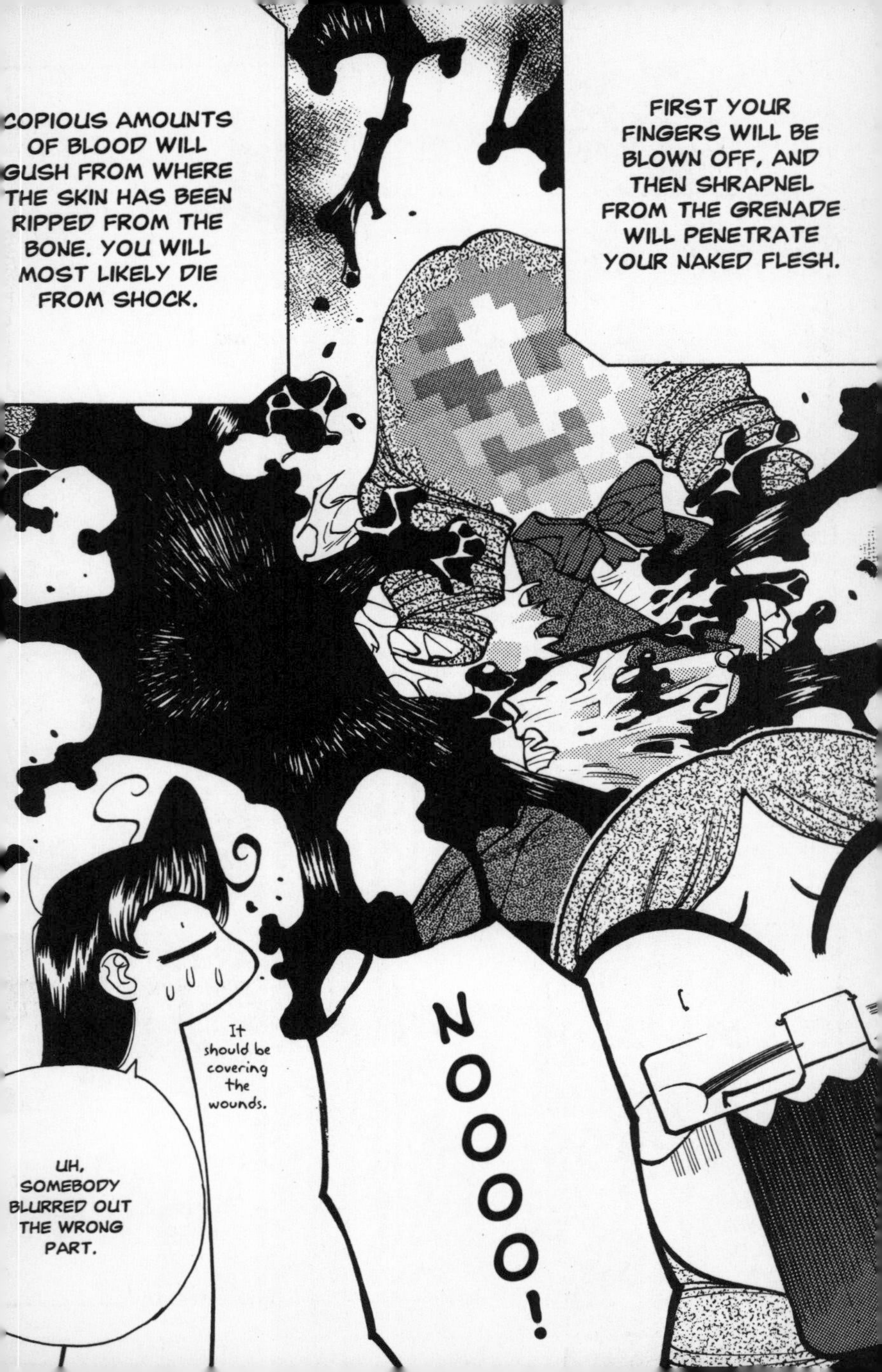
FIRST YOUR FINGERS WILL BE BLOWN OFF, AND THEN SHRAPNEL FROM THE GRENADE WILL PENETRATE YOUR NAKED FLESH.
COPIOUS AMOUNTS OF BLOOD WILL GUSH FROM WHERE THE SKIN HAS BEEN RIPPED FROM THE BONE. YOU WILL MOST LIKELY DIE FROM SHOCK.
NOOOOO!
It should be covering the wounds.
UH, SOMEBODY BLURRED OUT THE WRONG PART.

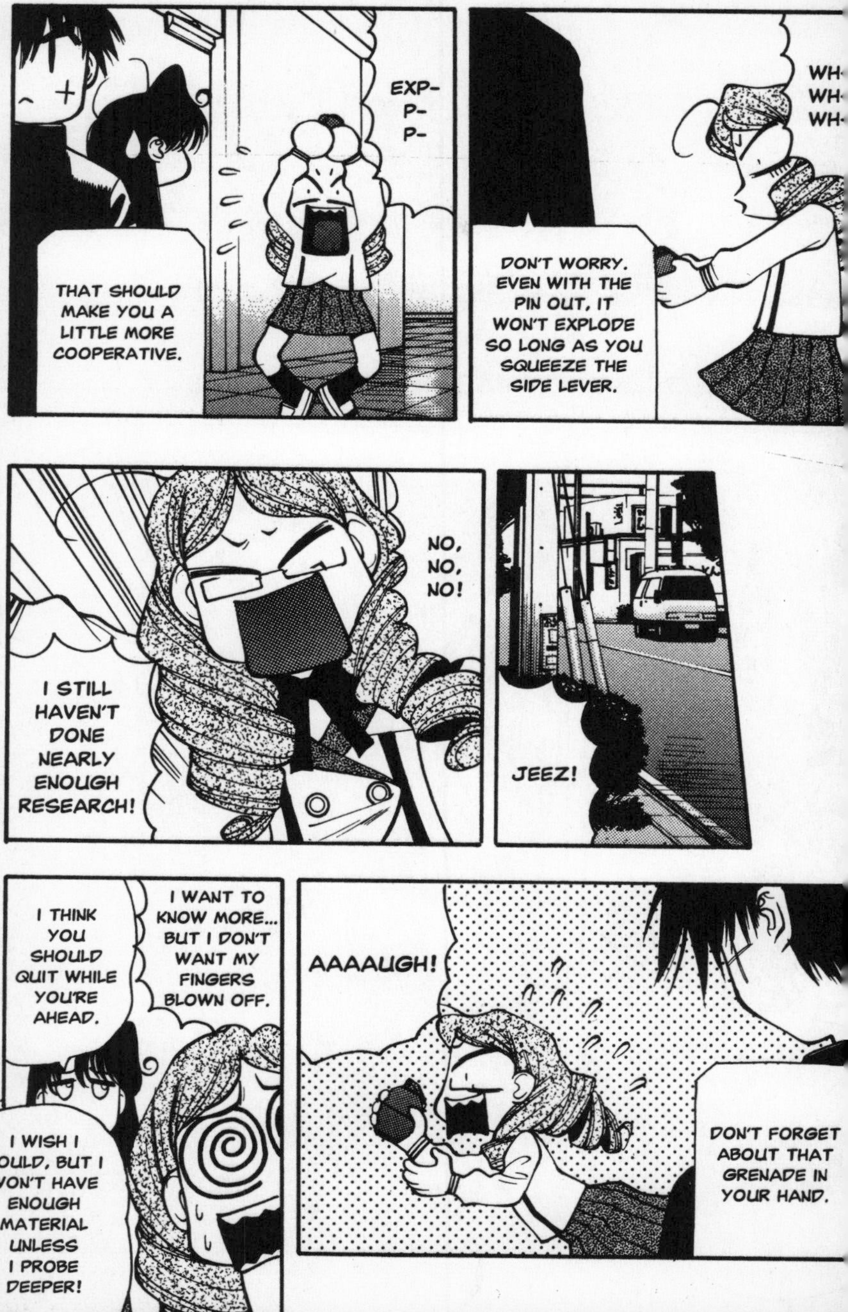

THAT SHOULD MAKE YOU A LITTLE MORE COOPERATIVE.
EXP- P- P-
WH- WH- WH-
DON'T WORRY. EVEN WITH THE PIN OUT, IT WON'T EXPLODE SO LONG AS YOU SQUEEZE THE SIDE LEVER.
NO, NO, NO!
I STILL HAVEN'T DONE NEARLY ENOUGH RESEARCH!
JEEZ!
I THINK YOU SHOULD QUIT WHILE YOU'RE AHEAD.
I WANT TO KNOW MORE... BUT I DON'T WANT MY FINGERS BLOWN OFF.
I WISH I COULD, BUT I WON'T HAVE ENOUGH MATERIAL UNLESS I PROBE DEEPER!
AAAAUGH!
DON'T FORGET ABOUT THAT GRENADE IN YOUR HAND.

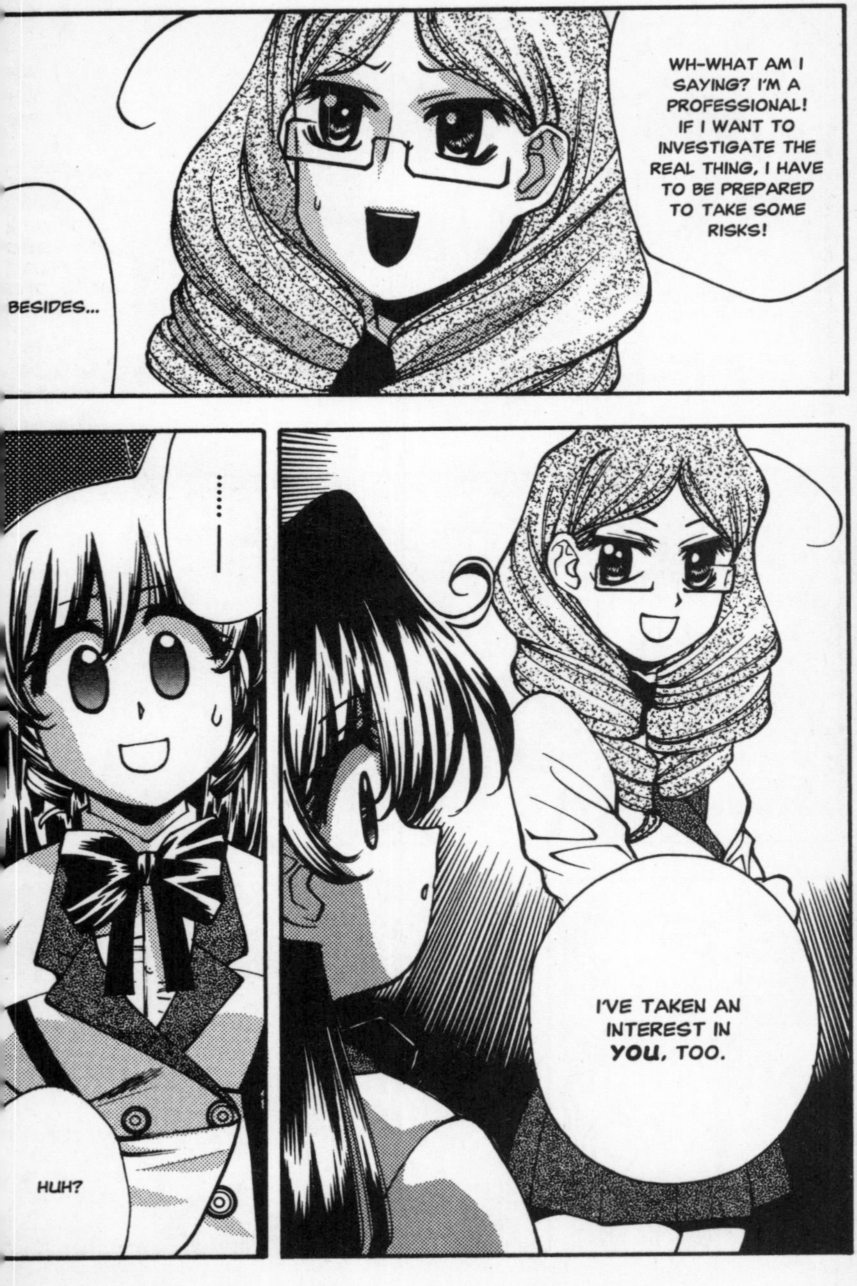
WH-WHAT AM I SAYING? I'M A PROFESSIONAL! IF I WANT TO INVESTIGATE THE REAL THING, I HAVE TO BE PREPARED TO TAKE SOME RISKS!
BESIDES...
I'VE TAKEN AN INTEREST IN YOU, TOO.
......!
HUH?

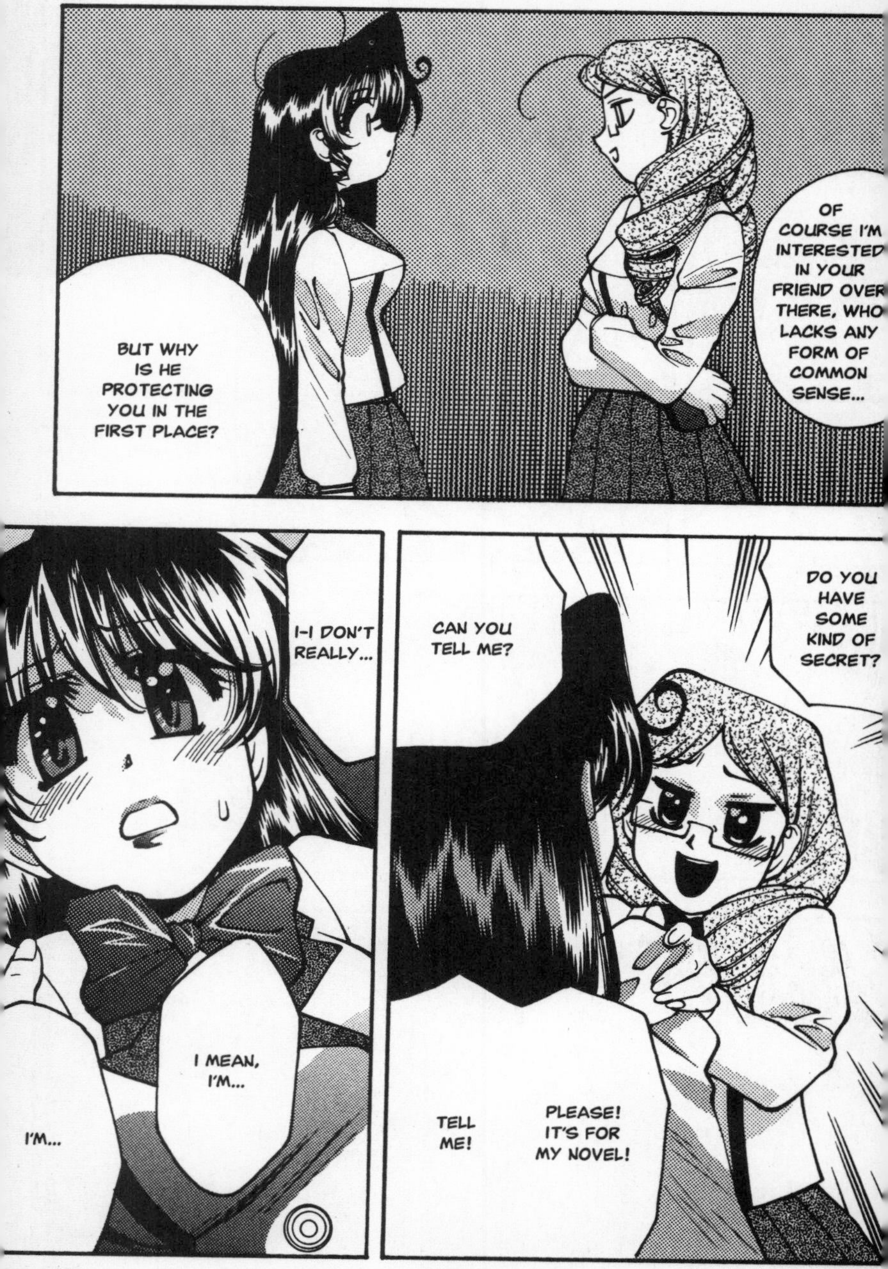
OF COURSE I'M INTERESTED IN YOUR FRIEND OVER THERE, WHO LACKS ANY FORM OF COMMON SENSE...
BUT WHY IS HE PROTECTING YOU IN THE FIRST PLACE?
DO YOU HAVE SOME KIND OF SECRET?
CAN YOU TELL ME?
PLEASE! IT'S FOR MY NOVEL!
TELL ME!
I-I DON'T REALLY...
I MEAN, I'M...
I'M...

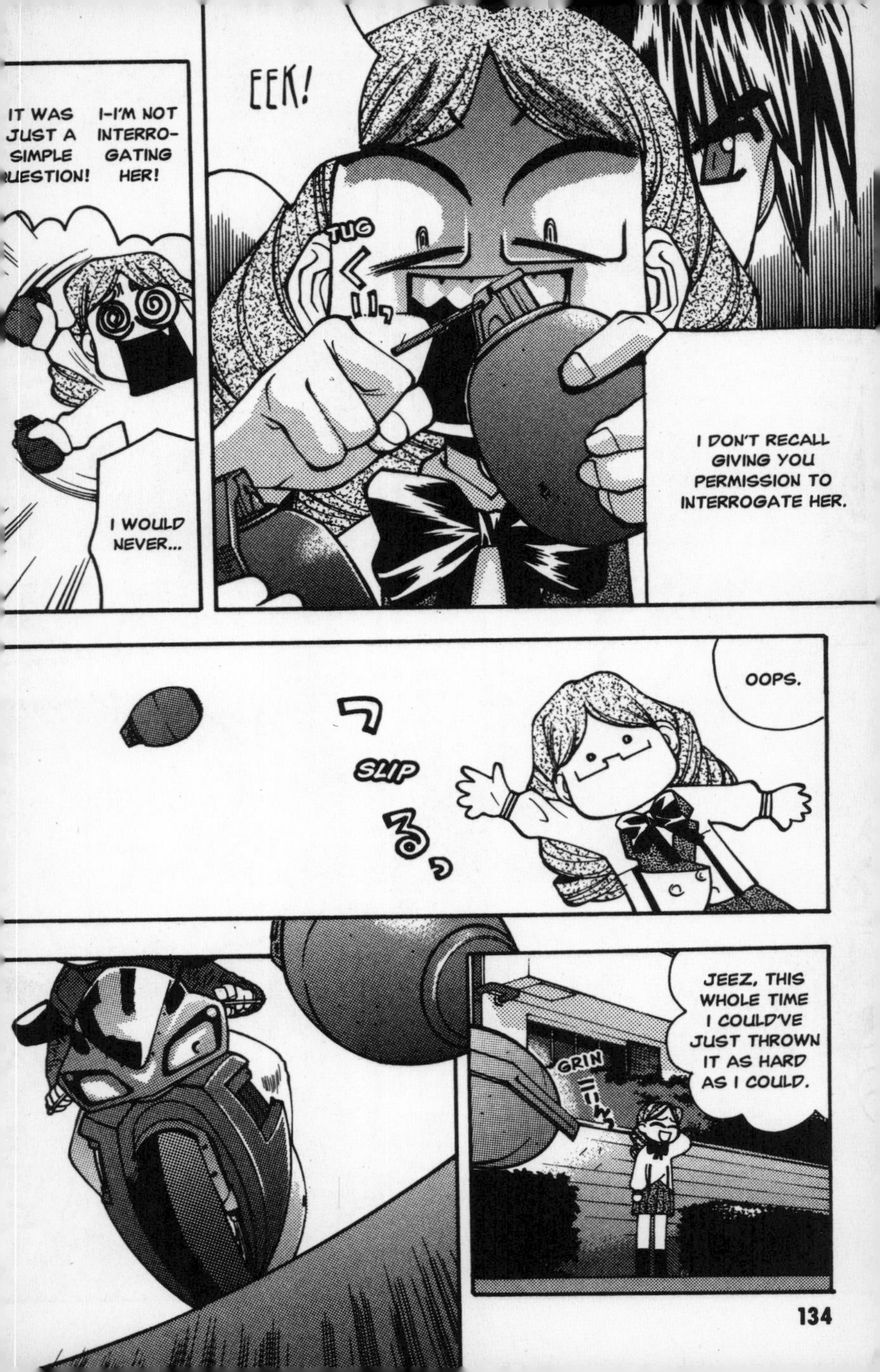
I DON'T RECALL GIVING YOU PERMISSION TO INTERROGATE HER.
EEK!
TUG
I-I'M NOT INTERROGATING HER!
IT WAS JUST A SIMPLE QUESTION!
I WOULD NEVER...
OOPS.
SLIP
JEEZ, THIS WHOLE TIME I COULD'VE JUST THROWN IT AS HARD AS I COULD.
GRIN

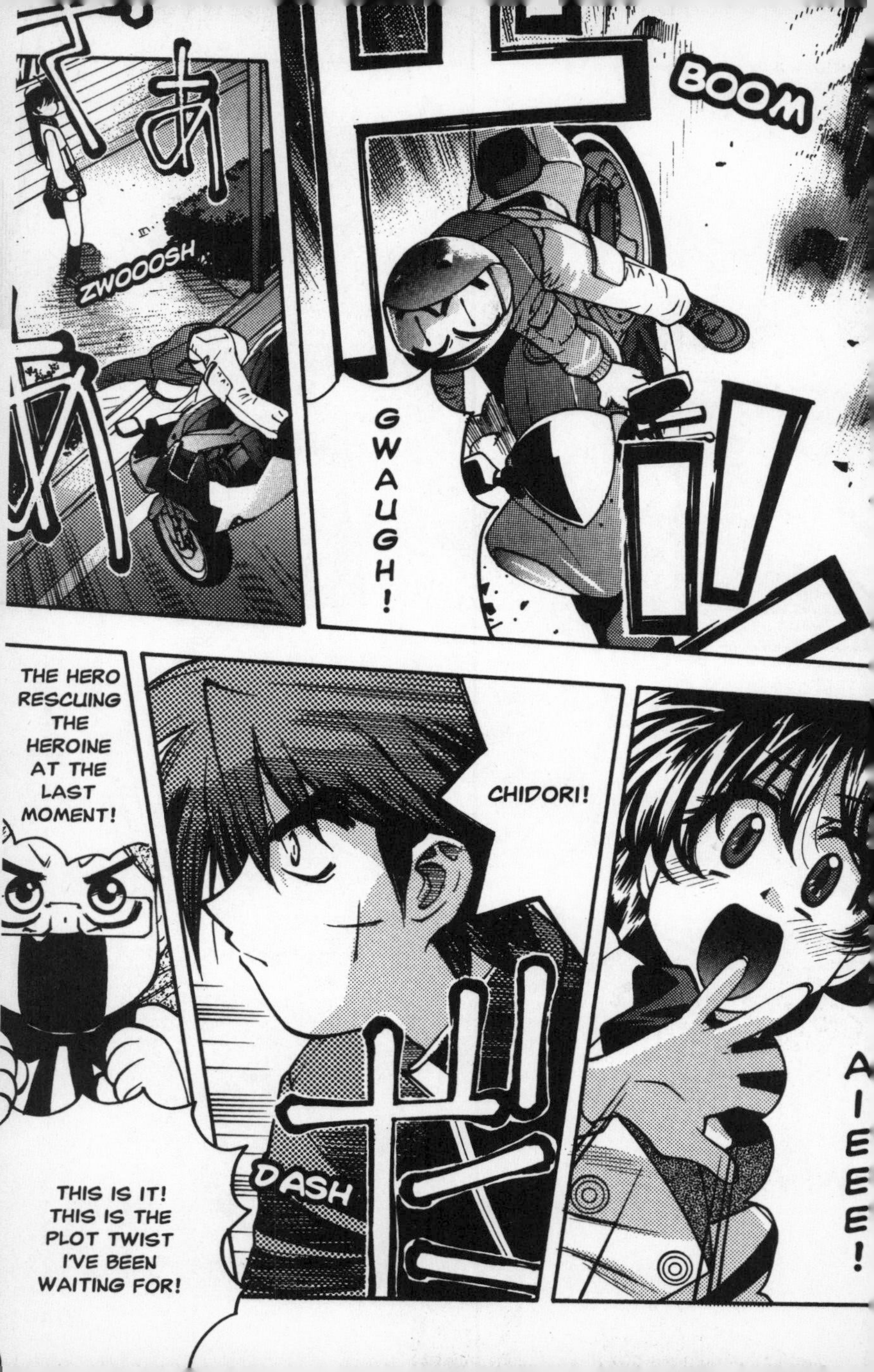

BOOM
ZWOOOSH
GWAUGH!
THE HERO RESCUING THE HEROINE AT THE LAST MOMENT!
THIS IS IT! THIS IS THE PLOT TWIST I'VE BEEN WAITING FOR!
CHIDORI!
DASH
AIEEE!

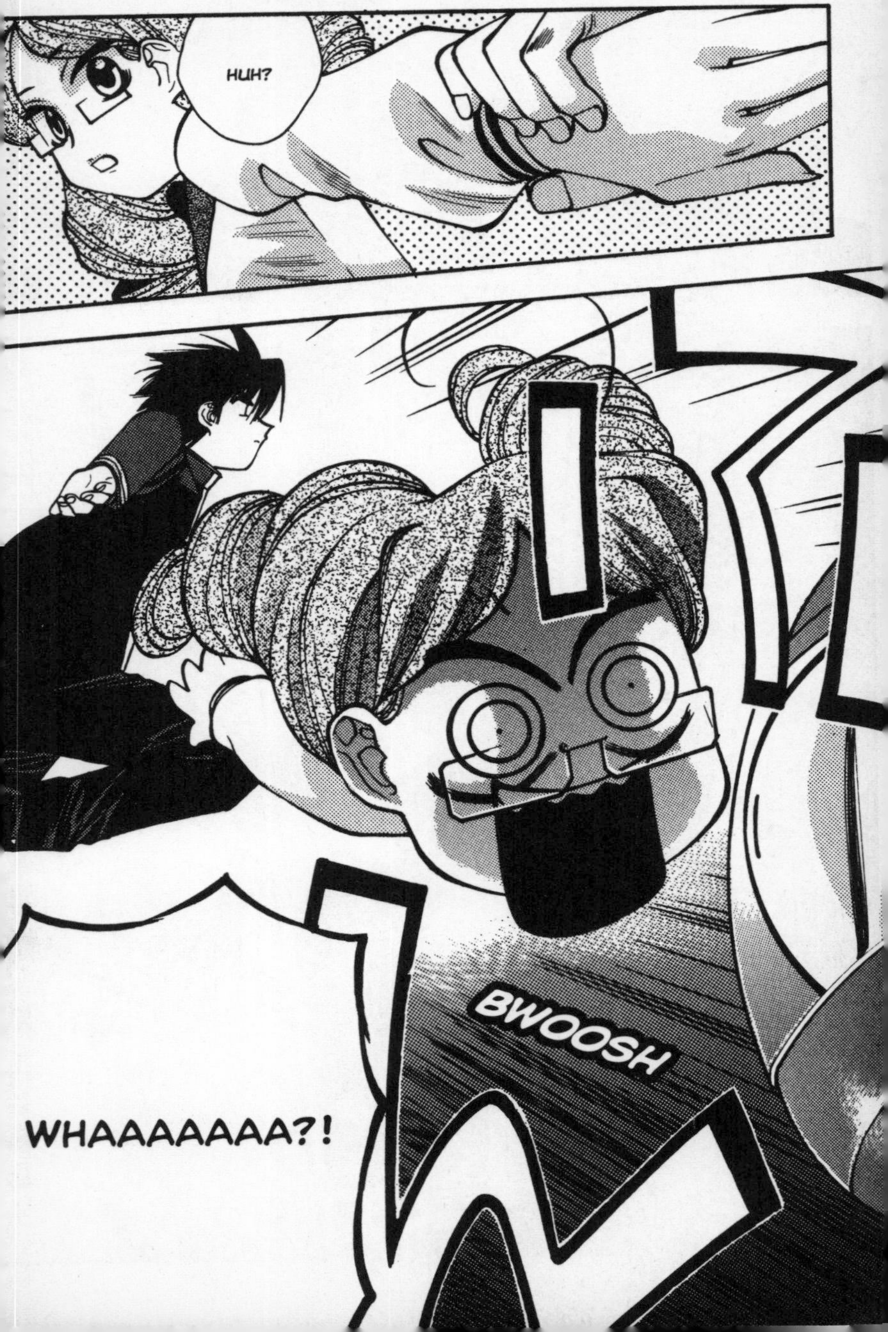
HUH?
BWOOSH
WHAAAAAAA?!

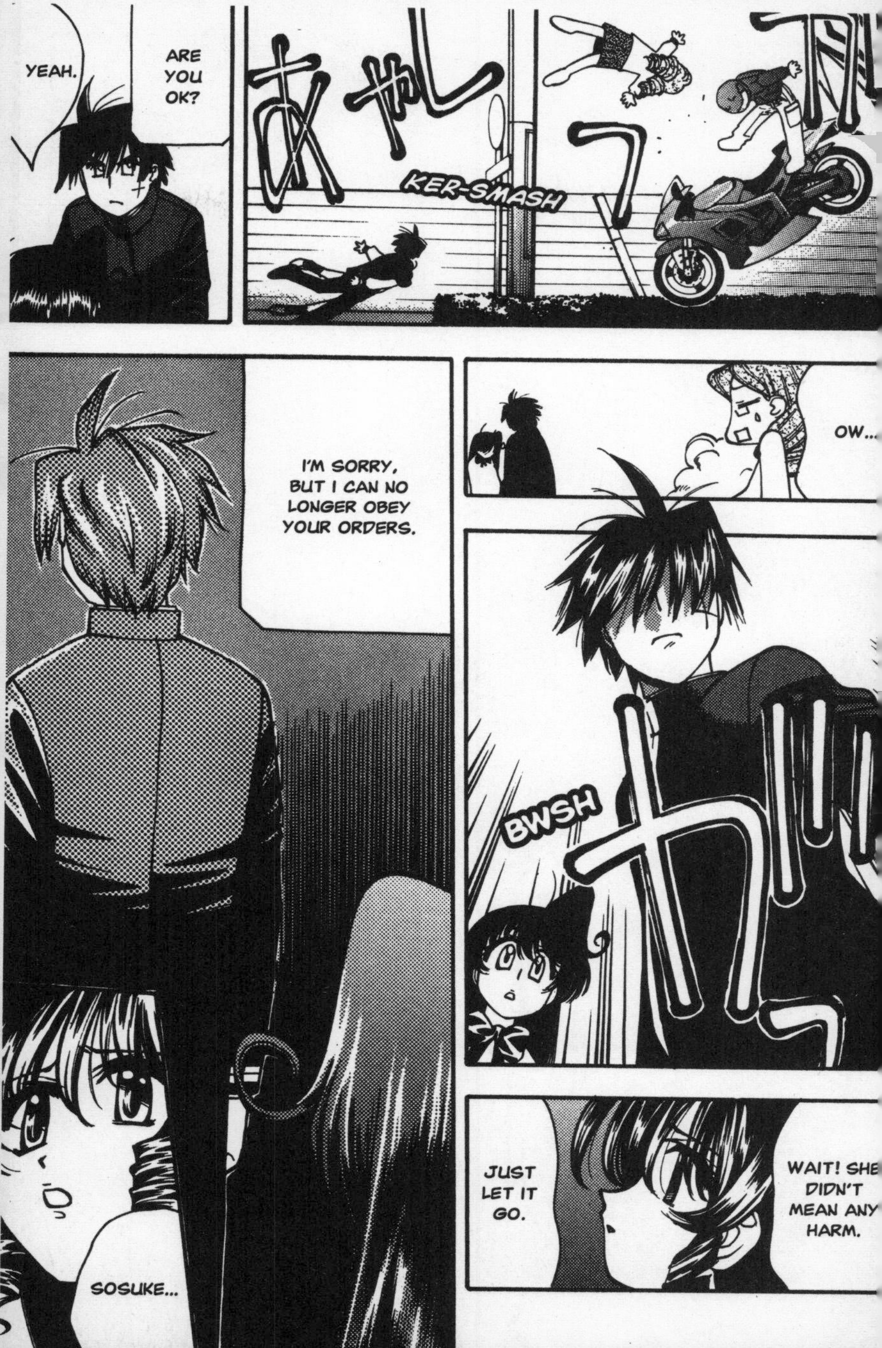
KER-SMASH
ARE YOU OK?
YEAH.
OW...
BWSH
WAIT! SHE DIDN'T MEAN ANY HARM.
JUST LET IT GO.
I'M SORRY, BUT I CAN NO LONGER OBEY YOUR ORDERS.
SOSUKE...

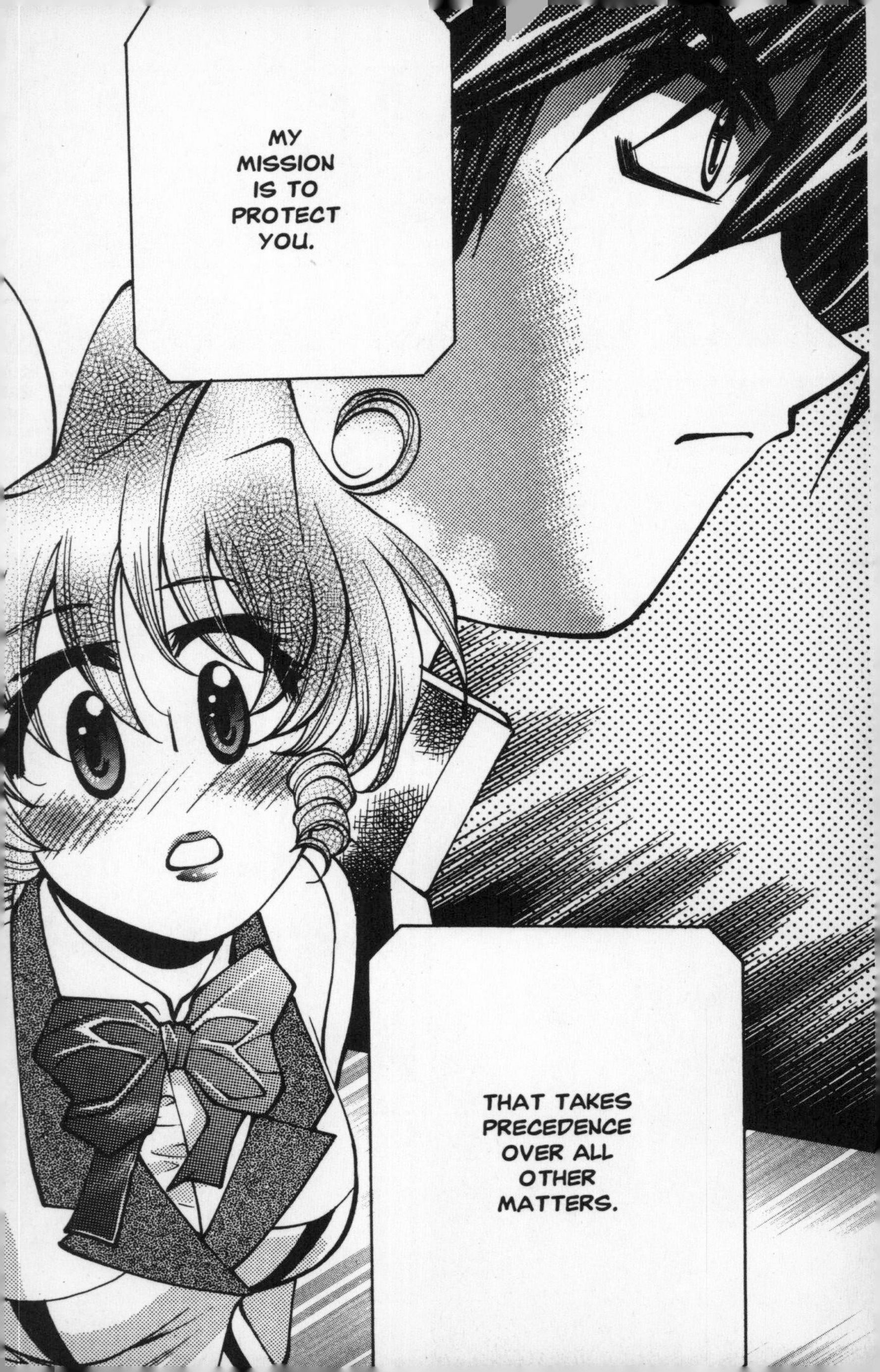
MY MISSION IS TO PROTECT YOU.
THAT TAKES PRECEDENCE OVER ALL OTHER MATTERS.

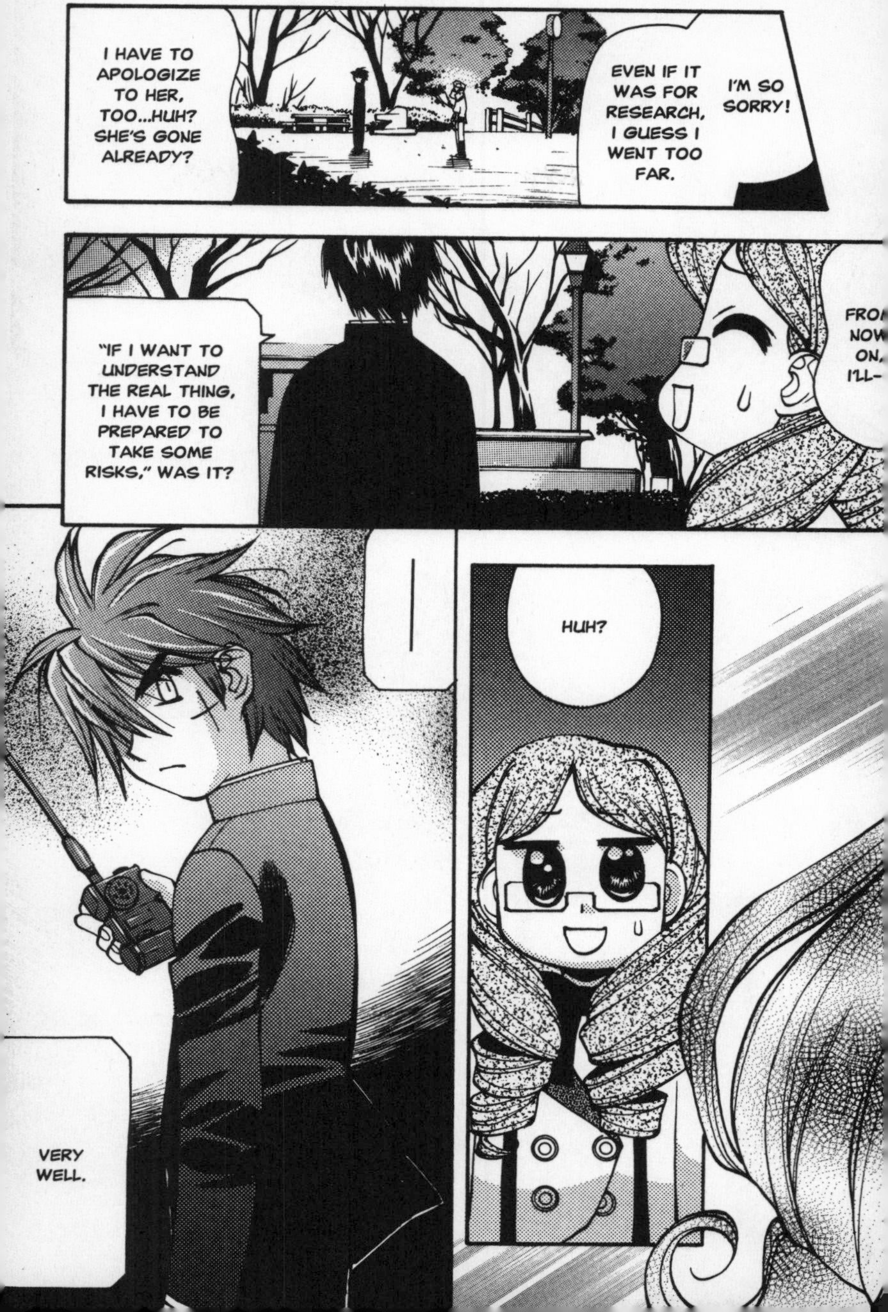
I'M SO SORRY!
EVEN IF IT WAS FOR RESEARCH, I GUESS I WENT TOO FAR.
I HAVE TO APOLOGIZE TO HER, TOO...HUH? SHE'S GONE ALREADY?
FROM NOW ON, I'LL–
"IF I WANT TO UNDERSTAND THE REAL THING, I HAVE TO BE PREPARED TO TAKE SOME RISKS," WAS IT?
HUH?
VERY WELL.

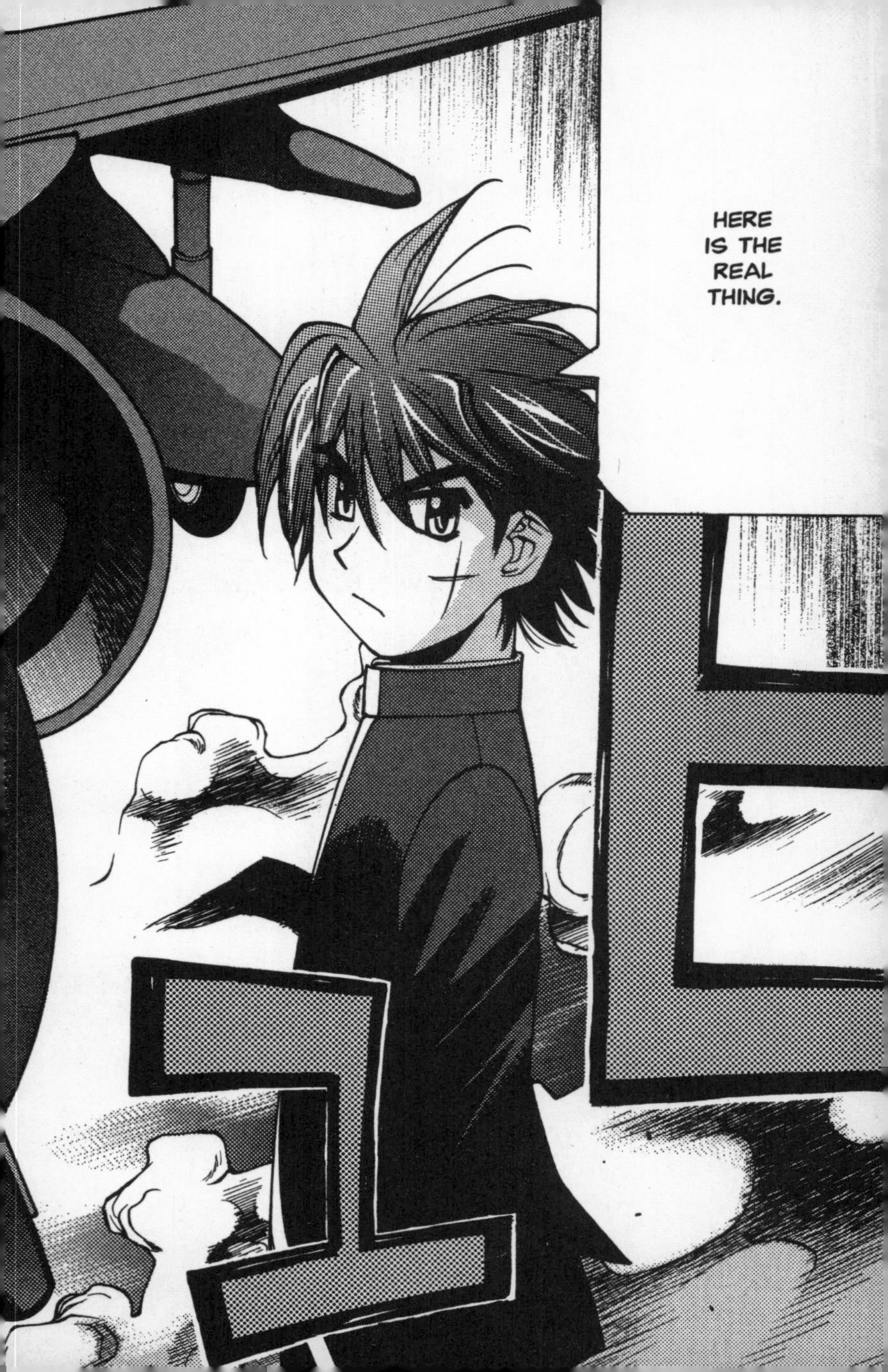
HERE IS THE REAL THING.

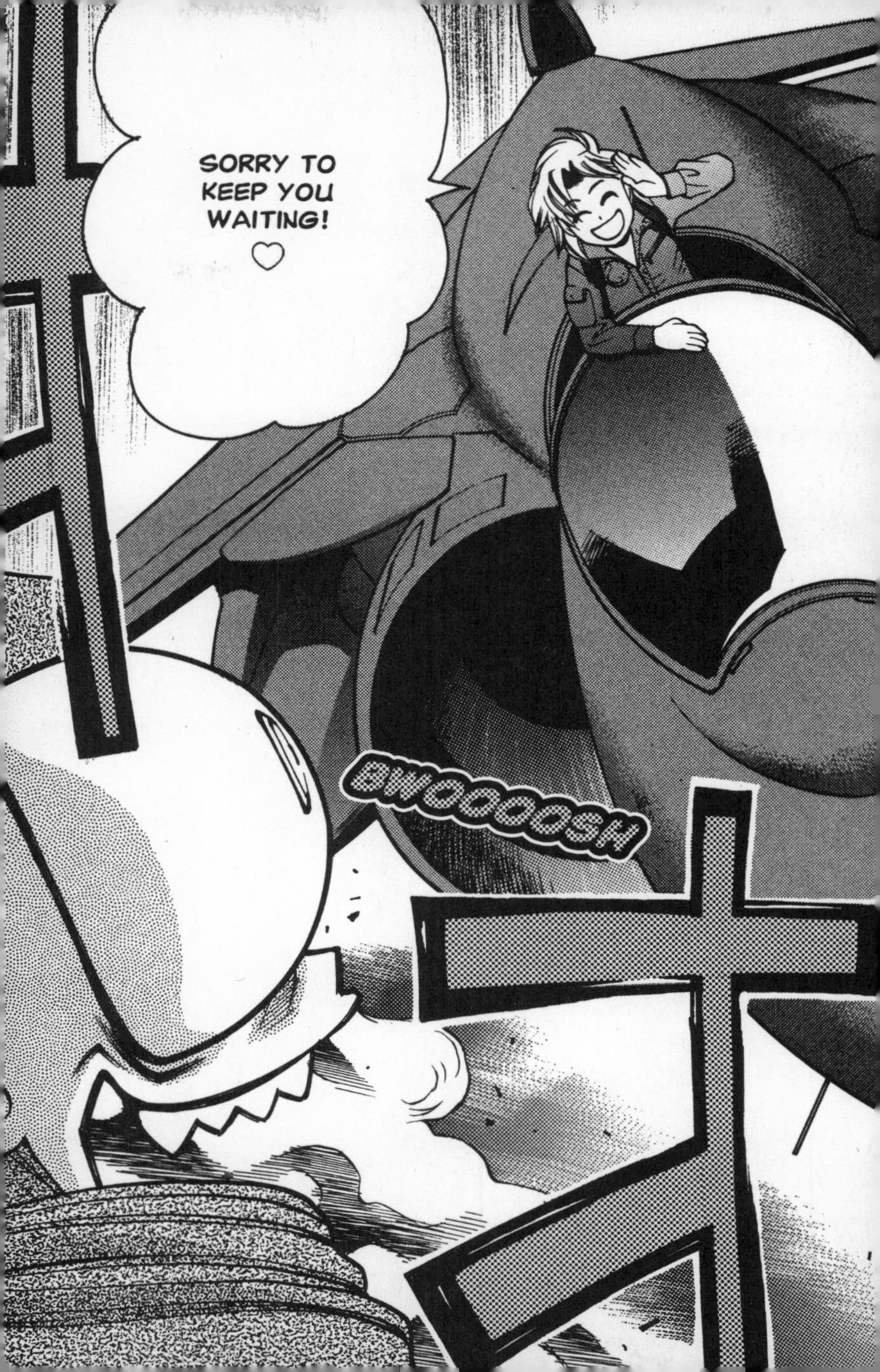
SORRY TO KEEP YOU WAITING! ♡
BWOOOOSH

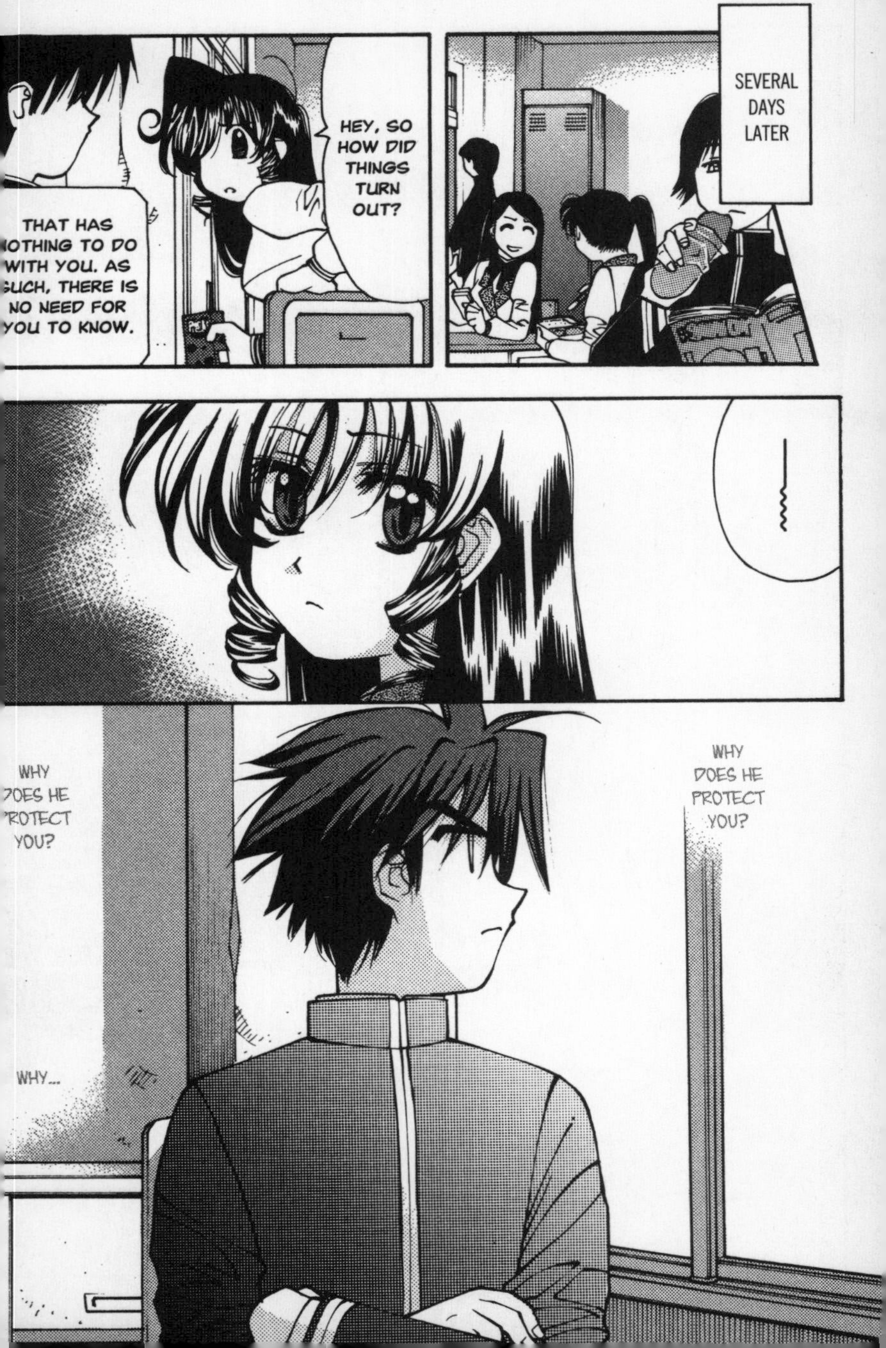

SEVERAL DAYS LATER
HEY, SO HOW DID THINGS TURN OUT?
THAT HAS NOTHING TO DO WITH YOU. AS SUCH, THERE IS NO NEED FOR YOU TO KNOW.
...
WHY DOES HE PROTECT YOU?
WHY DOES HE PROTECT YOU?
WHY...

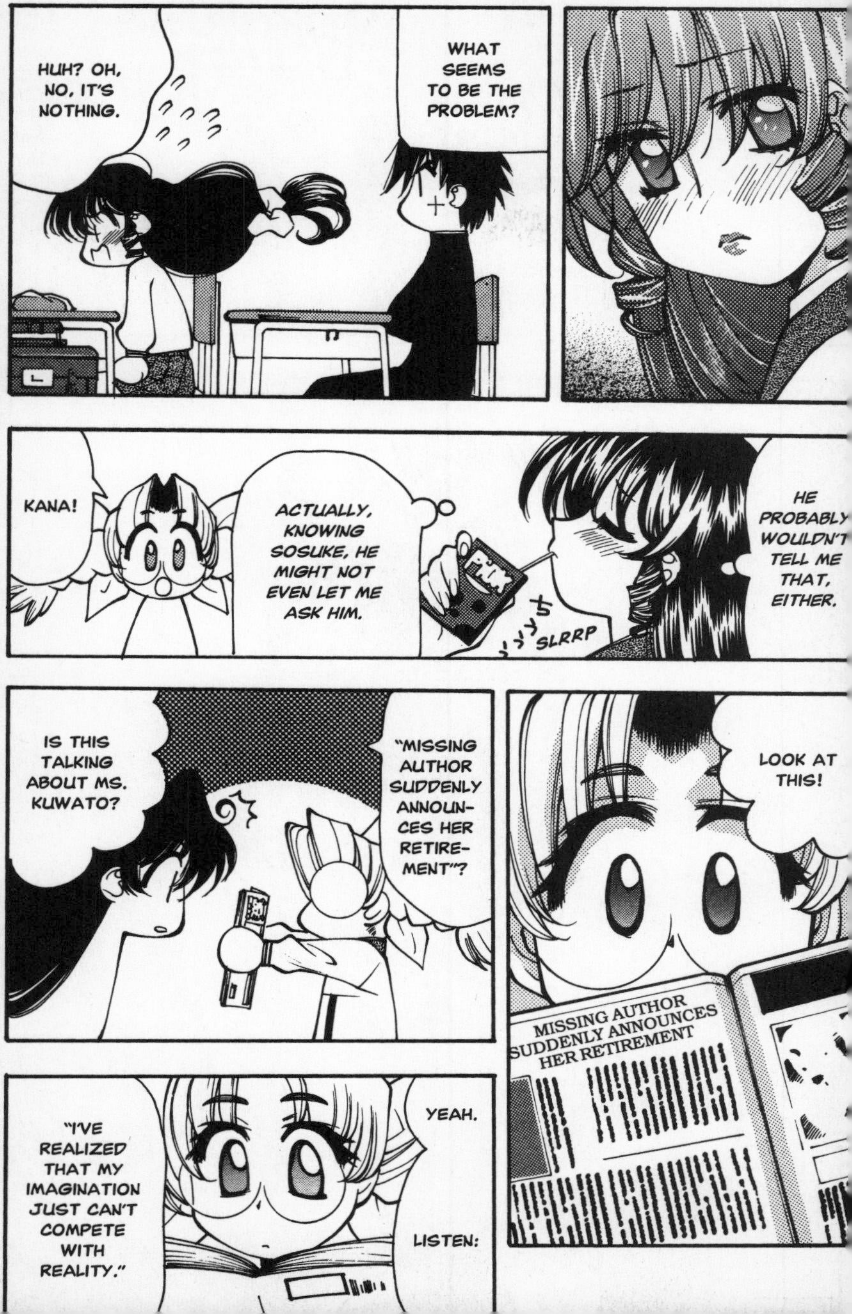
WHAT SEEMS TO BE THE PROBLEM?
HUH? OH, NO, IT'S NOTHING.
HE PROBABLY WOULDN'T TELL ME THAT, EITHER.
SLRRP
ACTUALLY, KNOWING SOSUKE, HE MIGHT NOT EVEN LET ME ASK HIM.
KANA!
LOOK AT THIS!
MISSING AUTHOR SUDDENLY ANNOUNCES HER RETIREMENT
"MISSING AUTHOR SUDDENLY ANNOUN-CES HER RETIRE-MENT"?
IS THIS TALKING ABOUT MS. KUWATO?
YEAH.
LISTEN:
"I'VE REALIZED THAT MY IMAGINATION JUST CAN'T COMPETE WITH REALITY."

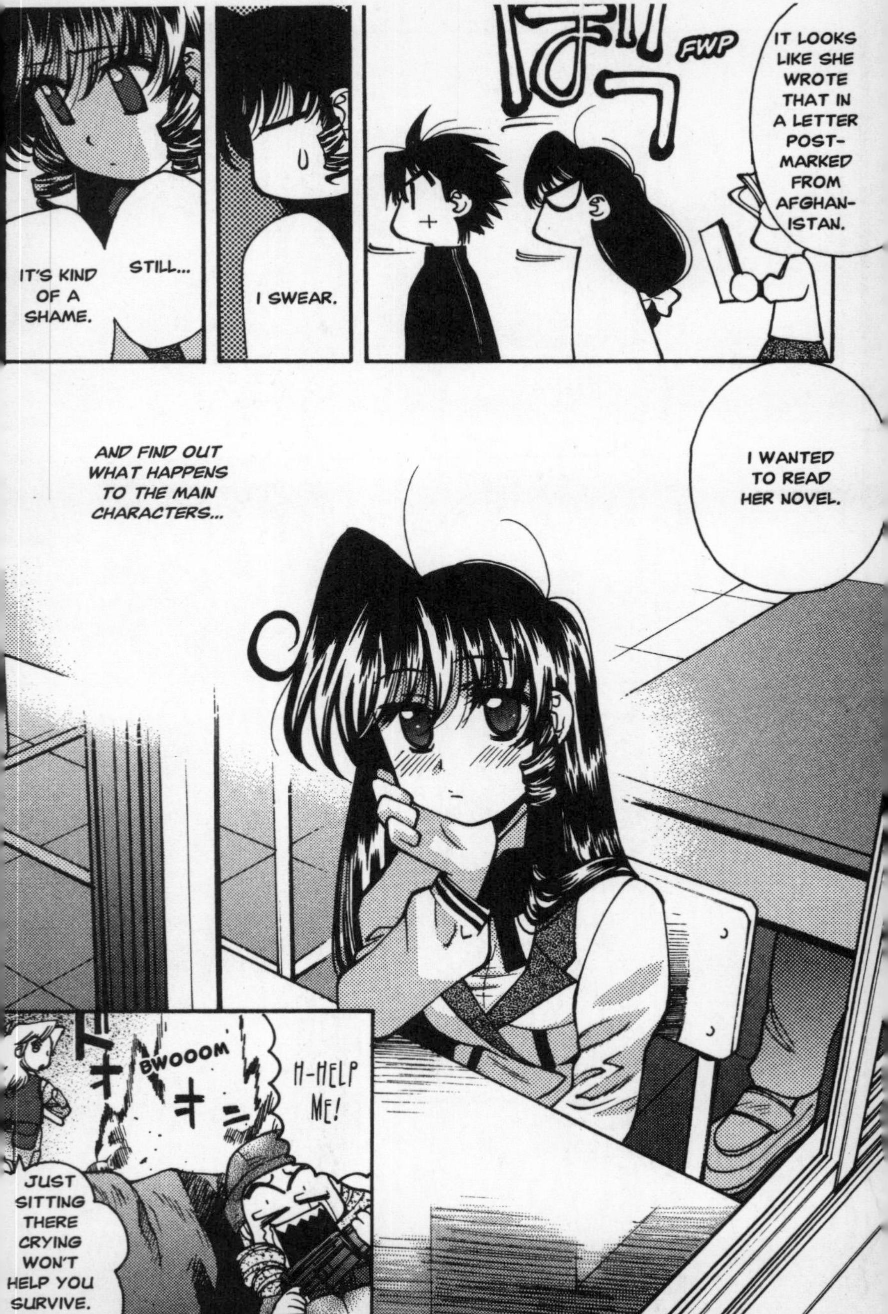

IT LOOKS LIKE SHE WROTE THAT IN A LETTER POST-MARKED FROM AFGHAN-ISTAN.
FWP
I SWEAR.
STILL...
IT'S KIND OF A SHAME.
I WANTED TO READ HER NOVEL.
AND FIND OUT WHAT HAPPENS TO THE MAIN CHARACTERS...
H-HELP ME!
BWOOOM
JUST SITTING THERE CRYING WON'T HELP YOU SURVIVE.

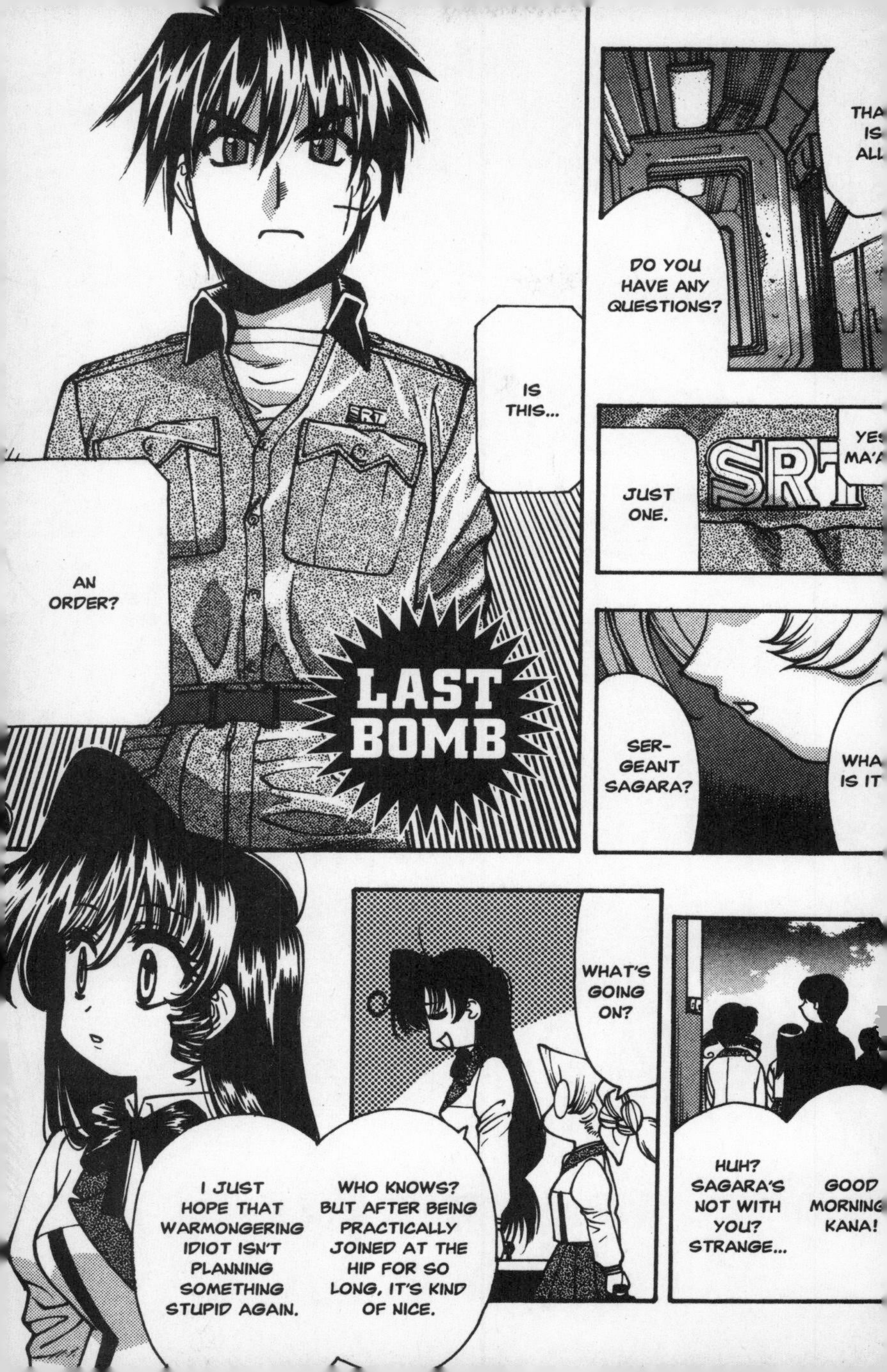
THA
IS
ALL
DO YOU HAVE ANY QUESTIONS?
YES
MA'A
JUST ONE.
WHA
IS IT
SER-GEANT SAGARA?
IS THIS...
AN ORDER?
LAST BOMB
GOOD MORNING KANA!
HUH? SAGARA'S NOT WITH YOU? STRANGE...
WHAT'S GOING ON?
WHO KNOWS? BUT AFTER BEING PRACTICALLY JOINED AT THE HIP FOR SO LONG, IT'S KIND OF NICE.
I JUST HOPE THAT WARMONGERING IDIOT ISN'T PLANNING SOMETHING STUPID AGAIN.

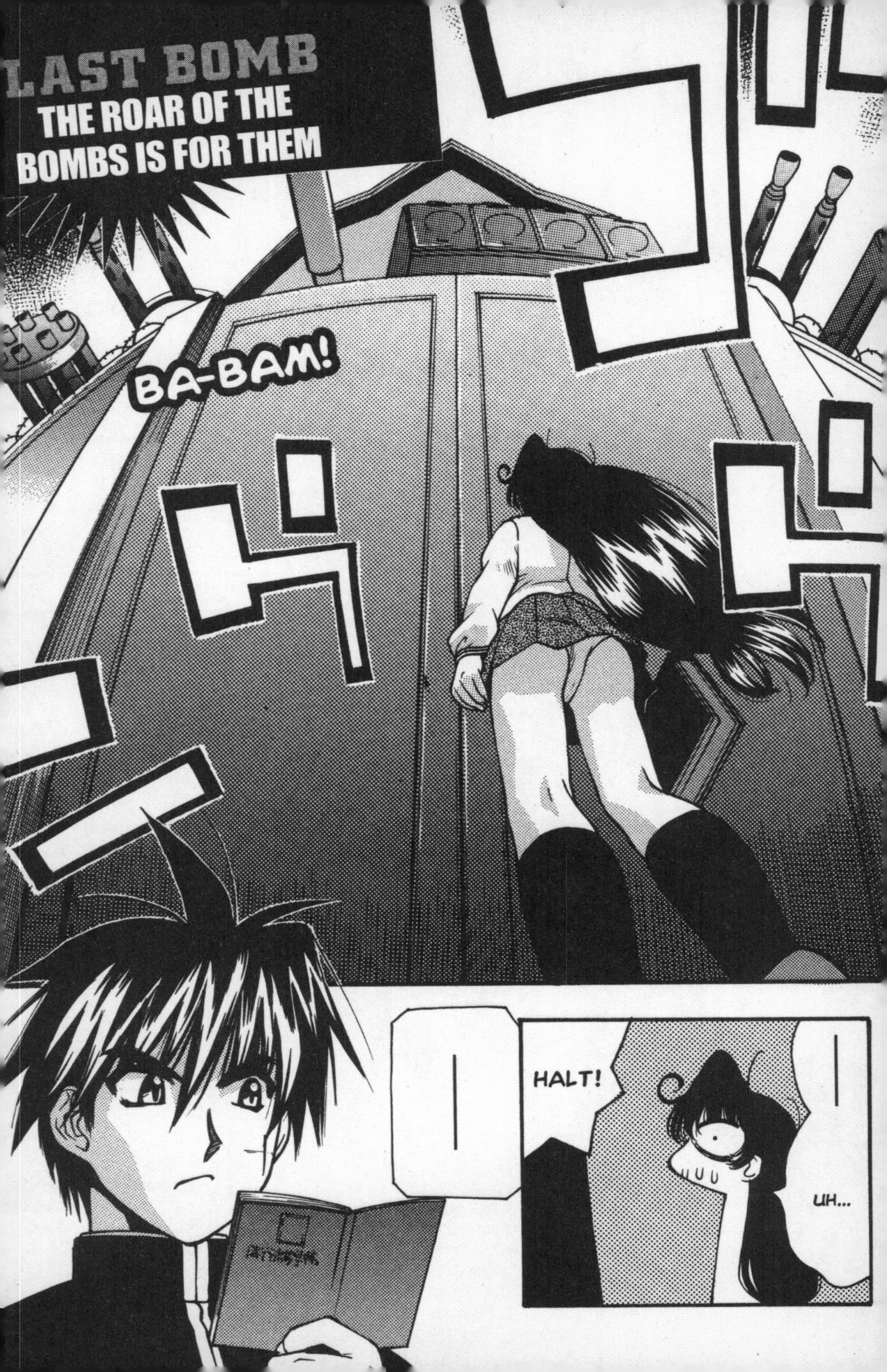
LAST BOMB
THE ROAR OF THE BOMBS IS FOR THEM
BA-BAM!
HALT!
UH...

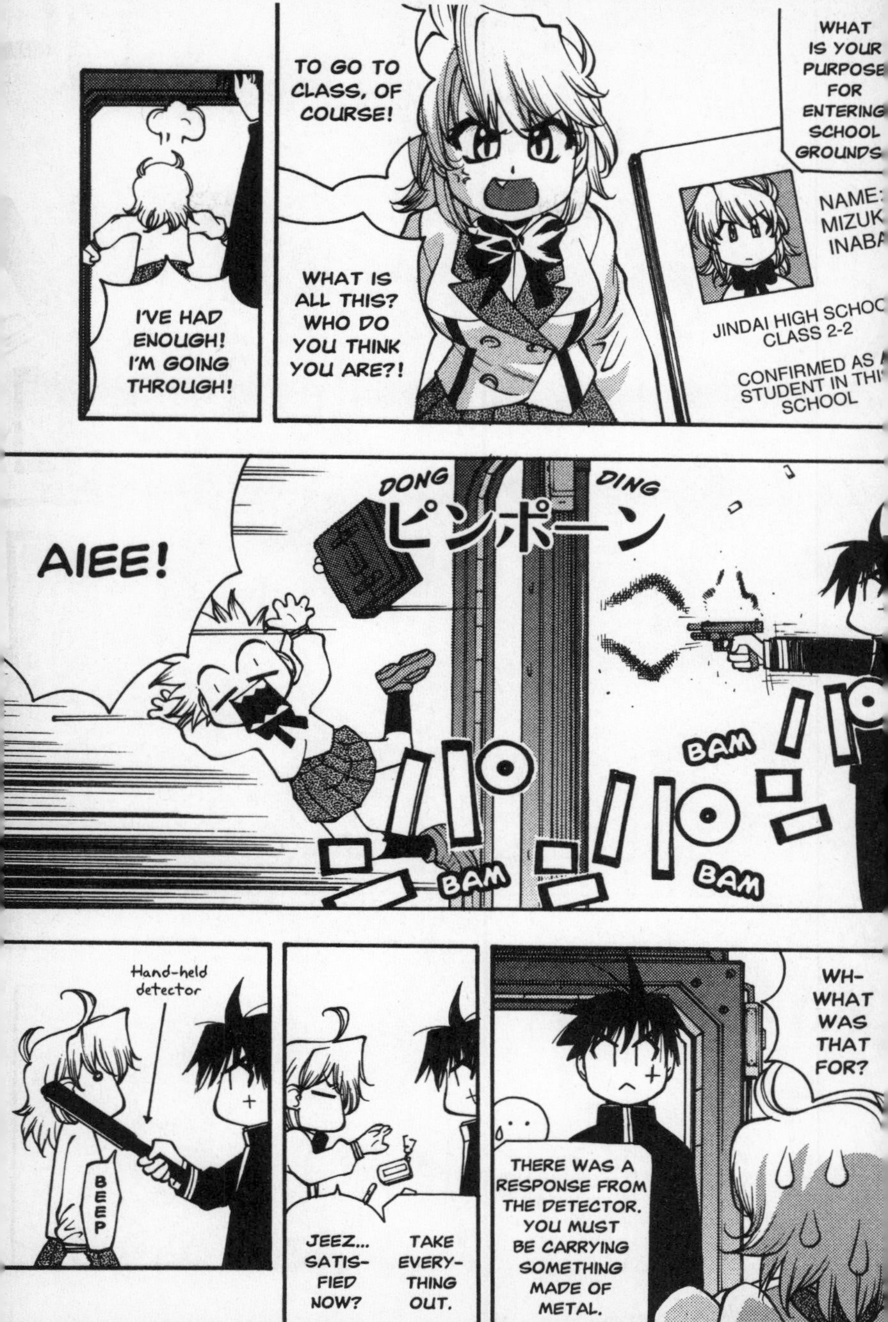

WHAT IS YOUR PURPOSE FOR ENTERING SCHOOL GROUNDS
NAME: MIZUK INABA
JINDAI HIGH SCHOC CLASS 2-2
CONFIRMED AS STUDENT IN THI SCHOOL
TO GO TO CLASS, OF COURSE!
WHAT IS ALL THIS? WHO DO YOU THINK YOU ARE?!
I'VE HAD ENOUGH! I'M GOING THROUGH!
DING
DONG
ピンポーン
AIEE!
BAM
BAM
BAM
WH- WHAT WAS THAT FOR?
THERE WAS A RESPONSE FROM THE DETECTOR. YOU MUST BE CARRYING SOMETHING MADE OF METAL.
TAKE EVERY- THING OUT.
JEEZ... SATIS- FIED NOW?
Hand-held detector
BEEP

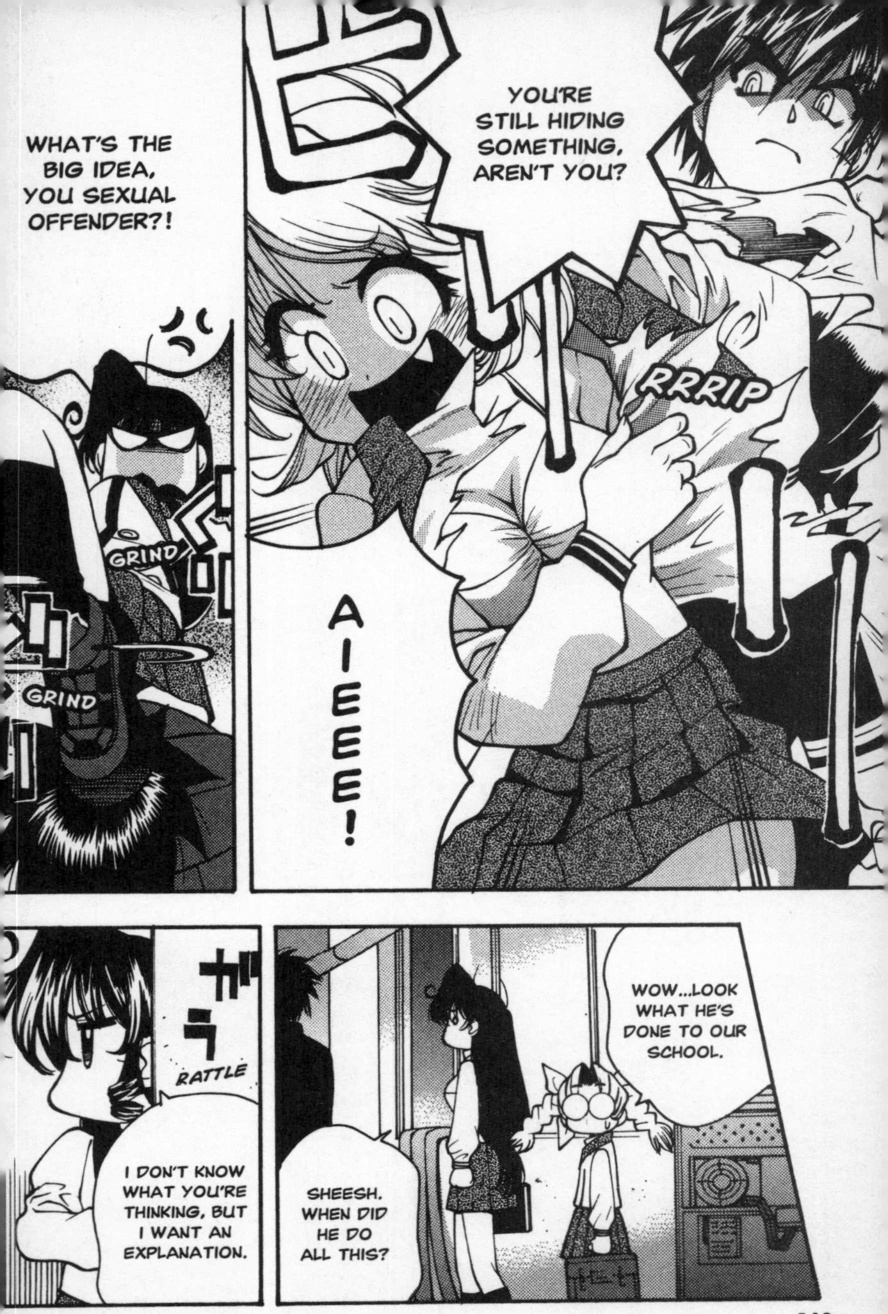
YOU'RE STILL HIDING SOMETHING, AREN'T YOU?
RRRIP
AIEEE!
WHAT'S THE BIG IDEA, YOU SEXUAL OFFENDER?!
GRIND
GRIND
WOW...LOOK WHAT HE'S DONE TO OUR SCHOOL.
SHEESH. WHEN DID HE DO ALL THIS?
RATTLE
I DON'T KNOW WHAT YOU'RE THINKING, BUT I WANT AN EXPLANATION.

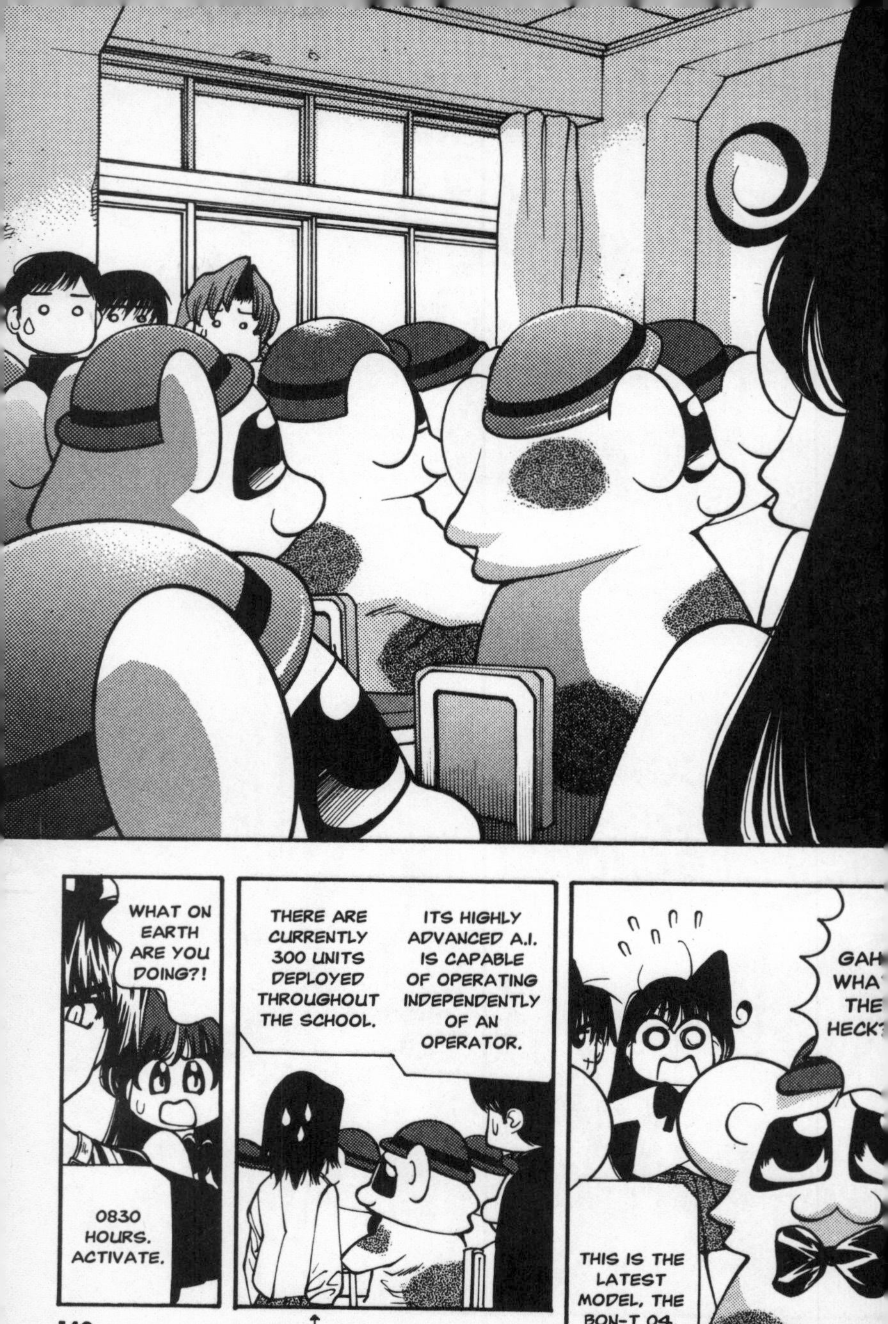
GAH WHA THE HECK?
THIS IS THE LATEST MODEL, THE BON-T 04.
ITS HIGHLY ADVANCED A.I. IS CAPABLE OF OPERATING INDEPENDENTLY OF AN OPERATOR.
THERE ARE CURRENTLY 300 UNITS DEPLOYED THROUGHOUT THE SCHOOL.
WHAT ON EARTH ARE YOU DOING?!
0830 HOURS. ACTIVATE.

↑
In another classroom

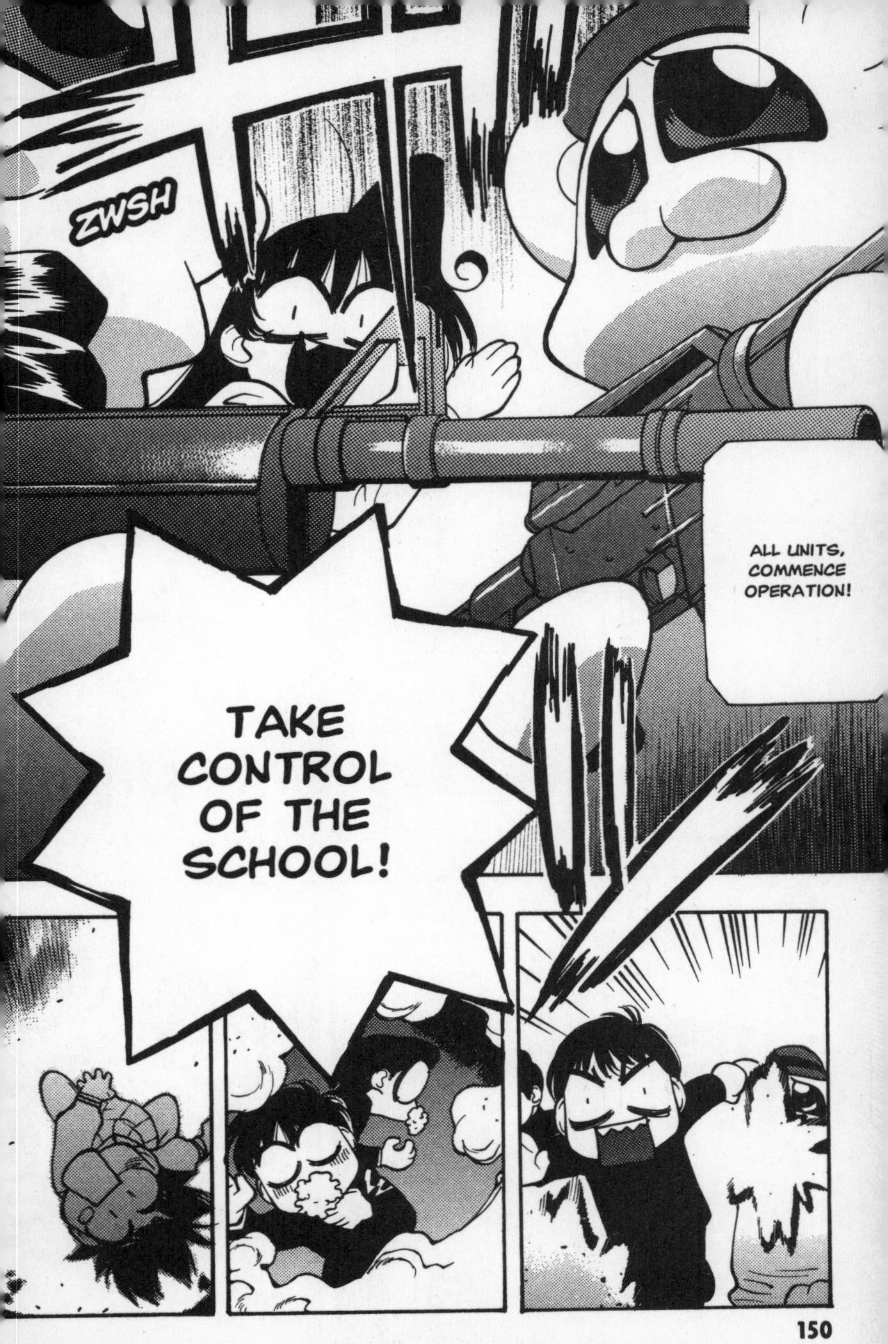
ZWSH
ALL UNITS, COMMENCE OPERATION!
TAKE CONTROL OF THE SCHOOL!

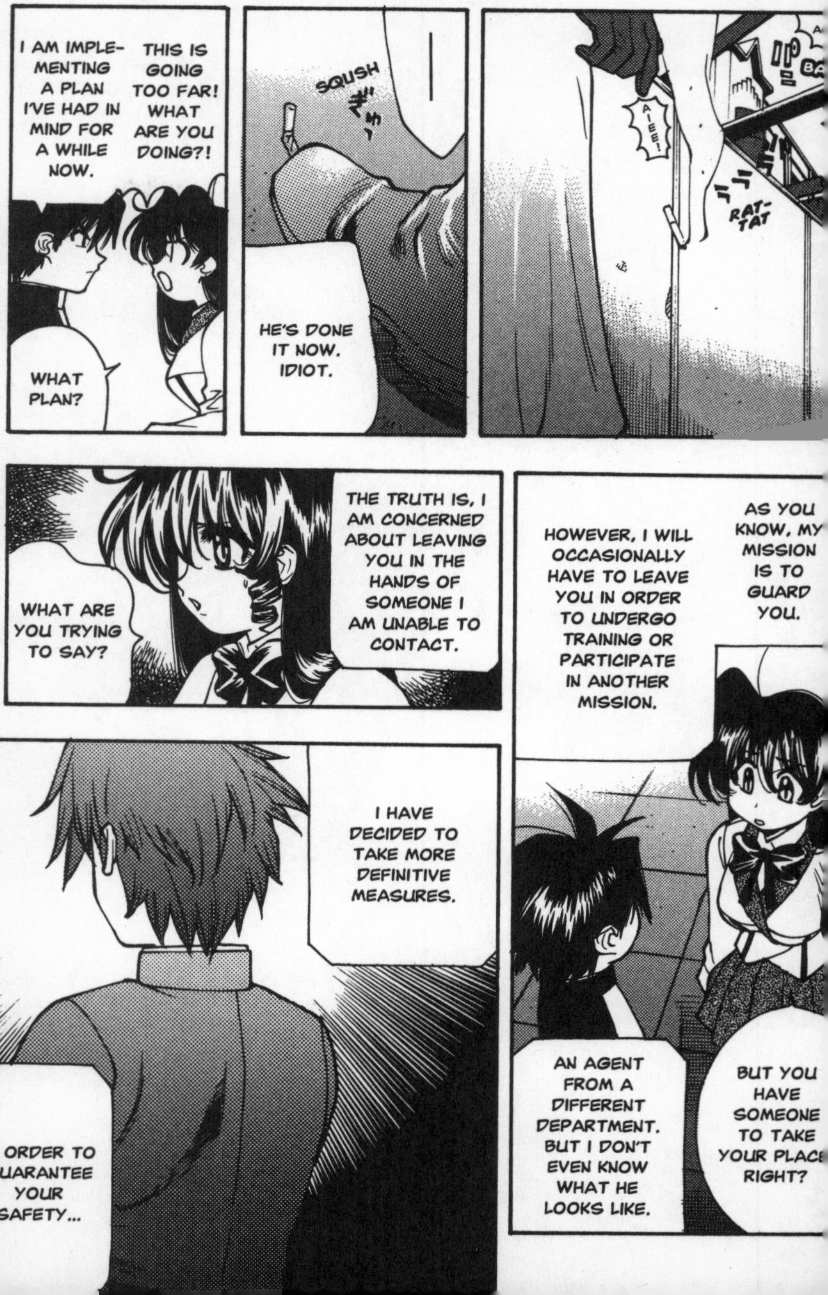

AIEE!
RAT-TAT
SQUSH
HE'S DONE IT NOW. IDIOT.
THIS IS GOING TOO FAR! WHAT ARE YOU DOING?!
I AM IMPLEMENTING A PLAN I'VE HAD IN MIND FOR A WHILE NOW.
WHAT PLAN?
AS YOU KNOW, MY MISSION IS TO GUARD YOU.
HOWEVER, I WILL OCCASIONALLY HAVE TO LEAVE YOU IN ORDER TO UNDERGO TRAINING OR PARTICIPATE IN ANOTHER MISSION.
BUT YOU HAVE SOMEONE TO TAKE YOUR PLACE RIGHT?
AN AGENT FROM A DIFFERENT DEPARTMENT. BUT I DON'T EVEN KNOW WHAT HE LOOKS LIKE.
THE TRUTH IS, I AM CONCERNED ABOUT LEAVING YOU IN THE HANDS OF SOMEONE I AM UNABLE TO CONTACT.
WHAT ARE YOU TRYING TO SAY?
I HAVE DECIDED TO TAKE MORE DEFINITIVE MEASURES.
IN ORDER TO GUARANTEE YOUR SAFETY...

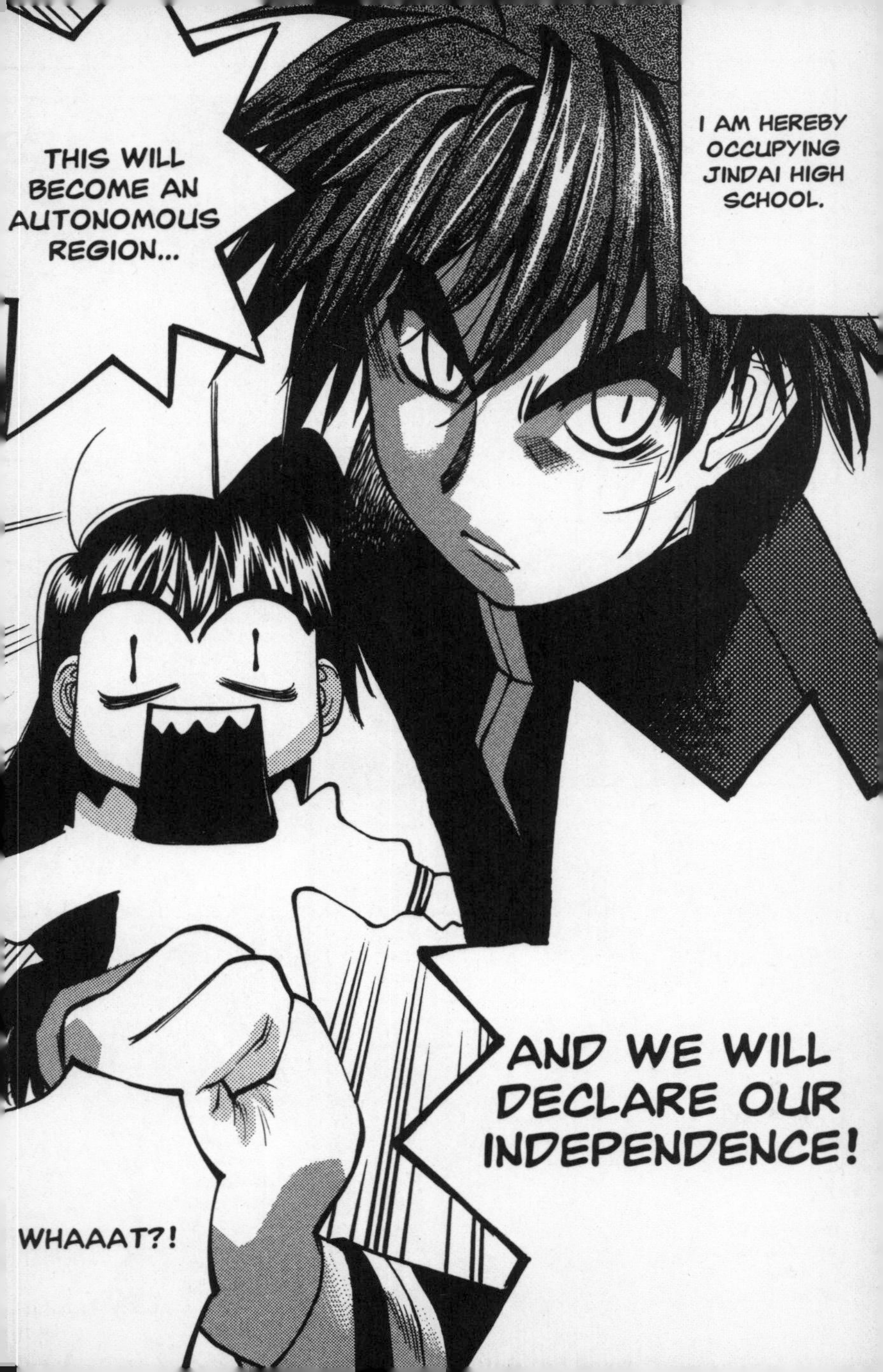
I AM HEREBY OCCUPYING JINDAI HIGH SCHOOL.
THIS WILL BECOME AN AUTONOMOUS REGION...
AND WE WILL DECLARE OUR INDEPENDENCE!
WHAAAT?!

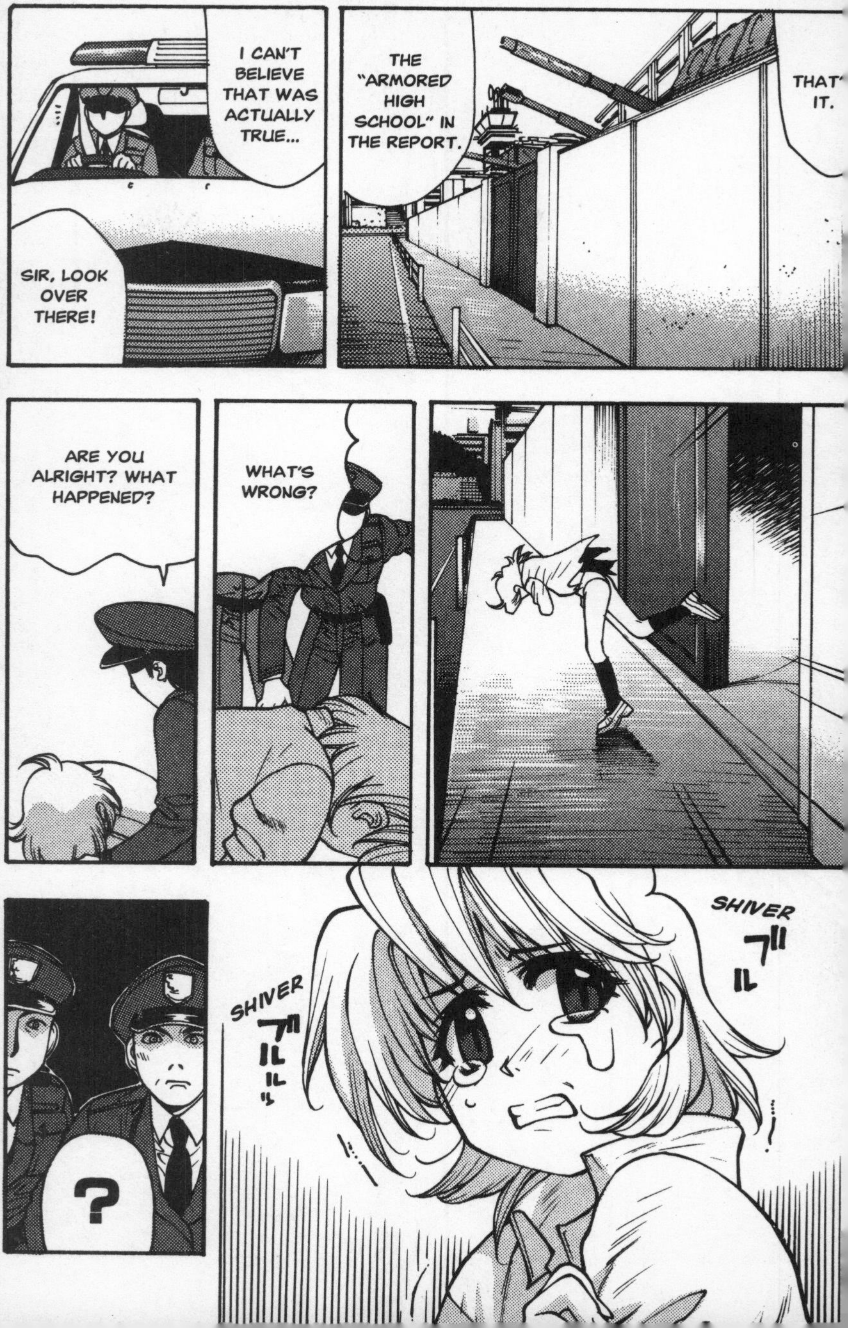
THAT'S IT.
THE "ARMORED HIGH SCHOOL" IN THE REPORT.
I CAN'T BELIEVE THAT WAS ACTUALLY TRUE...
SIR, LOOK OVER THERE!
WHAT'S WRONG?
ARE YOU ALRIGHT? WHAT HAPPENED?
SHIVER
SHIVER
?

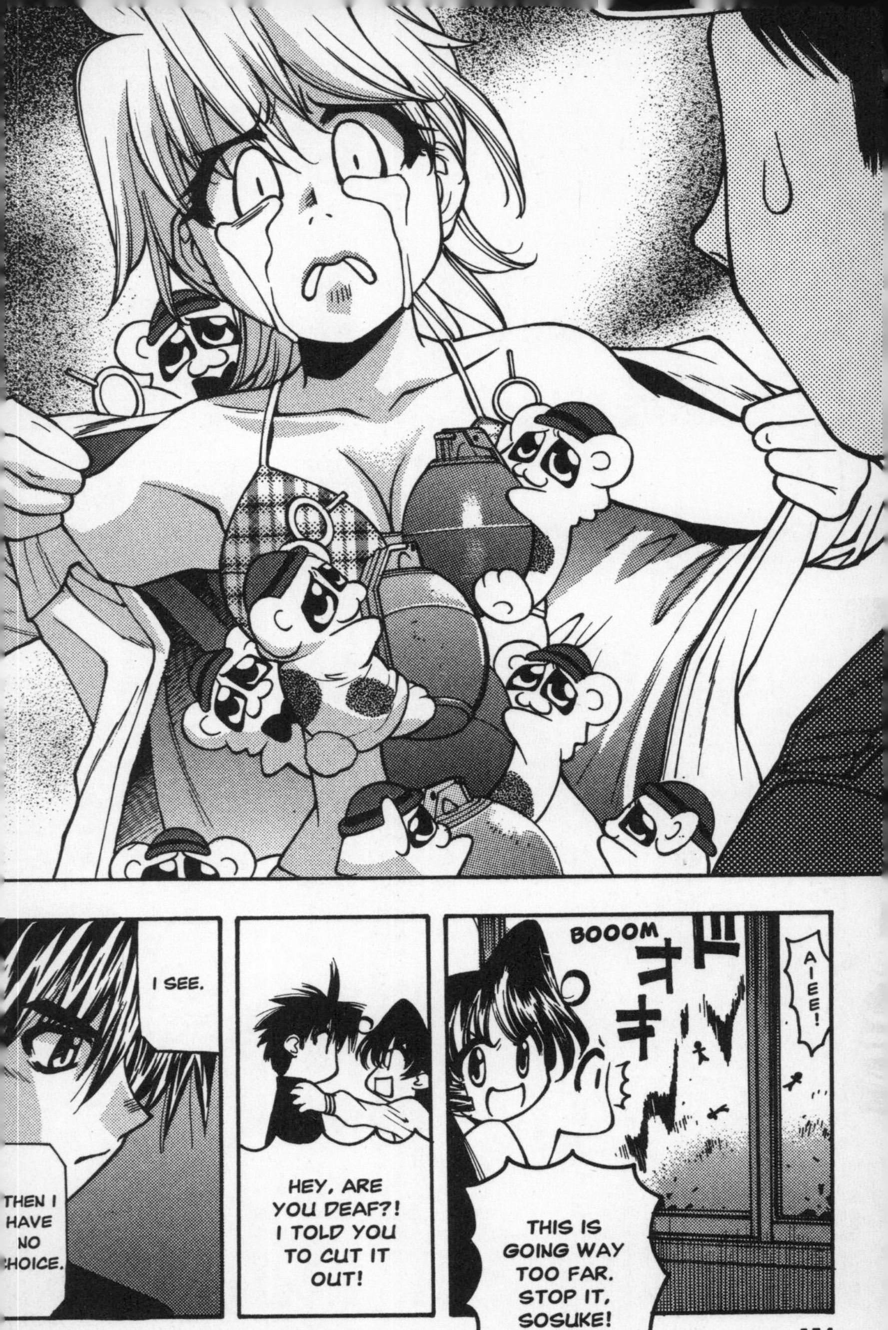
BOOOM
AIEEE!
THIS IS GOING WAY TOO FAR. STOP IT, SOSUKE!
HEY, ARE YOU DEAF?! I TOLD YOU TO CUT IT OUT!
I SEE.
THEN I HAVE NO CHOICE.

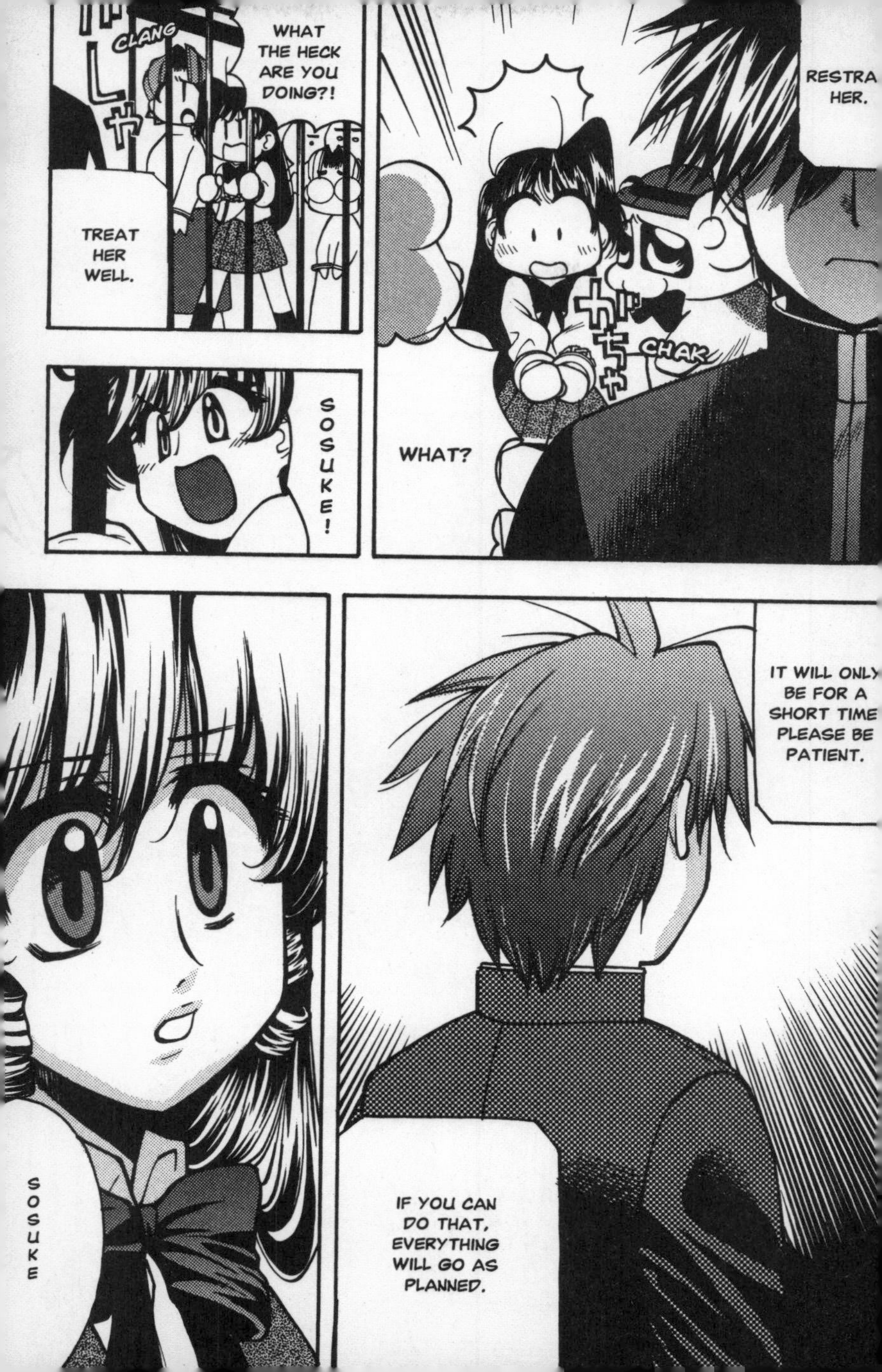

RESTRA HER.
CHAK
WHAT?
WHAT THE HECK ARE YOU DOING?!
CLANG
TREAT HER WELL.
SOSUKE!
IT WILL ONLY BE FOR A SHORT TIME PLEASE BE PATIENT.
IF YOU CAN DO THAT, EVERYTHING WILL GO AS PLANNED.
SOSUKE

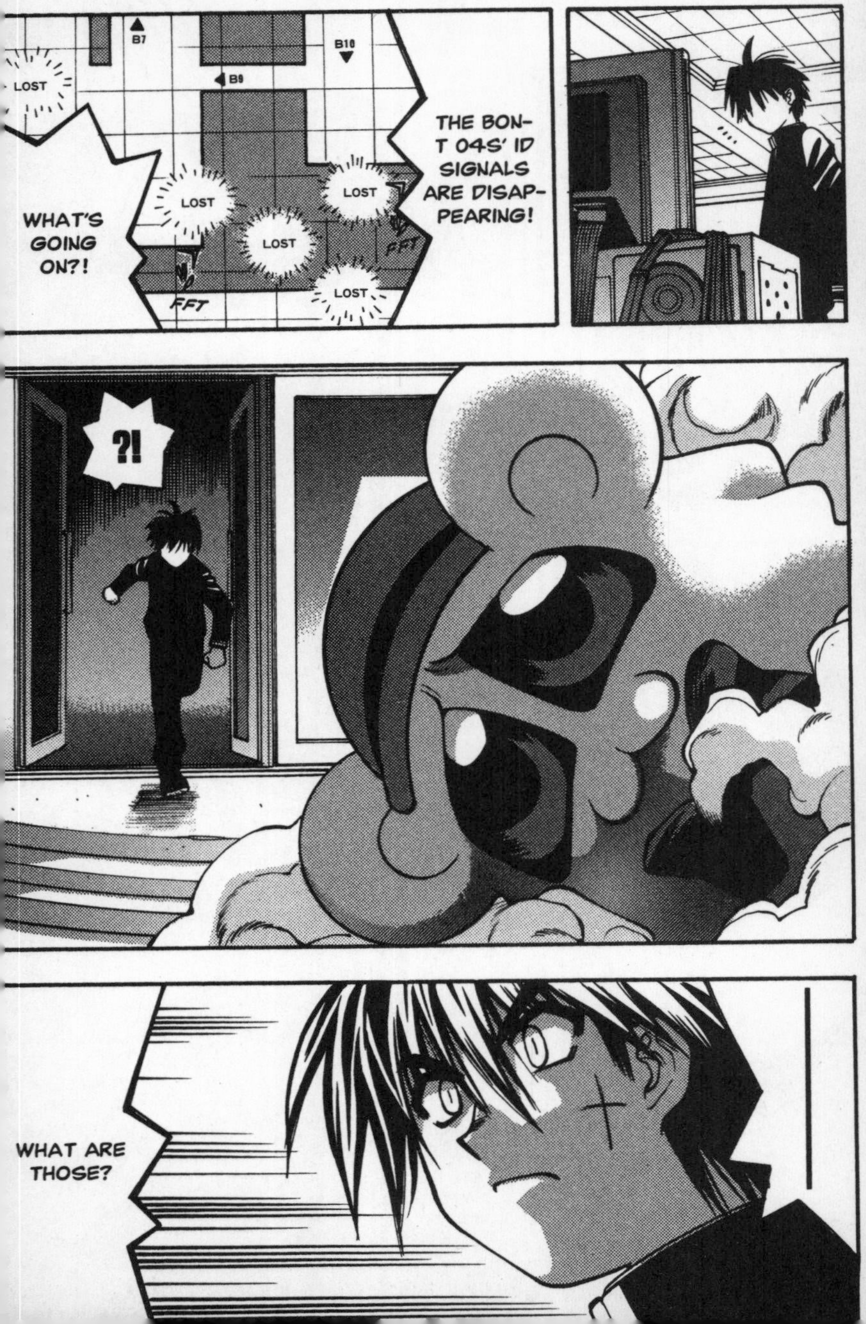
THE BON-T 04S' ID SIGNALS ARE DISAP-PEARING!
B10
B7
B9
LOST
WHAT'S GOING ON?!
LOST
LOST
LOST
LOST
FFT
FFT
?!
WHAT ARE THOSE?

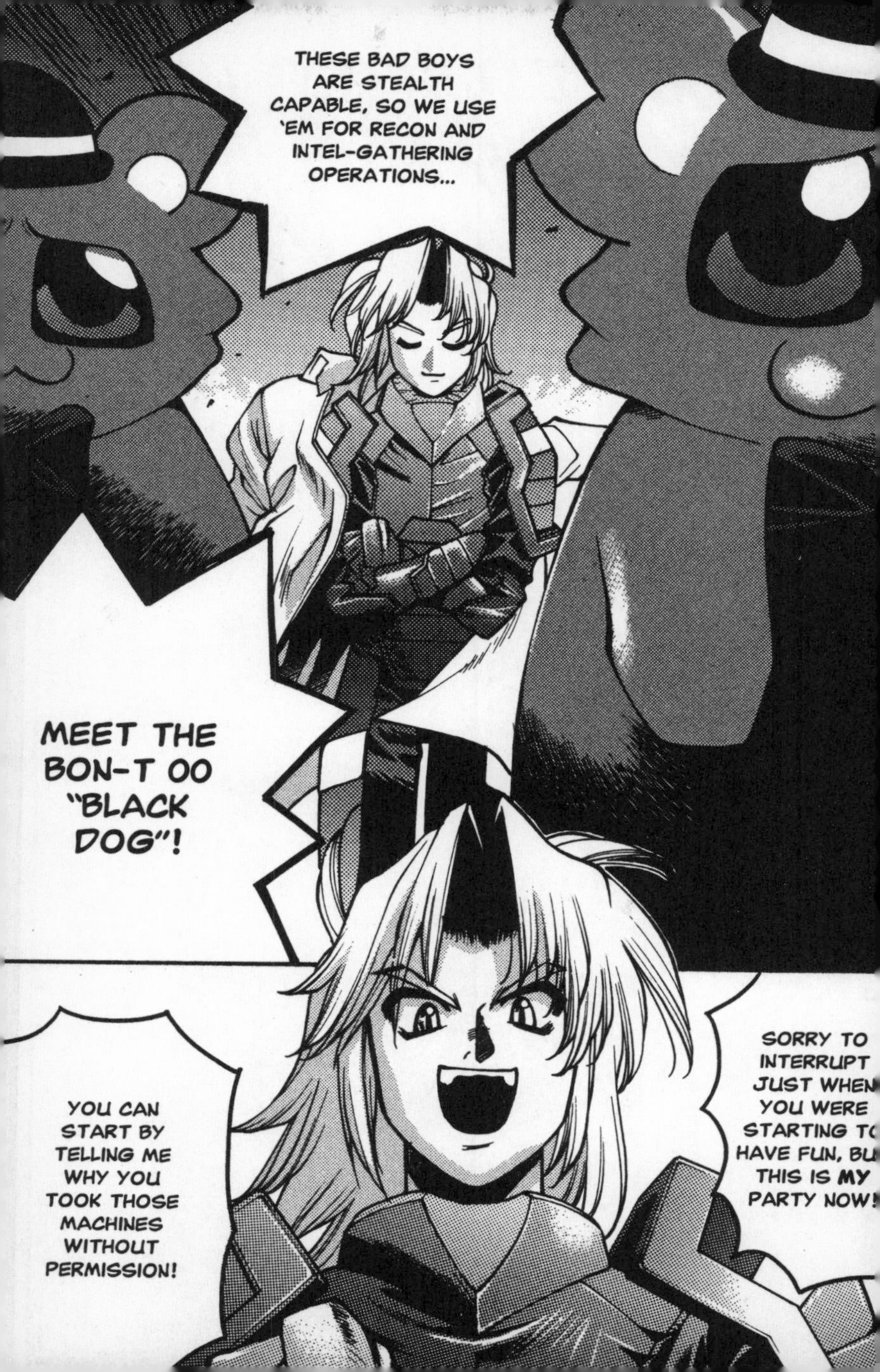
THESE BAD BOYS ARE STEALTH CAPABLE, SO WE USE 'EM FOR RECON AND INTEL-GATHERING OPERATIONS...
MEET THE BON-T 00 "BLACK DOG"!
SORRY TO INTERRUPT JUST WHEN YOU WERE STARTING TO HAVE FUN, BUT THIS IS MY PARTY NOW!
YOU CAN START BY TELLING ME WHY YOU TOOK THOSE MACHINES WITHOUT PERMISSION!

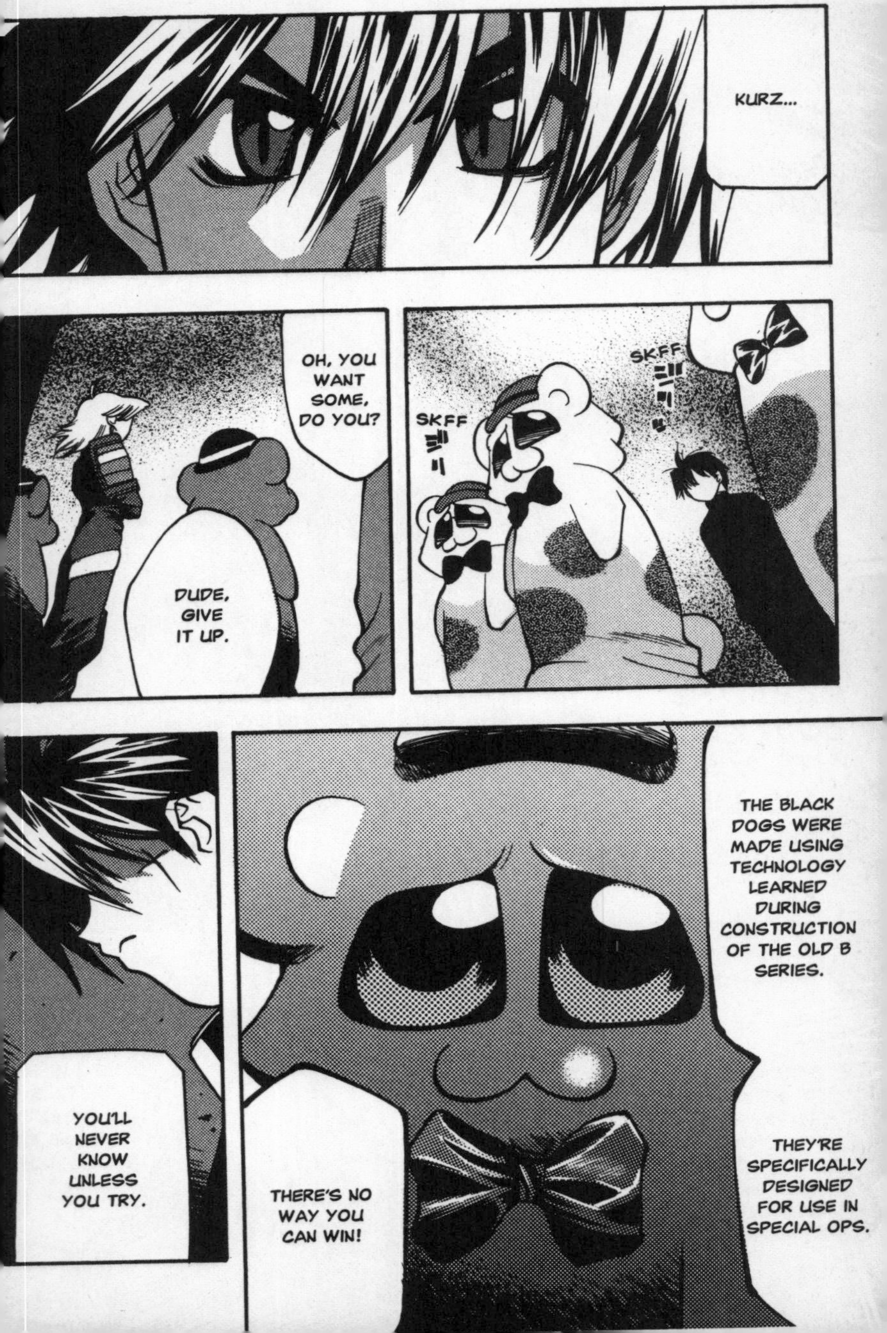
KURZ...
SKFF
SKFF
OH, YOU WANT SOME, DO YOU?
DUDE, GIVE IT UP.
THE BLACK DOGS WERE MADE USING TECHNOLOGY LEARNED DURING CONSTRUCTION OF THE OLD B SERIES.
THEY'RE SPECIFICALLY DESIGNED FOR USE IN SPECIAL OPS.
THERE'S NO WAY YOU CAN WIN!
YOU'LL NEVER KNOW UNLESS YOU TRY.

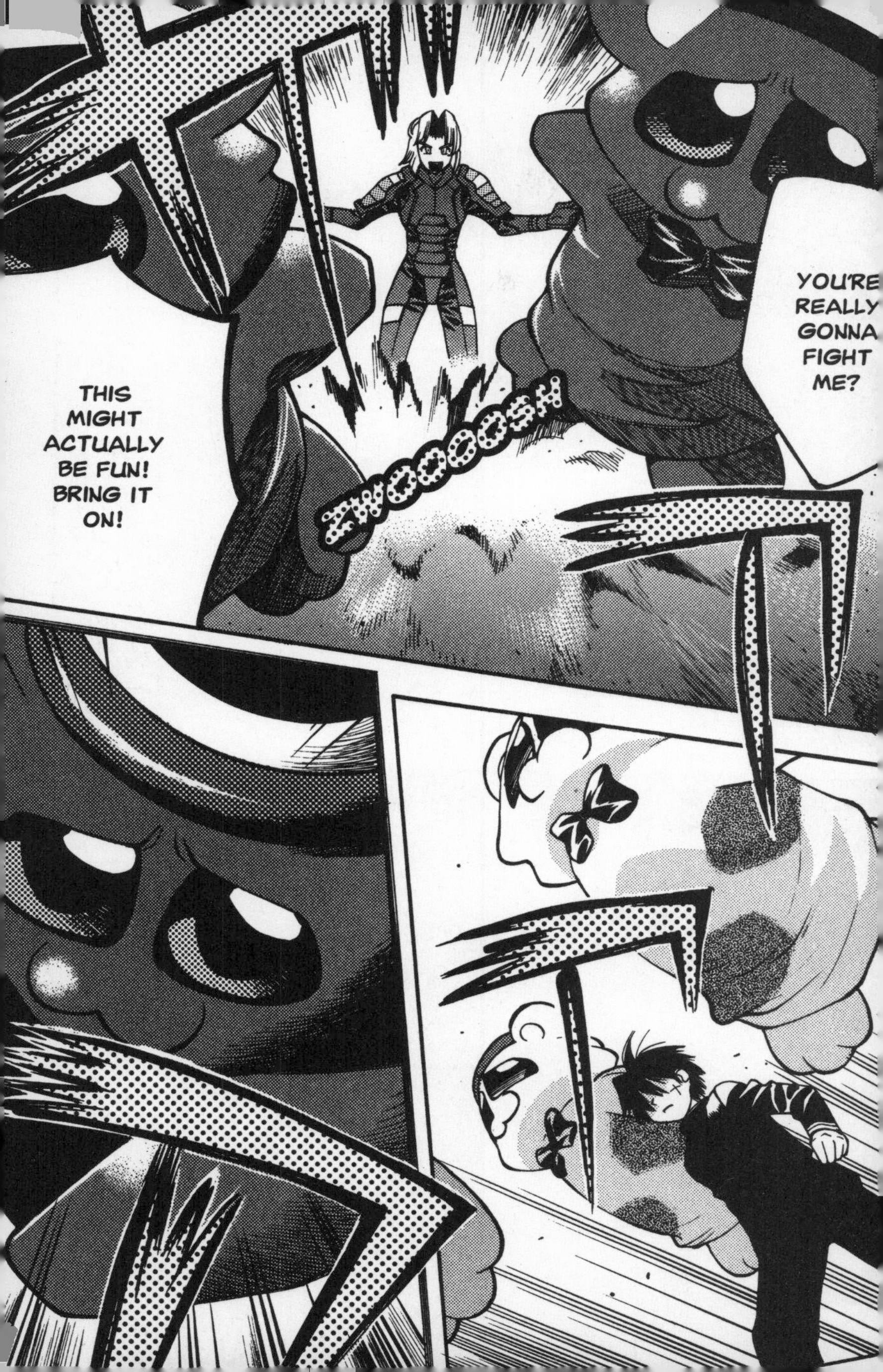
YOU'RE REALLY GONNA FIGHT ME?
THIS MIGHT ACTUALLY BE FUN! BRING IT ON!
ZWOOOOSH

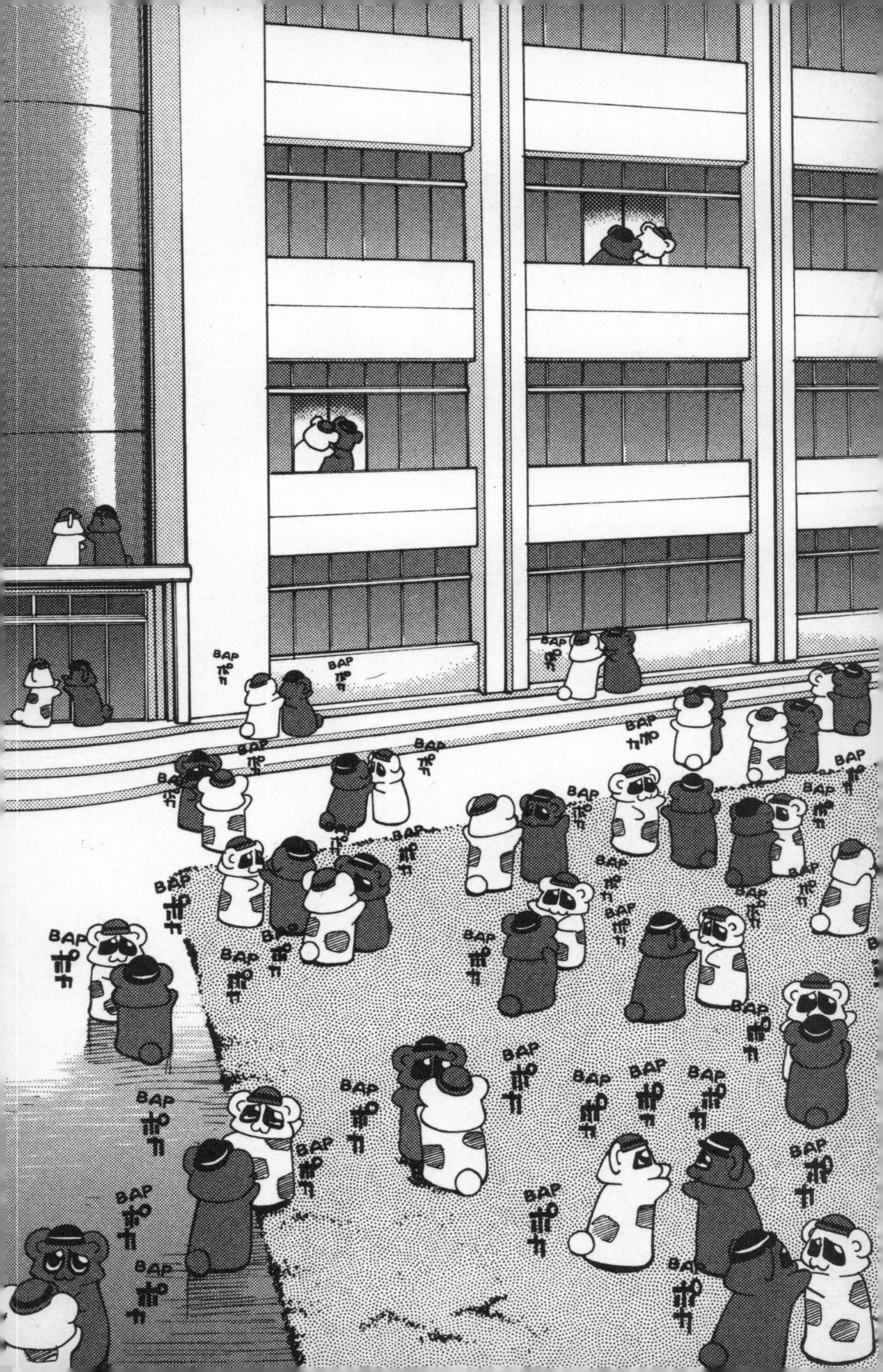
BAP ポカ
BAP ポカ
BAP ポカ
BAP ポカ
BAP ポカ
BAP ポカ
BAP ポカ
BAP ポカ
BAP ポカ
BAP ポカ
BAP ポカ
BAP ポカ
BAP ポカ
BAP ポカ
BAP ポカ
BAP ポカ
BAP ポカ
BAP ポカ
BAP ポカ
BAP ポカ
BAP ポカ
BAP ポカ
BAP ポカ
BAP ポカ
BAP ポカ
BAP ポカ
BAP ポカ
BAP ポカ
BAP ポカ
BAP ポカ
BAP ポカ
BAP ポカ
BAP ポカ
BAP ポカ
BAP ポカ
BAP ポカ
BAP ポカ
BAP ポカ

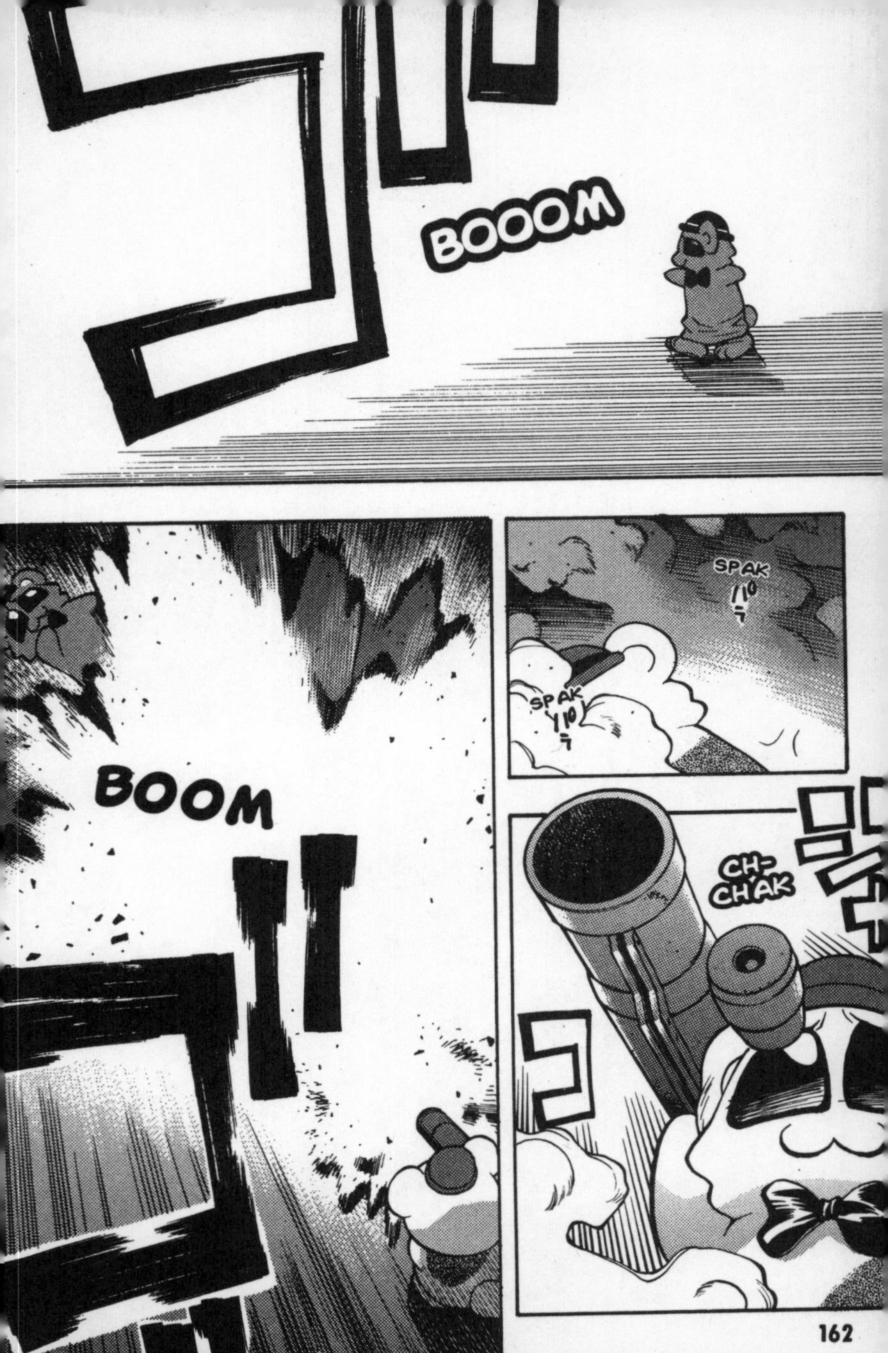
BOOOM
SPAK
SPAK
BOOM
CH-CHAK

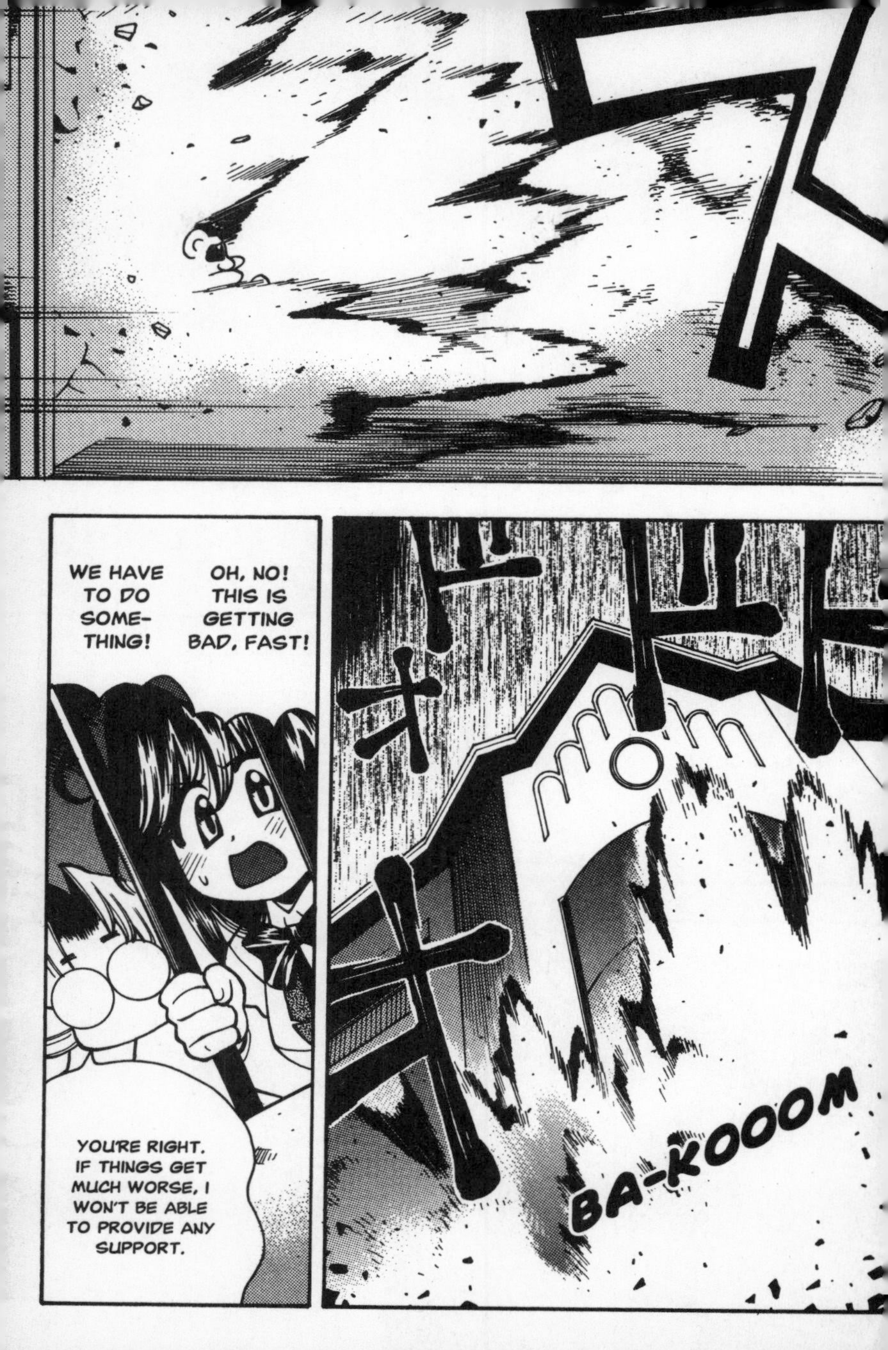
BA-KOOOM
OH, NO! THIS IS GETTING BAD, FAST!
WE HAVE TO DO SOME-THING!
YOU'RE RIGHT. IF THINGS GET MUCH WORSE, I WON'T BE ABLE TO PROVIDE ANY SUPPORT.

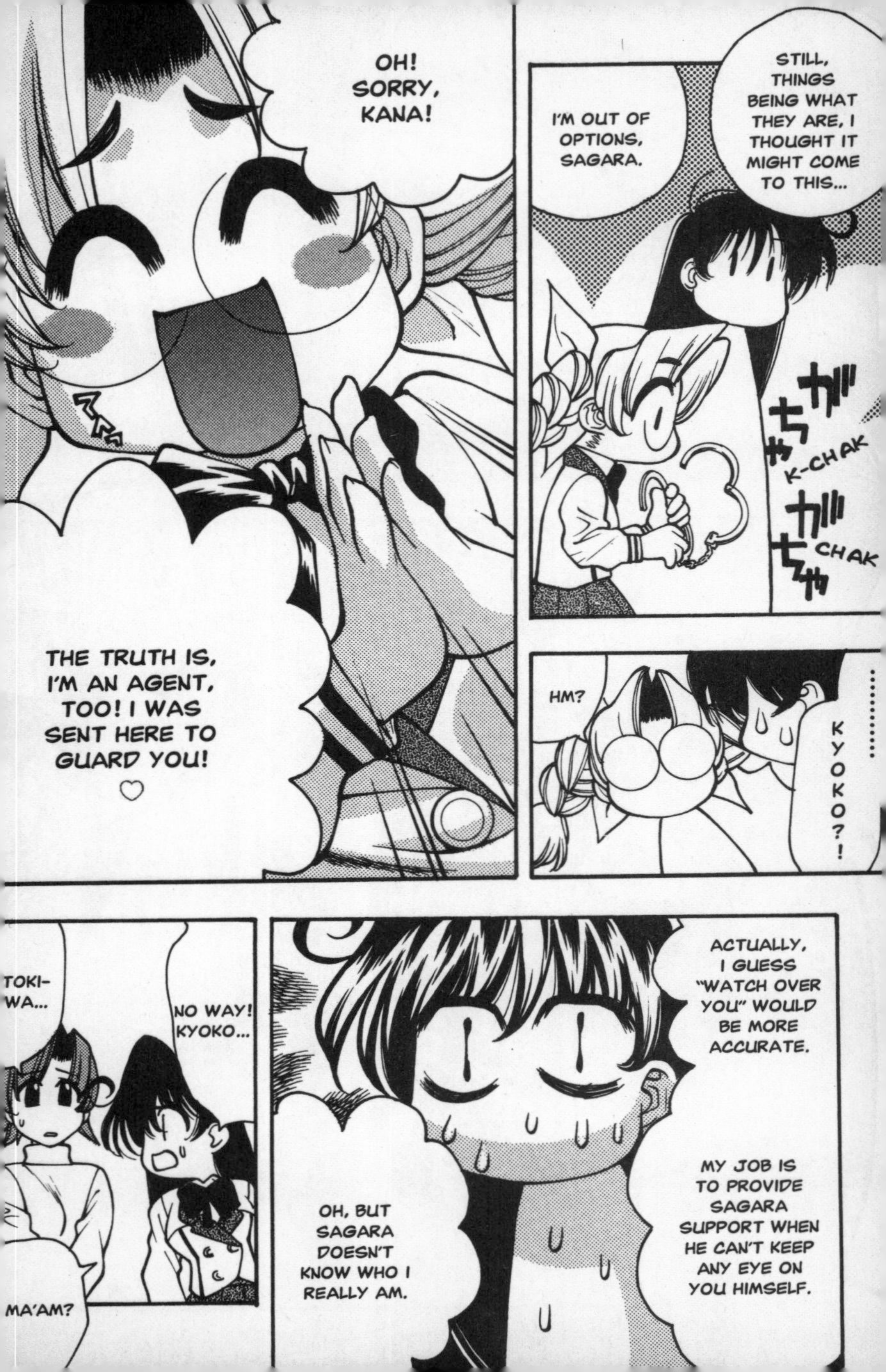

STILL, THINGS BEING WHAT THEY ARE, I THOUGHT IT MIGHT COME TO THIS...
I'M OUT OF OPTIONS, SAGARA.
K-CHAK
CHAK
HM?
KYOKO?!
OH! SORRY, KANA!
THE TRUTH IS, I'M AN AGENT, TOO! I WAS SENT HERE TO GUARD YOU! ♡
ACTUALLY, I GUESS "WATCH OVER YOU" WOULD BE MORE ACCURATE.
MY JOB IS TO PROVIDE SAGARA SUPPORT WHEN HE CAN'T KEEP ANY EYE ON YOU HIMSELF.
OH, BUT SAGARA DOESN'T KNOW WHO I REALLY AM.
NO WAY! KYOKO...
TOKI-WA...
MA'AM?

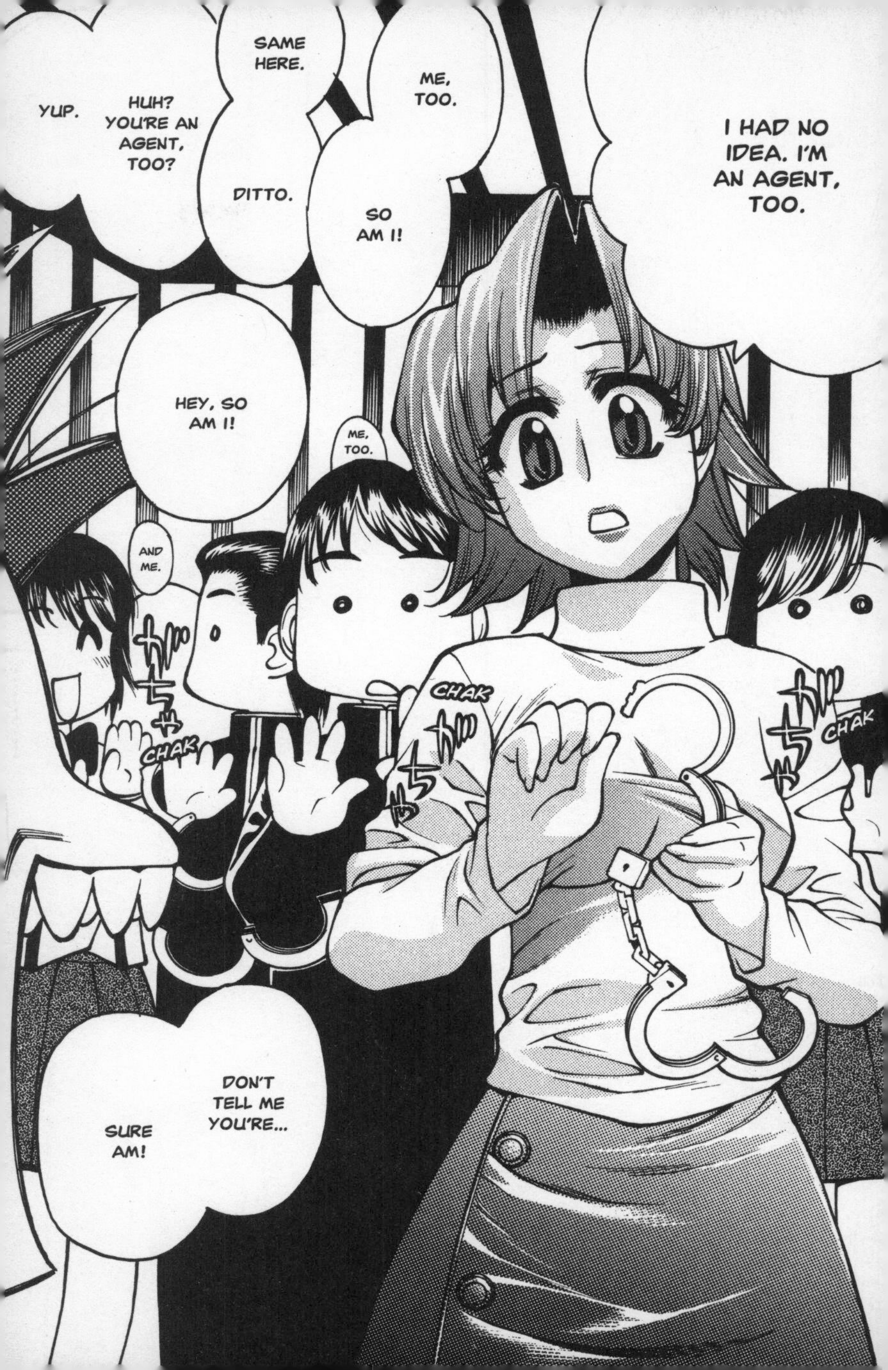
I HAD NO IDEA. I'M AN AGENT, TOO.
ME, TOO.
SO AM I!
SAME HERE.
DITTO.
HUH? YOU'RE AN AGENT, TOO?
YUP.
HEY, SO AM I!
ME, TOO.
AND ME.
CHAK
CHAK
CHAK
DON'T TELL ME YOU'RE...
SURE AM!

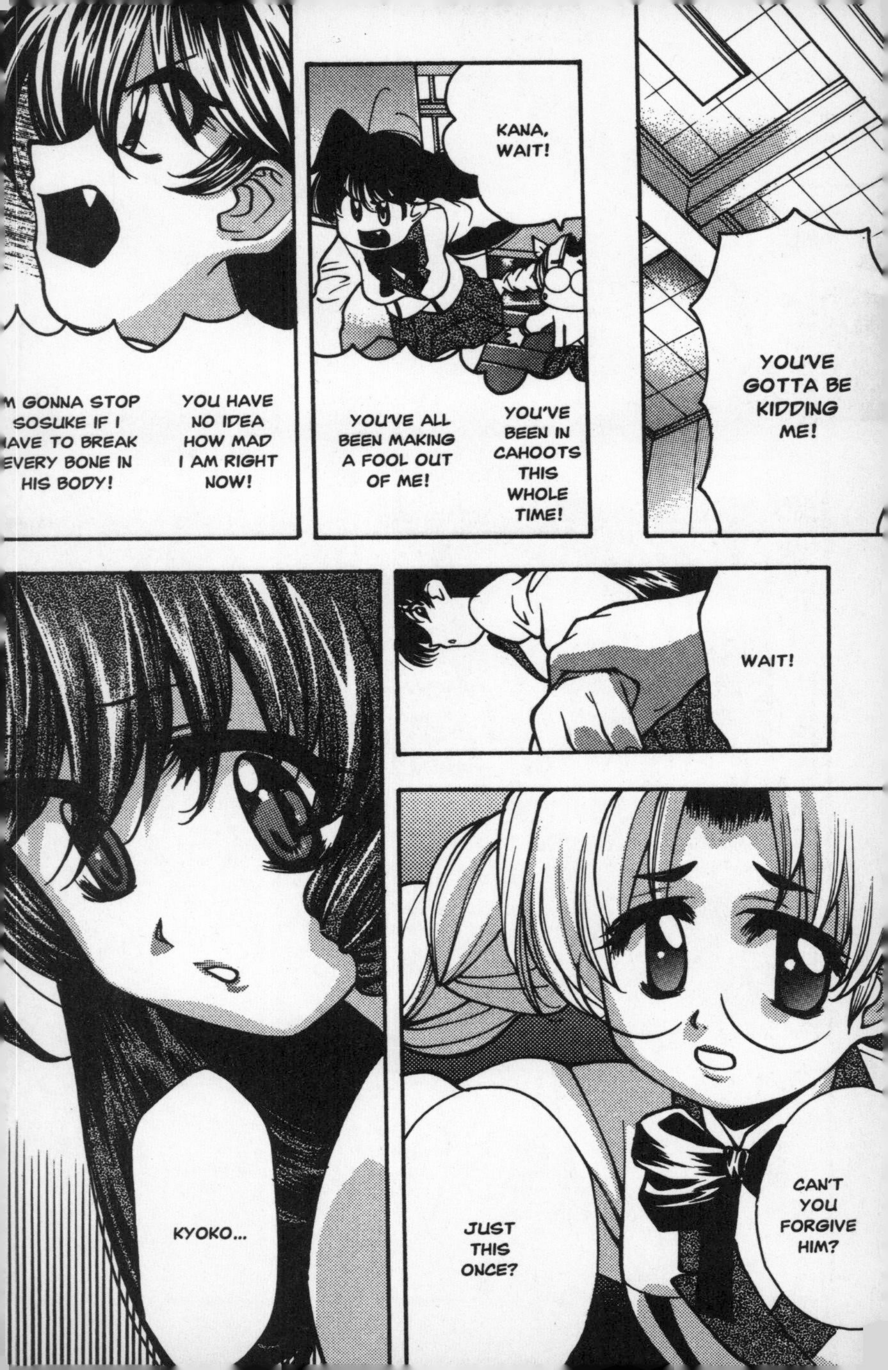
YOU'VE GOTTA BE KIDDING ME!
KANA, WAIT!
YOU'VE BEEN IN CAHOOTS THIS WHOLE TIME!
YOU'VE ALL BEEN MAKING A FOOL OUT OF ME!
YOU HAVE NO IDEA HOW MAD I AM RIGHT NOW!
M GONNA STOP SOSUKE IF I AVE TO BREAK EVERY BONE IN HIS BODY!
WAIT!
CAN'T YOU FORGIVE HIM?
JUST THIS ONCE?
KYOKO...

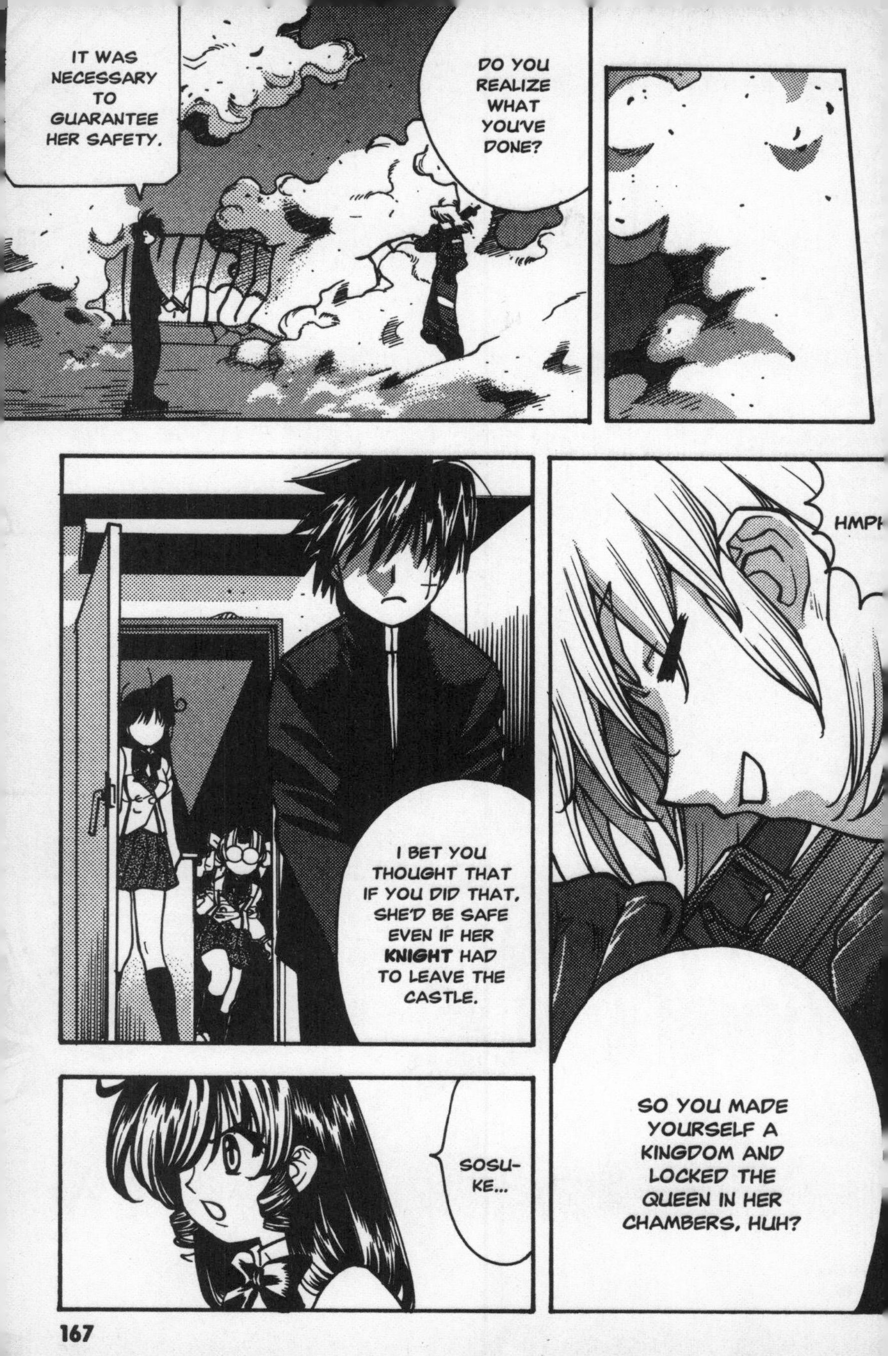

DO YOU REALIZE WHAT YOU'VE DONE?
IT WAS NECESSARY TO GUARANTEE HER SAFETY.
HMPH
SO YOU MADE YOURSELF A KINGDOM AND LOCKED THE QUEEN IN HER CHAMBERS, HUH?
I BET YOU THOUGHT THAT IF YOU DID THAT, SHE'D BE SAFE EVEN IF HER KNIGHT HAD TO LEAVE THE CASTLE.
SOSU-KE...

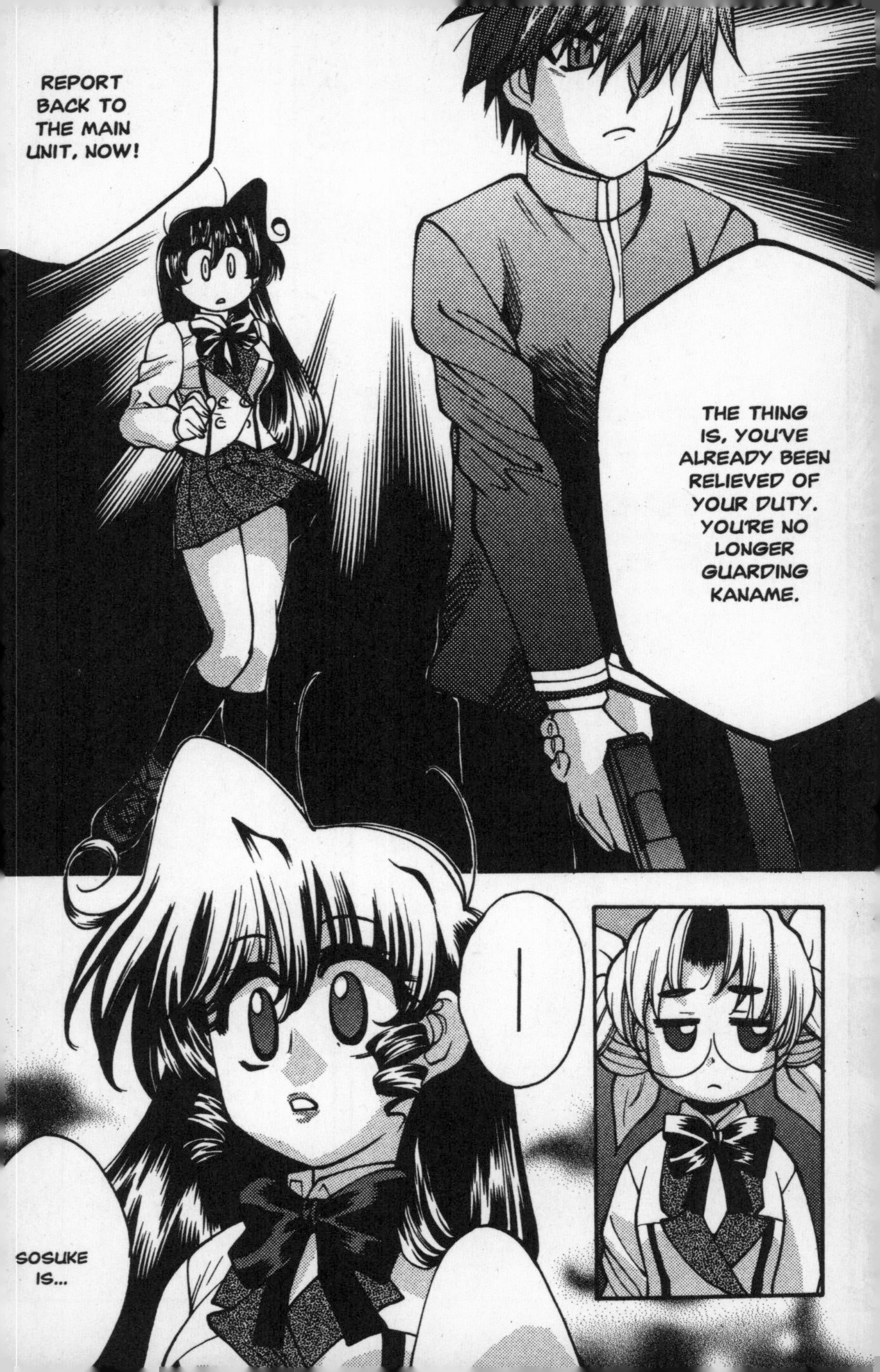
THE THING IS, YOU'VE ALREADY BEEN RELIEVED OF YOUR DUTY. YOU'RE NO LONGER GUARDING KANAME.
REPORT BACK TO THE MAIN UNIT, NOW!
SOSUKE IS...

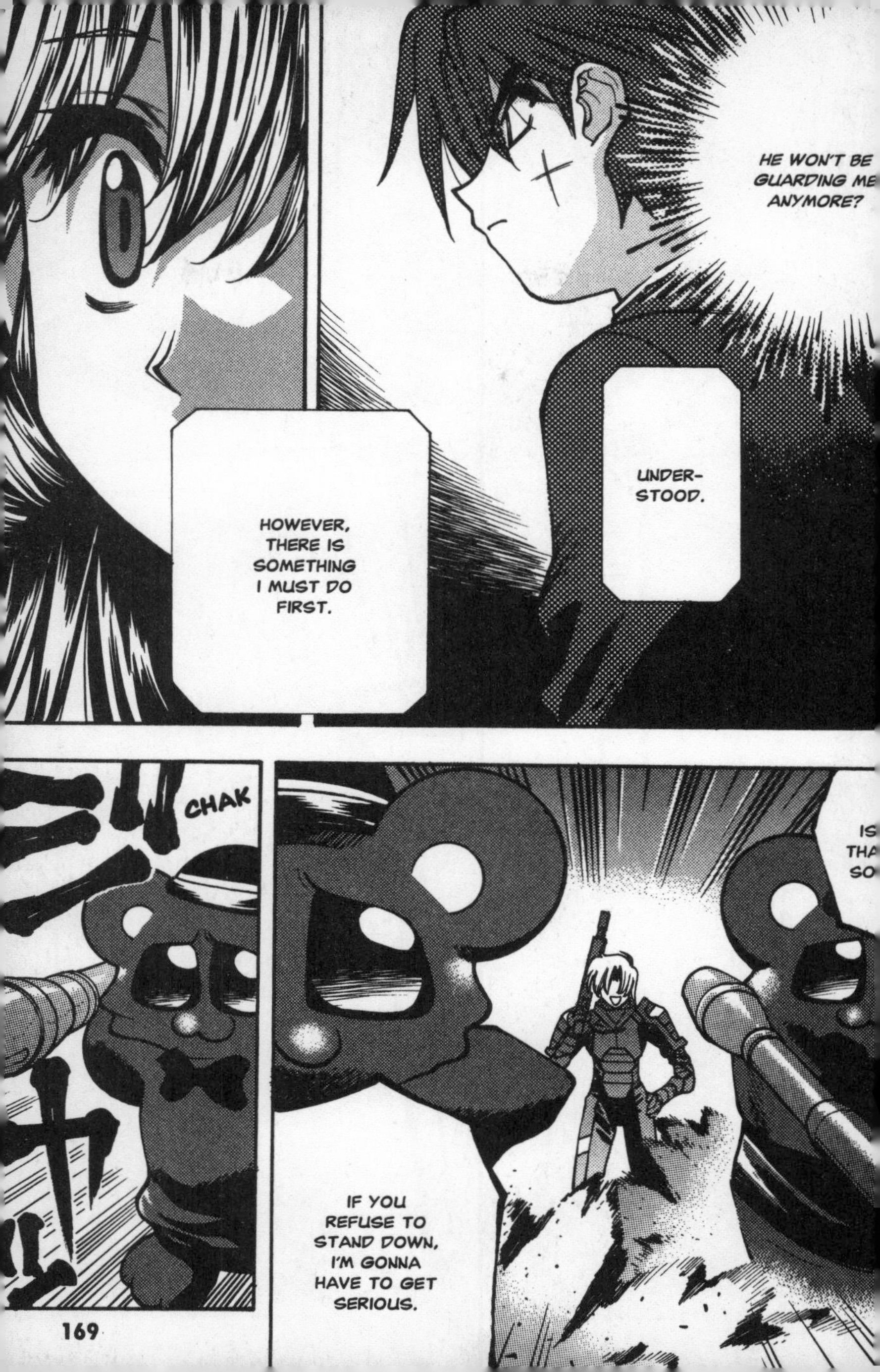
HE WON'T BE GUARDING ME ANYMORE?
UNDER-STOOD.
HOWEVER, THERE IS SOMETHING I MUST DO FIRST.
IS THA SO
IF YOU REFUSE TO STAND DOWN, I'M GONNA HAVE TO GET SERIOUS.
CHAK

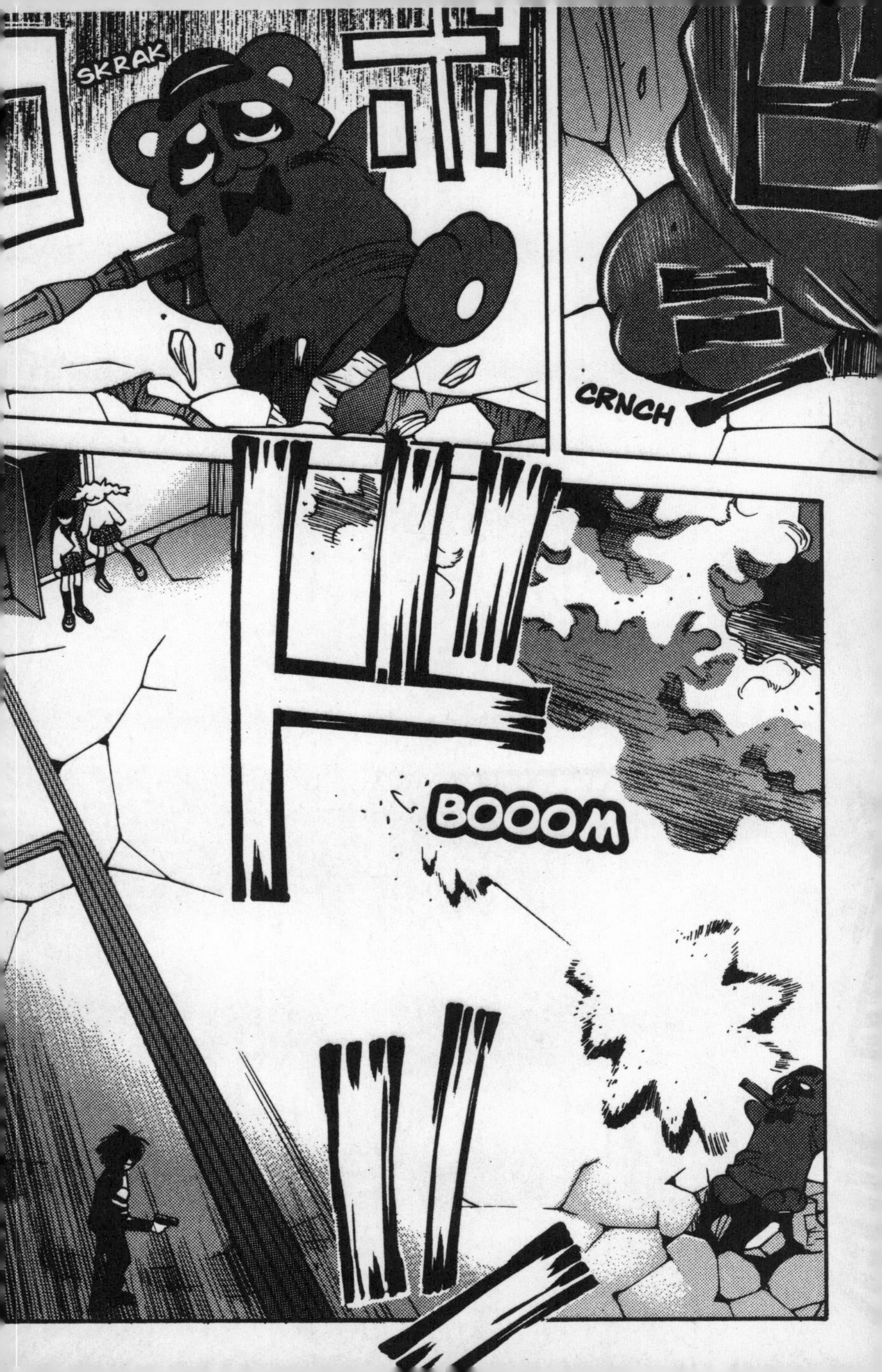
SKRAK
CRNCH
BOOOM

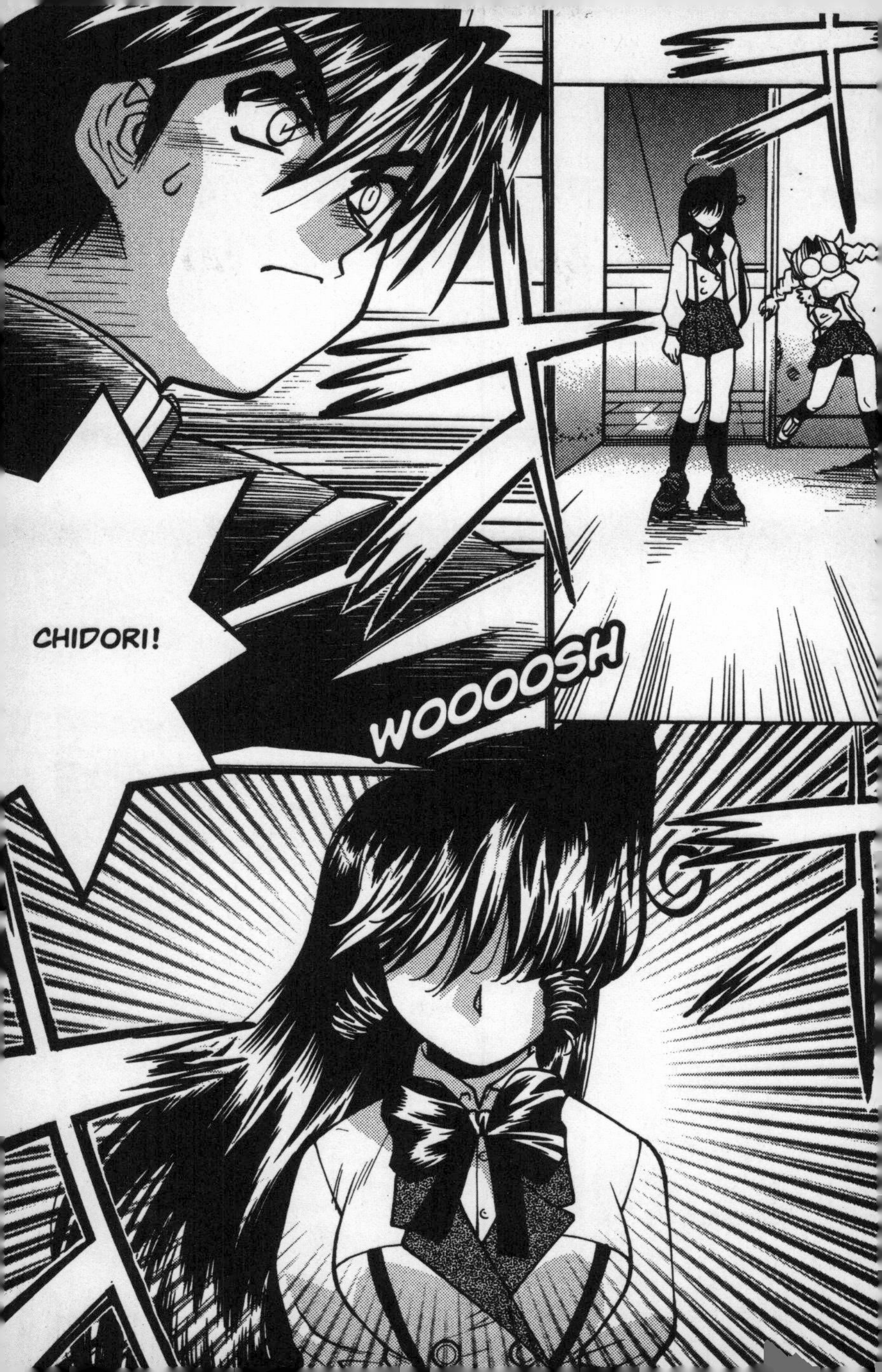
CHIDORI!
WOOOOOSH

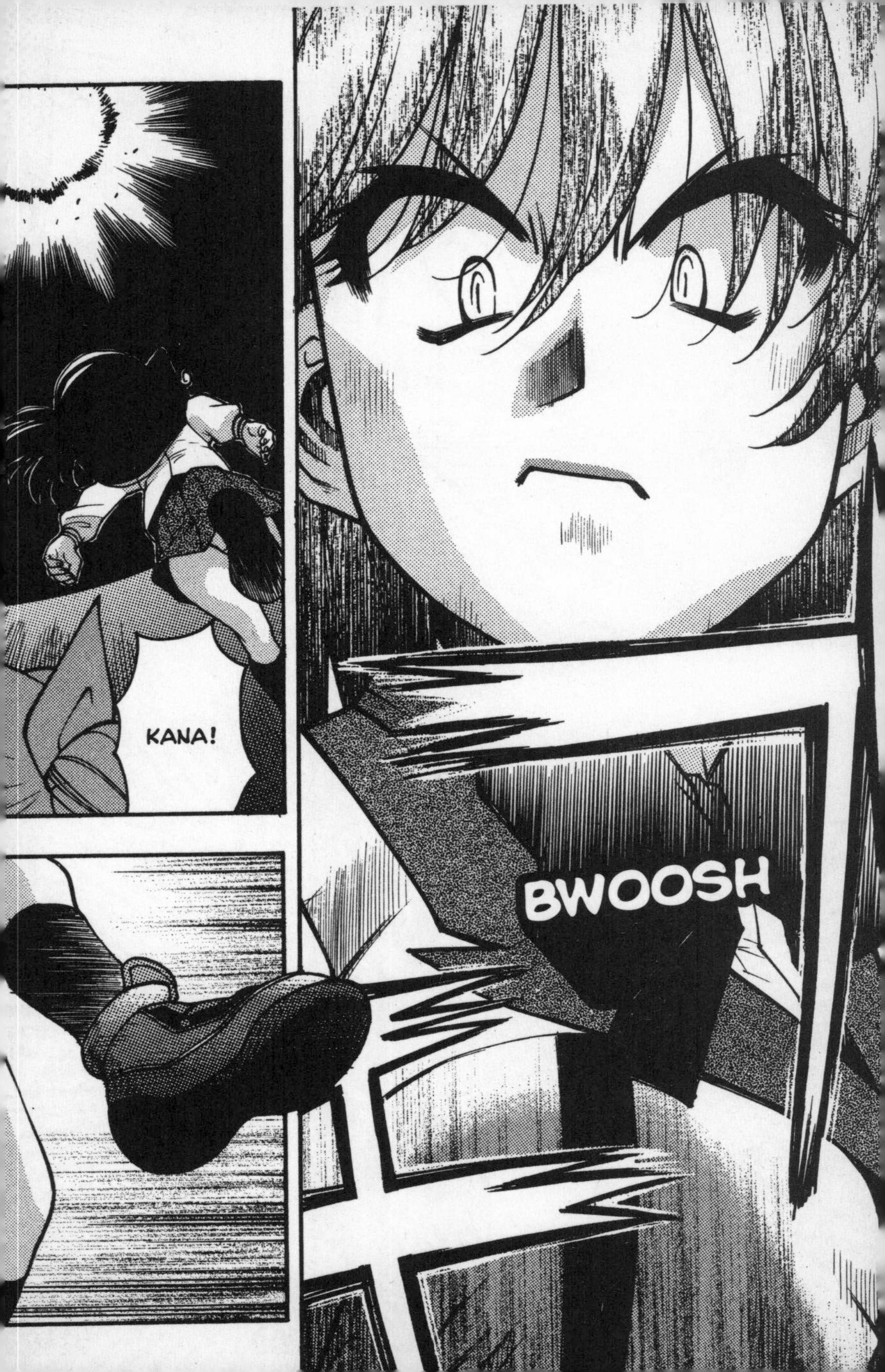
BWOOSH
KANA!

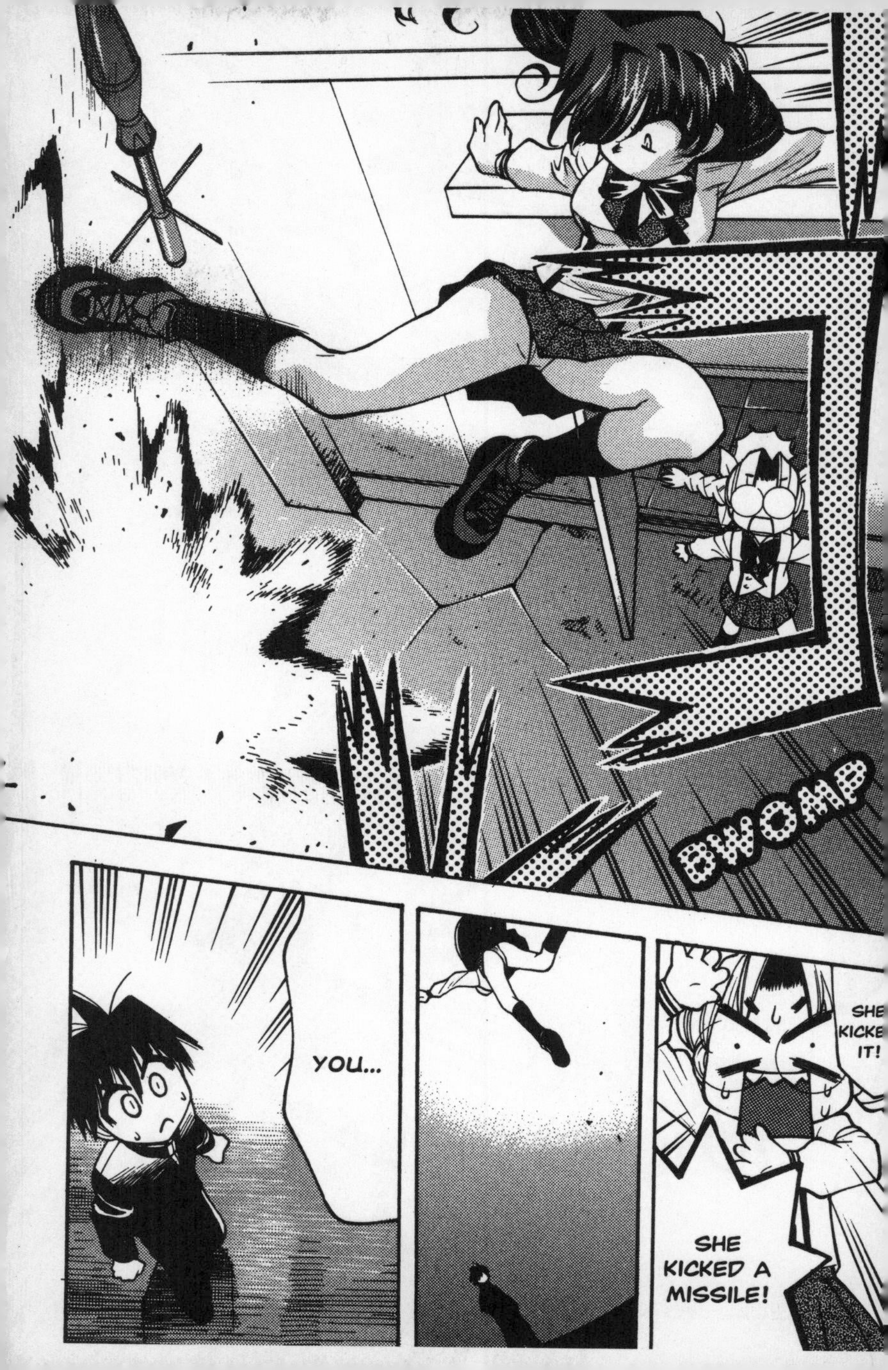
DWOMP
SHE KICKED IT!
SHE KICKED A MISSILE!
YOU...

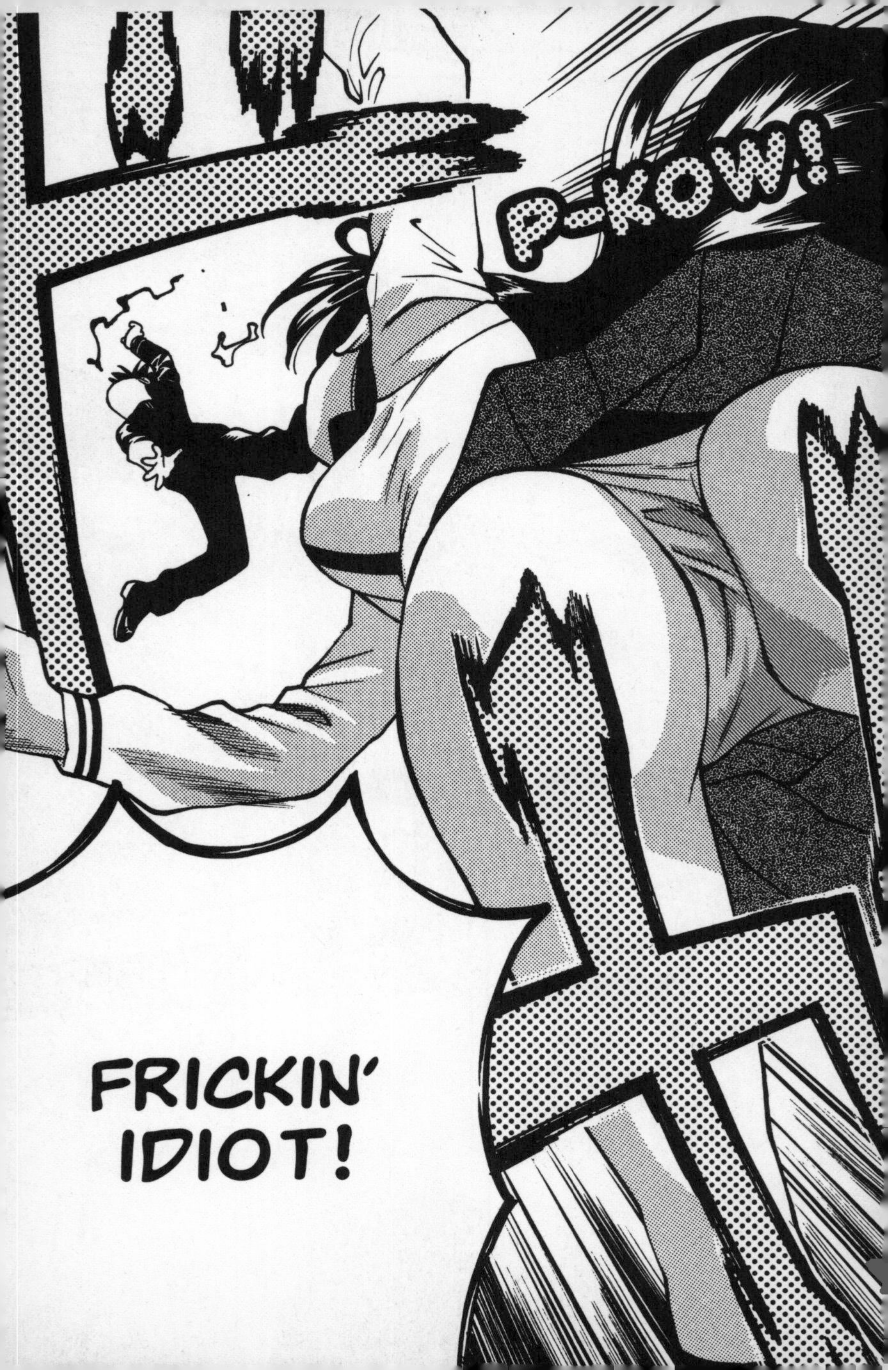
P-KOW!
FRICKIN' IDIOT!

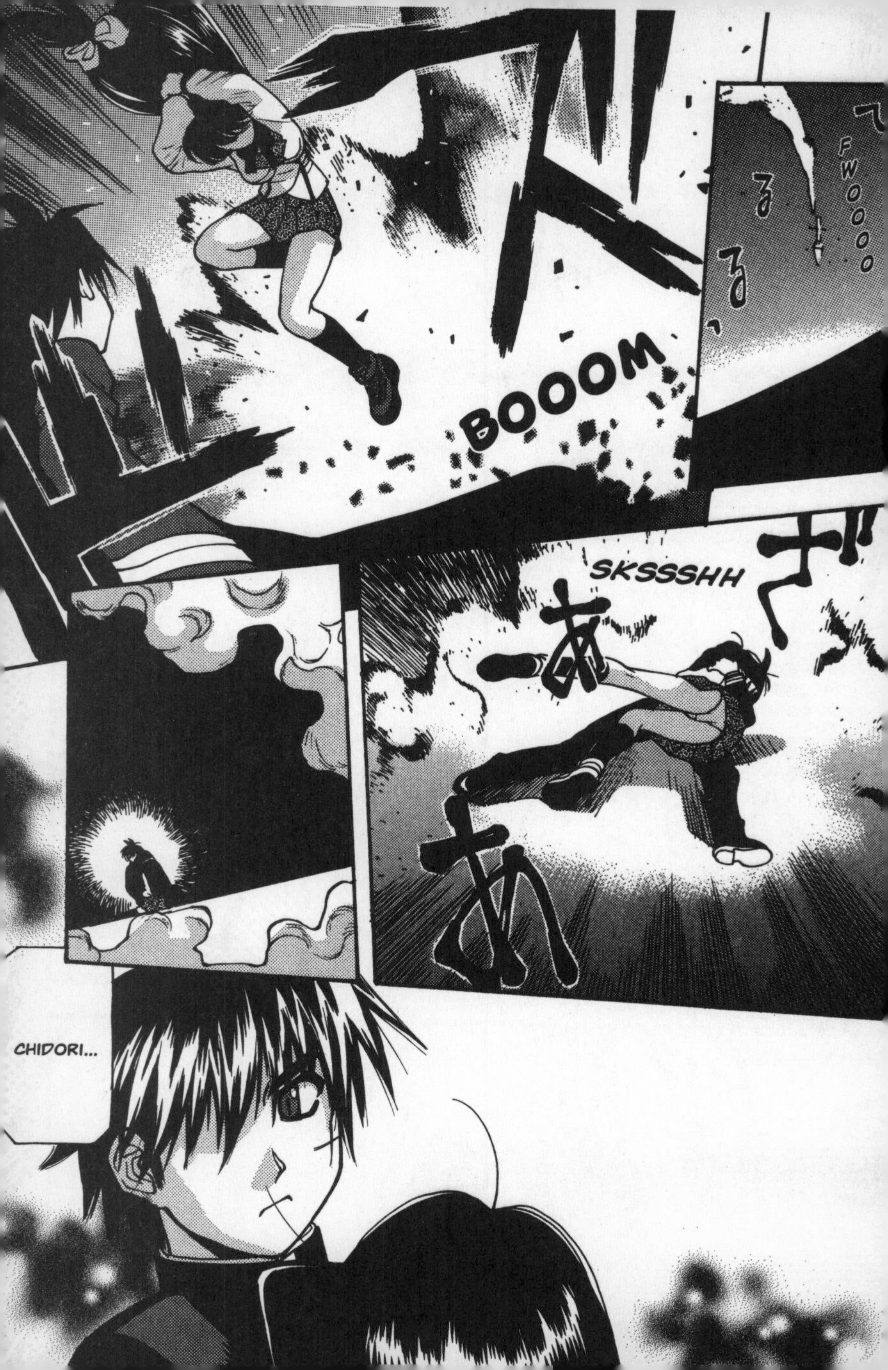

FWOOOOO
BOOOM
SKSSSHH
CHIDORI...

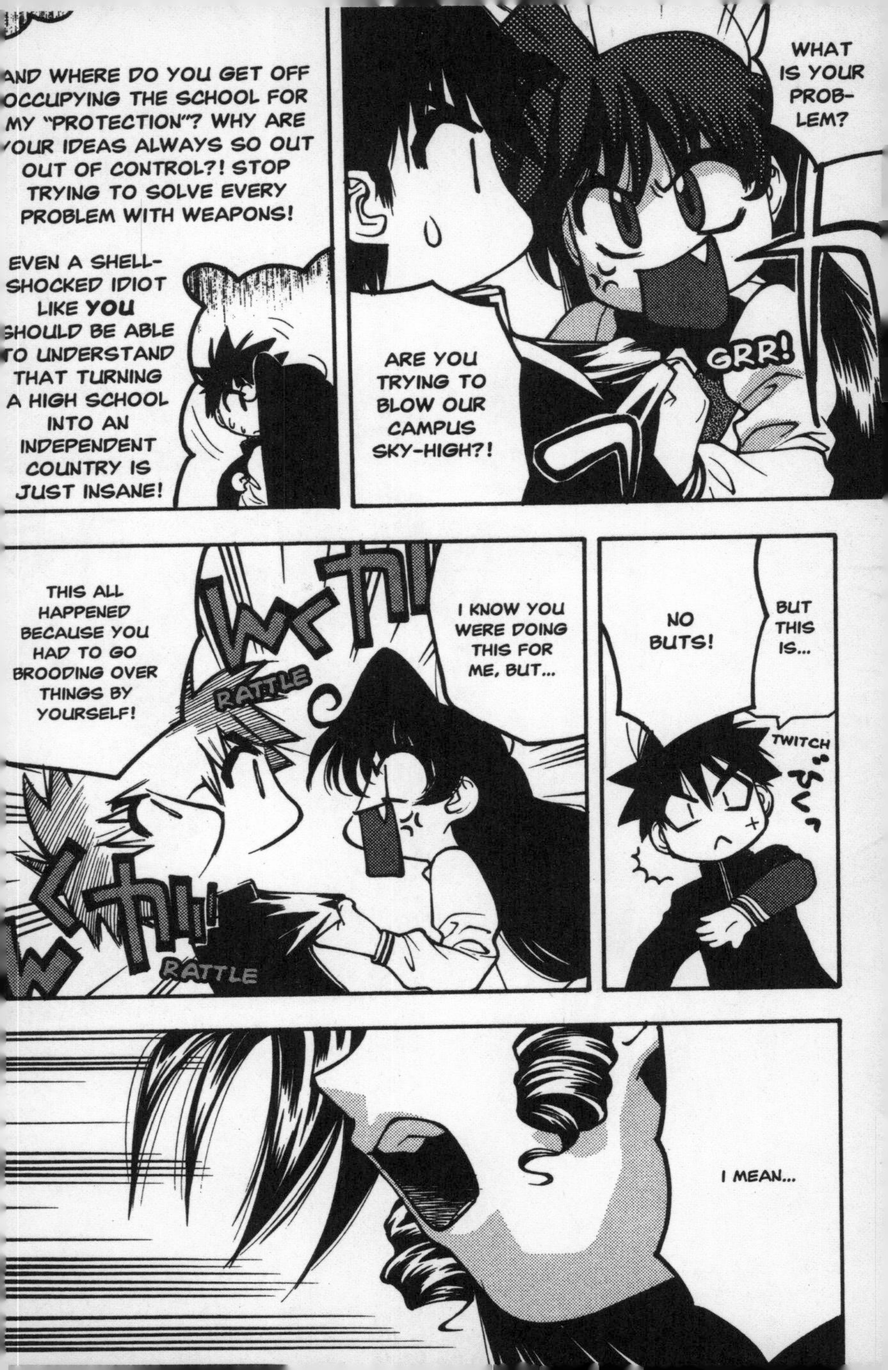
WHAT IS YOUR PROBLEM?
ARE YOU TRYING TO BLOW OUR CAMPUS SKY-HIGH?!
GRR!
AND WHERE DO YOU GET OFF OCCUPYING THE SCHOOL FOR MY "PROTECTION"? WHY ARE YOUR IDEAS ALWAYS SO OUT OUT OF CONTROL?! STOP TRYING TO SOLVE EVERY PROBLEM WITH WEAPONS!
EVEN A SHELL-SHOCKED IDIOT LIKE **YOU** SHOULD BE ABLE TO UNDERSTAND THAT TURNING A HIGH SCHOOL INTO AN INDEPENDENT COUNTRY IS JUST INSANE!
BUT THIS IS...
NO BUTS!
TWITCH
I KNOW YOU WERE DOING THIS FOR ME, BUT...
THIS ALL HAPPENED BECAUSE YOU HAD TO GO BROODING OVER THINGS BY YOURSELF!
RATTLE
RATTLE
I MEAN...

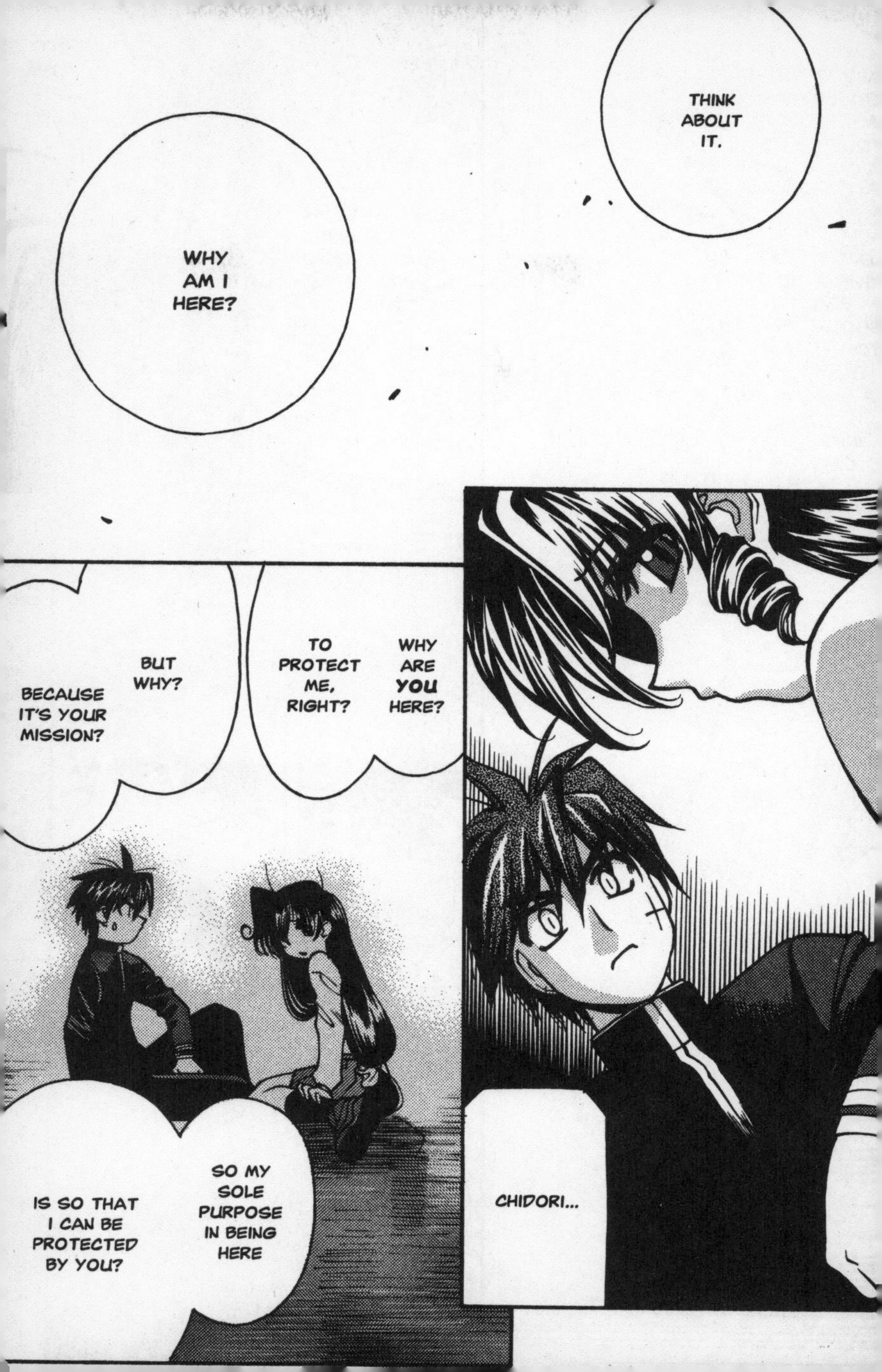
THINK ABOUT IT.
WHY AM I HERE?
WHY ARE YOU HERE?
TO PROTECT ME, RIGHT?
BUT WHY?
BECAUSE IT'S YOUR MISSION?
CHIDORI...
SO MY SOLE PURPOSE IN BEING HERE
IS SO THAT I CAN BE PROTECTED BY YOU?

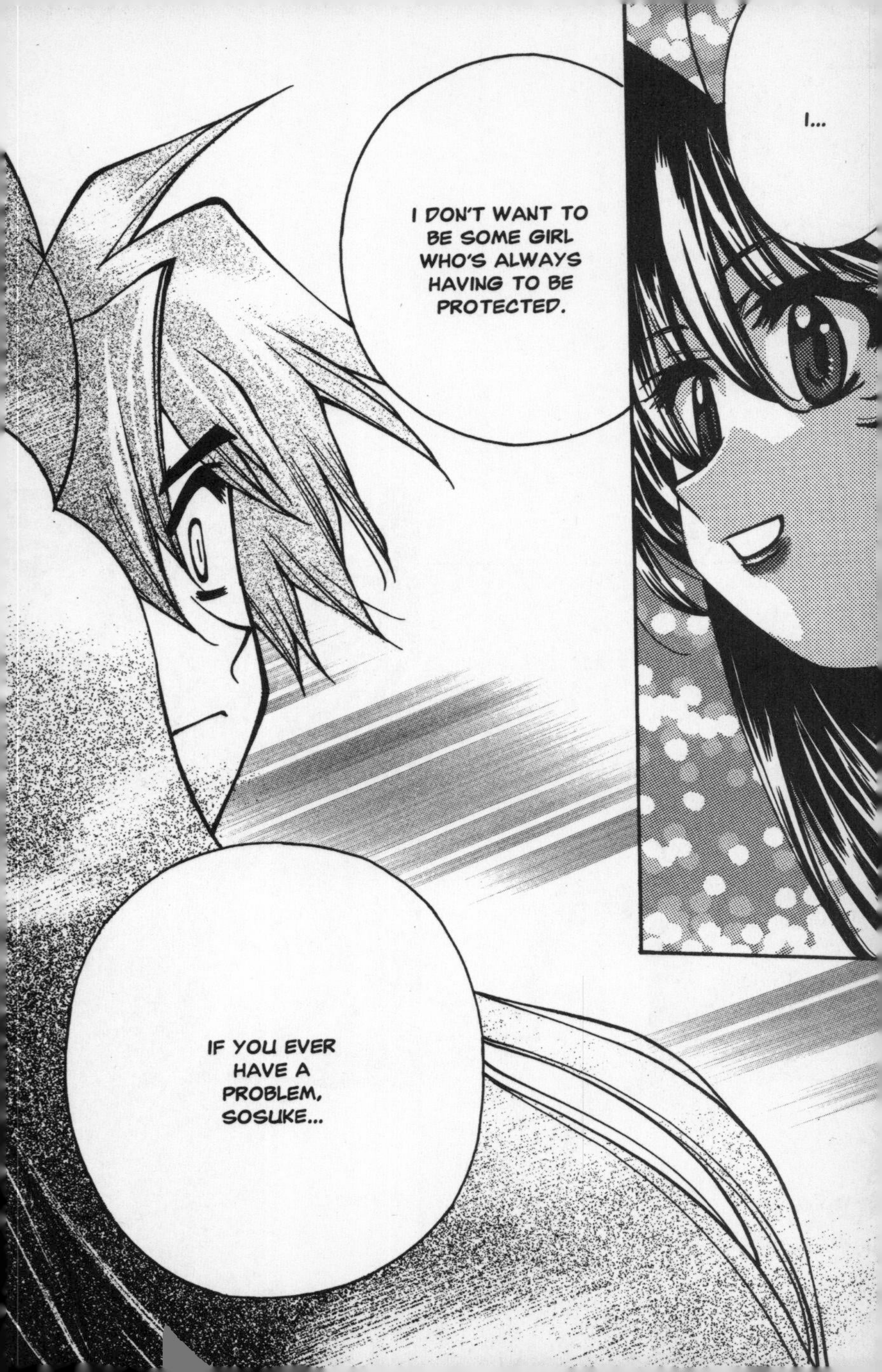
I...
I DON'T WANT TO BE SOME GIRL WHO'S ALWAYS HAVING TO BE PROTECTED.
IF YOU EVER HAVE A PROBLEM, SOSUKE...

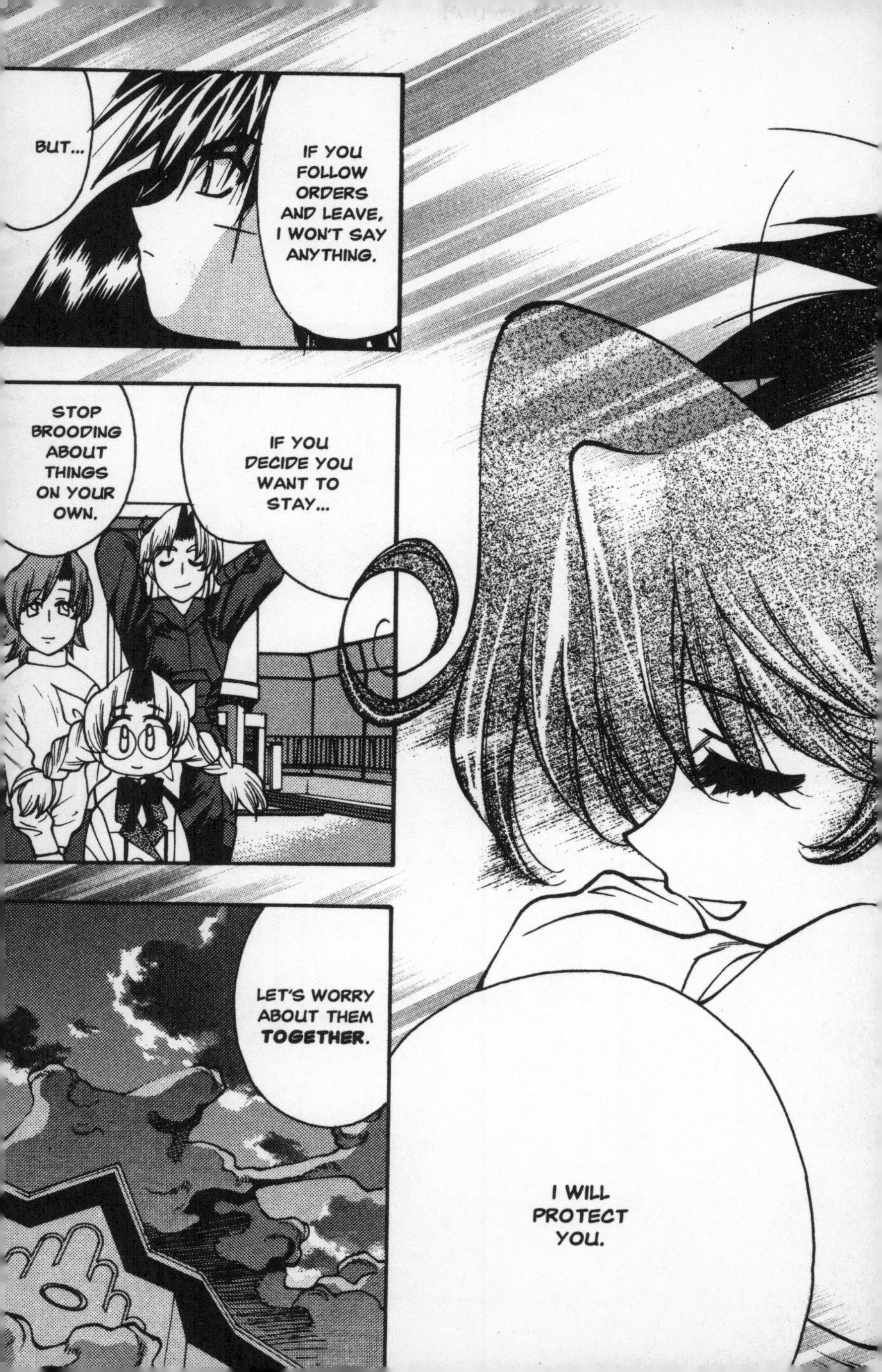
IF YOU FOLLOW ORDERS AND LEAVE, I WON'T SAY ANYTHING.
BUT...
I WILL PROTECT YOU.
IF YOU DECIDE YOU WANT TO STAY...
STOP BROODING ABOUT THINGS ON YOUR OWN.
LET'S WORRY ABOUT THEM **TOGETHER**.

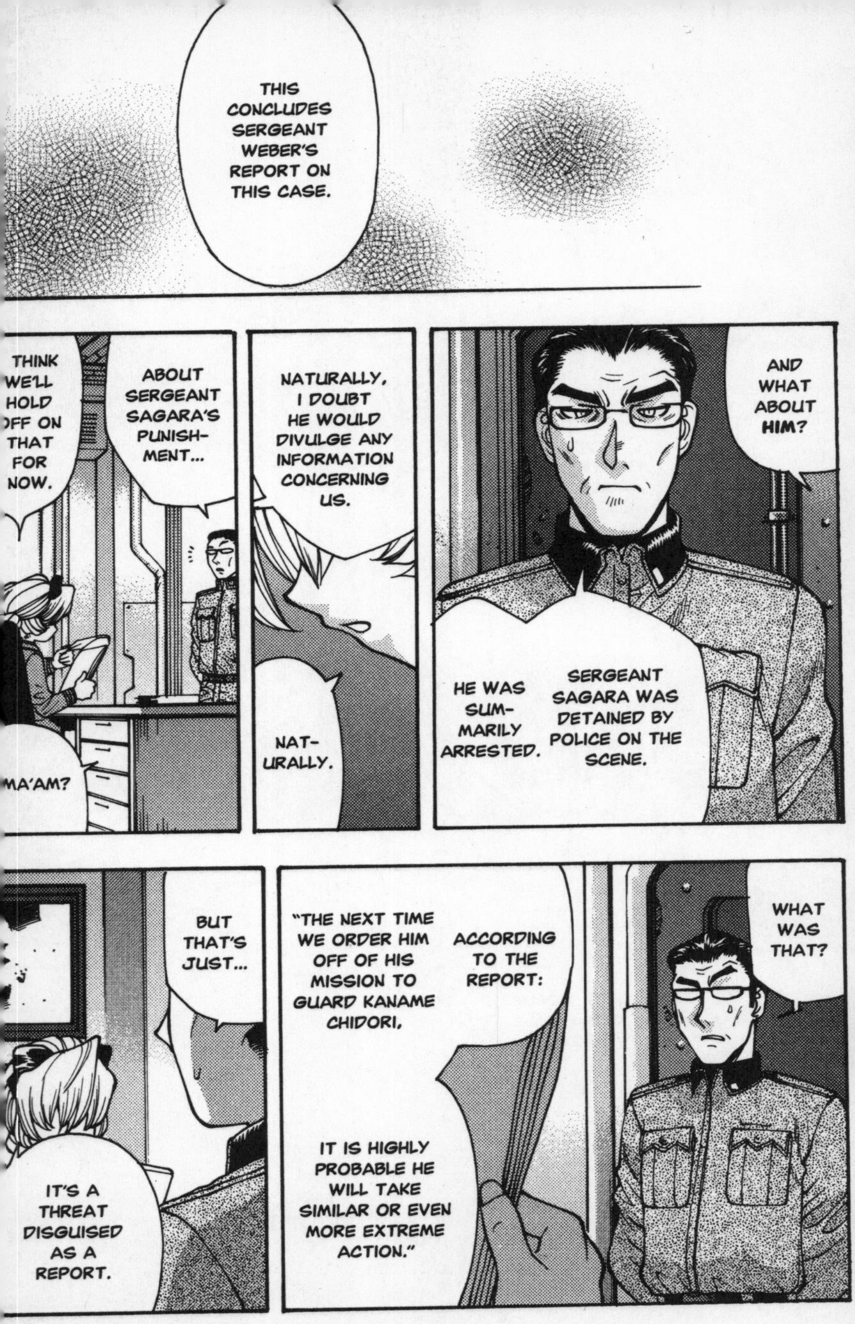
THIS CONCLUDES SERGEANT WEBER'S REPORT ON THIS CASE.
AND WHAT ABOUT HIM?
SERGEANT SAGARA WAS DETAINED BY POLICE ON THE SCENE.
HE WAS SUMMARILY ARRESTED.
NATURALLY, I DOUBT HE WOULD DIVULGE ANY INFORMATION CONCERNING US.
NATURALLY.
ABOUT SERGEANT SAGARA'S PUNISHMENT...
THINK WE'LL HOLD FF ON THAT FOR NOW.
MA'AM?
WHAT WAS THAT?
ACCORDING TO THE REPORT:
"THE NEXT TIME WE ORDER HIM OFF OF HIS MISSION TO GUARD KANAME CHIDORI,
IT IS HIGHLY PROBABLE HE WILL TAKE SIMILAR OR EVEN MORE EXTREME ACTION."
BUT THAT'S JUST...
IT'S A THREAT DISGUISED AS A REPORT.

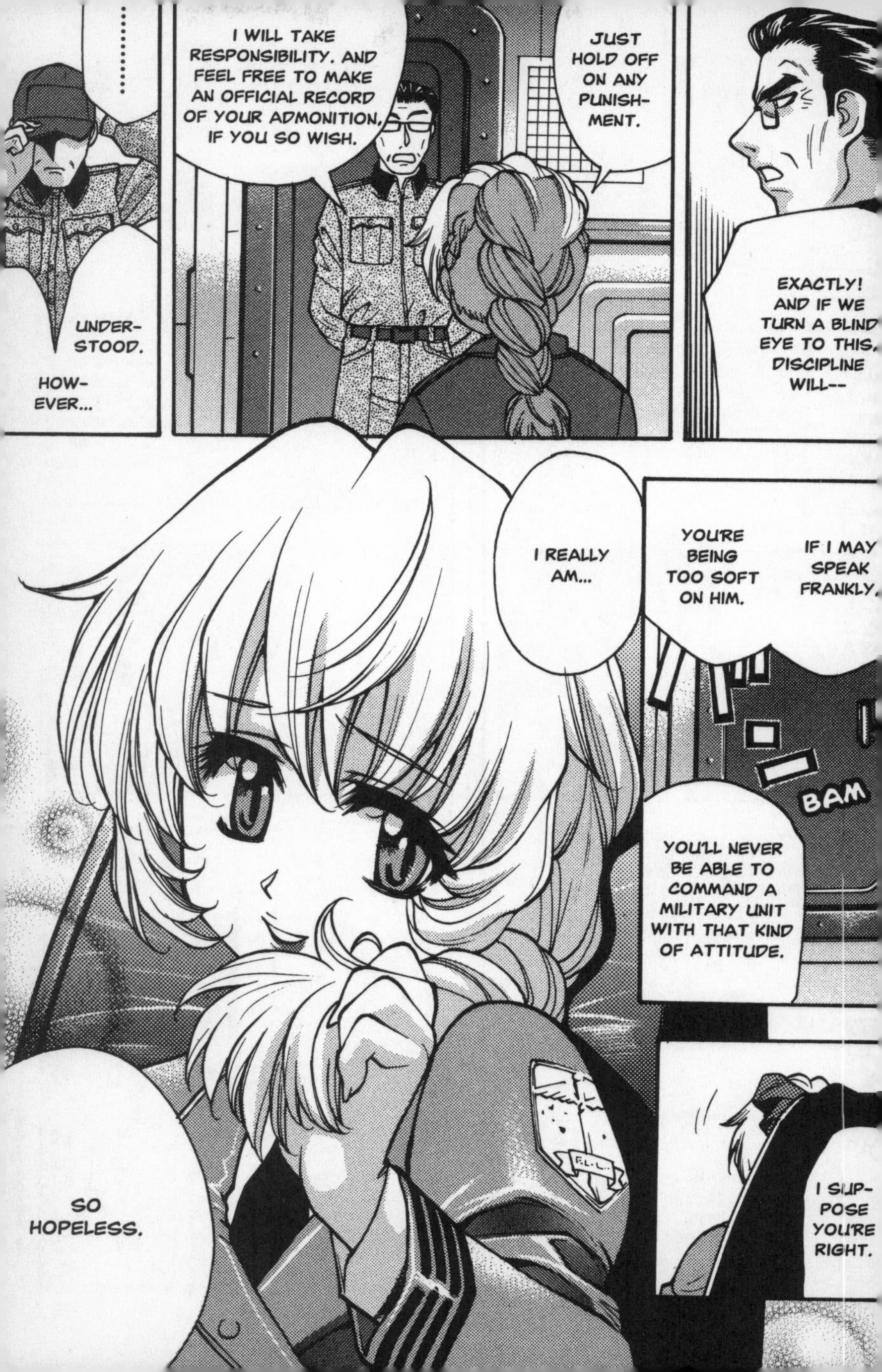
EXACTLY! AND IF WE TURN A BLIND EYE TO THIS, DISCIPLINE WILL--
JUST HOLD OFF ON ANY PUNISHMENT.
I WILL TAKE RESPONSIBILITY. AND FEEL FREE TO MAKE AN OFFICIAL RECORD OF YOUR ADMONITION, IF YOU SO WISH.
......
UNDER-STOOD.
HOW-EVER...
IF I MAY SPEAK FRANKLY,
YOU'RE BEING TOO SOFT ON HIM.
I REALLY AM...
BAM
YOU'LL NEVER BE ABLE TO COMMAND A MILITARY UNIT WITH THAT KIND OF ATTITUDE.
I SUP-POSE YOU'RE RIGHT.
SO HOPELESS.

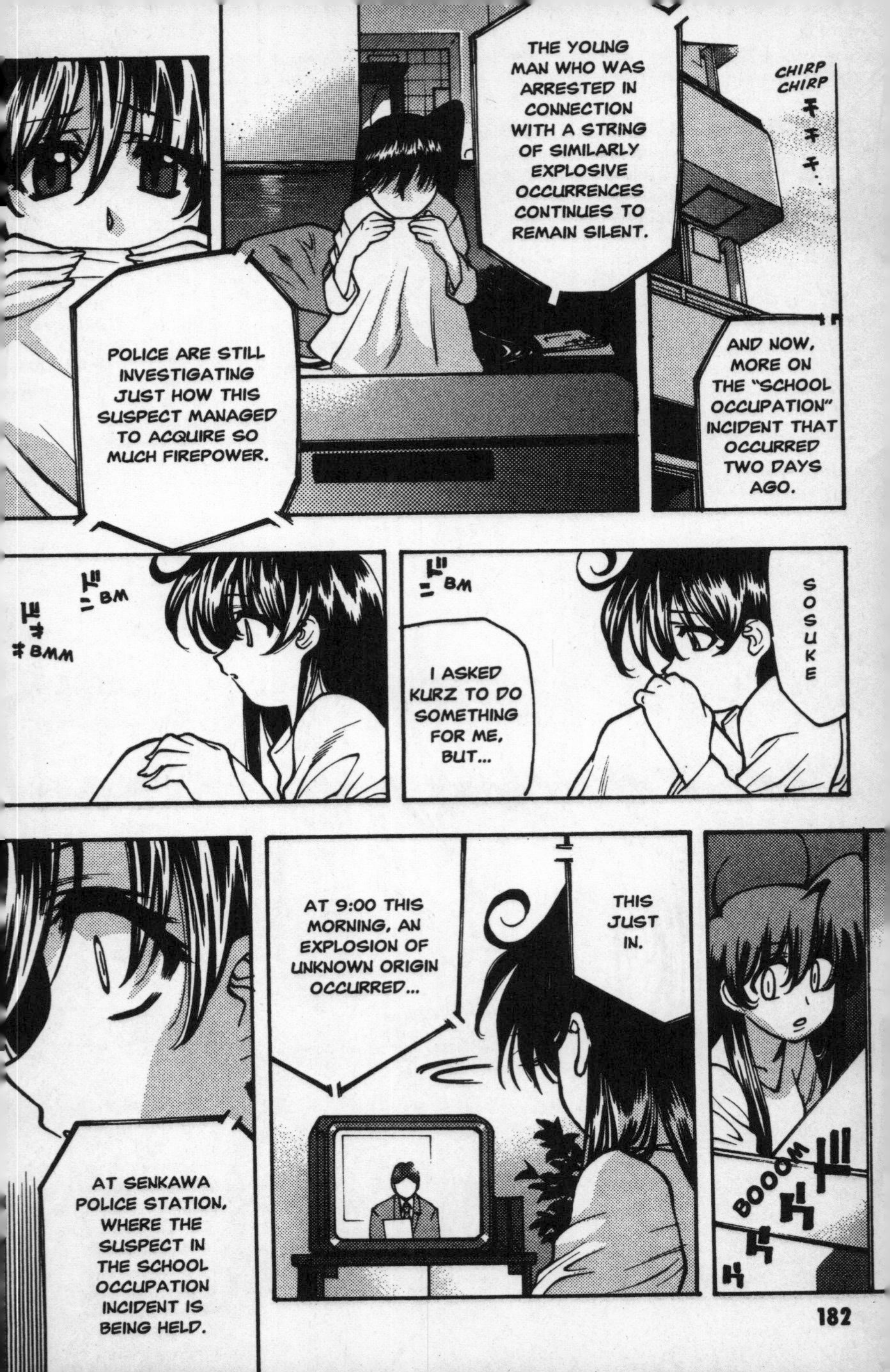
CHIRP CHIRP
チチチ…
THE YOUNG MAN WHO WAS ARRESTED IN CONNECTION WITH A STRING OF SIMILARLY EXPLOSIVE OCCURRENCES CONTINUES TO REMAIN SILENT.
POLICE ARE STILL INVESTIGATING JUST HOW THIS SUSPECT MANAGED TO ACQUIRE SO MUCH FIREPOWER.
AND NOW, MORE ON THE "SCHOOL OCCUPATION" INCIDENT THAT OCCURRED TWO DAYS AGO.
SOSUKE
I ASKED KURZ TO DO SOMETHING FOR ME, BUT...
ドン BM
ドン BM
ドオ BMM
BOOOM
ドドド
THIS JUST IN.
AT 9:00 THIS MORNING, AN EXPLOSION OF UNKNOWN ORIGIN OCCURRED...
AT SENKAWA POLICE STATION, WHERE THE SUSPECT IN THE SCHOOL OCCUPATION INCIDENT IS BEING HELD.

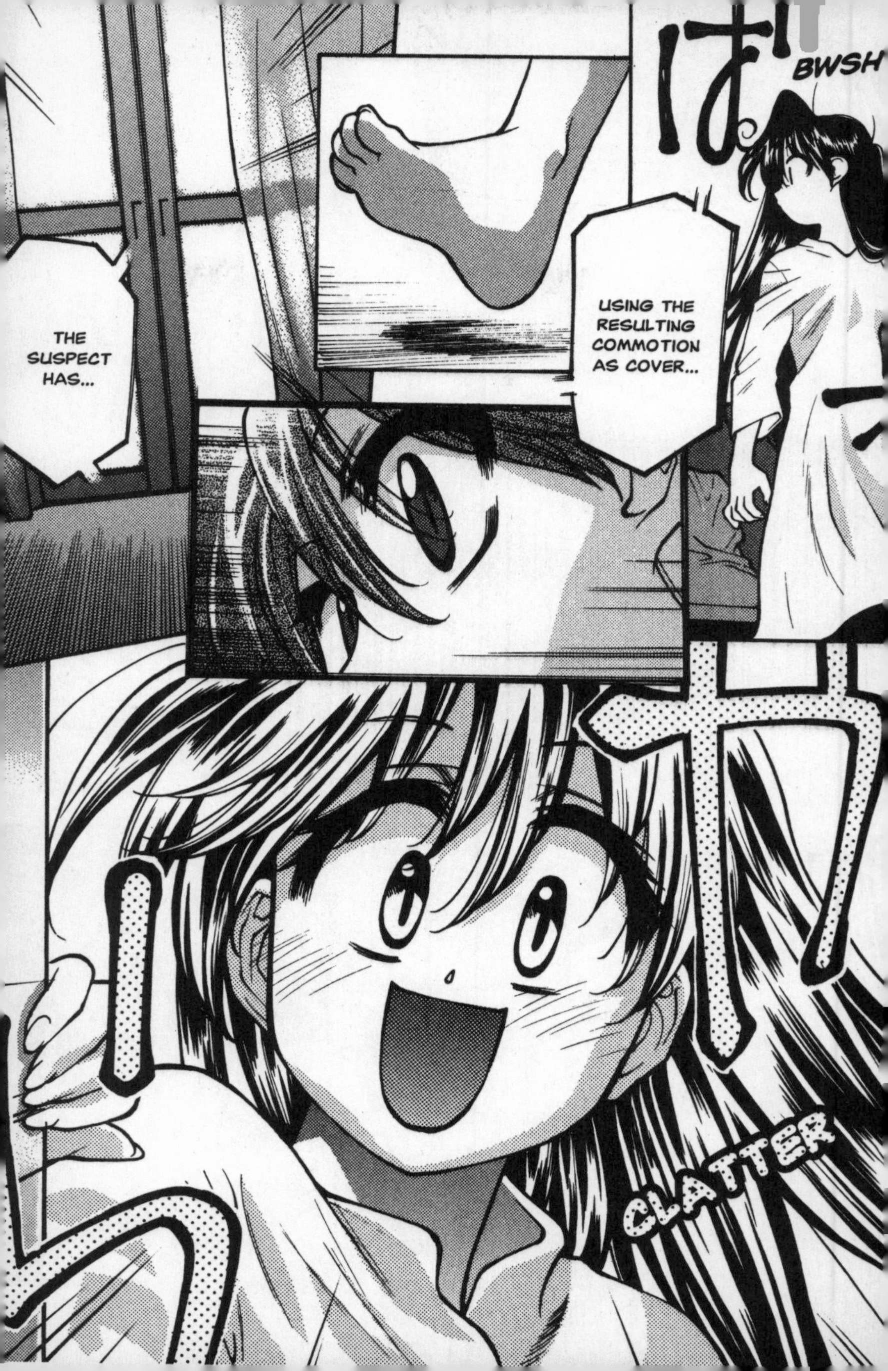

ぱ
BWSH
USING THE RESULTING COMMOTION AS COVER...
THE SUSPECT HAS...
CLATTER

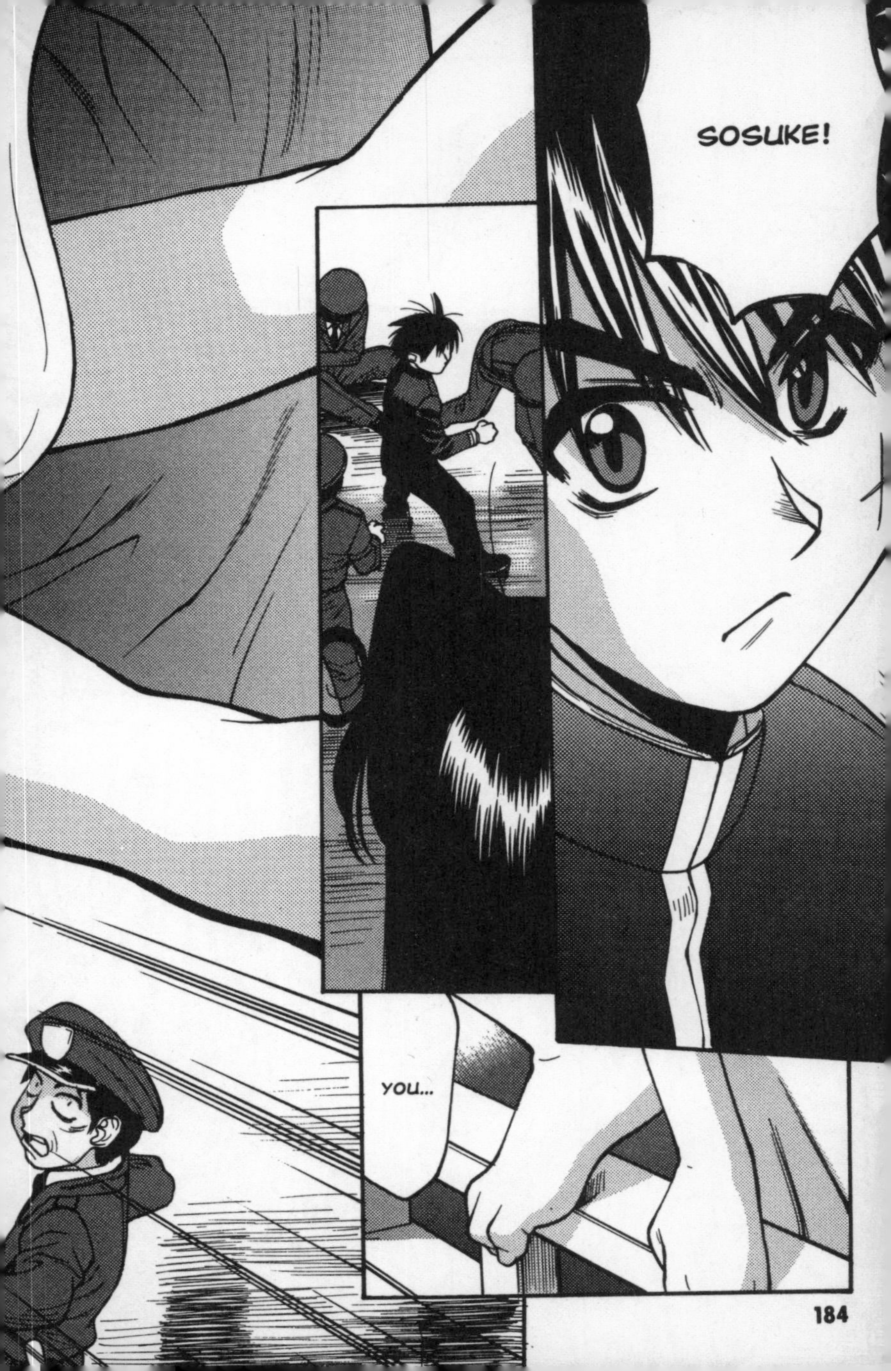
SOSUKE!
YOU...

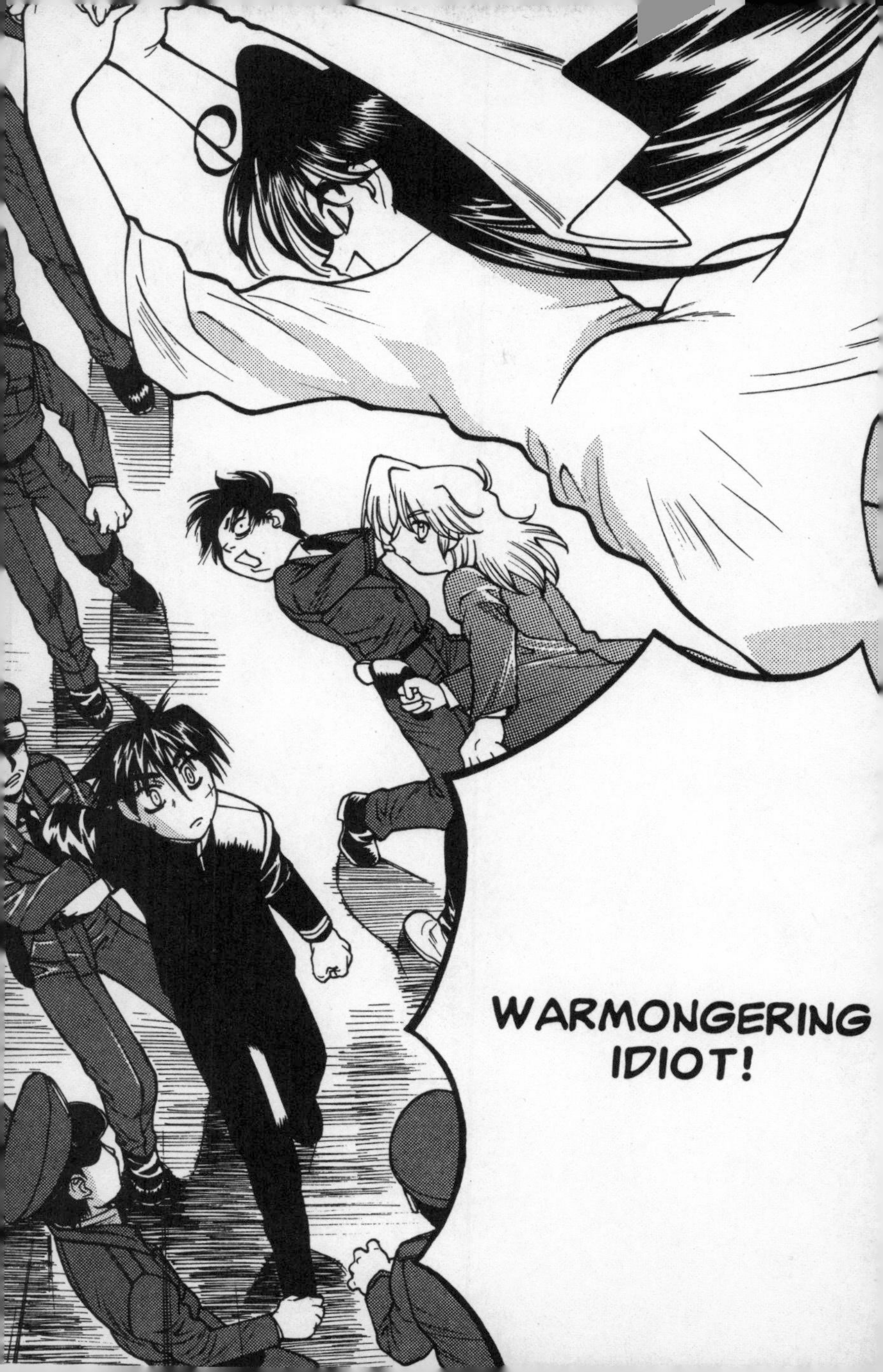
WARMONGERING IDIOT!

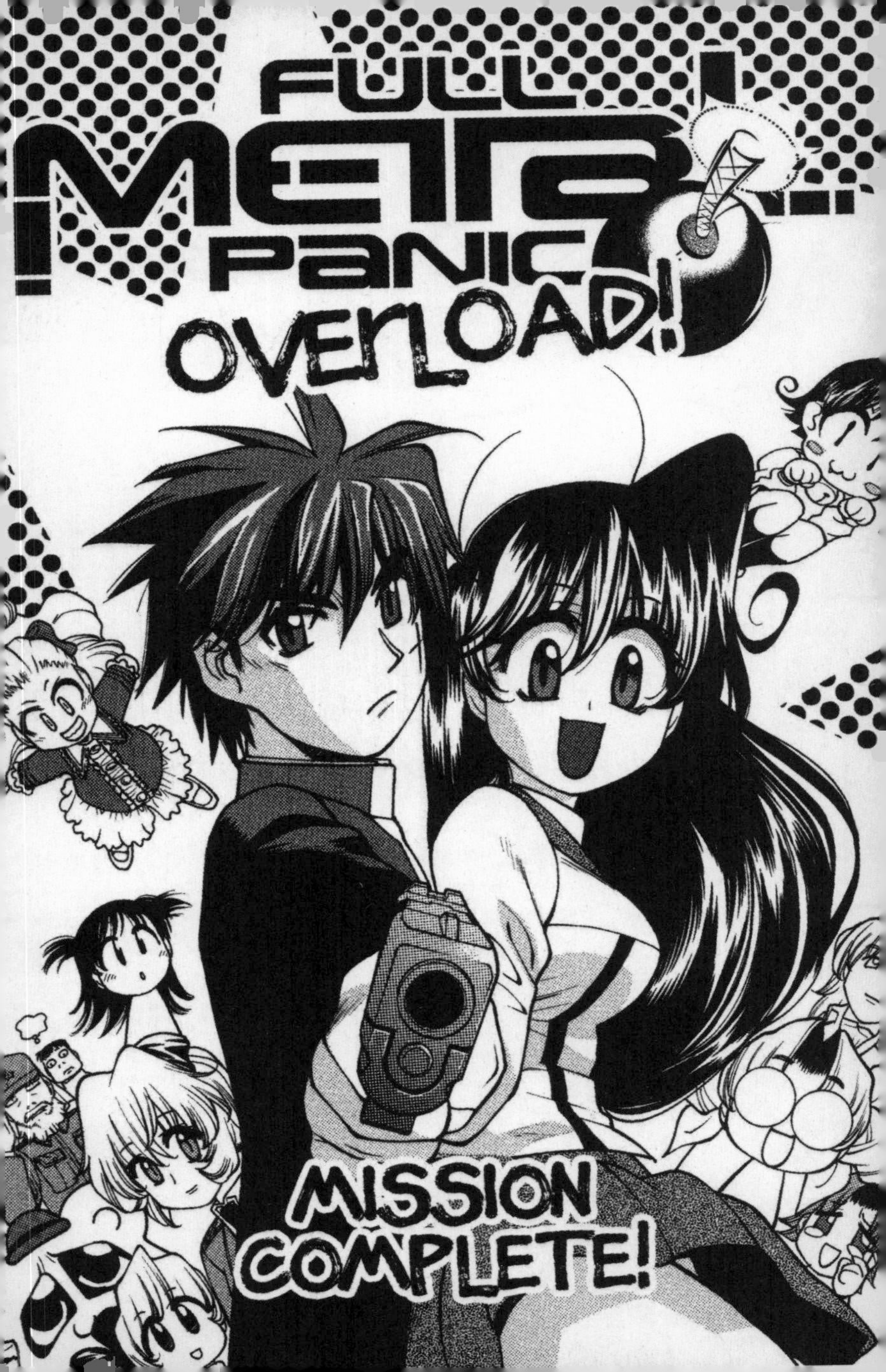
FULL METAL PANIC
OVERLOAD!
MISSION COMPLETE!

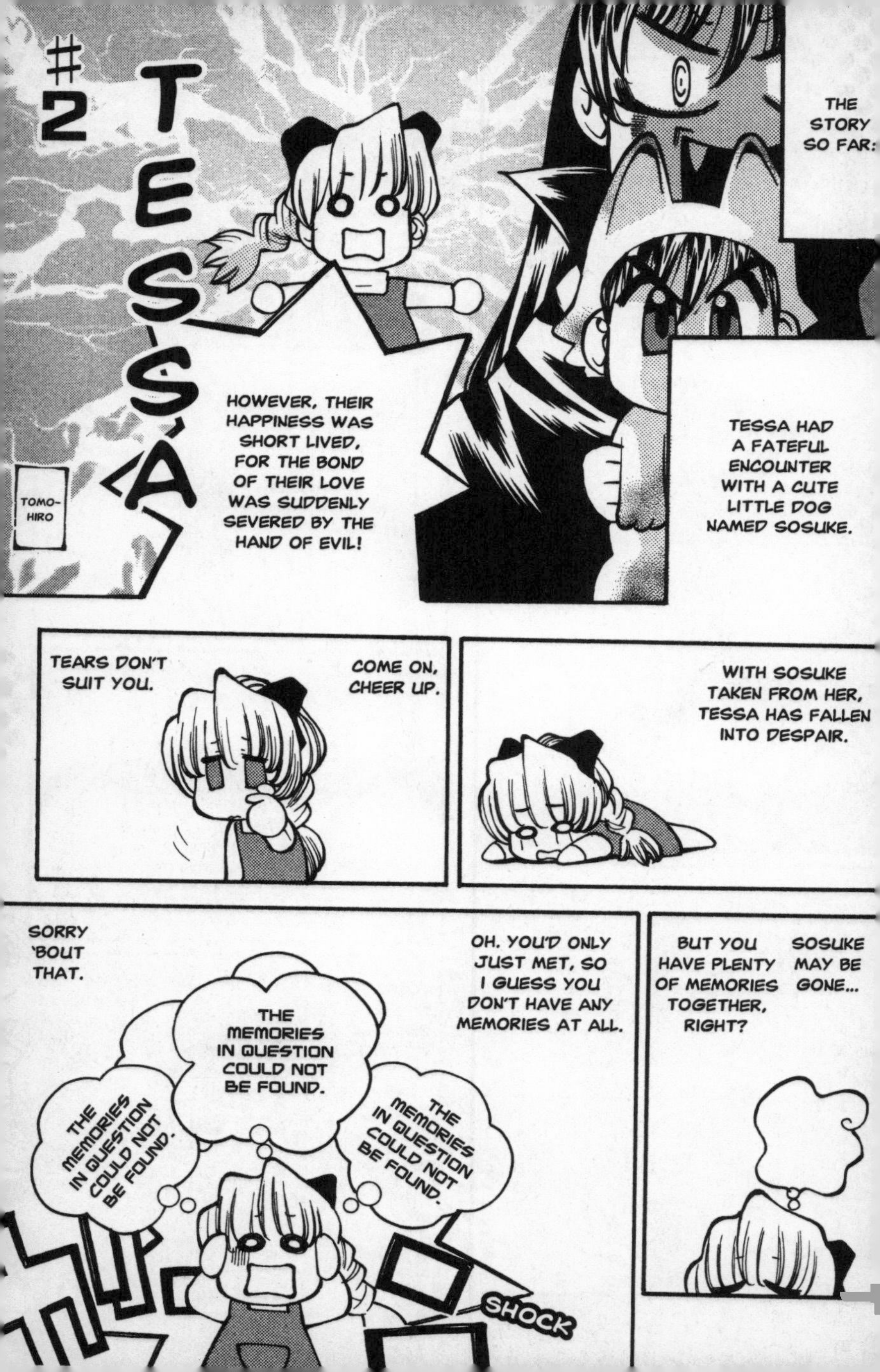

THE STORY SO FAR:
#2 TESSA
TOMO-HIRO
TESSA HAD A FATEFUL ENCOUNTER WITH A CUTE LITTLE DOG NAMED SOSUKE.
HOWEVER, THEIR HAPPINESS WAS SHORT LIVED, FOR THE BOND OF THEIR LOVE WAS SUDDENLY SEVERED BY THE HAND OF EVIL!
WITH SOSUKE TAKEN FROM HER, TESSA HAS FALLEN INTO DESPAIR.
COME ON, CHEER UP.
TEARS DON'T SUIT YOU.
SOSUKE MAY BE GONE...
BUT YOU HAVE PLENTY OF MEMORIES TOGETHER, RIGHT?
OH. YOU'D ONLY JUST MET, SO I GUESS YOU DON'T HAVE ANY MEMORIES AT ALL.
SORRY 'BOUT THAT.
THE MEMORIES IN QUESTION COULD NOT BE FOUND.
THE MEMORIES IN QUESTION COULD NOT BE FOUND.
THE MEMORIES IN QUESTION COULD NOT BE FOUND.
SHOCK

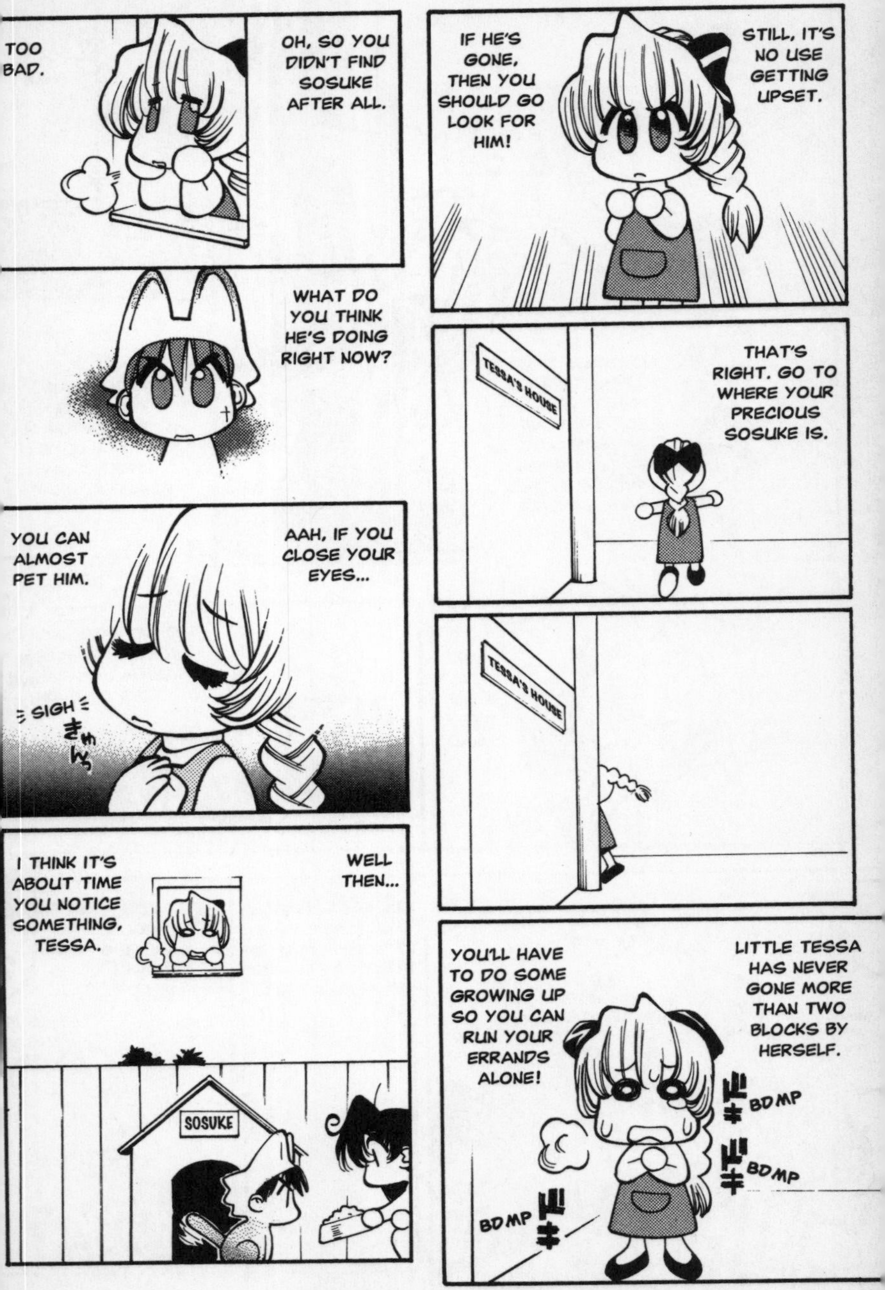

STILL, IT'S NO USE GETTING UPSET.
IF HE'S GONE, THEN YOU SHOULD GO LOOK FOR HIM!
TESSA'S HOUSE
THAT'S RIGHT. GO TO WHERE YOUR PRECIOUS SOSUKE IS.
TESSA'S HOUSE
LITTLE TESSA HAS NEVER GONE MORE THAN TWO BLOCKS BY HERSELF.
YOU'LL HAVE TO DO SOME GROWING UP SO YOU CAN RUN YOUR ERRANDS ALONE!
BDMP
BDMP
BDMP
OH, SO YOU DIDN'T FIND SOSUKE AFTER ALL.
TOO BAD.
WHAT DO YOU THINK HE'S DOING RIGHT NOW?
AAH, IF YOU CLOSE YOUR EYES...
YOU CAN ALMOST PET HIM.
SIGH
きゅん
WELL THEN...
I THINK IT'S ABOUT TIME YOU NOTICE SOMETHING, TESSA.
SOSUKE

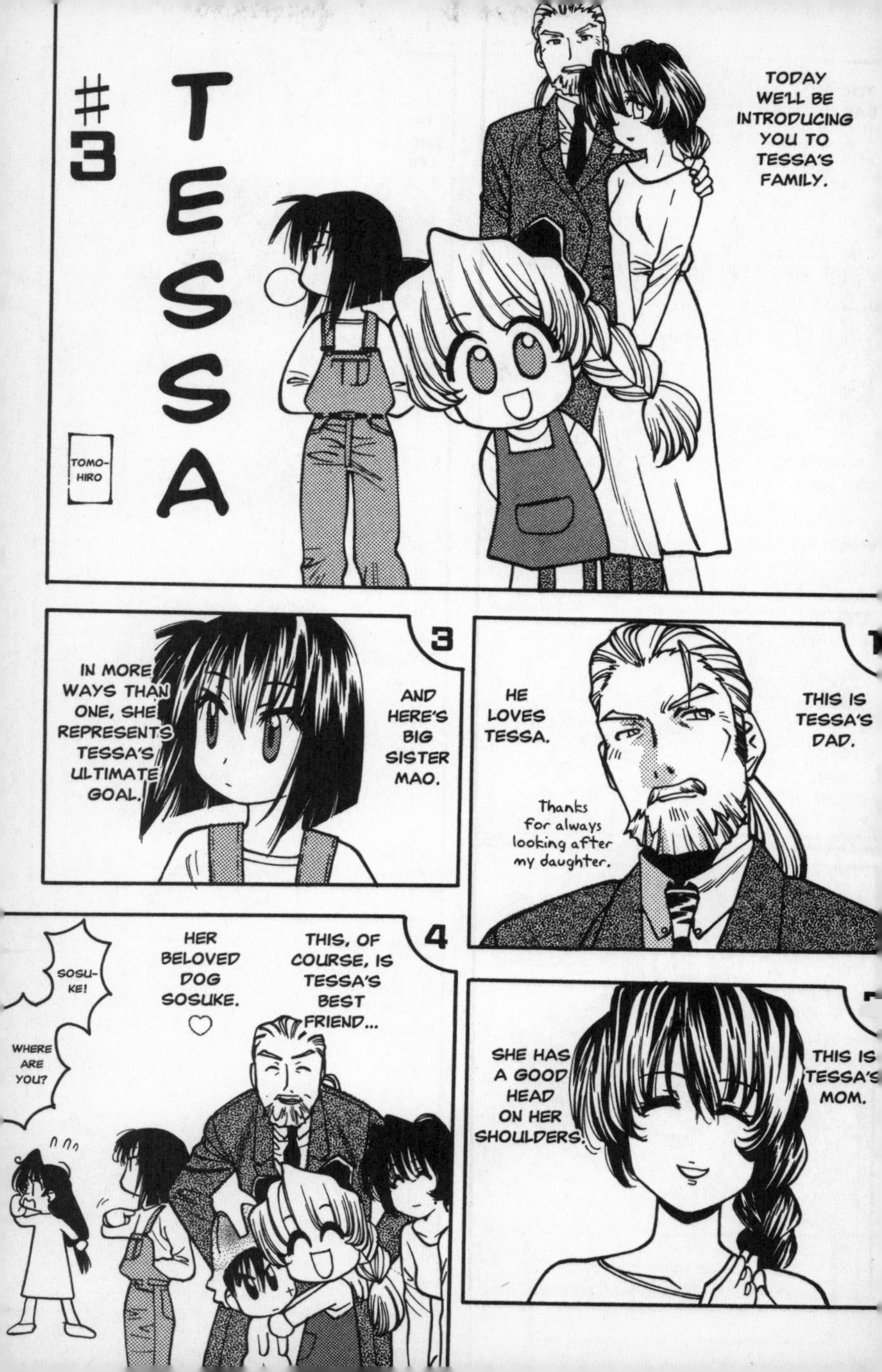

#3 TESSA
TOMO-HIRO
TODAY WE'LL BE INTRODUCING YOU TO TESSA'S FAMILY.
1
THIS IS TESSA'S DAD.
HE LOVES TESSA.
Thanks for always looking after my daughter.
2
THIS IS TESSA'S MOM.
SHE HAS A GOOD HEAD ON HER SHOULDERS.
3
AND HERE'S BIG SISTER MAO.
IN MORE WAYS THAN ONE, SHE REPRESENTS TESSA'S ULTIMATE GOAL.
4
THIS, OF COURSE, IS TESSA'S BEST FRIEND...
HER BELOVED DOG SOSUKE. ♡
SOSU-KE!
WHERE ARE YOU?

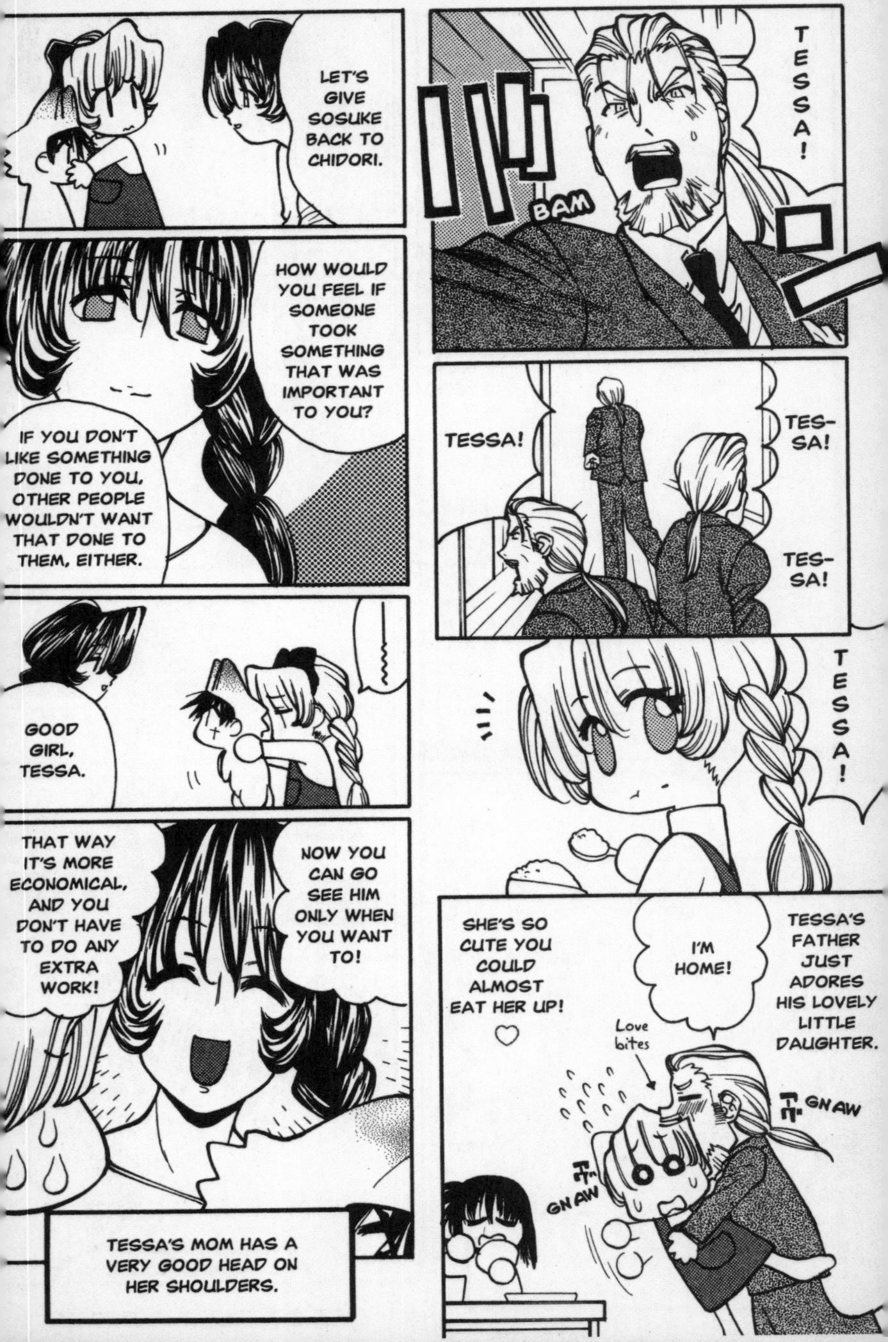
TESSA!
BAM
TESSA!
TES-SA!
TES-SA!
TESSA!
TESSA'S FATHER JUST ADORES HIS LOVELY LITTLE DAUGHTER.
I'M HOME!
SHE'S SO CUTE YOU COULD ALMOST EAT HER UP!
Love bites
GNAW
GNAW
LET'S GIVE SOSUKE BACK TO CHIDORI.
HOW WOULD YOU FEEL IF SOMEONE TOOK SOMETHING THAT WAS IMPORTANT TO YOU?
IF YOU DON'T LIKE SOMETHING DONE TO YOU, OTHER PEOPLE WOULDN'T WANT THAT DONE TO THEM, EITHER.
GOOD GIRL, TESSA.
NOW YOU CAN GO SEE HIM ONLY WHEN YOU WANT TO!
THAT WAY IT'S MORE ECONOMICAL, AND YOU DON'T HAVE TO DO ANY EXTRA WORK!
TESSA'S MOM HAS A VERY GOOD HEAD ON HER SHOULDERS.

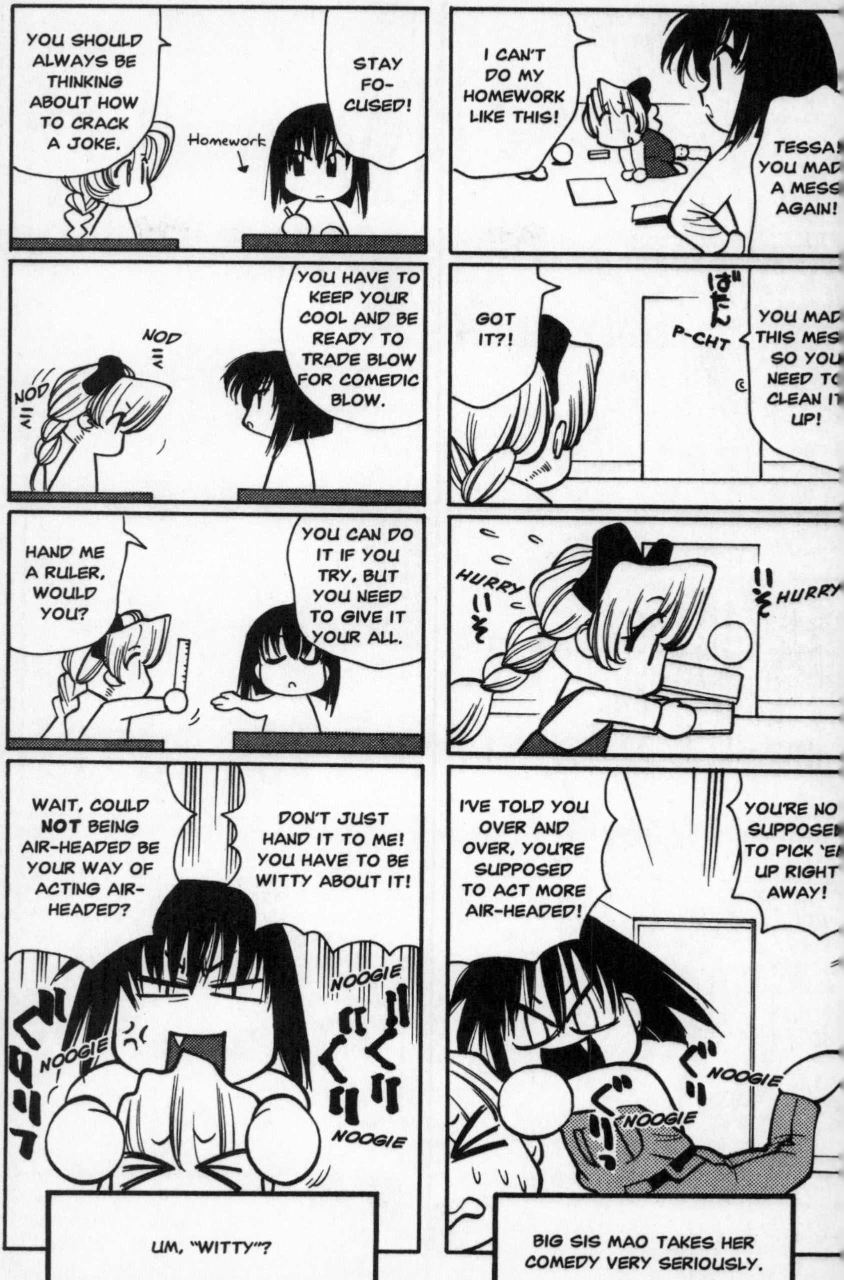
TESSA! YOU MAD A MESS AGAIN!
I CAN'T DO MY HOMEWORK LIKE THIS!
YOU MAD THIS MES SO YOU NEED TO CLEAN IT UP!
ばたん
P-CHT
GOT IT?!
HURRY
HURRY
YOU'RE NO SUPPOSE TO PICK 'E UP RIGHT AWAY!
I'VE TOLD YOU OVER AND OVER, YOU'RE SUPPOSED TO ACT MORE AIR-HEADED!
NOOGIE
NOOGIE
BIG SIS MAO TAKES HER COMEDY VERY SERIOUSLY.
STAY FO-CUSED!
YOU SHOULD ALWAYS BE THINKING ABOUT HOW TO CRACK A JOKE.
Homework
YOU HAVE TO KEEP YOUR COOL AND BE READY TO TRADE BLOW FOR COMEDIC BLOW.
NOD
NOD
YOU CAN DO IT IF YOU TRY, BUT YOU NEED TO GIVE IT YOUR ALL.
HAND ME A RULER, WOULD YOU?
DON'T JUST HAND IT TO ME! YOU HAVE TO BE WITTY ABOUT IT!
WAIT, COULD **NOT** BEING AIR-HEADED BE YOUR WAY OF ACTING AIR-HEADED?
NOOGIE
NOOGIE
NOOGIE
UM, "WITTY"?

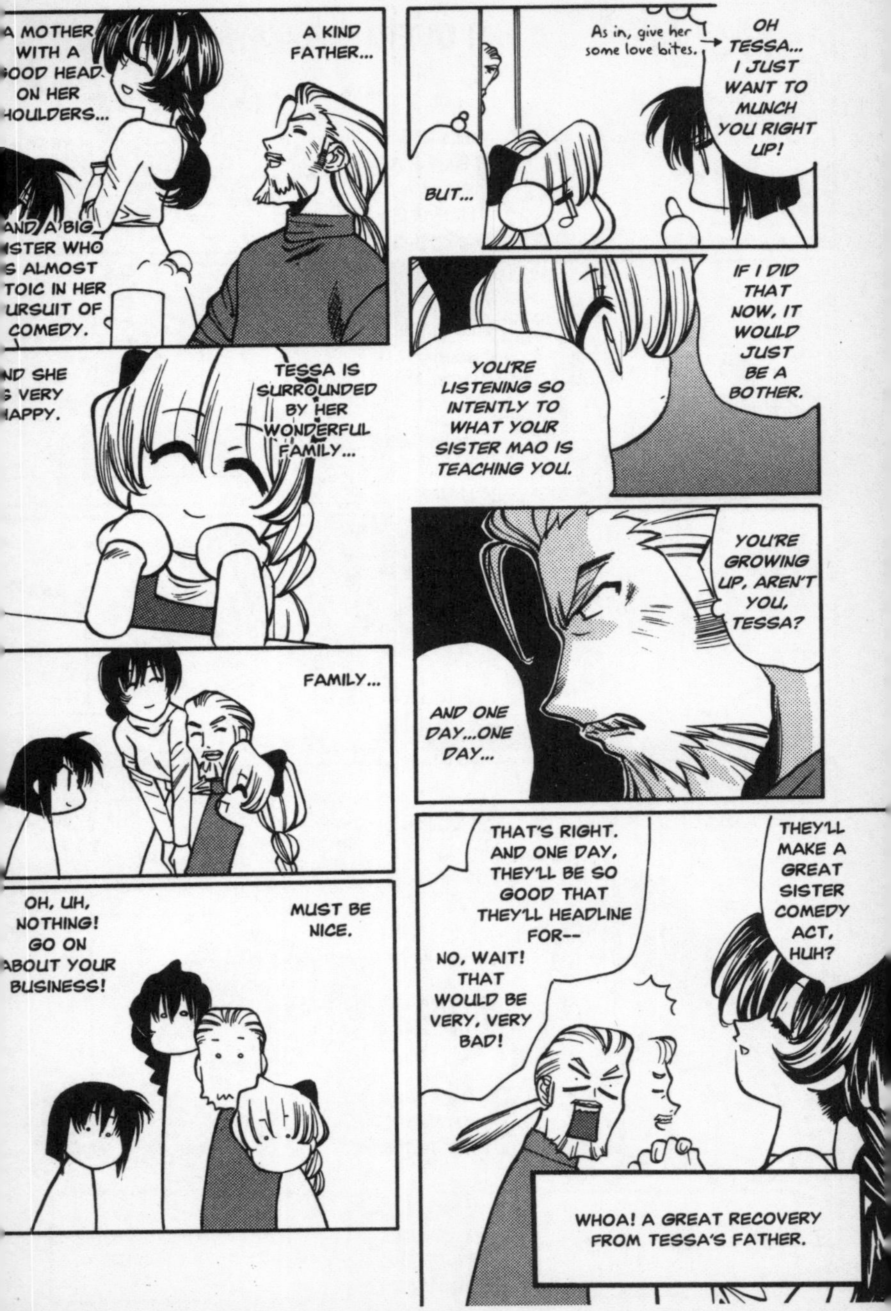

A MOTHER WITH A OOD HEAD ON HER HOULDERS...
A KIND FATHER...
AND A BIG ISTER WHO S ALMOST TOIC IN HER URSUIT OF COMEDY.
ND SHE S VERY APPY.
TESSA IS SURROUNDED BY HER WONDERFUL FAMILY...
FAMILY...
MUST BE NICE.
OH, UH, NOTHING! GO ON ABOUT YOUR BUSINESS!
OH TESSA... I JUST WANT TO MUNCH YOU RIGHT UP!
As in, give her some love bites.
BUT...
IF I DID THAT NOW, IT WOULD JUST BE A BOTHER.
YOU'RE LISTENING SO INTENTLY TO WHAT YOUR SISTER MAO IS TEACHING YOU.
YOU'RE GROWING UP, AREN'T YOU, TESSA?
AND ONE DAY...ONE DAY...
THEY'LL MAKE A GREAT SISTER COMEDY ACT, HUH?
THAT'S RIGHT. AND ONE DAY, THEY'LL BE SO GOOD THAT THEY'LL HEADLINE FOR--
NO, WAIT! THAT WOULD BE VERY, VERY BAD!
WHOA! A GREAT RECOVERY FROM TESSA'S FATHER.

FULL METAL PANIC! OVERLOAD! VOLUME FIVE

© 2003 Tomohiro NAGAI • Shouji GATOU
© 2003 Shikidouji
Originally published in Japan in 2003 by
KADOKAWA SHOTEN PUBLISHING CO., LTD., Tokyo.
English translation rights arranged with
KADOKAWA SHOTEN PUBLISHING CO., LTD., Tokyo.

Editor **JAVIER LOPEZ**
Translator **AMY FORSYTH**
Graphic Artist **SCOTT HOWARD**

Editorial Director **GARY STEINMAN**
Creative Director **JASON BABLER**
Print Production Manager **BRIDGETT JANOTA**
Production Coordinator **MARISA KREITZ**

International Coordinators **TORU IWAKAMI & MIYUKI KAMIYA**

President, CEO & Publisher **JOHN LEDFORD**

Email: editor@adv-manga.com
www.adv-manga.com

www.advfilms.com

For sales and distribution inquiries please call 1.800.282.7202

ADV ™
MANGA
is a division of A.D. Vision, Inc.
5750 Bintliff Drive, Suite 210, Houston, Texas 77036

English text © 2006 published by A.D. Vision, Inc. under exclusive license.
ADV MANGA is a trademark of A.D. Vision, Inc.

ISBN: 1-4139-0342-8
First printing, May 2006
10 9 8 7 6 5 4 3 2 1
Printed in Canada

Full Metal Panic! Overload! Vol. 05

P. 12

(1) Kimchee

Kimchee (or kimchi) is a traditional Korean dish of spicy pickled vegetables, generally cabbage. It is often used, either as is or in a concentrated paste, in *nabe*-style soups (called *chige* in Korean).

2) Red miso

Miso is a paste of fermented soybeans most often used in soups. There are several different varieties, of which white and red are arguably the most often used.

P. 23

Blue Fluted

"Blue Fluted" is the name of Royal Copenhagen's trademark design.

P. 25

Half Lace

"Half Lace," another of Royal Copenhagen's designs, is a variation on Blue Fluted.

P. 29

Kyonchin, My Love

The name of the Kyoko-devoted fan site is reminiscent of *Ally, My Love*, the Japanese title for *Ally McBeal*. Incidentally, "Kyonchin" is a cute-sounding nickname derived from "Kyoko."

P. 31

Takoyaki

Takoyaki consists of small pieces of octopus tentacle inside a "ball" made of quick-fried batter. It is usually topped with dried seaweed flakes, bonito shavings and/or sauce and mayonnaise.

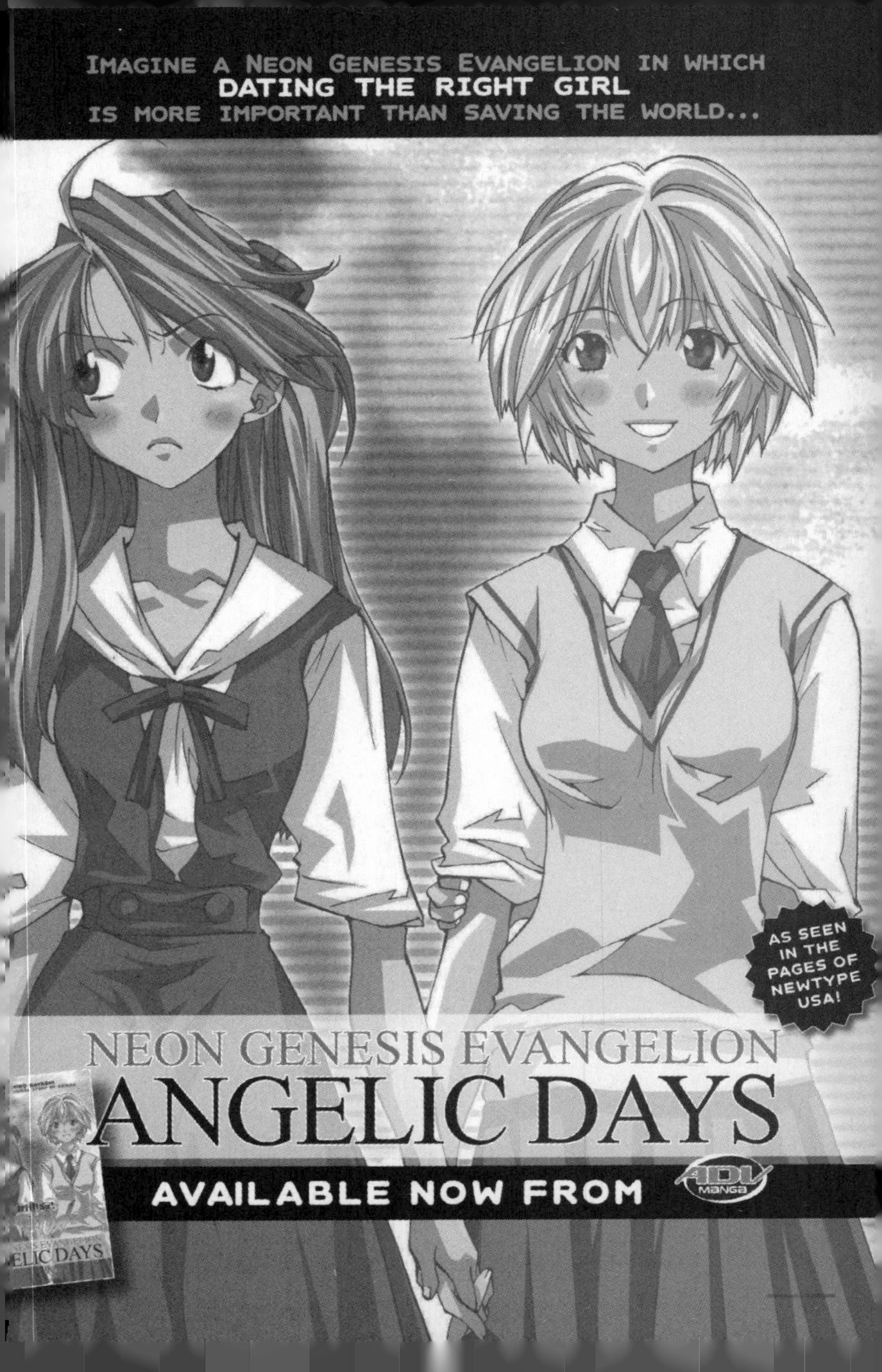
IMAGINE A NEON GENESIS EVANGELION IN WHICH
DATING THE RIGHT GIRL
IS MORE IMPORTANT THAN SAVING THE WORLD...
AS SEEN IN THE PAGES OF NEWTYPE USA!
NEON GENESIS EVANGELION
ANGELIC DAYS
AVAILABLE NOW FROM
ADV MANGA

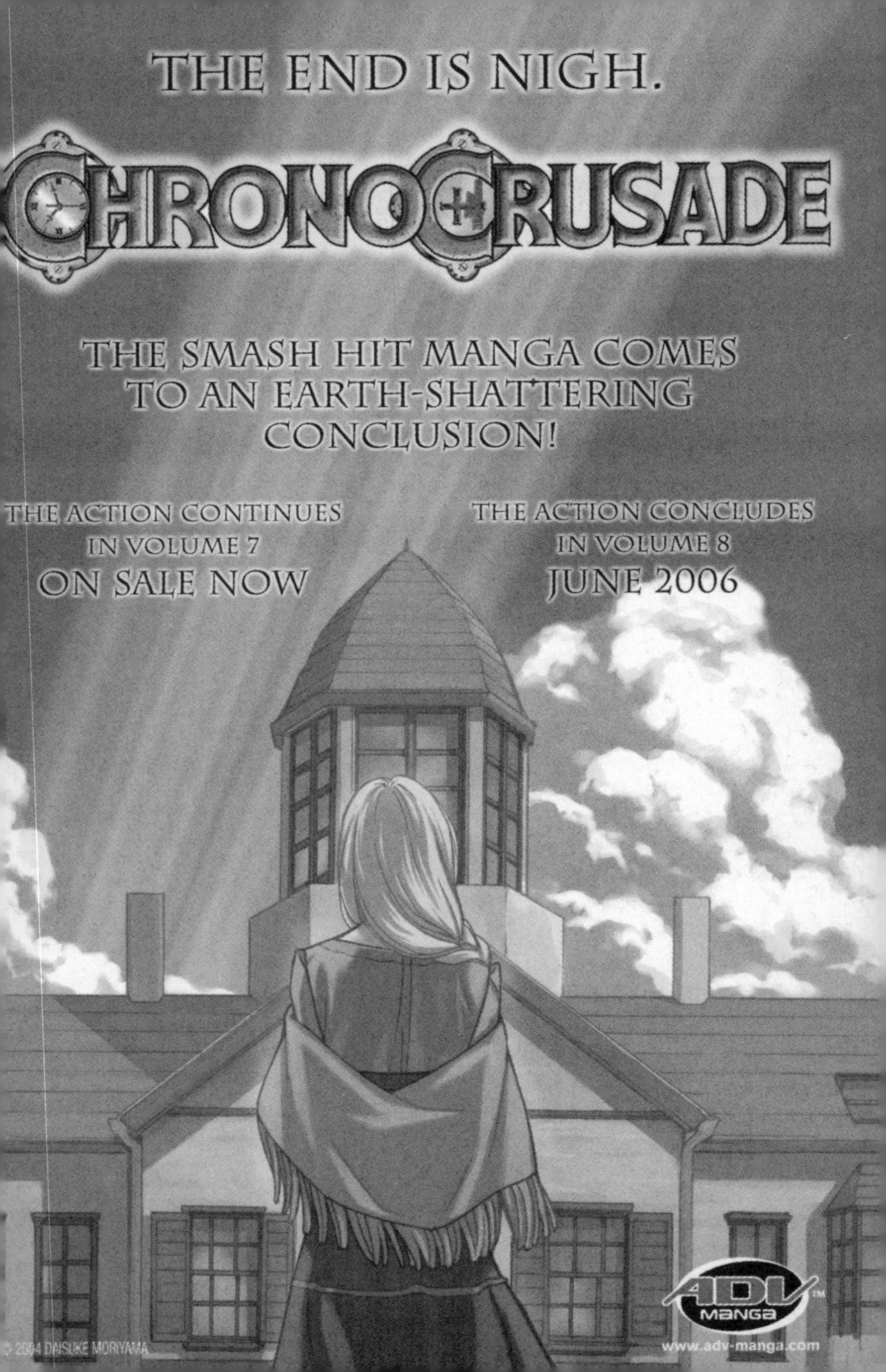

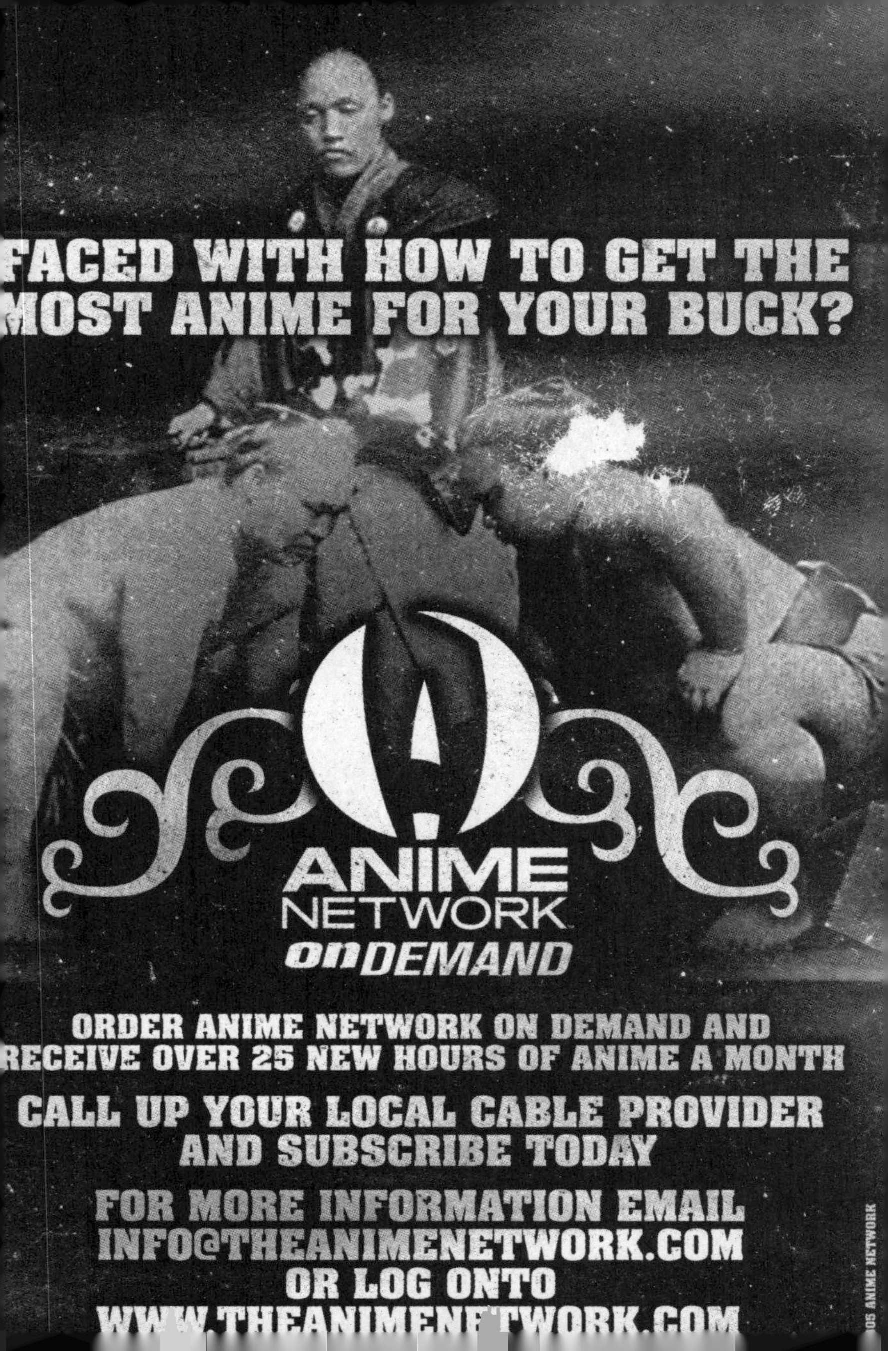

FACED WITH HOW TO GET THE MOST ANIME FOR YOUR BUCK?
ANIME NETWORK
onDEMAND
ORDER ANIME NETWORK ON DEMAND AND RECEIVE OVER 25 NEW HOURS OF ANIME A MONTH
CALL UP YOUR LOCAL CABLE PROVIDER AND SUBSCRIBE TODAY
FOR MORE INFORMATION EMAIL INFO@THEANIMENETWORK.COM OR LOG ONTO WWW.THEANIMENETWORK.COM
05 ANIME NETWORK